FASHIONING AMERICA

FASHIO
AMER

Edited by Michelle Tolini Finamore

Crystal Bridges Museum of American Art Bentonville, Arkansas
The University of Arkansas Press Fayetteville, Arkansas 2022

ONING

ICA

GRIT *to* GLAMOUR

CONTENTS

DIRECTOR'S FOREWORD

We live fashion. From our everyday work clothes pulled from department store racks to stylish seasonal looks crafted by runway designers to kicks from the latest sneaker drop, fashion is the artistic medium we spend most of our lives in.

Guest curated by fashion art historian Dr. Michelle Finamore for Crystal Bridges, *Fashioning America* is Crystal Bridges' first fashion exhibition. The exhibition pushes the boundaries of American art at Crystal Bridges by focusing on one of the most intimate art forms, one that shapes our sense of self and relationships to others. You will find histories of Native American and self-emancipated Black designers, learn how we shifted culturally from customized clothing to standardizing sizing for mass production, and discover family histories drawing connections between immigration and the fashion industry, along with so much more. We are excited for our audiences to dive deeply into these essays and immerse themselves in these underexamined and underrepresented fashion histories. It is thrilling to learn about the designers, wearers, workers, and stories that make up the robust history of what we wear, that demonstrate why every thread matters. We are proud to present this impactful exhibition and publication. Audiences from Bentonville and beyond will experience American fashion as art for all, celebrating its presence on the global stage.

A project that centers fashion as an art form and highlights the contributions of Black, Indigenous, and other designers of color—as well as those of immigrant, queer identified, and women designers—aligns powerfully with the vision of Crystal Bridges to welcome all. We are grateful for the designers' participation in this groundbreaking exhibition, which celebrates over two hundred years of American contributions to the world of fashion. From denim's working-class grit and streetwear's versatile utility, to ready-to-wear's standard-sized stylings and glamour's opulent detailing, the landscape of American fashion is as vast as the nation itself—and its reach and allure are global.

We are especially grateful to Hamish Bowles, editor in chief of the *World of Interiors* and global editor at large for *Vogue* magazine, and collector Jimmy Raye for the generous and extensive loans from their private collections. Thank you to every individual and institution who supported this exhibition by generously lending the many precious works for display, as well as the staff and sponsors who made the show possible. We deeply appreciate Dr. Finamore's initiative and trust in Crystal Bridges to champion her vision for telling a new story of American fashion. Textile conservator Claudia P. Iannuccilli's steadfast work throughout the run-up to the exhibition was exceptional. Designer Ruben Toledo provided extraordinary guidance, insight, and imaginative ideas for the design of the exhibition. We are honored to host the works of so many brilliant designers and makers who will inspire audiences to think of the art in the fashion they wear every day.

We are especially grateful for the exhibition's generous sponsorship by Terri and Chuck Erwin; the Bogle family; Blakeman's Fine Jewelry; Dillards, Inc.; Gelmart International; Jim and Susan von Gremp; Shannon and Charles Holley; Neal and Gina Pendergraft; JT and Imelda Rose; Diane and Mark Simmons; and Tony Waller. We are also thankful for the support we received through our tenth-anniversary exhibition season, which benefited from sponsorship by the Coca-Cola Company; Goldman Sachs; Tyson Foods; Tyson Family Foundation; the Willard and Pat Walker Charitable Foundation; Walmart; James Dyke and Helen Porter; Christie's; Stout Executive Search; Trott Family Philanthropies; Del Monte Foods, Inc.; Sotheby's; Chuck and Terri Erwin; Shelby and Frederick Gans; Sybil Robson Orr; ConAgra Brands; the Kroenke Family Foundation; the Bogle family; Rick and Beverly Chapman; Pat Cooper; Valorie and Randy Lawson / Lawco Energy Group; and Kelly and Marti Sudduth. This publication could not have been possible without Acquavella Galleries' ongoing sponsorship and commitment to the Crystal Bridges publication program.

Rod Bigelow
Executive Director and Chief Diversity and Inclusion Officer
Crystal Bridges Museum of American Art

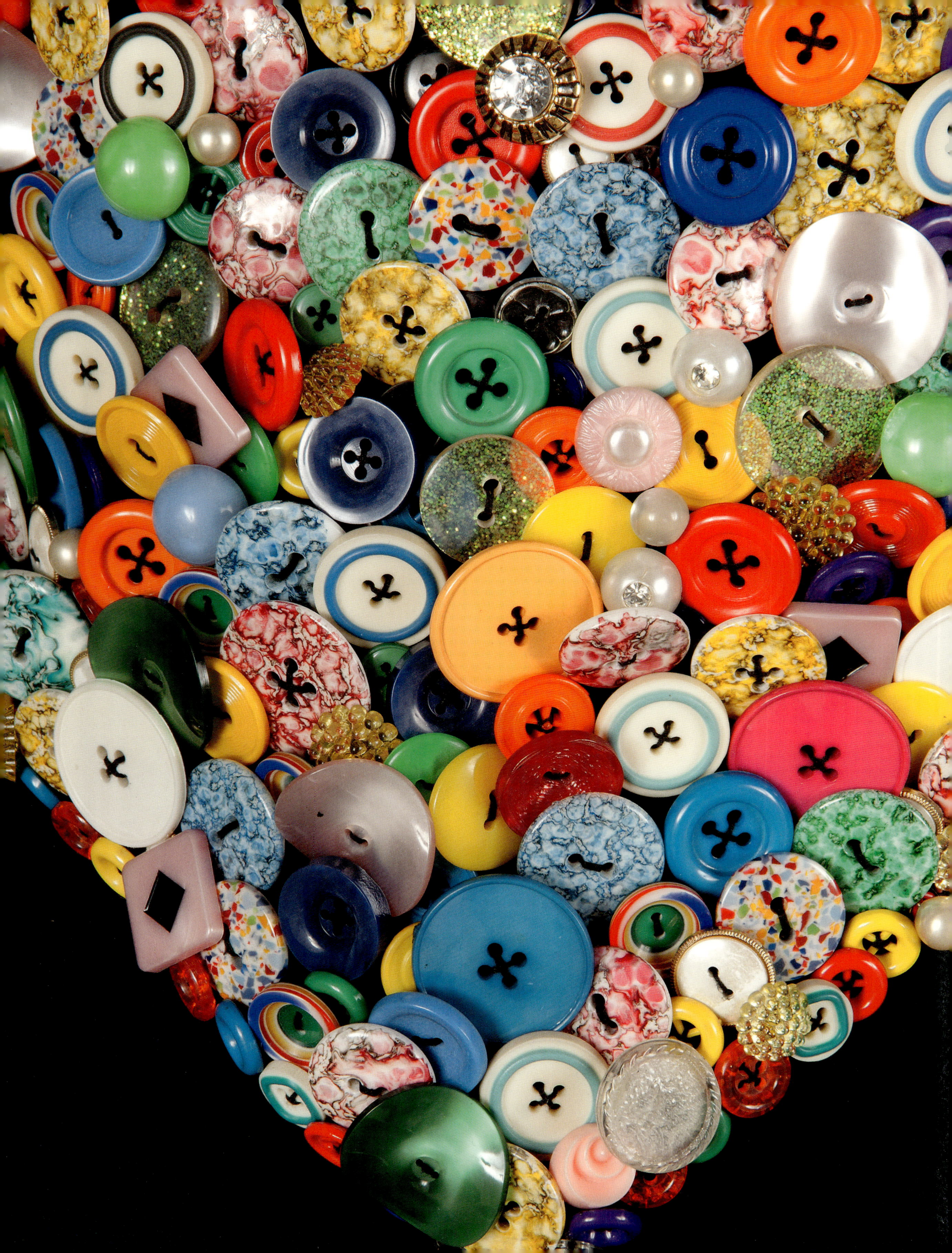

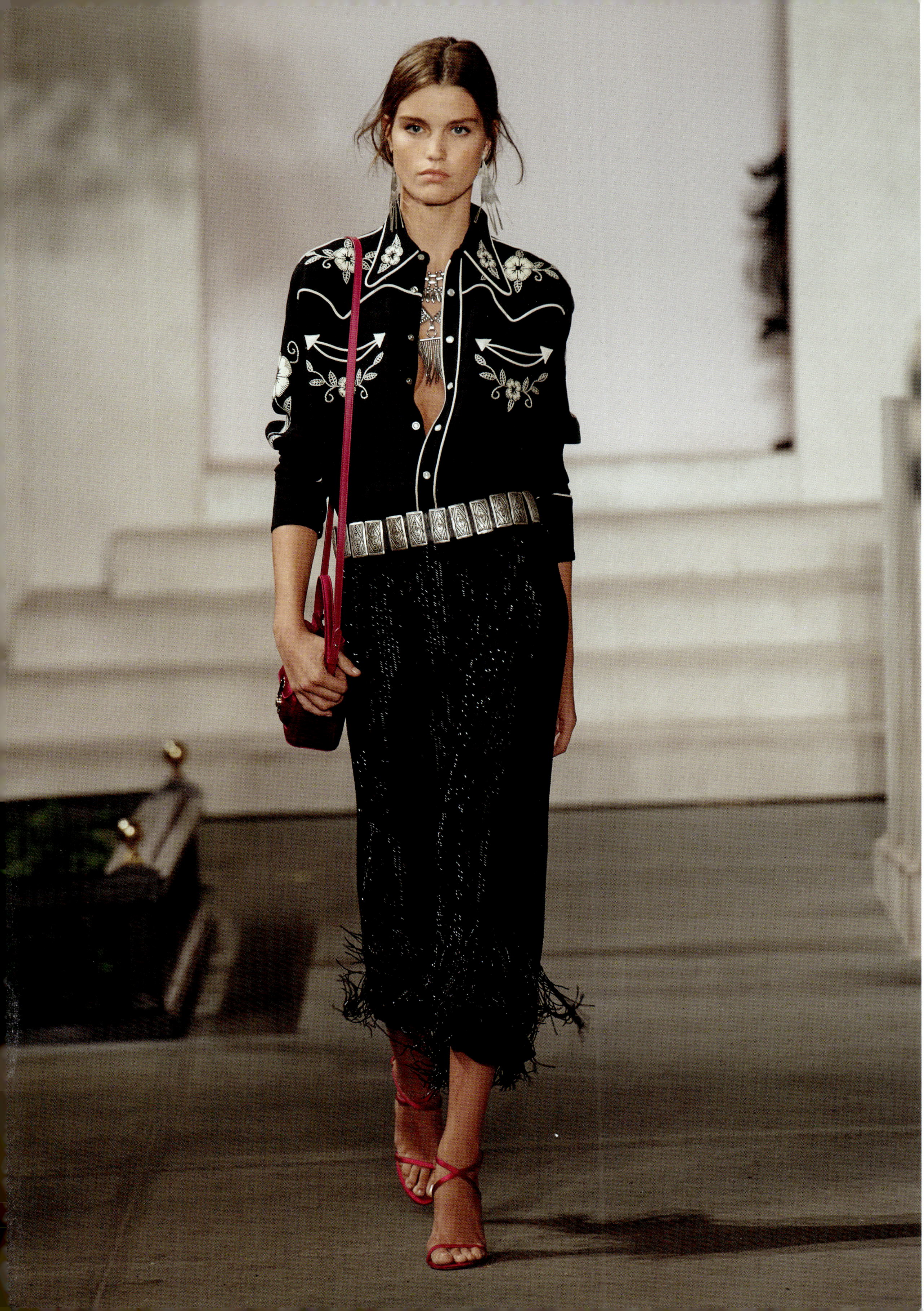

ACKNOWLEDGMENTS

Fashioning America: Grit to Glamour is Crystal Bridges Museum of American Art's first fashion exhibition, and I am grateful to the museum for entrusting me with the project. Fashion exhibitions are particularly complex, especially one that is a sweeping overview of more than two hundred years of American creativity. The participants on this journey, both internally and externally, consistently rose to the challenge, and I cannot adequately express my gratitude for all who have helped bring *Fashioning America* to fruition.

Planning and implementing an exhibition is challenging in normal times, but even more so during a global pandemic. I am thankful that Crystal Bridges was willing to keep moving forward with all the uncertainty that the art world has experienced over these past two years. I am grateful to Alice Walton for spear-heading a museum that is vibrant, progressive, and welcoming, and to chairperson Olivia Walton, who has been an enthusiastic supporter of *Fashioning America*.

Rod Bigelow, executive director and chief diversity and inclusion officer, has been a keen supporter of the exhibition from the start, and his faith in the project and encouragement to amplify both the exhibition and the new perspectives it offers have been inspiring. I am especially grateful for the collaboration of chief curator Austen Barron Bailly, who has been instrumental in shepherding this project through Crystal Bridges with careful attention to bigger-picture issues. Deputy director Jill Wagar and senior director Sandy Edwards have been wonderfully supportive colleagues throughout the project.

Xuxa Rodríguez has been my fabulous on-the-ground curator and took on this exhibition in the midst of the transition to her new role as assistant curator of contemporary art at Crystal Bridges. Quite simply, I could not have done it without her. Her enthusiasm and positivity throughout the exhibition-planning process made being a curator from afar more manageable. In her department, curatorial assistant Victor Gomez has been a vital member of the *Fashioning America* team as well.

In envisioning my dream scenario for a fashion installation, the first person who came to mind was designer and illustrator extraordinaire Ruben Toledo. And true to form, Ruben has infused the exhibition with his creative energy and distinctive vision. Ruben is also a lender to the show, and I am happy that we could pay tribute to the inspirational and unparalleled talent of his wife and creative partner, Isabel Toledo. Ruben worked very closely with the remarkable design team at Crystal Bridges, and Jessi Mueller was a fantastic collaborator, bringing her design talent to the process. After Jessi's departure, Alvaro Amat stepped in and joined Margo Jones, Aine McMahon, and Olivia Walton in making this exhibition a reality.

Claudia Iannuccilli has been a champion conservator. Her unerring eye and incredible dressing skills always result in beautifully refined exhibitions. She consistently went above and beyond her role as a contract conservator, from schlepping mannequins from Brooklyn to Rhode Island and Massachusetts, to examining objects in collections all over New England.

Tackling the subject of American fashion writ large had its challenges, but the clear-eyed vision and distinctive perspectives of the authors helped shape this book into something new and exciting. I am exceedingly grateful for the contributions and scholarship of all of the writers, who enthusiastically agreed to participate on a relatively tight time frame: Sonya Abrego, Amber-Dawn Bear Robe, Torren Gatson, Emma McClendon, Angely Mercado, Tiffany Momon, Lauren Downing Peters, Xuxa Rodríguez, and Elizabeth Way.

The production of the catalogue would never have happened without the careful attention of publications staff at the University of Arkansas Press, including David Scott Cunningham, Janet Foxman, Martin Fox, and Liz Lester. Gina Broze deserves kudos for dealing with the image rights, and this book would not be here today without the dedication and hard work of curatorial project manager Taylor Peckțal at Crystal Bridges.

Special acknowledgment is due editor Domenick Ammirati. His careful eye, remarkable editing, and sensitivity to the material resulted in a more refined tribute to American fashion. Designer Jena Sher was an enthusiastic and imaginative partner in bringing the book to life.

There are so many other staff members at Crystal Bridges who have been instrumental to the exhibition's planning and implementation process. Words cannot express my gratitude for exhibitions manager Andi Phillips, whose cheerful direction, attention, and organization kept the exhibition moving along. Registrar Leesha Alston has been a patient and appreciated presence throughout the planning, and director of exhibitions and interpretation Robin Groesbeck has been a wonderful and insightful colleague. Head of interpretation Stace Treat has been a cheerleader for this exhibition from the beginning, and I have benefited from his guidance and perspective.

Other Crystal Bridges staff members have been superb colleagues and partners, including Tonya Jackson, Loria Oliver, Emily Ironside, Emilio Fabico, Elizabeth Selders, Diana Walpole, KC Hurst, Erica Harmon, Tiffanie Harris, Juniper Patel, Aine McMahon, Valerie Lazelier, Marissa Reyes, Paul Scoggan, and Dave O'Ryan and his collections team.

With the challenge of trying to tell a more nuanced story related to American fashion, private lenders immediately came to mind. Their collections include "iconic" designers as well as those who fall outside the canon. I extend deeply felt gratitude to lenders Hamish Bowles and Jimmy Raye, whose rich collections helped me to curate an exhibition with stimulating and unexpected content. Both Hamish and Jimmy are wellsprings of knowledge and deeply passionate about their respective collections. Jimmy spent many hours with me poring through drawers, boxes, and trunks. Hamish is always so generous in sharing his treasures with the world, and his curator Molly Sorkin has been a fantastic colleague throughout the process.

Institutional lenders have been instrumental in telling the broader historical story and have generously shared their resources with *Fashioning America*. I am thankful for the help of all of these curators and conservators: Elaine Nichols, Drew Talley, and Laura Mina at the National Museum of African American History and Culture; Brandy Culp, Mary Busick, and Casey Mallinckrodt at the Wadsworth Atheneum; Virginia Theerman at The Charleston Museum; and Kevin Jones, Christina Johnson, and Leigh Wishner at FIDM Museum.

I am appreciative of the assistance I received from various colleagues at archives across the country, including Tracey Panek at the Levi Strauss & Co. Archives and Bette-Ann Gwathmey and Allison Johnson at Ralph Lauren. The wonderful archivists at Phillips-Van Heusen (PVH)—including Becca Love, Suzanne Shapiro, Jessica Garber, and Vanessa Barber—were all so helpful in finding pieces by Tommy Hilfiger, Calvin Klein, Warner, and Olga.

Collectors who graciously lent objects for the exhibition include Alexander Chesebro (whose vast knowledge of corset history was invaluable and seemingly endless), Robert Black, Lisa Perry, and Praise Santos McKenna. I must include a special shout-out to Bryan Hembree of the Fayetteville Roots Festival, whose enthusiasm for the exhibition resulted in the loan of a striking Nudie suit from Neal Pendergraft and connections with the talented team at Fort Lonesome tailors. Tiffany Dubin has been a generous supporter of the exhibition on so many levels, and I value both her enthusiasm and friendship. Liana Krupp, who has been my partner in crime on various projects, lent a stunning Virgil Abloh for Off-White ensemble that is a heartfelt tribute to a designer the fashion world lost too soon.

A host of scholars and curators have provided vital assistance and perspective, and I extend sincere thanks for their kindness. Providing Native American designers with a platform within the broader context of American fashion was always at the top of my mind, and I am grateful to Peabody Essex Museum scholar Karen Kramer, curator of the groundbreaking 2015 exhibition *Native Fashion Now*, who was so generous with her knowledge and connections. Curatorial colleagues who enthusiastically answered my queries about various aspects of American fashion and aided my research include Olivia Scott, Raissa Bretaña, Jessica Desany Ganong at the Concord Museum, Edith Serkownek at Kent State University, Doneeca Thurston at the Lynn Museum/Lynn Arts, Carla Smith at the Lincoln Presidential Library, Eric Darnell Pritchard at the University of Arkansas, Chloe Gerson at Brandeis University, and Petra Slinkard and Paula Richter at the Peabody Essex Museum. Christina Erteszek, the daughter of the lingerie designer Olga, willingly shared stories and material from her mother's archive. At Crystal Bridges, Polly Nordstrand, curator of Native American art, and Mindy Besaw, curator of American art, have also been generous with their time and knowledge.

There are many colleagues in the contemporary fashion world who have been part of the process, including Steven Kolb, Ashley Brooke-Sandall, Anna Chae at the Council of the Fashion Designers of America, and Ralph Pucci and his daughter Nicole Pucci. Locally, the pioneering Robin Wallis Atkinson at Interform and her dynamic team for Northwest Arkansas Fashion Week have been important collaborators.

Isabel Toledo once observed, "Fashion is what time looks like." The contemporary designers in *Fashioning America* embody history past and present while representing issues related to inclusion and exclusion. I appreciate their participation and that of all members of their design teams: Olivia Anthony; Amanda Bruegl and Erik Brodt of Ginew; Natalie Chanin and Catherine Counts at Alabama Chanin; Ji Won Choi and Sustainable Fashion Arm Milan s.r.l.; Manuel Cuevas and Weltsy Chong; Fort Lonesome's

Kathie Sever and Stephani Rose; Stephanie Adleson Mora at Libertine; Patricia Michaels; Viktoria Modesta and Ben Price; Jamie Okuma; Virgil Ortiz and Tish Agoyo; Kerby Jean-Raymond and Omari Williams at Pyer Moss; Walé Oyéjidé of Ikiré Jones; Mimi Prober; Savage X Fenty; Christian Siriano and Bianca Bianconi; Anna Sui and Isabelle Sui; and Shelly Xu.

There are so many players involved in large museum exhibitions, and I hope that I have managed to name all who contributed to this one. I take responsibility for any omissions and apologize in advance for anyone I may have forgotten. I realize there will be countless others who may participate in *Fashioning America* after this book goes to press, and I am grateful for their contributions even if I cannot name them here.

And last, but never least, special thanks to Dan, Oliver, and Madeleine.

Michelle Tolini Finamore

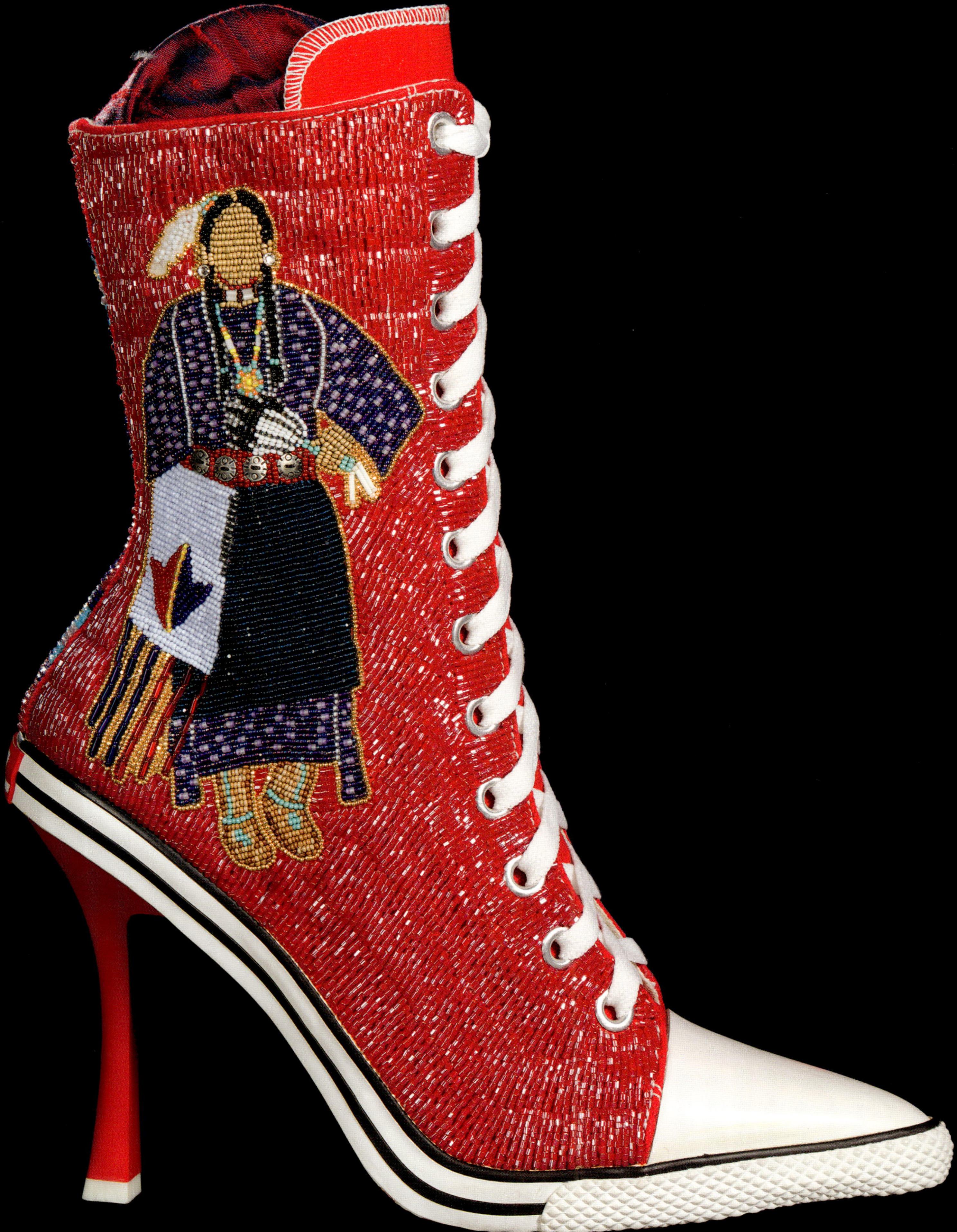

Introduction

REFASHIONING AMERICA

Michelle Tolini Finamore

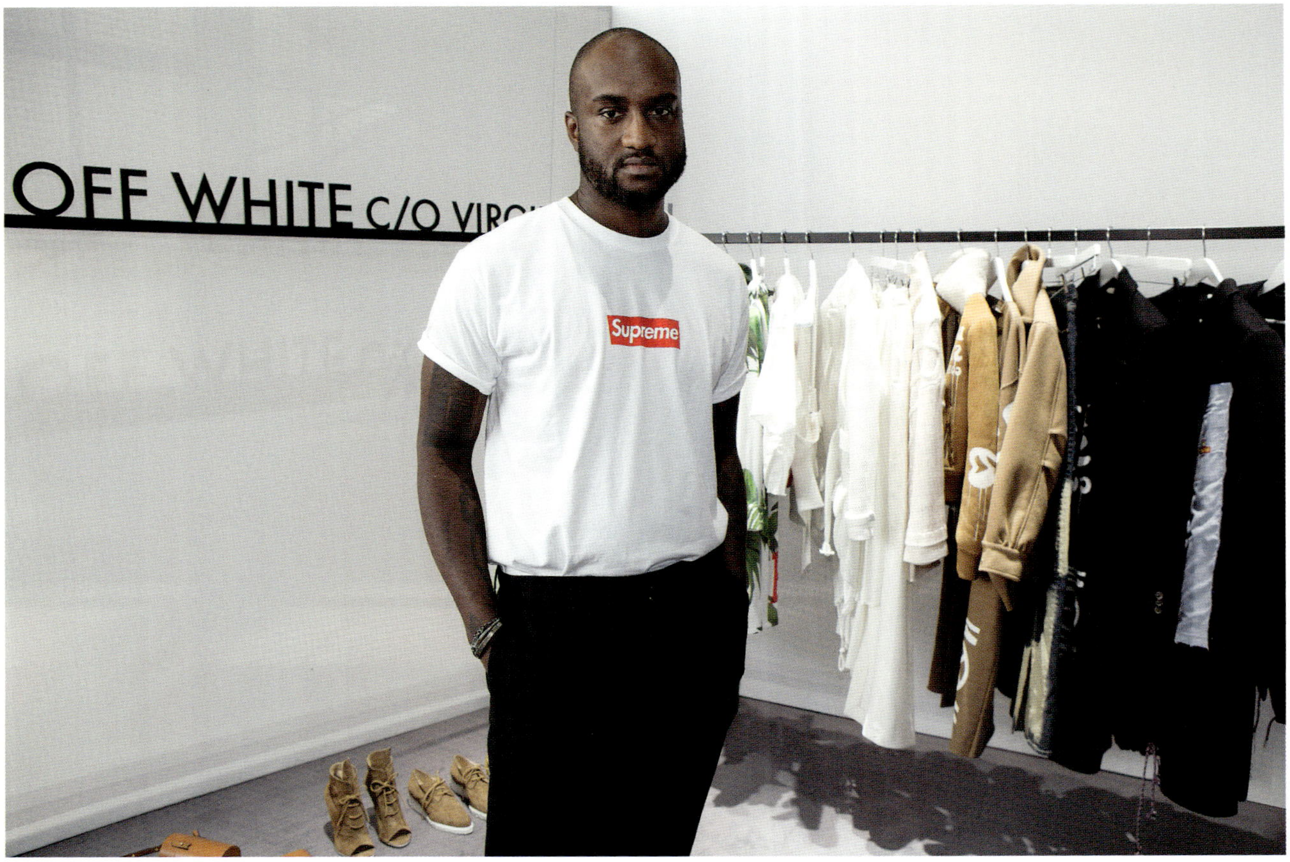

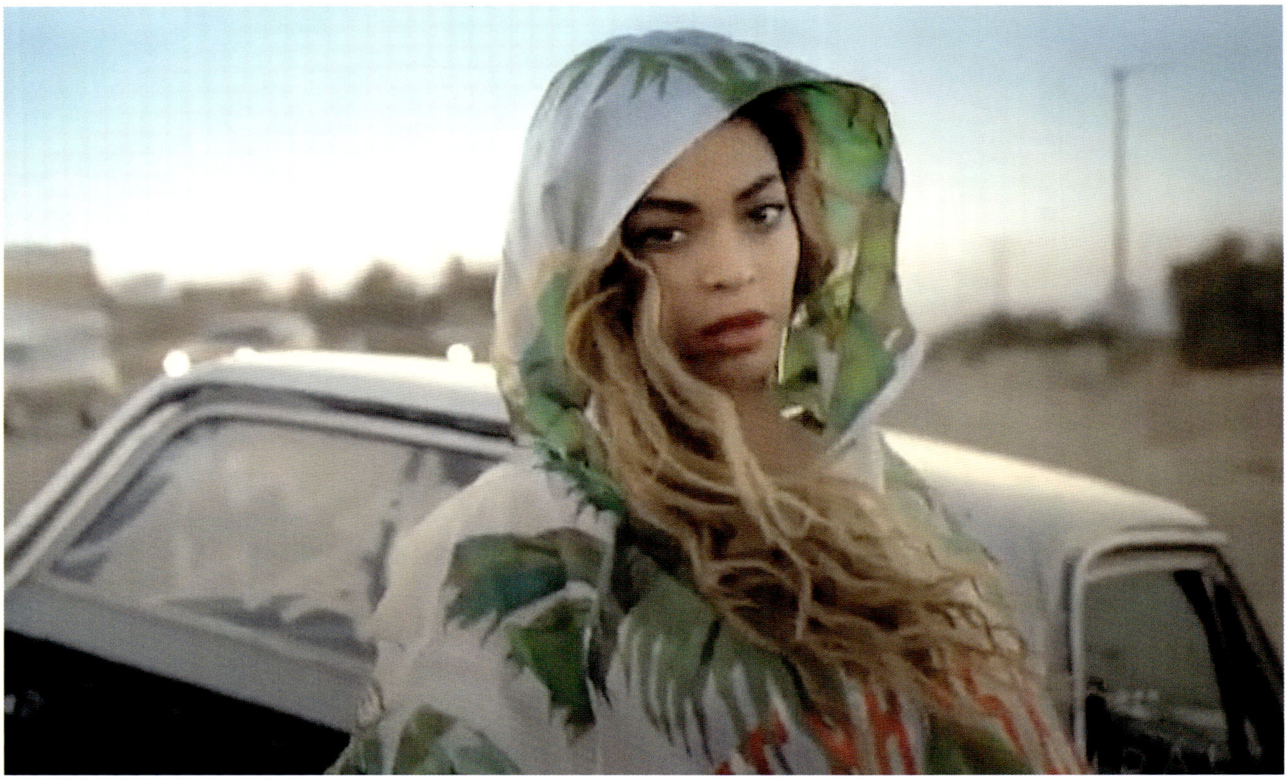

top Virgil Abloh for LVMH Fashion Designers Prize in Paris, France, with Off-White "Moving Still" collection behind him, 2015.

bottom Beyoncé wearing Nebraska hoodie from the collection in "Feeling Myself" video, 2015.

FASHION AND STORYTELLING

In 2015, Illinois-born streetwear designer Virgil Abloh sent models down the runway in garments with vibrant banana-leaf patterns overlaid with the word *Nebraska* in a collegiate typeface. Typical of the artist's mantra that "you can evoke meaning by crashing two things together," this collection for his brand Off-White found inspiration in the aesthetics of Big Ten university culture, the Beverly Hills Hotel's decor, and an "abstracted cheerleading silhouette."[1] Rejecting the idea that Middle America is a fashion "flyover" zone, Abloh took conventional American sportswear and turned it into high fashion. Like his brand's name, which implies something ambiguous, the designs deliberately defy categorization.

Abloh's melding of streetwear grit and Hollywood glamour shares an affinity with American fashion writ large, which is not easily defined. If we reject the idea that the subject revolves around a "greatest hits" of designer names, how do we make sense of it? Over the last ten years, the field has begun to reckon with a narrative that has traditionally privileged the courts of Europe, Parisian ateliers, and the United States' colonialist legacy as setting the standard. In reality, American fashion is not a single monolithic narrative but a matrix of converging and diverging narratives. It involves stories of immigration, innovation, independence, hard work, and self-invention, of harmony and dissonance, of difficulty and opportunity, and many unsung heroes.

One of the best aspects of working as a curator is the conversations I get to have with designers who speak passionately about the ways they translate contemporary sociocultural issues into the clothing we wear. Of course, these conversations are only possible with living designers, which raises a question: Who can speak for those whose history has not been preserved? For them, information has to be gleaned from very limited sources, often with no extant examples of their work. What of makers, for example, whose existence is documented solely in "criminal" records? In their essay for *Fashioning America*, Tiffany Momon and Torren Gatson delve into advertisements posted by enslavers seeking the self-emancipated in Charleston, South Carolina, and uncover the stories of myriad African Americans who worked in fashion-related occupations in the pre–Civil War era. Momon and Gatson have initiated the Black Craftspeople Digital Archive, an online resource for sharing new research in the field. Their work, and that of other scholars, significantly extends the narrative of American fashion while at the same time laying bare how much is still to be uncovered. If we overlay their research with the stories of the countless unnamed enslaved people and sharecroppers who were the engine of the American cotton industry, and the factory workers who toiled in the ready-to-wear industry, it is evident that the story will never be complete.

Each garment in *Fashioning America* embodies a multiplicity of players: designers, makers, wearers, collectors, and storytellers. Consider another piece of clothing: a beaded and embroidered silk House of Bianchi wedding gown from 1964. Cofounded by Italian immigrant Phyllis Bianchi Lange in 1949, Bianchi grew to become one of the premier wedding-dress designers and manufacturers in the United States, outfitting countless brides for their big day—including my mother, who wore a Bianchi gown when she married my father in 1964.

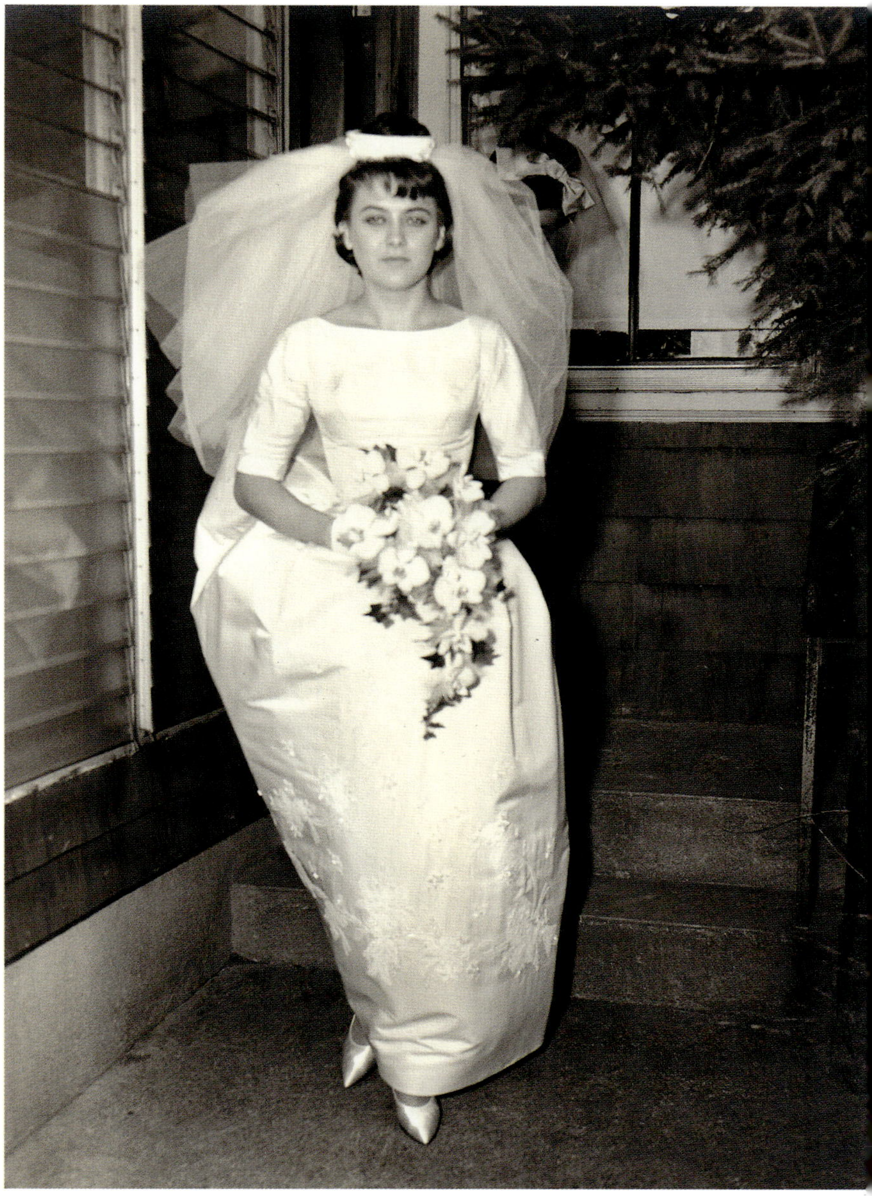

House of Bianchi, wedding dress worn by Anne Zoladkowski Tolini, 1964.

By 1971, Bianchi was carried in more than five hundred stores across the country, and (as my father relayed to me quite proudly, even though the dress my mother wore at her wedding was borrowed), the brand was found only in high-end department stores like Bonwit Teller and Saks Fifth Avenue.[2] House of Bianchi epitomizes the great American success story, but beyond its broad outlines lies a much richer and deeper tale, a story that includes the lives of the workers who toiled behind the scenes to make fairy-tale frocks. These workers included two generations of my own family. My great-aunt Olga Marazzi Tolini took a job as an embroiderer for Bianchi and continued working there for much of her life. Although it is no longer possible to ask her about her time there, the material memory of her expert embroidery—ropes of faux pearls, tiny rhinestones, and strings of crystal bugle beads—has moved from her attic to mine. My father and his brother, meanwhile, grew up in an Italian American neighborhood in Dorchester, Massachusetts, after their grandparents came to America as part of the great wave of Italians who came to the United States in the early twentieth century. They too worked at Bianchi, in afterschool jobs: my father made deliveries and my uncle operated cutting machines.

This arrangement of familial relations and multiple generations working for the same company, often hewing along ethnic lines, remains common among new immigrants today. As Angely Mercado points out in her reflections on Dominican immigrants working in the shoe factories of Lawrence, Massachusetts, newcomers to this country often simply follow the work. It was true for my mother's family as well, when they came from Communist-era Poland in 1963 to the Boston area and took jobs afforded by familial connections. After "moving up" from Dorchester to the suburbs, my mother held a range of office and retail jobs (including at the Boston-based Converse). Ultimately, she followed the siren song of the wedding dress, working for Bianchi's competitor Priscilla of Boston before eventually opening up her own wedding-gown shop north of the city. Buying trips and visits to fashion showrooms, as well as working in the shop itself, were a constant throughout my high school and college years.

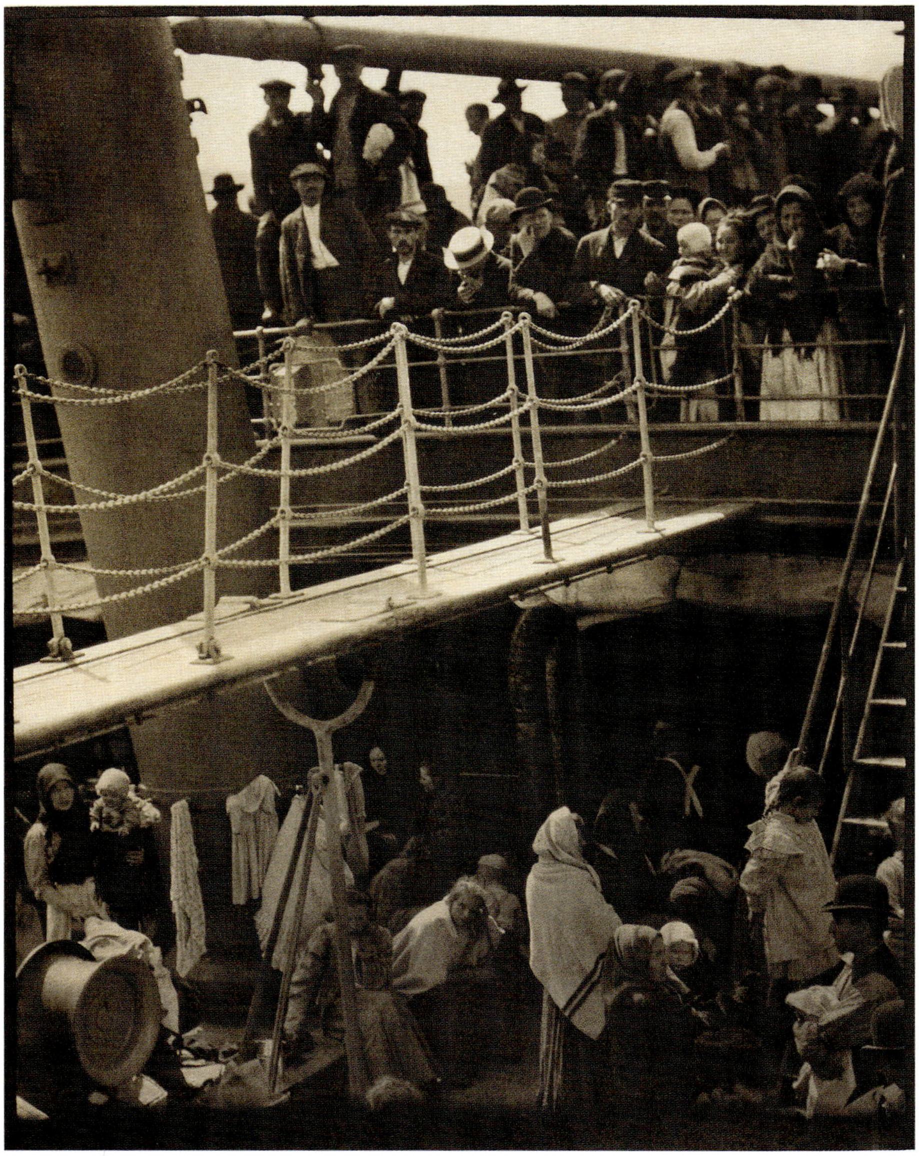

Alfred Stieglitz, *The Steerage*, 1907 (printed before 1913). Photogravure, 13 ⅛ × 10 ½ in. (33.3 × 26.7 cm). Alfred Stieglitz Collection, Co-owned by Fisk University, Nashville, Tennessee, and Crystal Bridges Museum of American Art, Bentonville, Arkansas, ASC 2012.85.

The dress that my mother wore at her wedding embodies a number of the varied and intersecting narratives that are reflected in *Fashioning America*: the immigrant experience, entrepreneurship, factory labor, self-invention, the history of ready-to-wear, standardized sizing, department-store history, the lives of behind-the-scenes workers, and last, but not least, the idea that a dress can sell a dream.

Through a cross-section of objects and imagery, *Fashioning America* aims to bring lesser-known designers and new research perspectives into conversation with standard histories and to expand the geographical scope of our sense of fashion in the United States. The contributors to this book are complicating the American fashion story by

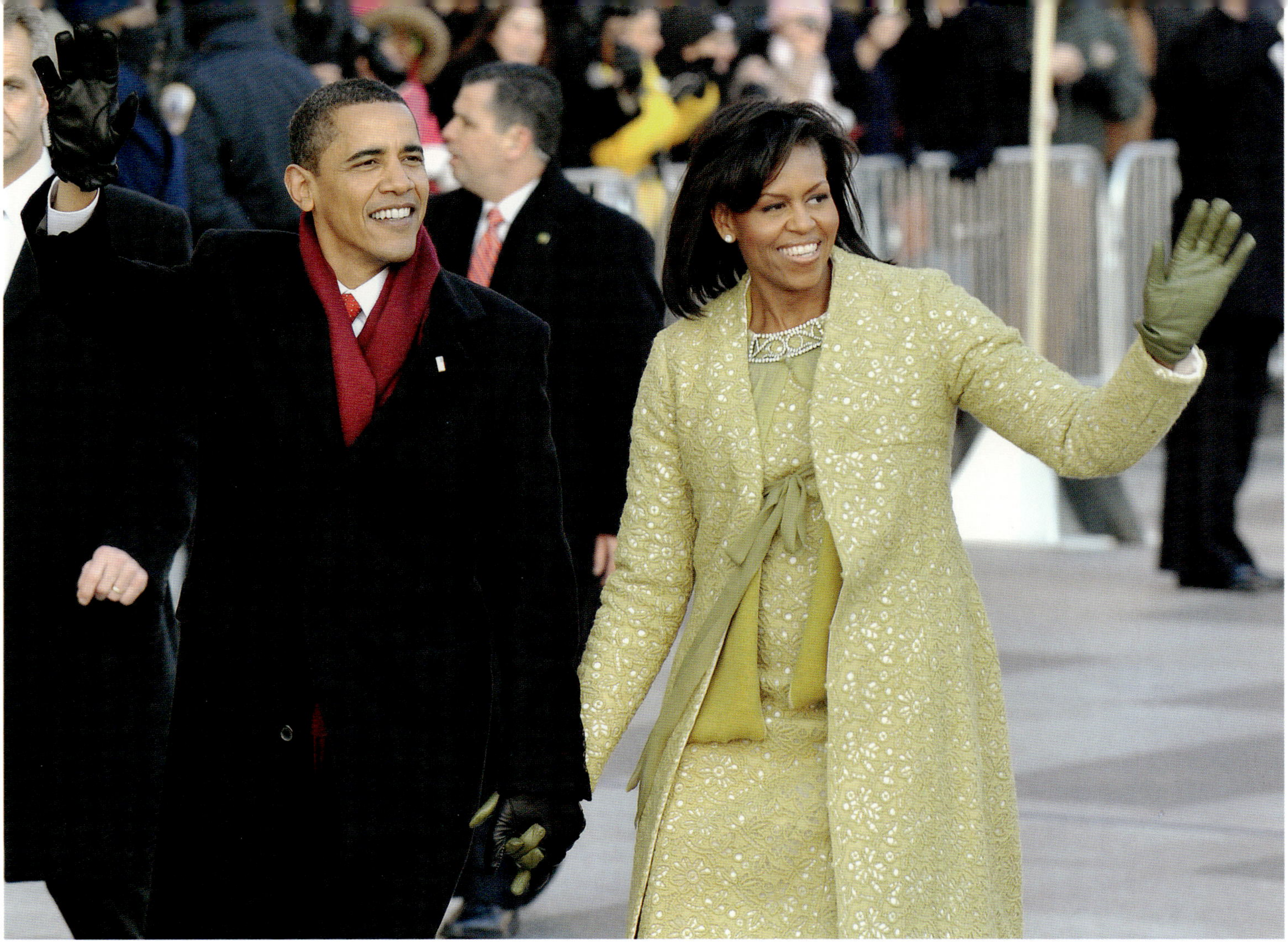

Isabel Toledo, ensemble designed for Michelle Obama for the 2009 presidential inauguration, 2008–9. Felted wool, silk linings, pashmina, and cotton. Isabel and Ruben Toledo Archives.

addressing subjects as varied as Indigenous fashion, how the history of standardized sizing and notions of whiteness have contributed to ideals of beauty, immigrant labor in the shoe industry, and the history of Black designers and tradespeople in fashion. Fashion designer Isabel Toledo, a Cuban American refugee and the designer of Michelle Obama's 2009 Inaugural ensemble, neatly sums up the hybrid nature of American dress:

> Our American population is made up of different ethnic, racial and religious backgrounds all living in such a wide range of terrains. The diversity of lifestyles and all the various economic classes that can participate in fashion contribute to fashion's richness. All this great delicious mix is what makes this country so modern and so interconnected and able to pioneer the future. This clash of intentions and difference in purpose is freedom for the soul.[3]

Fashioning America focuses on garments that represent this American spirit of entrepreneurship and invention, as well as those recognizable international exports of American style: Indigenous dress, denim jeans, westernwear, ready-to-wear fashion, streetwear, and the glamour of Hollywood. The series of stories that follows aims to unpack and explore these American archetypes.

House of Bianchi epitomizes the great American success story, but beyond its broad outlines lies a much richer and deeper tale, a story that includes the lives of the workers who toiled behind the scenes to make fairy-tale frocks.

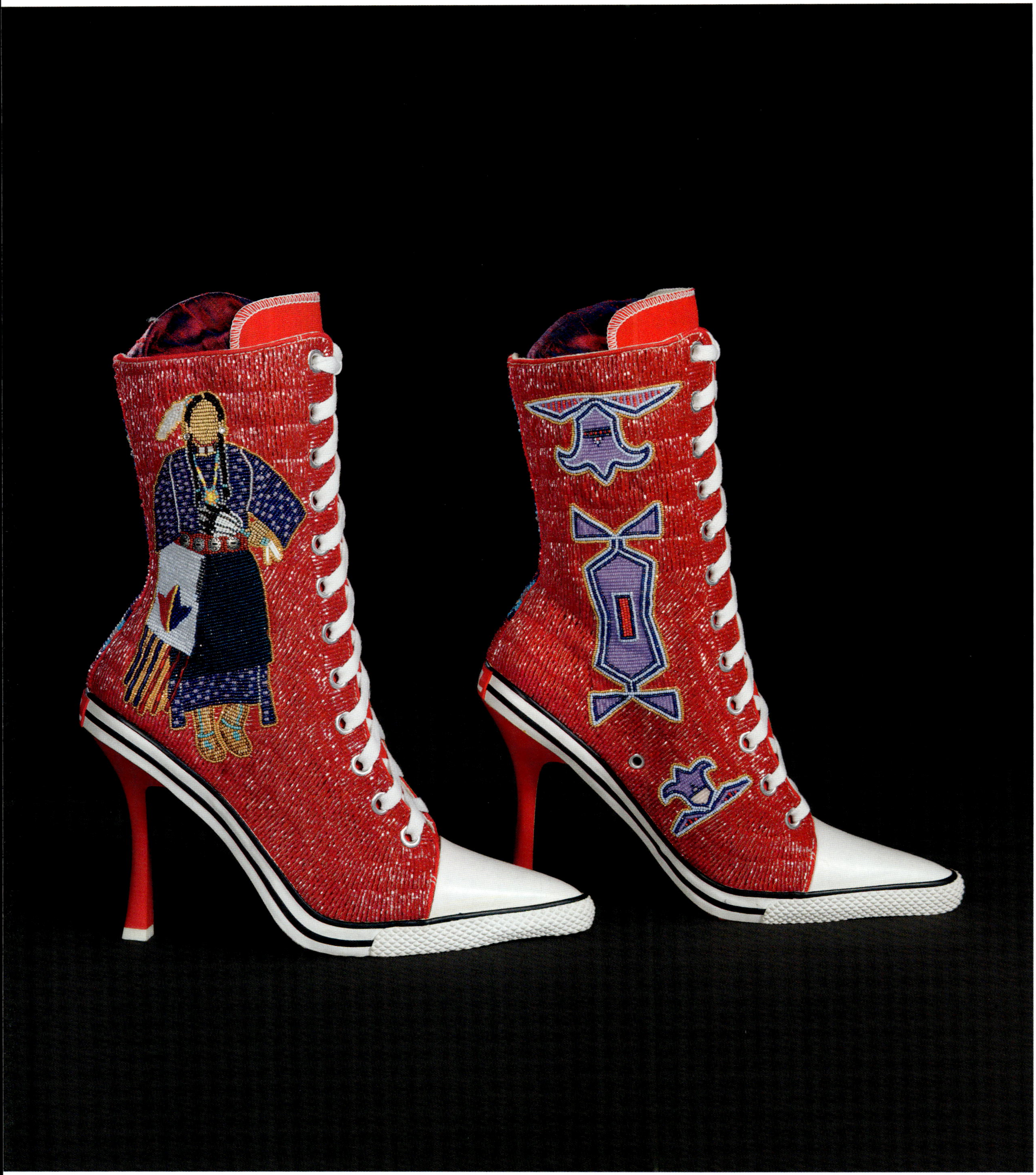

Teri Greeves, *Abstraction: Kiowa by Design*, 2014. Beads on canvas high-heeled sneakers, each 11 ½ × 10 × 4 in. (29.2 × 25.4 × 10.2 cm). Crystal Bridges Museum of American Art, Bentonville, Arkansas, 2021.40.

STORY 1
INDIGENOUS FASHION

Logically, the story of American design should begin with Indigenous design; as the Ojibwe fashion writer and stylist Christian Allaire has observed, Native Americans are the original couturiers in this country.[4] Long before European contact, Indigenous peoples were crafting handmade garments, engaging in complex weaving processes, and creating intricate beadwork and quillwork, among many other textile-oriented arts. In her essay in *Fashioning America*, Siksika Nation art historian Amber-Dawn Bear Robe explores the persistence of Native aesthetic lineage in the face of centuries of adversity and persecution.

It is particularly challenging to piece together Indigenous contributions to nineteenth-century American fashion within the context of the Reservation (1850–87) and Assimilation (1887–1934) periods. As a result, Indigenous work has rarely, if ever, been wrapped into larger fashion histories. Interrogating one expression of Native craft, Haudenosaunee (Iroquois) beaded bags, reveals the complicated nature of this narrative. The bags were made in the thousands for the tourist market and evolved into hybrid forms that adapted to both European styling and the use of trade goods such as glass and metallic beads. They became so prized that daguerreotypes of white women proudly displaying their beaded Native purses abound. The fascination with Native beadwork eventually made its way into nineteenth-century needlework manuals and women's magazines such as *Godey's Lady's Book*, which encouraged American women to try their hand at beadwork in the "Indian style."[5] With their multilayered history, the bags raise questions: Which is the Native piece and which is the work of a home handcrafter? What is Native American? What is American?

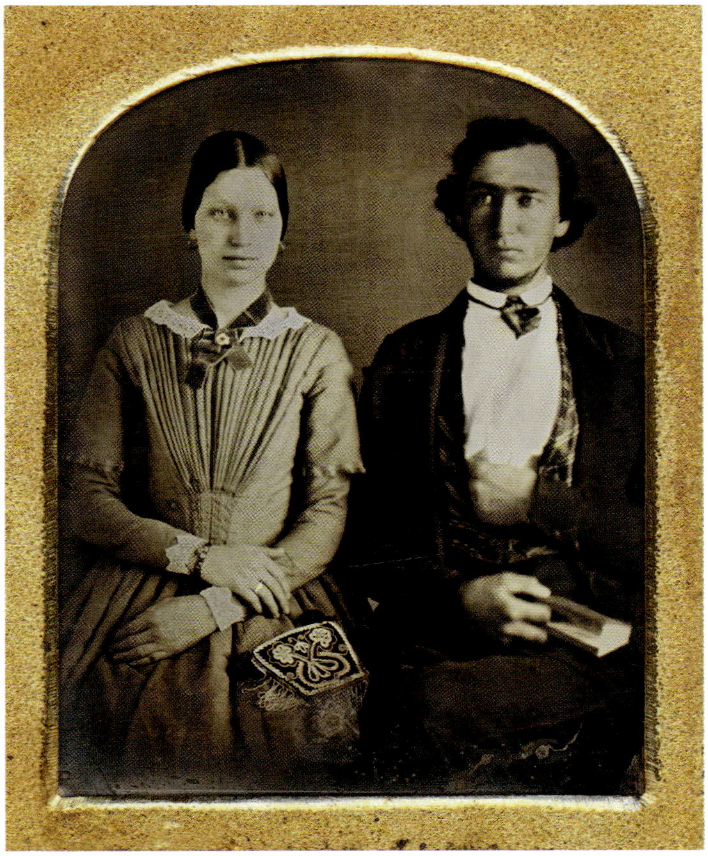

Couple with Haudenosaunee (Iroquois) beaded bag, ca. 1845. Daguerreotype. Collection of Gerry Biron.

These questions are still valid today. Even with an increased respect for Indigenous fashion, consumers do not fully grasp the nuances of appropriation versus appreciation, nor the fallacy of a generic "Indian" style. In the 1970s, at the height of the hippie movement, the San Francisco–based counterculture magazine *Rags* assessed the situation: "The Indian kids are aware of the mass rip-offs of their fringe, beaded headbands and buckskin moccasins by the country's hipsters. They do indeed dig the feedback but would rather see that designing done by Indians themselves."[6]

Even with an increased respect for Indigenous fashion, consumers do not fully grasp the nuances of appropriation versus appreciation, nor the fallacy of a generic "Indian" style.

Awareness of the plight of Native peoples was broadening, yet it was also a time when their "look" was being co-opted for hippie attire. Native designers today still grapple with being reduced to a single "Indian" style, when in reality there are more than five hundred tribal groups in the United States. It is this complexity that Kiowa artist Teri Greeves confronts in her 2014 beaded high-heeled sneakers *Abstraction: Kiowa by Design*.

Greeves trained in the Kiowa and Shoshone beadwork traditions and applies that handcraft to everyday objects from the non-Native world. In *Abstraction*, she exposes the tension inherent in Native design past and present by placing the image of a woman in traditional Kiowa dress on the surface of shoes that recall fashion designer Norma Kamali's 1980s imaginative high-heeled sneakers that turned the most functional of footwear into high fashion. Greeves's shoes move beyond mere function, however, becoming sculptural objects that tell multiple stories related to the use of Native abstract imagery as inspiration for American modernist art by reappropriating these patterns for her own purposes.

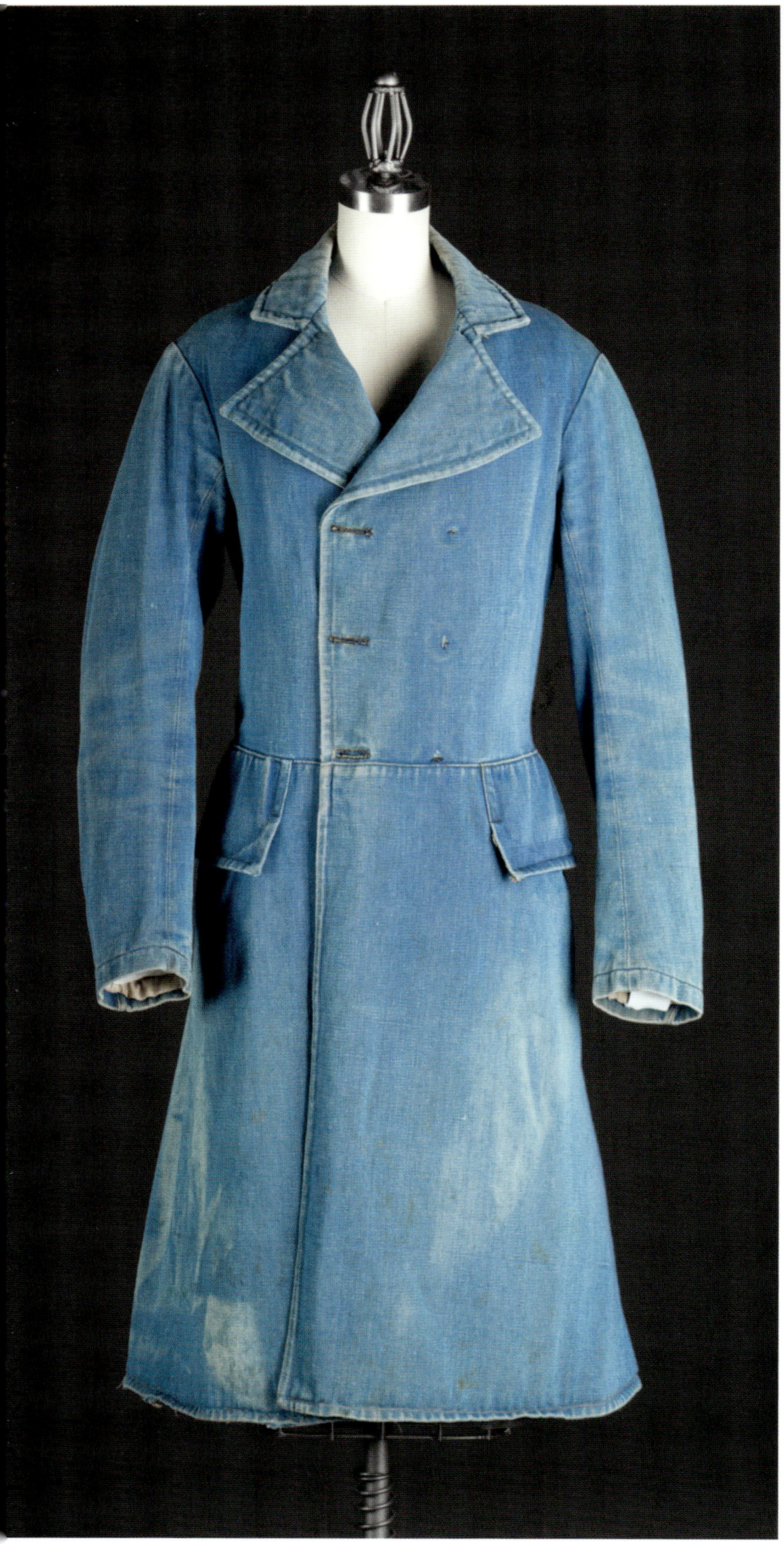

above Unknown, denim frock coat, 1850s. Denim. FIDM Museum Purchase. Courtesy of FIDM Museum at the Fashion Institute of Design & Merchandising, Los Angeles.

opposite Norman Rockwell, *Rosie the Riveter*, 1943. Oil on canvas, 52 × 40 in. (138.1 × 101.6 cm). Crystal Bridges Museum of American Art, Bentonville, Arkansas, 2007.178.

STORY 2
DENIM JEANS AND WESTERNWEAR

Denim jeans, invented in America and popularized by innovators such as German immigrant Levi Strauss, are arguably the world's most ubiquitous American fashion item. Their history, however, is broadly international, with the garment's evolution encompassing sailor cloth from Genoa (called *bleu de Gênes*, from which the word *jeans* is derived), *serge de Nîmes* from France, and dungaree fabric from India. America's participation in the global marketplace has deep roots, especially in the early days of colonialist expansion when the United States had to import cottons, laces, silks, wool, and even denim from abroad until textile production became more established. The word *denim* itself generally refers to a heavy cotton twill fabric that is dyed blue, originally with indigo, a dyestuff native to India, Asia, and Africa. Although historically linked with the American West and gold mining, denim jeans eventually found willing consumers of all sorts because of their practicality as casualwear.

By midcentury, associations with rebels, motorcycle riders, and subcultural style, popularized by film idols like Marlon Brando in *The Wild One* (1953) and James Dean in *Rebel without a Cause* (1955), gave way to a hippie counterculture in which jeans became canvases for self-expression via painting, embroidery, and other ornamentation. The 1980s designer-jean movement followed, spearheaded by American companies such as Calvin Klein, Jordache, and Guess, turning jeans with prominent logos into one of the most desirable purchases of the era. And yet, despite all those iterations, denim is still inextricably linked with the time-honored westernwear ensemble of jeans, a cowboy hat, cowboy boots, and leather jacket and accessories. In her essay in this volume, Sonya Abrego insightfully examines this indelible imagery, explaining that it represents "the material index of the diversity of the American West" as a bricolage of Spanish Colonial vaquero garb that traveled up through Mexico and mingled with both European sartorial habits and Indigenous traditions such as fringed buckskin and fine silverwork. The bandana, another requisite westernwear item, has a lineage that extends to eighteenth-century textile imports from India. Both the traditional paisley pattern on

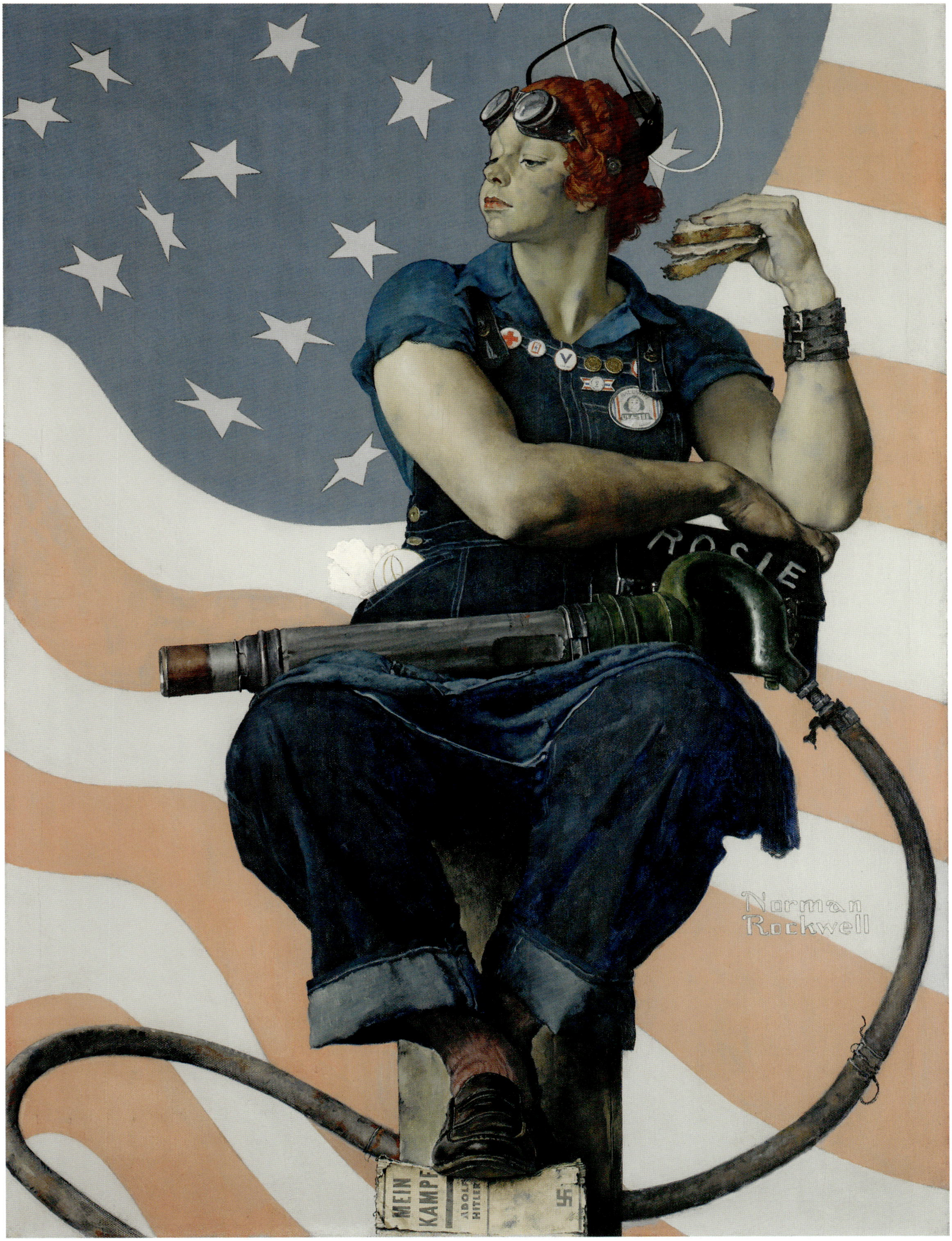
ROSIE
Norman Rockwell
MEIN KAMPF

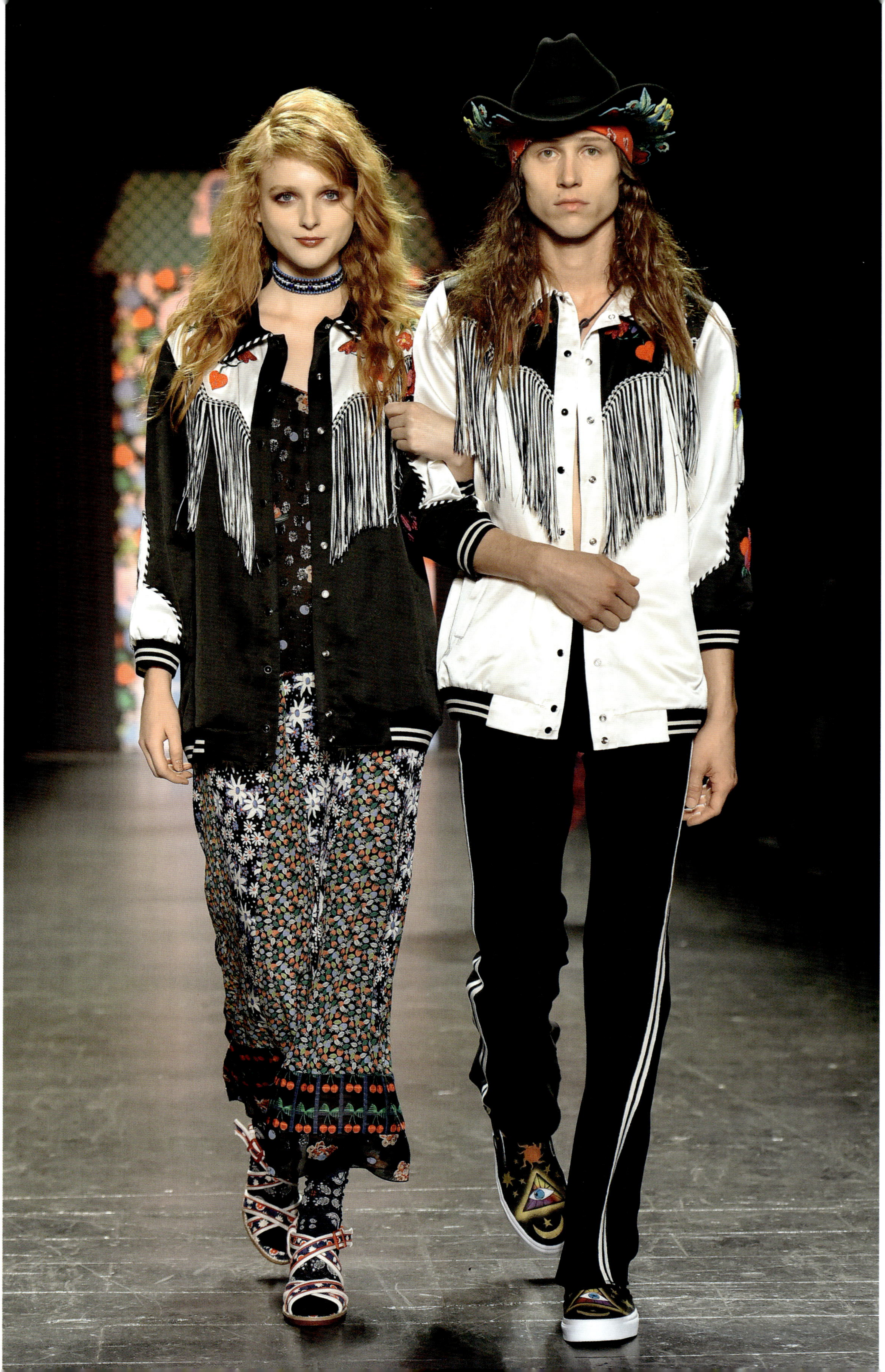

a red ground and the item's name itself, which comes from the Hindi word for tie-dying, *bhandu*, harken back to South Asian origins. The visual and craft traditions of Europe, Asia, and America are all interwoven in this archetypal American style.

Westernwear is so ubiquitous that it has consistently found expression in unexpected places: the "rhinestone cowboy" figure of the music industry, for example, which appears recurringly in the work of high-fashion figures. Detroit-born designer Anna Sui, for one, has acknowledged her indebtedness to the cowboy mythos and its hybridity as she spins it into a mashup of varied pop-culture influences:

> I am American, born in Suburbia, raised on pop culture. Sitcoms, rock 'n' roll, movie stars, I sucked up everything that mass media could unleash on me. . . . Optimism and Romance—they've always colored my Americana: cowboys, Indians, pioneers, soldiers demobbed from the Civil War into a frontier version of Victoriana.[7]

Sui's 2017 "Americana" collection, which merged functional westernwear with the rhinestone cowboy look, celebrated hand-craft techniques such as cross-stitch, embroidery, and crochet and included a collaboration with Los Angeles-based South Paradiso Organic Haberdashery on its detailed leatherwork.

STORY 3
READY-TO-WEAR

American innovation in ready-to-wear is one of the country's most significant contributions to global fashion history. The great pride in homegrown style and textile production goes back at least as far as George Washington, who, as a proponent of locally produced fabrics, wore American-made wool broadcloth from a Hartford, Connecticut, manufactory for his 1789 inauguration.[8] Although textile production was in its infancy at the time, the country's first Treasury Secretary, Alexander Hamilton, relayed the impressive range available in his 1791 report on "the subject of Manufactures":

> Great quantities of coarse cloths, coatings, serges, and flannels, linsey Woolseys, hosiery of Wool, cotton & thread, coarse fustians, jeans and Muslins, check[ed] and striped cotton and linen goods, . . . coarse shirtings, . . . and various mixtures of wool and cotton, and of Cotton & flax are made in the household way, and in many instances to an extent not only sufficient for the supply of the families in which they are made, but for sale, and (even in some cases) for exportation.[9]

At that time, a large portion of textiles and fashion-related goods were still made on a small scale in the home; one tour-de-force example is a circa 1759 dress originally owned and hand-embroidered by Abigail Wadsworth that was made from hand-loomed linen with an allover silk imagery depicting flora and fauna.

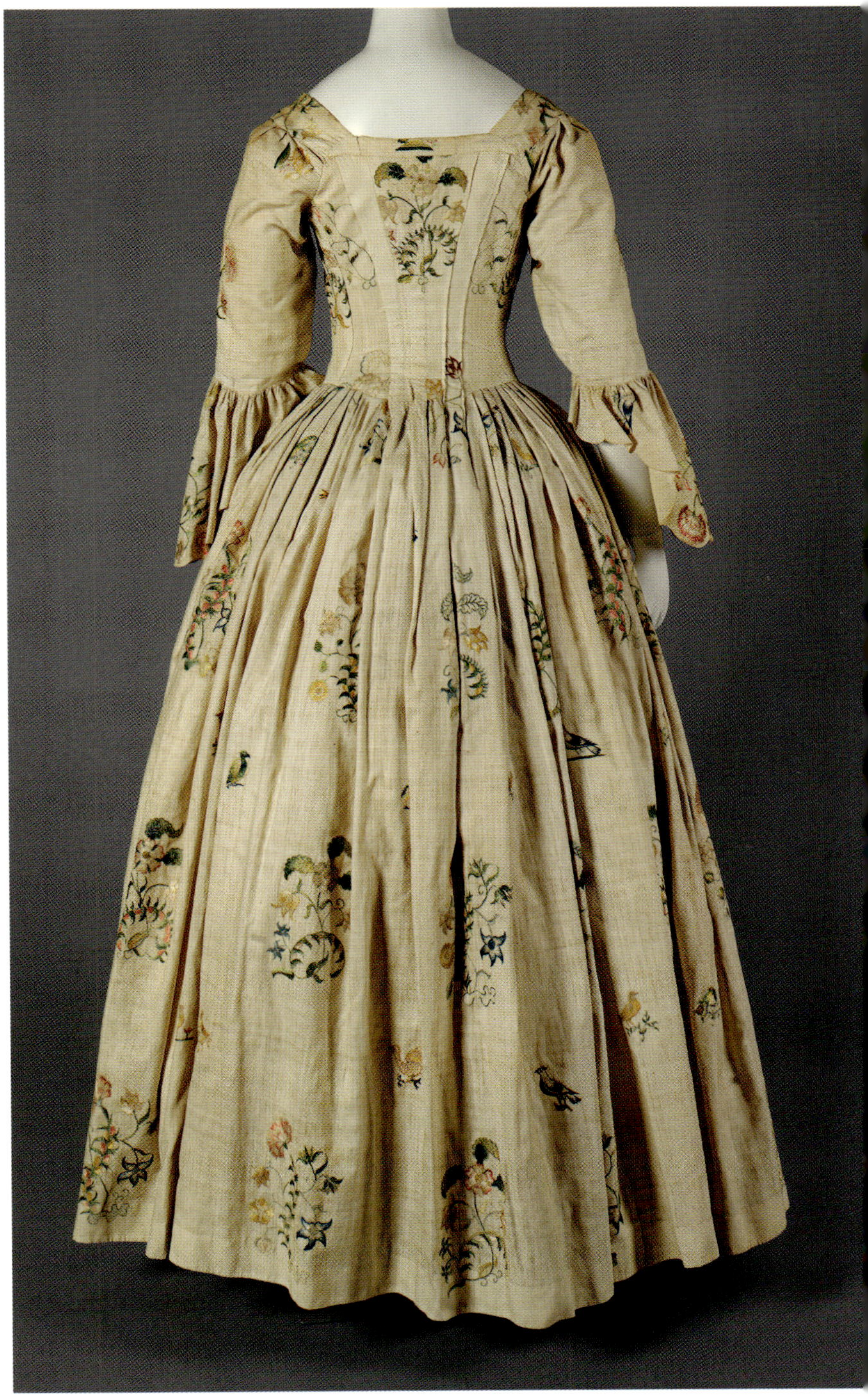

above Dress embroidered by Abigail Wadsworth, ca. 1759. Hand-loomed linen with silk embroidery. Wadsworth Atheneum Museum of Art, Hartford, Connecticut. Gift of Mrs. Fredric J. Agate.

opposite Anna Sui, westernwear ensembles, "Americana" collection, Spring 2017 Ready-to-Wear. Courtesy of Anna Sui.

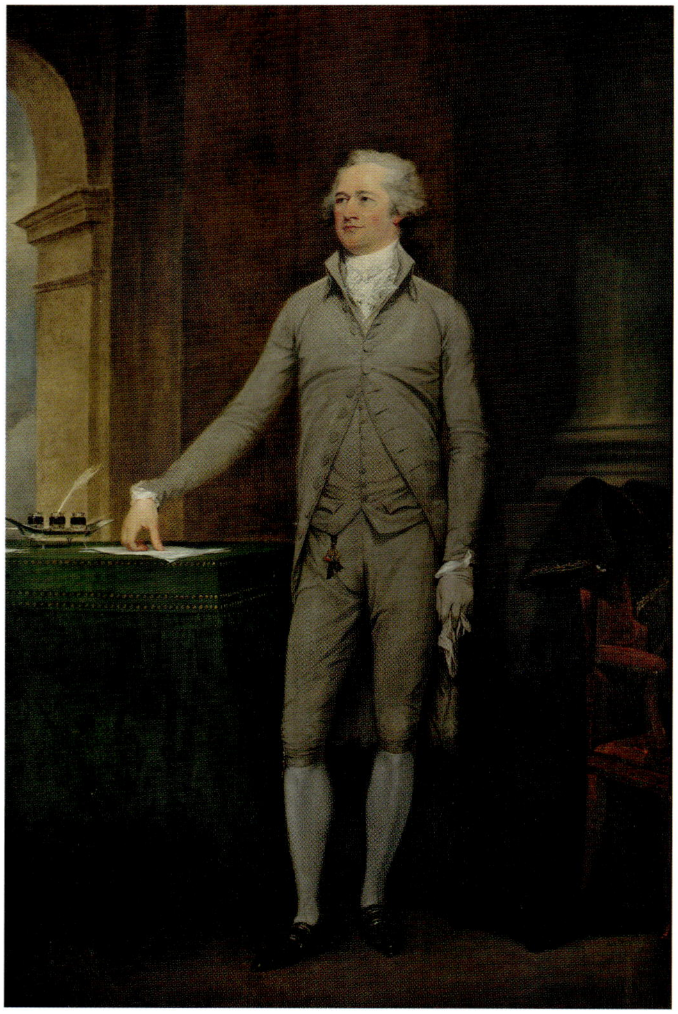

John Trumbull, *Portrait of Alexander Hamilton*, 1792. Oil on canvas, 86 ½ × 57 ½ in. (219.7 × 146.1 cm). Jointly owned by Crystal Bridges Museum of American Art, Bentonville, Arkansas, and the Metropolitan Museum of Art, New York, Gift of Credit Suisse, 2013.

Hamilton's ultimate goal was production on an industrial scale to help achieve economic autonomy from Europe and less dependence on goods from abroad. The seeds of the future powerhouse ready-to-wear industry were sown in Hamilton's 1791 report, which advocated increased mechanization, division of labor, and the employment of immigrants in textile factories.[10] For his own portrait by John Trumbull, Hamilton chose an unadorned gray suit that bore no traces of political messaging or embellishment that might imply European influence. Although there is no documentation of where it was made, the suit is intentionally simple and made with the type of fabric produced in the colonies at that time.

Real advances in ready-made clothing production occurred with the American invention of the sewing machine in 1846. The added improvement of continuous stitching in 1851 marked the beginning of the ready-to-wear era. In the 1860s, the demand for Civil War uniforms accelerated the pace of garment production, and by the middle of the decade, a vibrant ready-made industry had grown up in cities such as New York, Boston, Philadelphia, Chicago, Baltimore, and Cleveland, as well as in the state of Tennessee.[11] The burgeoning middle class were eager consumers of the ever-expanding variety of clothes: between 1860 and 1910, women's ready-made clothing production multiplied fifty times, whereas the United States' population increased only threefold.[12] Children's clothes, uniforms, cloaks, shirtwaists, and corsets were among the earliest ready-made garments, and the great waves of immigrants in the late nineteenth and twentieth centuries—which included Germans, Italians, Poles, and Russians—made up the vast majority of workers manufacturing them. Textile production increased throughout the late nineteenth and early twentieth centuries, with the United States manufacturing an impressive 597 million yards of silk and 135 million yards of rayon in 1929.[13]

The growth in the American textile industry was not a sheer success story, however, when one reckons with its human costs. Up until the Civil War, slavery in agricultural production was a key driver of the American fashion industry;[14] the Quakers notably refusing to wear garments made from cotton produced by enslaved people. The first water-powered cotton mill, built in 1793 in Rhode Island, used child labor—a practice that remained common, along with other appalling labor conditions. The infamous 1911 Triangle Shirtwaist Fire in New York resulted in the deaths of 146 garment workers, primarily young women and girls. The fire became a clarion call for industry-wide reform and inspired the establishment of the International Ladies' Garment Workers' Union (ILGWU) and the institution of factory safety standards.

In the 1920s, the fashionable silhouette evolved into something more easily mass-produced: a simple sheath. Skirts became shorter, corsetry became obsolete, and waistlines dropped, reflecting women's newfound physical and social freedoms—the ultimate modern dress for the New Woman. Coco Chanel is often credited with inventing the "little black dress," a myth rooted in a misreading of the phrase's first appearance, in *Vogue* in 1926. There, Chanel was described not as the originator of the garment—also memorably called a "fashion Ford"—but rather as an example of the standardization that was sweeping the industry: "Would one hesitate to buy an automobile because it could not be distinguished from another of the same brand? On the contrary,

opposite Quaker bonnet, 1850s. Straw and cotton. Jimmy Raye Collection, Salem, Massachusetts.

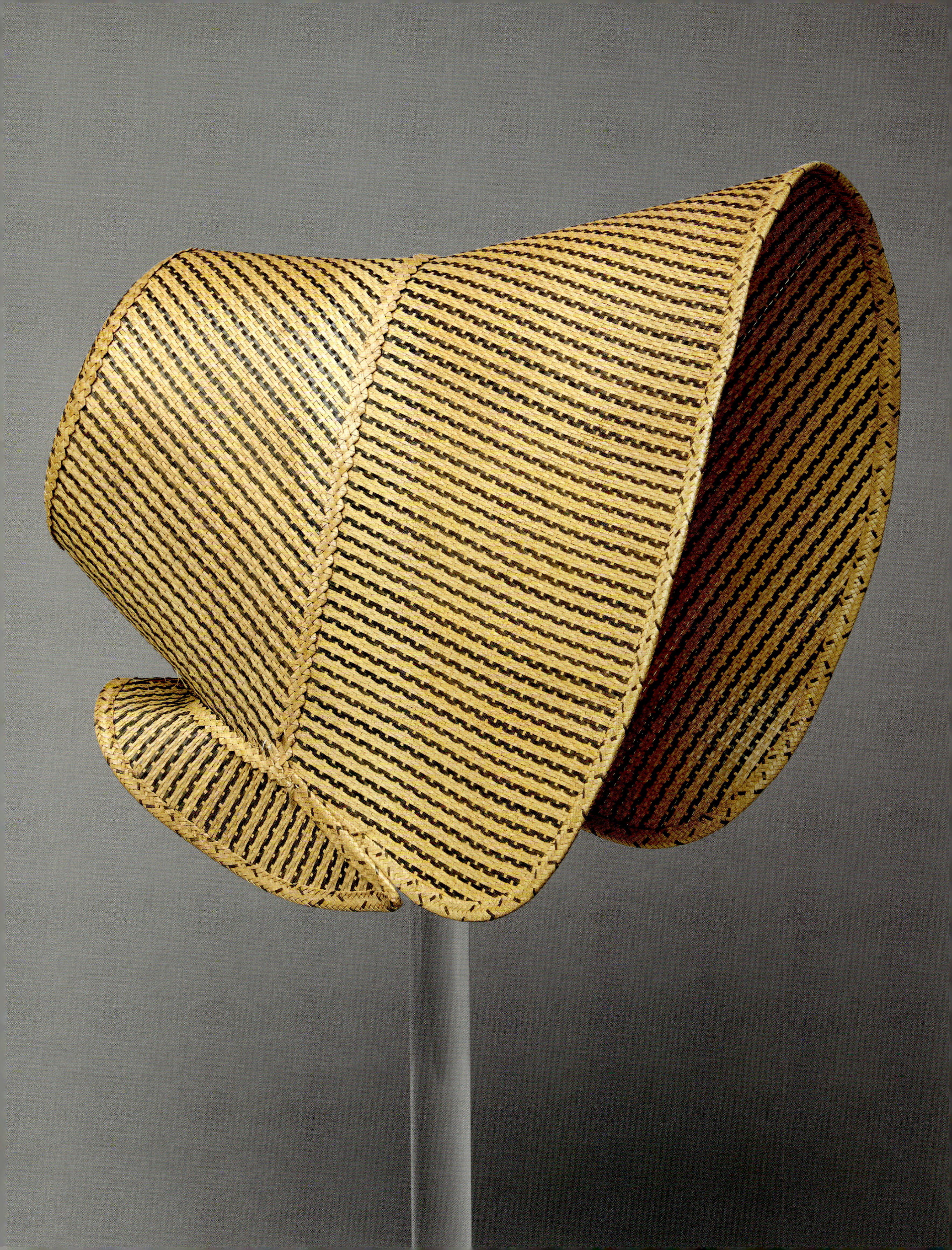

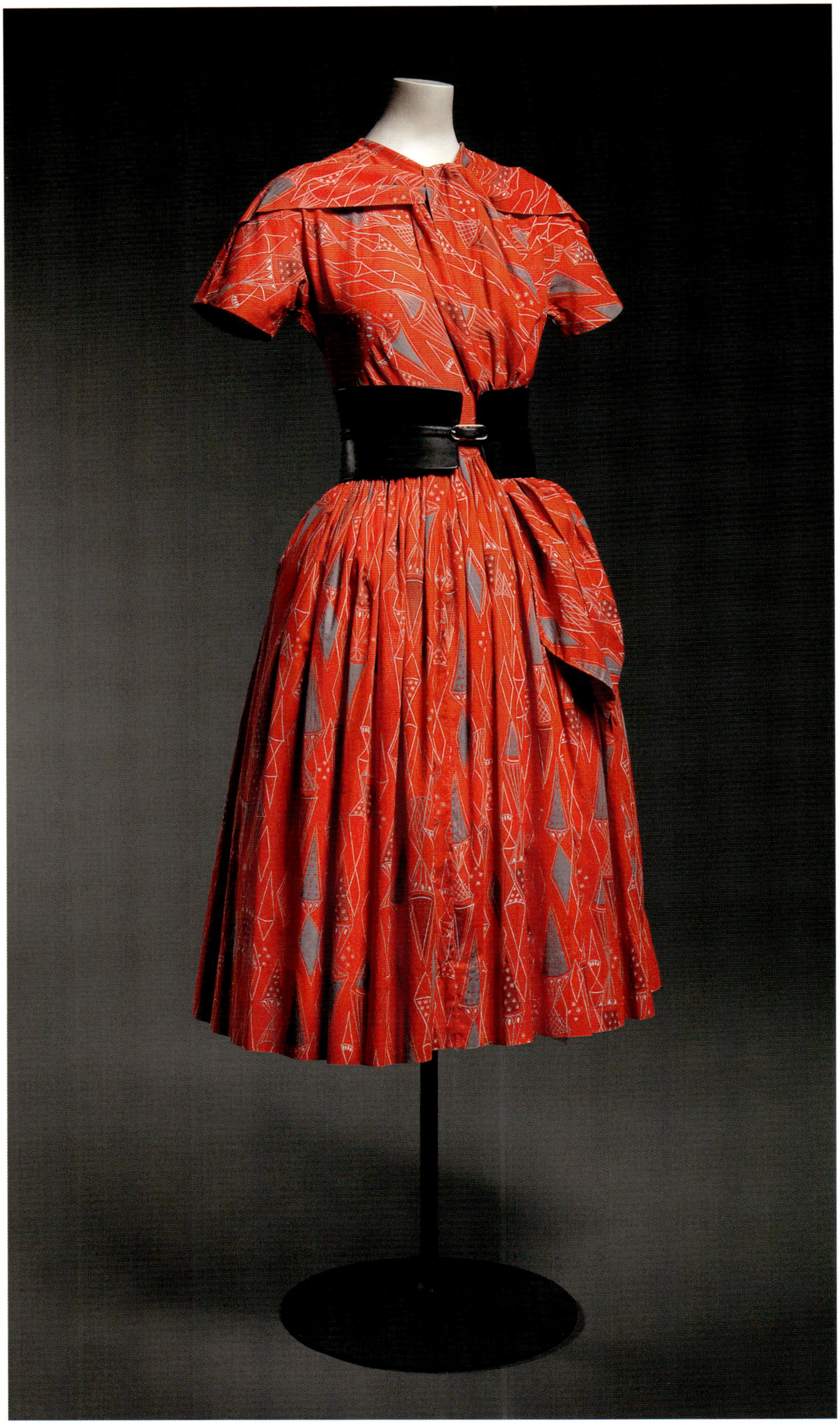

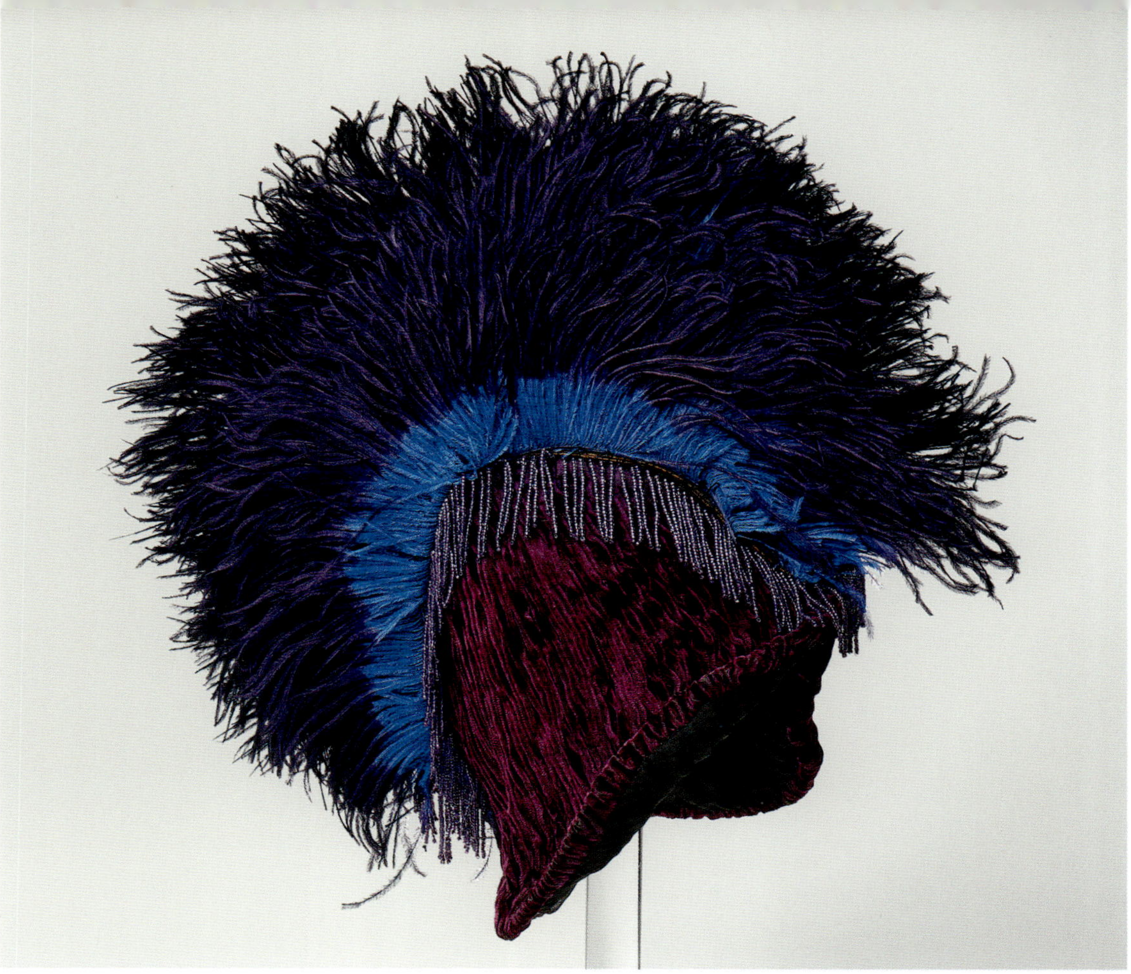

for the similarity constituted a guarantee of quality. Here is the Ford signed 'Chanel.' "[15] This comparison to an assembly line signals the growing appreciation for the great advances in mass production even within the prestigious world of haute couture.

American department stores, the great democratizers of the shopping experience, were key disseminators of accessibly priced American prêt-à-porter. A. T. Stewart's in New York, Wanamaker's in Philadelphia, Hudson's in Detroit, Marshall Field's in Chicago, and I. Magnin on the West Coast had been selling ready-made clothing since the nineteenth century. By the 1920s, even the upscale Bergdorf Goodman started carrying ready-to-wear, which was by then considered the modern way to dress. The export of American ready-made clothing continued apace throughout the twentieth century, and by the 1950s and 1960s, august European department stores had gotten on board: the Galeries Lafayette in Paris sold West Coast–based White Stag sportswear, Liberty of London carried Bonnie Cashin's functional fashion, and Harrods sold California-based designer Rudi Gernreich's avant-garde, pop-infused knitwear.

Department stores were also important incubators for countless designers who started their careers as in-house seamstresses, designers, and accessories makers. Many of the accessories in *Fashioning America* were created by unknown department-store designers for grand emporiums such as Marshall Field's, as well as for smaller local stores such as the Baltimore-based Sondheim, Frank & Co., which sold startlingly avant-garde millinery. In the 1930s, figures such as Dorothy Shaver at the department store Lord & Taylor were profoundly influential in celebrating American design, promoting the work of makers such as Sally Victor, Claire McCardell, and Pauline Trigère. Neiman Marcus was an important advocate of the work of Indigenous designer Lloyd Henri "Kiva" New, and both Ann Lowe and Halston worked at New York's Bergdorf Goodman. Bonwit Teller in Boston was a place of inspiration for a young Bill Cunningham, who started his career as a milliner in New York City before becoming the influential street-style photographer for the *New York Times*. In the 1970s and '80s, Henri Bendel's boutique program to promote emerging American designers helped launch

opposite Claire McCardell, day dress, ca. 1952. Printed cotton plainweave. FIDM Museum Collection: Gift of Shirley Dichek. Courtesy of FIDM Museum at the Fashion Institute of Design & Merchandising, Los Angeles.

above Sondheim, Frank & Co., hat worn by Lulu Glaser, 1920s. Velvet, silk, feathers, and beads. Jimmy Raye Collection, Salem, Massachusetts.

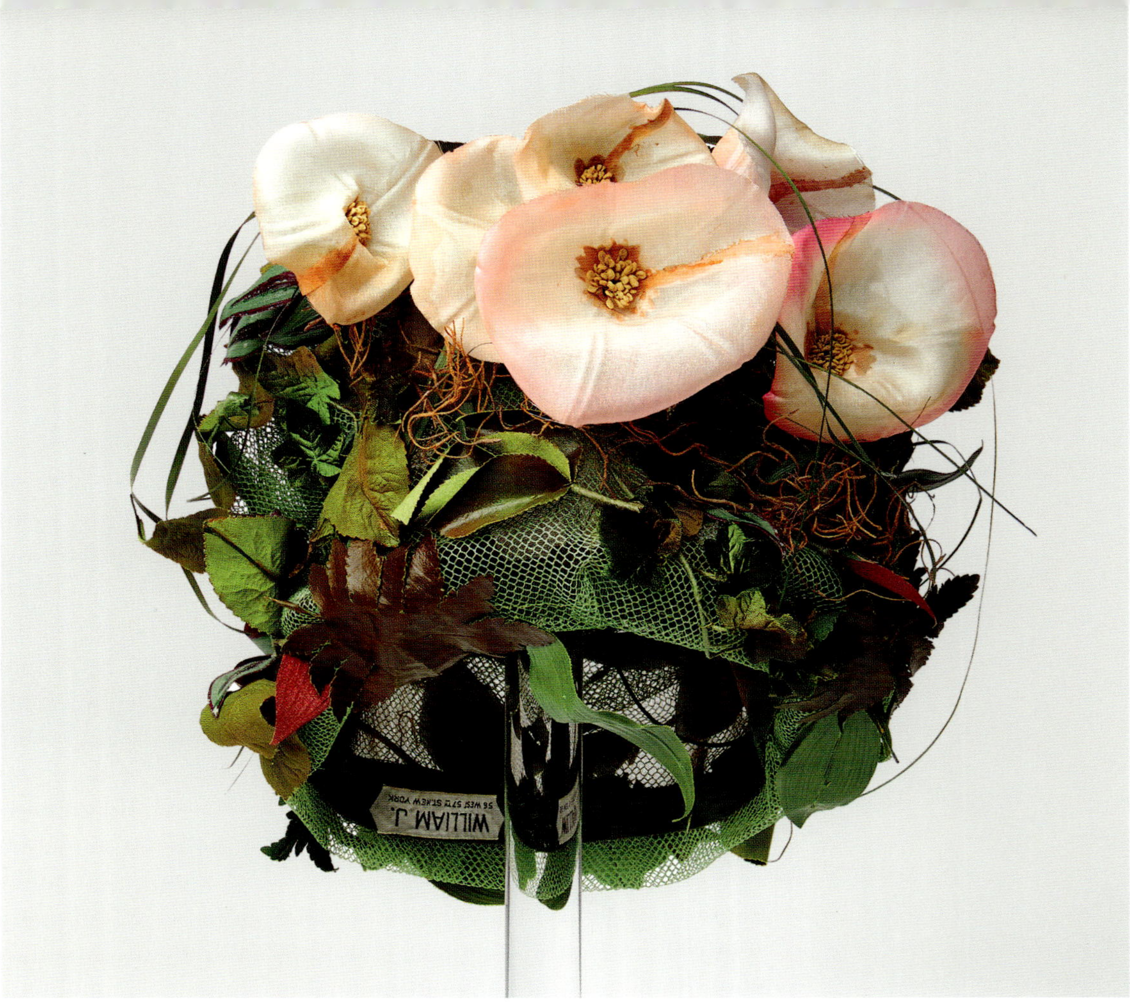

the careers of Fabrice Simon, Stephen Burrows, and Isabel Toledo, all of whose work is featured in this catalogue.

The expansion of ready-made retail and the great advances in garment production had another, unexpected impact. Standard sizes, essential for scaling up ready-to-wear output, changed the way wearers looked at their own bodies. In *Fashioning America*, Emma McClendon and Lauren Downing Peters delve into the history of standard sizing, opening up new perspectives on contemporary issues like self-fashioning and body positivity. One's bust might be close to a "perfect thirty-six" inches, they note, but that measurement fails to account for the wearer's cup size, shoulders, and the space between the collarbone and breast. An important shift occurred in the early twentieth century when consumers started to fit their bodies to their clothing rather than fitting clothes to their bodies. (Curating fashion exhibitions, one quickly learns that almost all mannequins need to be customized in some way to fit a garment on display—unless it is a contemporary runway piece, which will inevitably be a size two or four.) In the last decade, the fashion world has finally begun to respond to the idea that real bodies are never a standard size. American designers such as Christian Siriano are leading the way in promoting body inclusivity and positivity.

The sleeker silhouette that began to emerge in the 1920s, coupled with the coincident rise of Hollywood, encouraged a body consciousness and interest in physical fitness that helped promote a sporty, active, outdoorsy West Coast lifestyle. As a result, many innovative ready-to-wear sportswear and bathing-suit designers were based in or hailed from the West Coast. The swimwear industry was at the forefront of incorporating new textile technologies into their design, experimenting with knits and elasticized fibers that resulted in garments that fit like a second skin. In 1936, Margit Fellegi, head designer of Cole of California, invented stretchable bathing suits, which could be made in cotton and wool and shirred with Lastex, an elastic yarn covered with cotton, silk, or rayon threads. By the 1940s, California was on its way to becoming the biggest producer and exporter of bathing suits in the world; by the 1960s, a fashion editor could rightfully proclaim, "Of course California bathing suits are all over Europe."[16] The West Coast is also the birthplace

above William J. (Bill) Cunningham, hat, late 1940s or '50s. Net, silk, and buckram. Jimmy Raye Collection, Salem, Massachusetts.

opposite Marilyn Monroe wearing a Catalina bathing suit, 1950s.

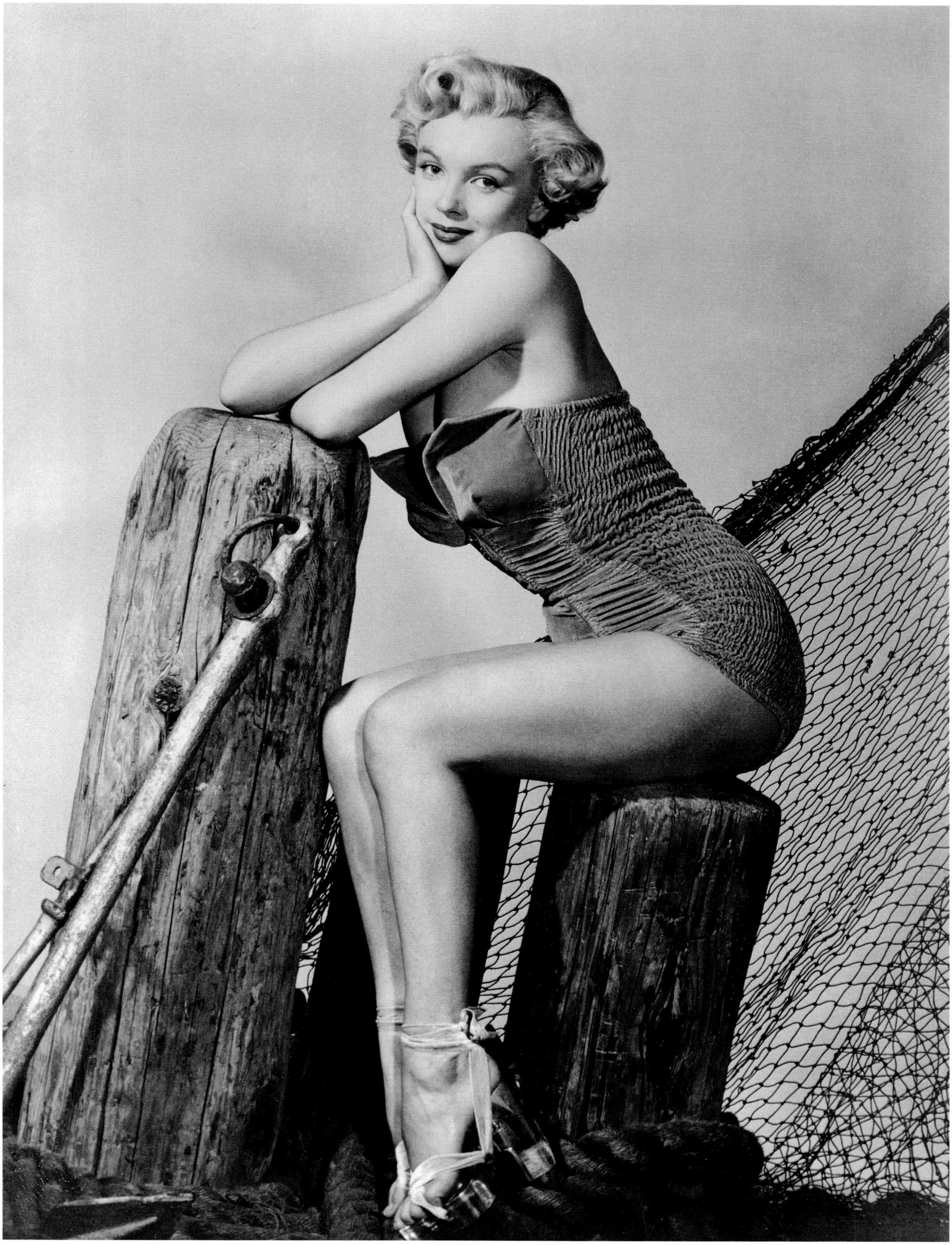

of surfing and skateboarding culture and a distinctive style of sportswear that emanated from the beach and street kids. Created by "non designer" surfers and boarders such as Shawn Stüssy and James Jebbia of Supreme, this style has retained its broad-based appeal and cool factor because it continues to operate outside the standard fashion system, even if today the look is far from subcultural.

STORY 4
STREETWEAR

Undoubtedly, the most significant American contributions to global style in the post–World War II era lie in streetwear. American street style as a distinct and influential form dates back at least to the 1940s and the zoot suit, with its baggy, pegged pants, extra-long jacket with extreme shoulder pads, and dangling key-chain, to be worn with "conked" or pompadoured hair. Originating in Harlem in the mid-1930s, it was embraced by African American and Latino youth as a deliberate countercultural marker. The extreme quantity of fabric the suit used was construed by some as wasteful during times of economic depression and wartime rationing, but these accusations of a supposed lack of patriotism were often simply a pretext for racial discrimination. This conflict came to a head in the summer of 1943. Violence erupted in Los Angeles when white sailors on leave targeted the local Latino population, often identifying them by their style of dress, which led to the conflicts remembered as the Zoot Suit Riots. Despite its negative associations in some quarters, the zoot suit worked its way into contemporary culture, finding expression in the entertainment industry, most famously with Cab Calloway singing and dancing in a zoot suit in the 1943 film *Stormy Weather*. The zoot suit foreshadowed subsequent developments in streetwear in its oversize styling, bold accessories, and distinctive headgear.

The stylistic innovations of 1980s and early 1990s rap and hip-hop performers have powerfully shaped American fashion in the years since. Designers such as April Walker and FUBU dressed stars and trendsetters like Salt-N-Pepa, LL Cool J, Big Daddy Kane, and the Fat Boys. One of the most influential figures of the period was Daniel Day, aka Dapper Dan, whose boutique in Harlem became *the* place for many hip-hop artists to purchase performance gear, street-savvy designs that co-opted the logos of Gucci, Louis Vuitton, and Fendi. These famous brands, and their associations with luxury, appealed to a range of clientele, but hip-hop artists were not necessarily made to feel welcome in high-end fashion stores. Nor did the clothes feature quite the right cuts: in Dapper Dan's words, he took the styles and "black-enized" them.[17] His first piece was a jacket made from a Gucci garment bag, the pliable canvas patterned with the iconic double G offering a perfect base for experimentation. Unable to afford extensive purchases of the bags, Dapper Dan taught himself the computer program Corel Draw and bought a sublimation printer to reproduce the logos on various fabrics and leathers that he then crafted into tracksuits and snorkel jackets. When his store appeared on the cable television show *Yo! MTV Raps* in 1988, he called it a "turning point in the relationship between street culture and the mainstream—everybody on the show was a Dapper Dan customer."[18] Hip-hop style soon moved from the street to the shopping mall and found a willing consumer base beyond urban centers.

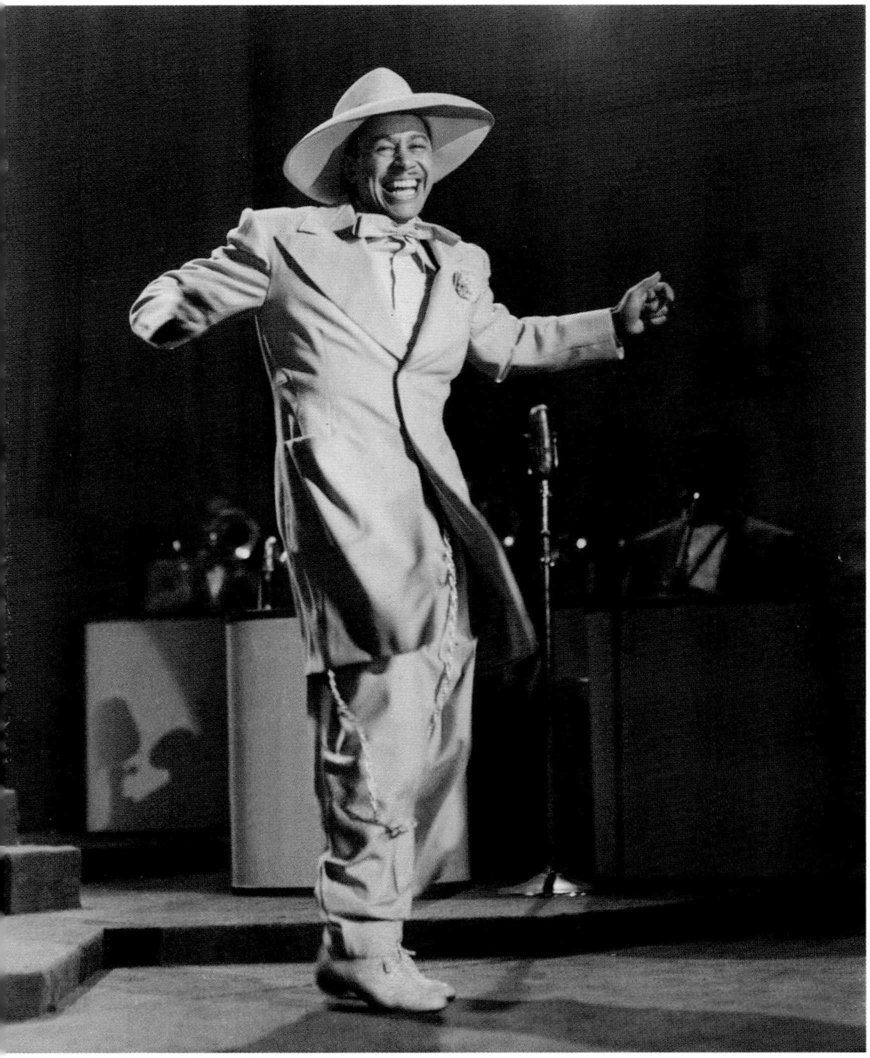

left Cab Calloway wearing a zoot suit in a musical performance from the 1943 motion picture *Stormy Weather*. The New York Public Library Digital Collections.

opposite Dapper Dan (left) and rapper Dave East at Dapper Dan Atelier in New York City for video shoot, September 2021.

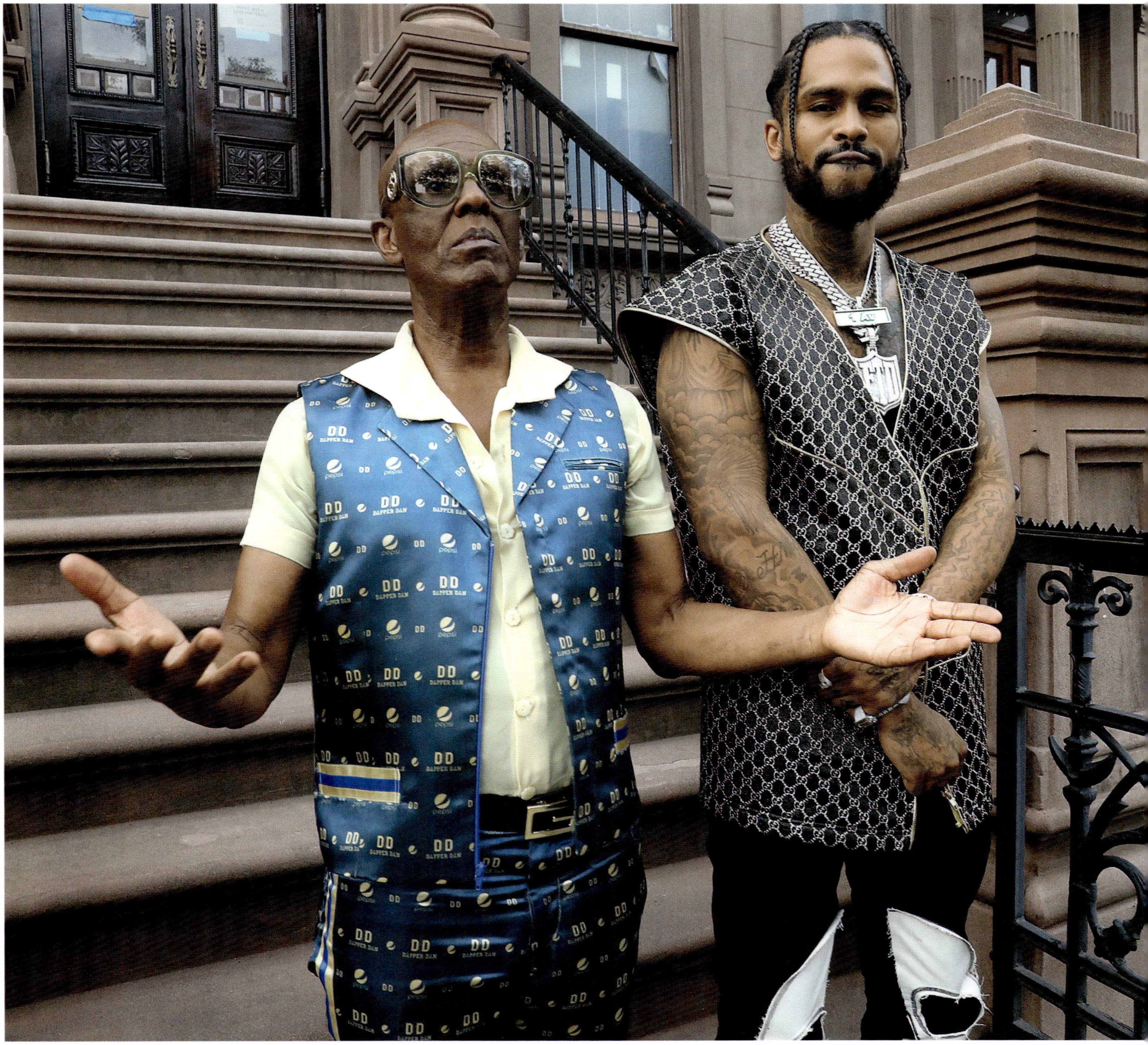
DD
DAPPER DAN

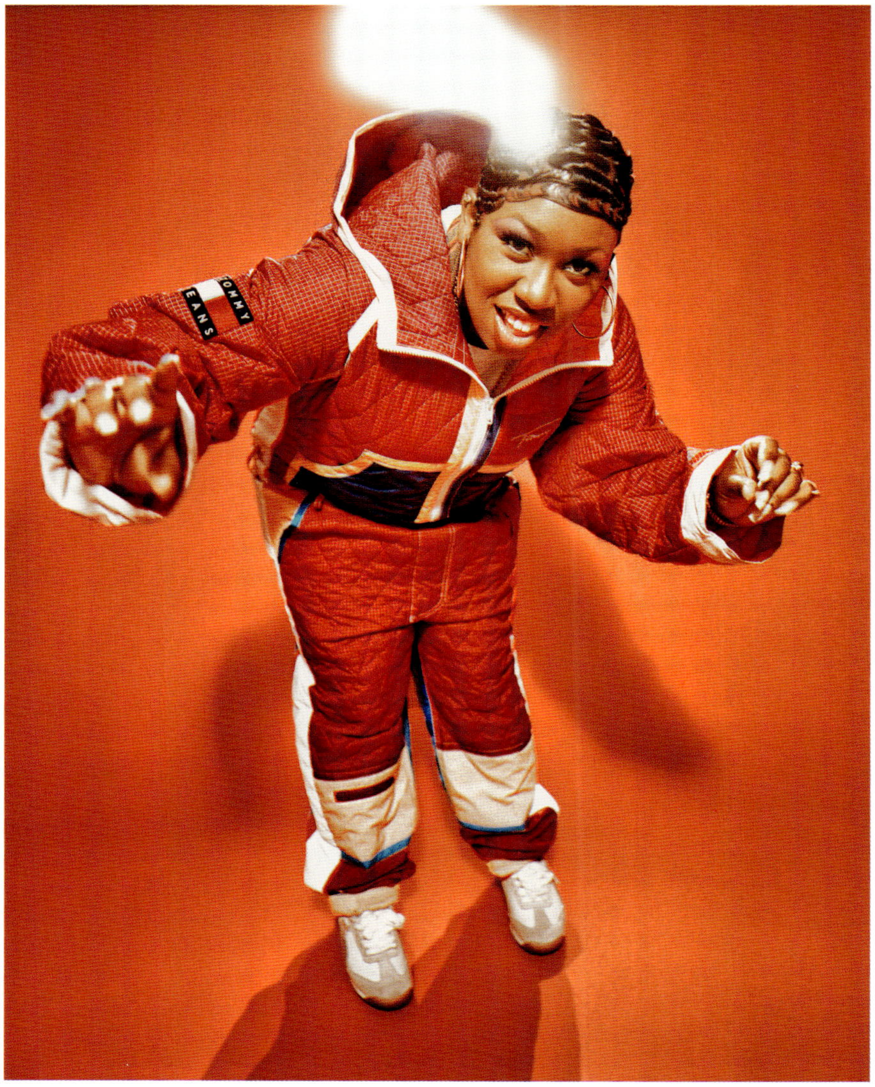

Hip-hop songs have remained replete with references to fashion and specific designers through the present, and its stars have birthed myriad trends. Hip-hop spawned the vogue for wearing oversize Ralph Lauren polo shirts and Tommy Hilfiger rugby shirts, effectively subverting two forms of dress that represented upper-class white culture. Hilfiger, ever tuned into the benefits of aligning with the music industry,[19] was one of the first mainstream designers to market directly to the hip-hop generation, dressing performers such as Missy Elliott and Snoop Dogg, for whom he famously provided an outsized rugby shirt for his first appearance on *Saturday Night Live*, in 1994. Hilfiger approached Dapper Dan to collaborate, but as he noted in his memoir, he had no interest in "more plantation stuff."[20] Dapper Dan was eventually driven out of the industry because of copyright infringement, but in an ironic twist of fate, he is now designing for Gucci. After its lead designer, Alessandro Michele, appropriated Dapper Dan's 1980s designs for his 2018 "Cruise" collection, the social-media outrage that followed resulted in a partnership between Michele and Dapper Dan for a new collection.

Today, designers have greater control of their own narratives. In this volume, Elizabeth Way takes up one example, that of Kerby Jean-Raymond and his label Pyer Moss, whose "spiritual sportswear" fuses streetwear with couture in garments that communicate powerful messages related to Black history. Another young designer, Olivia Anthony—the rare woman streetwear designer in a field still dominated by men—makes ensembles that feature the archetypal hallmarks of streetwear: oversize rugby shirts, sweatpants, branded sneakers, and bold accessories such as "doorknocker" earrings that are a key aspect of Black feminine street style.

above Missy Elliott wearing a Tommy Jeans by Tommy Hilfiger jumpsuit, 1997. Nylon. PVH Archives.

opposite Olivia Anthony for LIVSTREETWEAR, "A Love Letter to Our Culture" ensemble, 2021. Cotton and Spandex. Courtesy of LIVSTREETWEAR.

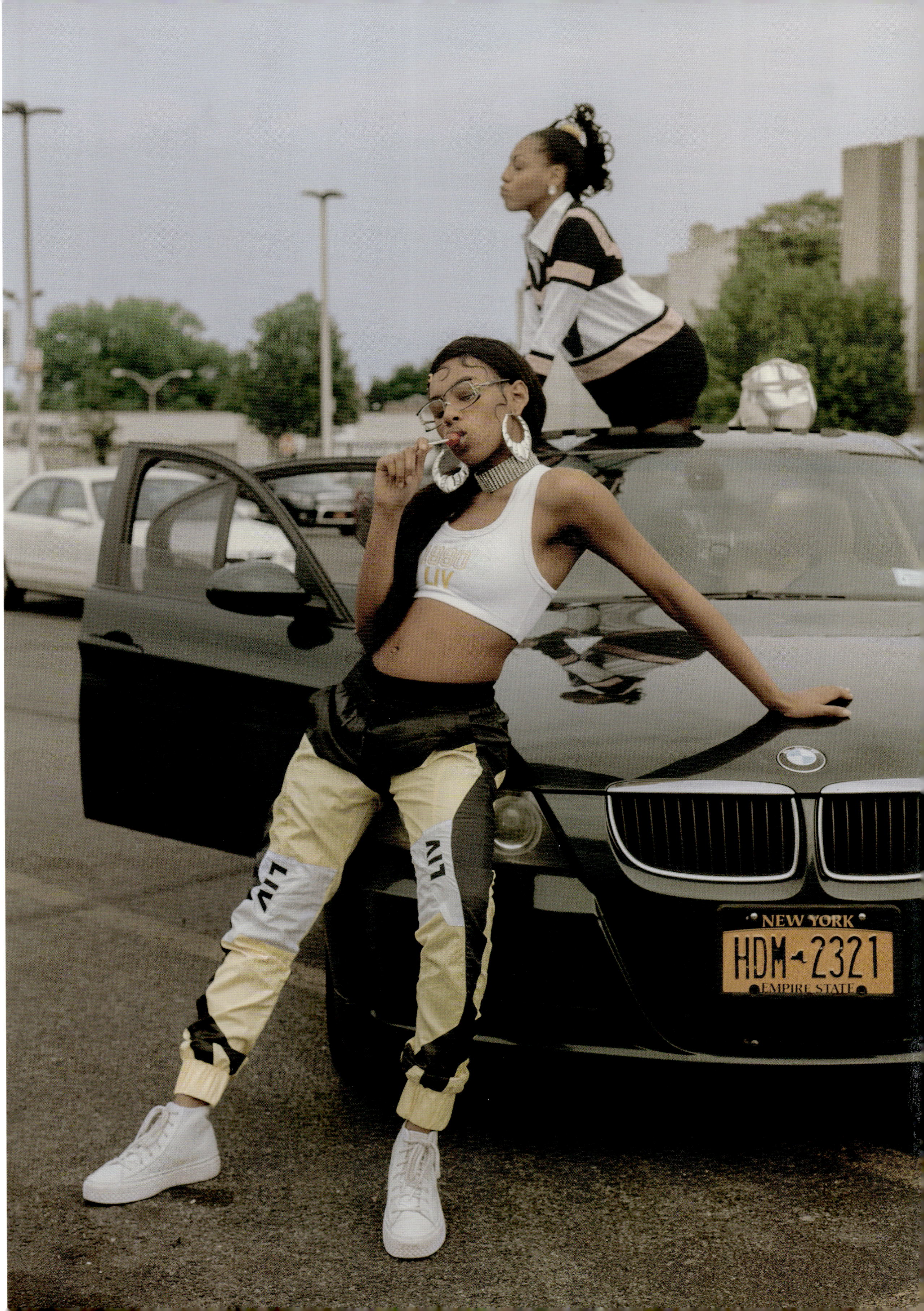

1990
LIV
NEW YORK
HDM 2321
EMPIRE STATE

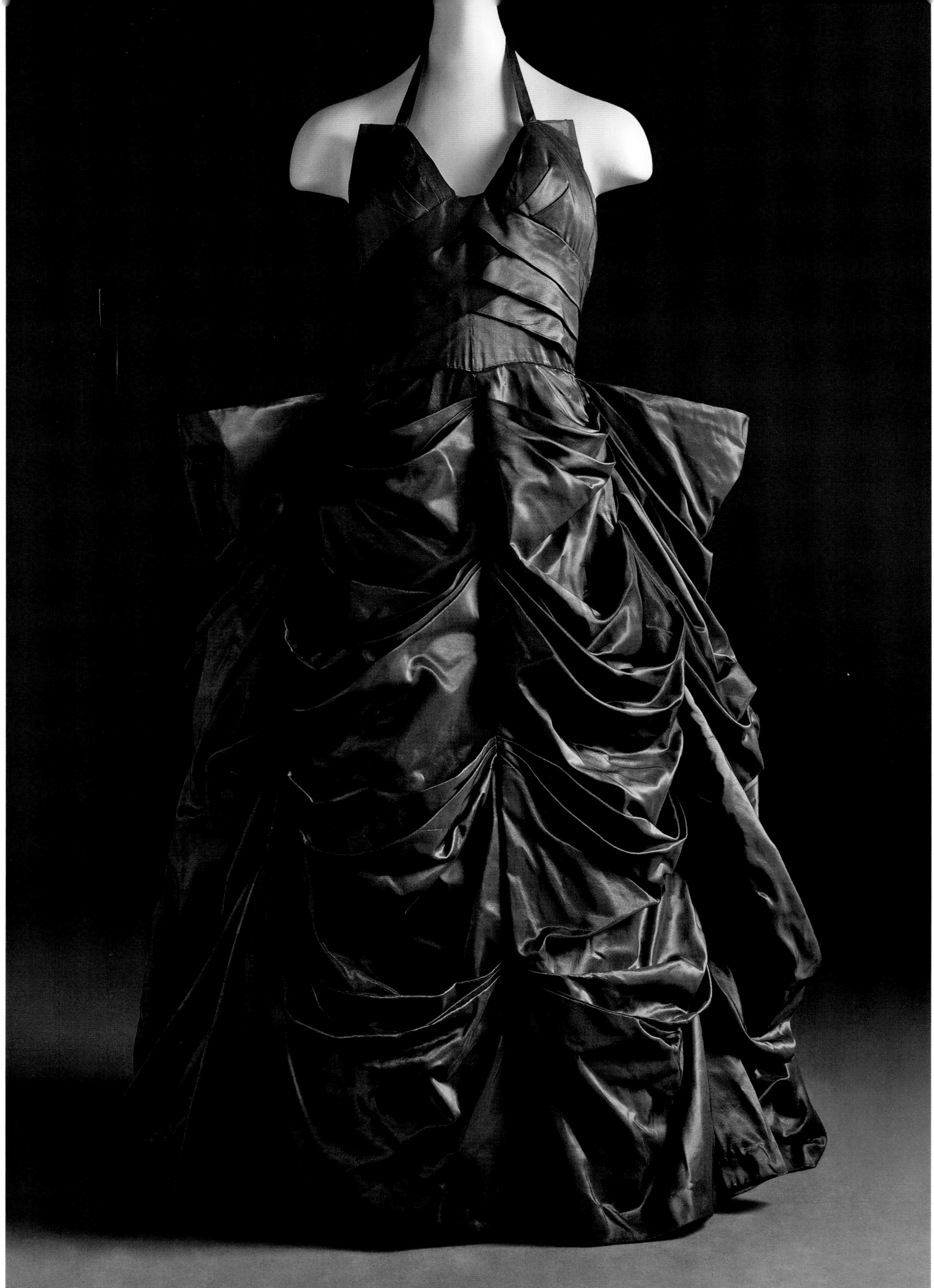

STORY 5
GLAMOUR

Film and music have been potent disseminators of American style on a global scale. Many fashion histories look at them as phenomena separate from fashion per se, citing the difference between fashion and "costume," but the line between the two has often been blurred, and each has undoubtedly influenced the other. One of the most famous twentieth-century Hollywood costume designers, Gilbert Adrian, became a powerful force in the fashion industry, setting trends with his "costume" work before bringing his uniquely glamorous style to the masses when he spearheaded his own fashion line beginning in 1941. Almost every designer of the twentieth and twenty-first centuries represented in *Fashioning America* has benefited at some point in their career from a connection to Hollywood or the music industry. Some have cultivated those connections explicitly, while others have gained cachet indirectly when their designs were featured in a film or on the red carpet.

As the aspirational "dream factory" of popular culture has grown in power and reach, so too has the accessibility of ready-made copies of the clothing seen on the silver screen. By 1937, the achievability of a Hollywood look was noted by George Orwell:

> The two things that have probably made the greatest difference are the movies and the mass-production of cheap, smart clothes since the war. You may have three half-pence in your pocket, not a prospect in the world . . . but in your new clothes you can stand on the street corner, indulging in a private daydream of yourself as Clark Gable or Greta Garbo.[21]

In 1938, *Vogue*, too, acknowledged the selling power of film: "Hollywood is certainly the most perfect visual medium of fashion propaganda that ever existed." It was the birthplace of a uniquely American brand of glamour, the inventor of the red carpet, and the popularizer of the full spectrum of iconic American fashion.

One surprising yet seemingly enduring form that captures American glamour while reflecting the influence of various hallmarks of fashion in the United States is the Nudie suit. According to one writer, "In the global narrative of fashion . . . [the Nudie suit] its clearly one of America's greatest contributions, period."[22]

opposite Adrian, evening gown, 1948. Silk taffeta. FIDM Museum Collection: Gift of Bob Diamond. Courtesy of FIDM Museum at the Fashion Institute of Design & Merchandising, Los Angeles.

The creation of Ukrainian Jewish immigrant Nuta Kotlyarenko, Nudie suits marry the sparkle and glitter of Eastern European folk dress and Hollywood glamour with cowboy attire. Nudie began his career designing costumes for New York City show-girls, but it was only after moving to Hollywood in 1940 that he carved out a niche for himself by creating meticulously beaded, rhinestone-studded, and embroidered suits. Famous musicians such as Elvis, Elton John, Gram Parsons, Hank Snow, and countless others have donned this distinctive form. Currently, Nudie suits are witnessing a revival, no doubt because performers outside the country-music genre such as Lil Nas X and Post Malone have worn them in recent years, and European couture houses such as Christian Dior, Gucci, and Yves Saint Laurent have shown their own versions on the runway. Various American contemporary designers are carrying the "torch of the Rodeo Tailor,"[23] including Nudie's former tailor Manuel Cuevas and Austin's Fort Lonesome, which specializes in vibrantly patterned, hand-built garments with chain-stitch embroidery that maintain "the continuum between art and fashion with a strong focus on heirloom quality and unexpected imagery."[24] Indianapolis-based Jerry Lee Atwood has dressed Lil Nas X for many music-video and public appearances in his "Street Cowboy" guise, and Nas's fusion of hip-hop and country style has effectively blurred the boundaries between two distinctively American styles of dress.

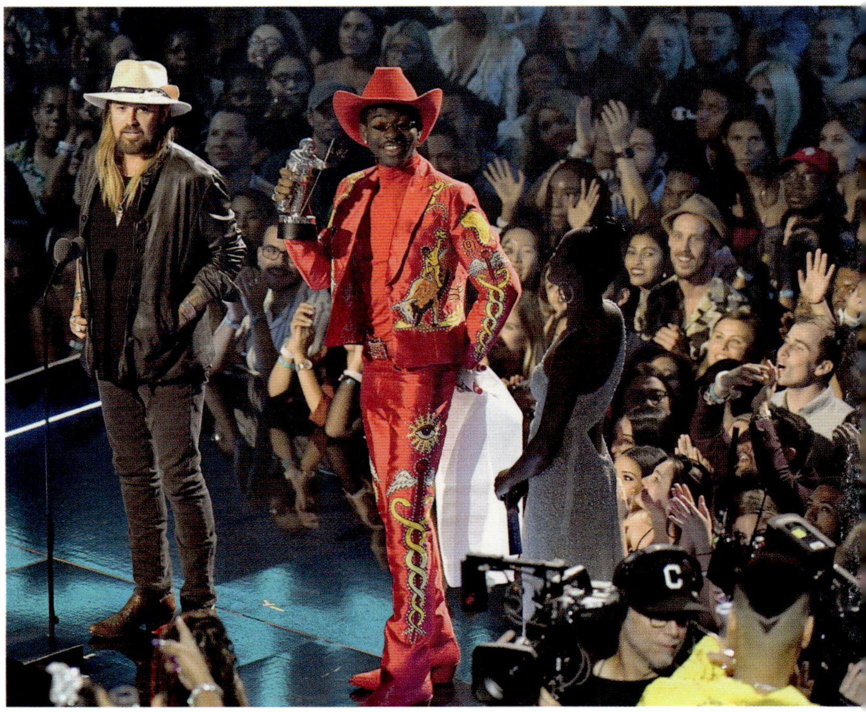

Lil Nas X wearing a Jerry Lee Atwood suit, with Billy Ray Cyrus at the 2019 MTV Music Video Awards.

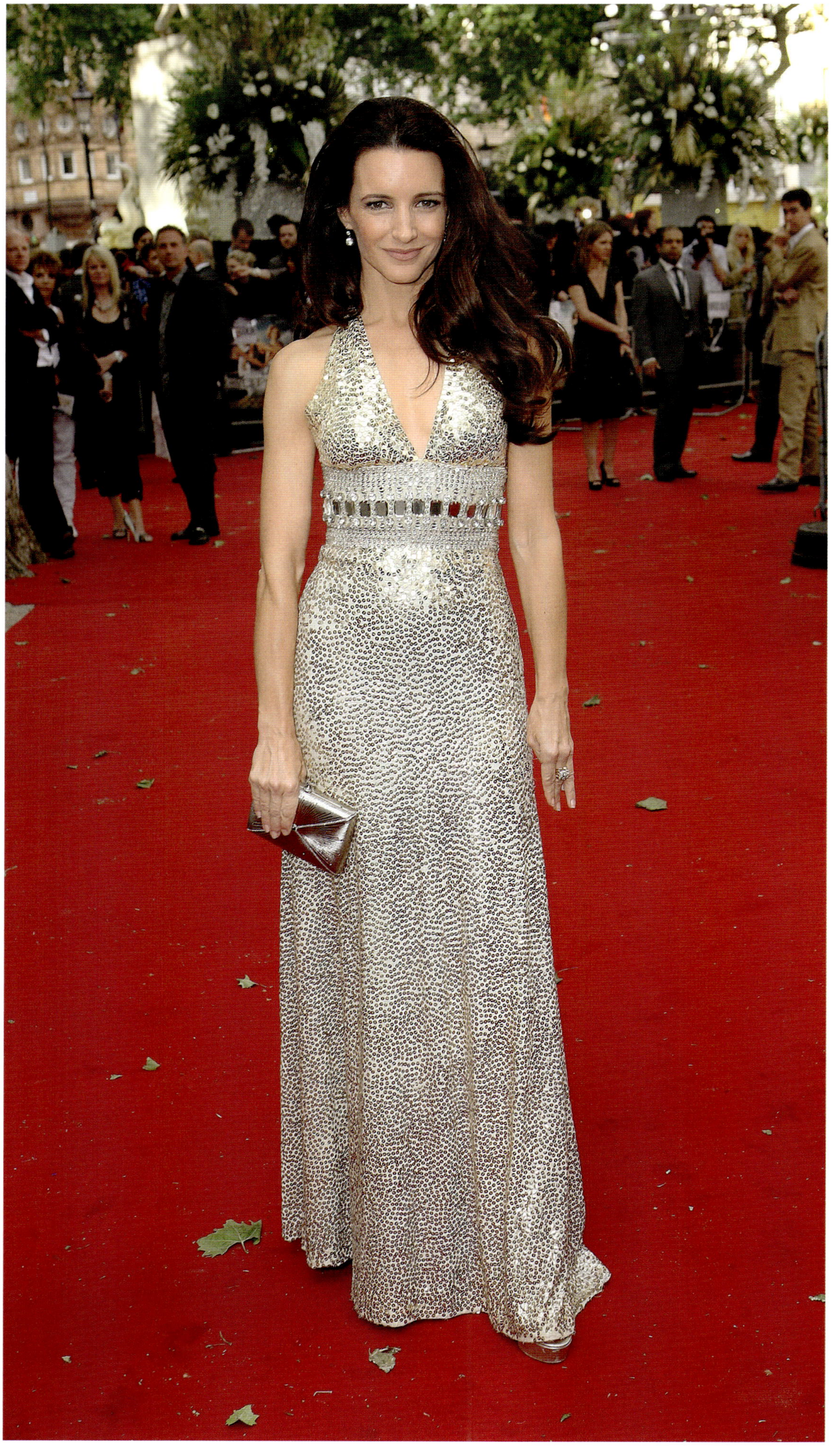

The red carpet itself should be regarded as an American fashion innovation. The phrase *red-carpet treatment* dates to 1902 and is derived from the use of plush red carpeting to direct passengers boarding the 20th Century Limited luxury train between New York and Chicago. It was Hollywood, however, that made the phenomenon larger than life. The red carpet was first used in 1961 at that year's Academy Awards ceremony, and it became a salient, internationally recognized locus of style after the first color-television broadcast of the Oscars in 1966.[25] Even in today's social-media-driven culture, the red carpet in its various expressions, particularly for Hollywood events, remains a premier site for voyeuristic fantasy and enjoys fanatical press coverage. *Fashioning America* includes a red-carpet dress by designer Norman Norell. One of the mid-twentieth century's major American designers, he began his career costuming stage and film stars, training with silent-film designer Natacha Rambova. Although he was known for minimalist design in the 1950s and '60s, he remained attuned to the power of screencraft. His sequined "mermaid" gowns, most famously worn by Marilyn Monroe and other stars, are considered classics of twentieth-century design and quintessential statements of Hollywood glamour. Their lasting allure causes them to resurface time and again on the red carpet, including when Kristin Davis wore a vintage Norell dress for the 2010 London premiere of the film *Sex and the City 2*.

REFASHIONING AMERICA

The enormous popularity of the TV/film series *Sex and the City* made it one of the most influential franchises for fashion in recent years. It featured the handiwork of costume designer Patricia Field, who famously mixed urban street style with high fashion. Field adorned Carrie with a classic bit of hip-hop iconography, a nameplate necklace and matching earrings, which became a signature look for Sarah Jessica Parker's on-screen persona. Its real source was not lost on observers, however, such as the fashion scholar Tanisha Ford: "Once a white woman like Patricia Field said it was fashion, the ghetto gold look was now a vintage something to emulate."[26]

Fashion has always drawn inspiration from varied sources, but the line between appropriation and appreciation is often obfuscated, and the origins of particular styles are not always clear. New interpretations of fashion history, often driven by designers themselves, are highlighting longstanding tensions that are newly coming to the fore. Xuxa Rodríguez's essay in *Fashioning America*, for example, explores how Eurocentric ideals of whiteness in traditional fashion practice have deeply affected our perceptions of beauty and style. Native American fashion designers in particular grapple with educating fashion consumers to think beyond "Native" graphic patterns and symbols to understand that the garments they produce tell deeper stories related to their history, culture, landscape, and their view of humanity's place in the world. Respected Indigenous designers such as Patricia Michaels, Jamie Okuma, and Virgil Ortiz have large followings; yet, as of 2020, the Council of Fashion Designers of America included no Indigenous designers. Amber-Dawn Bear Robe's essay in this volume describes the conflicts inherent in this transitional moment for the industry, taking the opportunity to imagine a future where inclusion will not be a separate platform and designers of color will have equal footing on the fashion stage.

With a contemporary fashion industry driven by global production and consumption, e-commerce, and social media, can we even define "Americanness" in fashion in 2022? It is a rare designer today who does not use cotton or polyester from China or embroidery from India, or have shoes made in Vietnamese factories. The rich international exchange of fashion ideas and design inspiration has a long history, with European couture houses looking to the United States for inspiration for decades. Salvatore Ferragamo, founder of one of the foremost purveyors of luxury footwear and innovative design, learned lessons related to mass production, star promotion, ergonomics, and practicality in his early days in America. Yves Saint Laurent incorporated American teen style into his 1970s collections, and French designer Karl Lagerfeld's 1990s mining of hip-hop style for Chanel paired large-scale gold chains, baggy jean shorts, and oversize logos with the brand's traditional plaid. Lagerfeld's transformative moves breathed life into what had been considered a staid couture house and helped Chanel regain its footing in the luxury market. Sneakers have swept the globe, with almost all high-end fashion houses carrying some lavish version of this once humble athletic footwear. In what could be called the apotheosis of American streetwear, fashion conglomerates that have traditionally hewed close to their luxury roots have been steadily hiring American designers to imbue their ateliers with street savvy, including, most famously, Louis Vuitton's hiring of the late Illinois-born designer and Off-White founder Virgil Abloh.

opposite Norman Norell, "Mermaid" dress, ca. 1966. Silk, metal, and synthetic. Worn by Kristin Davis at the UK premiere of *Sex and the City 2*, London, 2010.

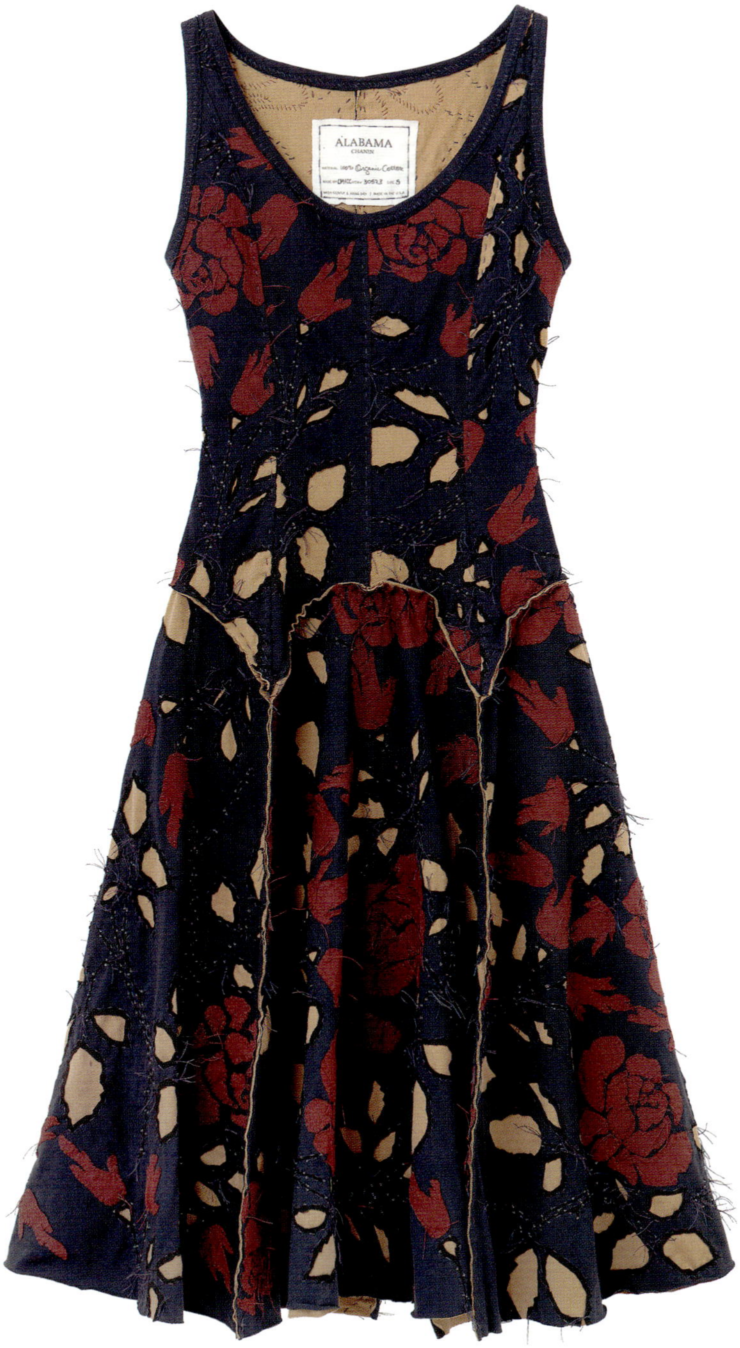

Despite these positive global cross-pollinations, there is a growing awareness that the current model of global fashion production has led to overconsumption of fast fashion, contributed to unfair labor practices, and become a factor in the climate crisis. The decline of fashion-related manufacturing in the United States—denim, to cite a prominent example, is no longer mass-produced in this country[27]—and decades of outsourcing have helped lead to questionable safety standards in factories abroad. The 2013 Rana Plaza building collapse in Dhaka, Bangladesh, in which at least 1,132 workers, mostly women, perished, was a modern-day Triangle Shirtwaist Factory fire.

The current model of global fashion production has led to over-consumption of fast fashion, contributed to unfair labor practices, and become a factor in the climate crisis.

Smaller design houses are now grappling with how to efficiently and cost-effectively produce within our borders. Although it will take many decades to reinvigorate textile industries in America, smaller producers are leading the way. Ginew, based in Portland, Oregon, is a Native-owned denim company cofounded by Erik Brodt (Ojibwe) and Amanda Bruegl (Oneida and Mohican) that reappropriates a textile with a challenging history and filters it through a uniquely Indigenous and modern lens. After achieving critical success in New York, Natalie Chanin set out to create a small-scale, sustainable textile business in her home state of Alabama. That company, Alabama Chanin, has spearheaded an organic-cotton cottage industry, uses upcycled materials in the workshop's garments, and employs local "generational sewers" to create the brand's distinctive appliqué and embroidery. Korean-born Oklahoma native Ji Won Choi, meanwhile, turns deadstock

above Natalie Chanin, Cynthia Rose Dress, 2021. One hundred percent organic cotton jersey, upcycled cotton T-shirts and organic fabric scraps from Alabama Chanin's design studio, clear seed beads, and Button Craft thread. Courtesy of Natalie Chanin for Alabama Chanin.

opposite Ji Won Choi, Jogakbo Dress, "Antecedent" collection, Summer 2021. Deadstock patchwork squares. IED Firenze students: V. Botarelli, A. Capoccetta, M. Catarzi, IED Istituto Europeo di Design S.p.A.

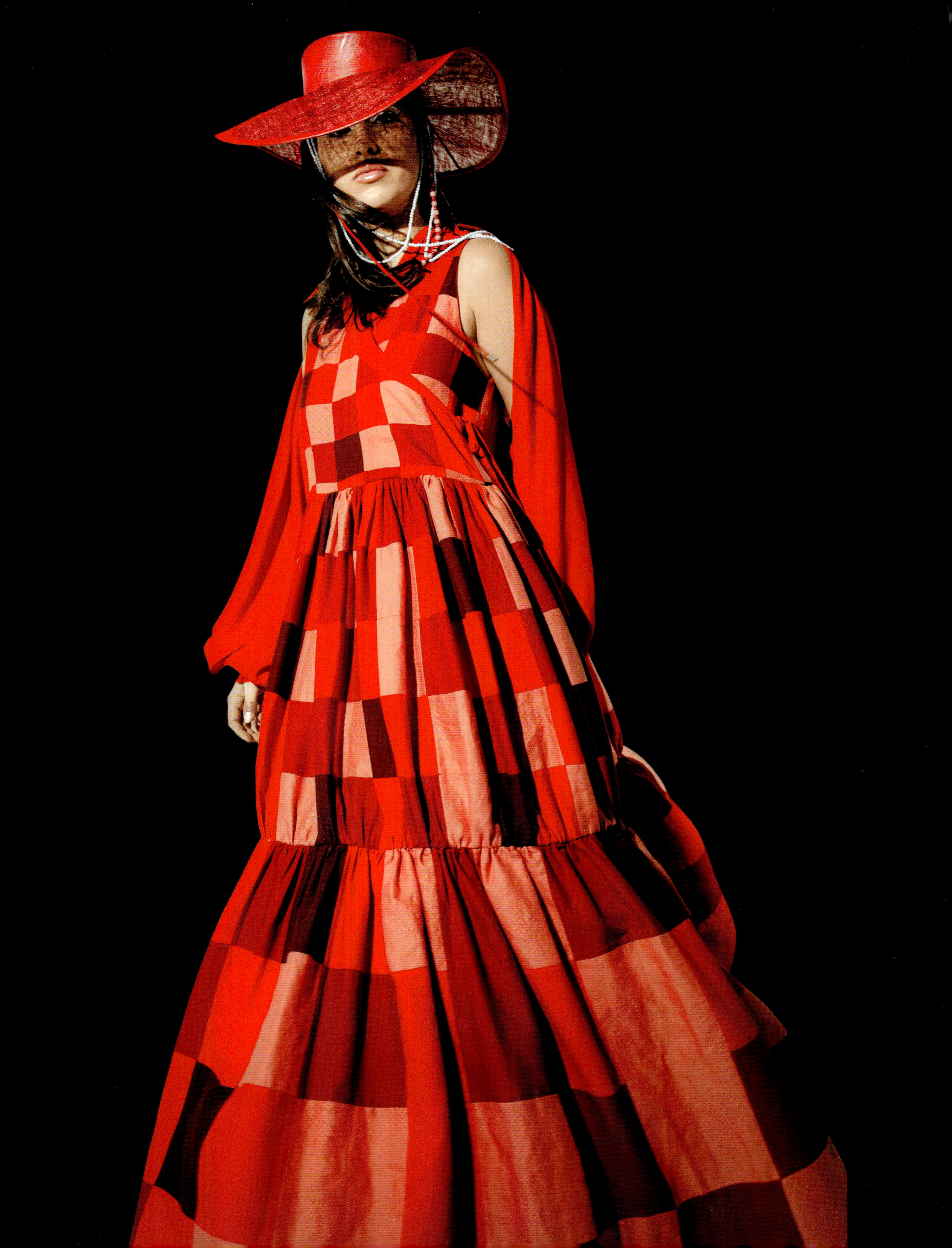

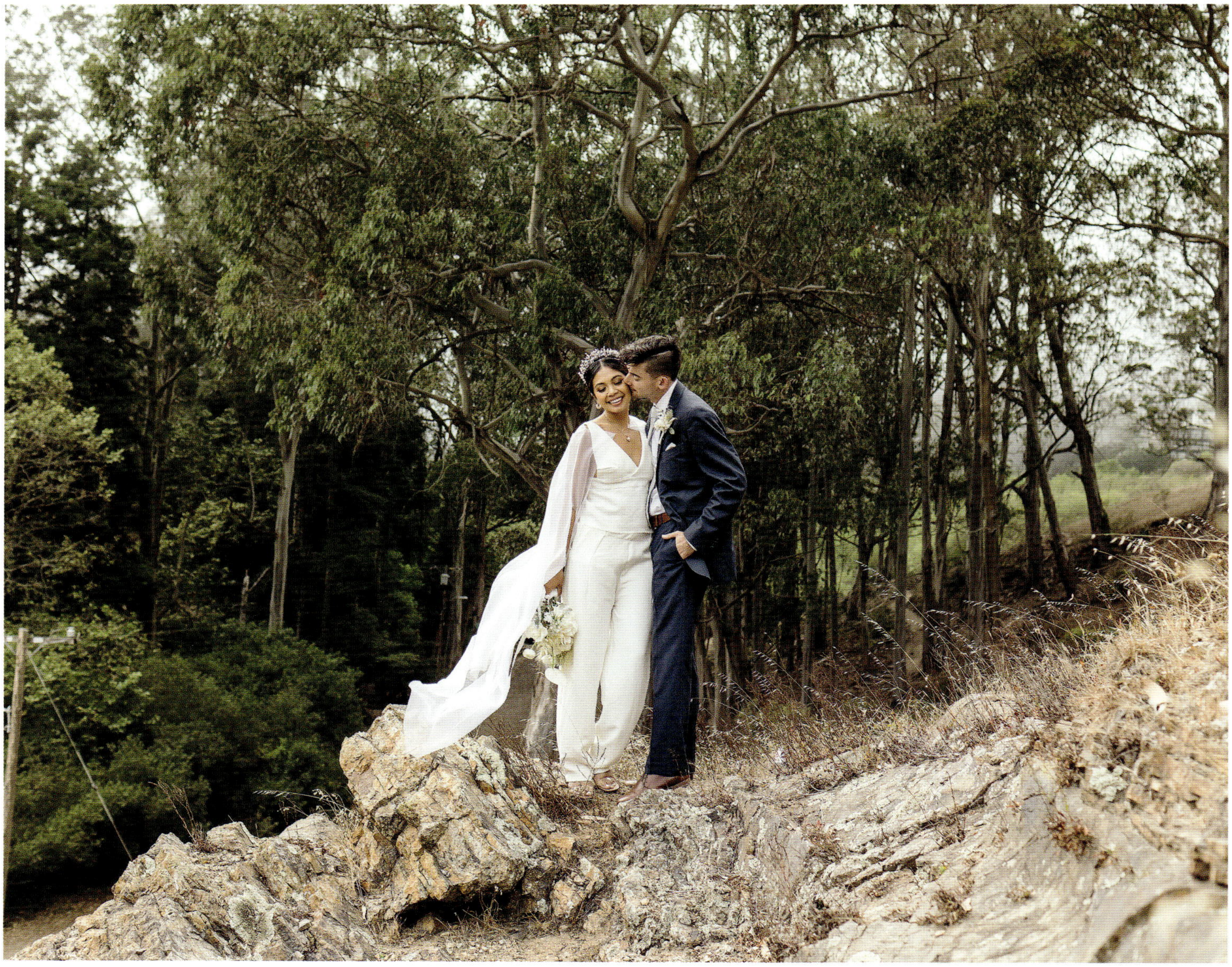

squares into an ethereal and striking dress that references *jogakbo*, a centuries-old Korean tradition of recycling fabric into patchwork wrapping cloths, and shares inspiration with American quilting.

Asian American designer Shelly Xu's zero-waste initiatives use every last scrap of fabric in even more efficient ways. The bridal pants ensemble she created for photographer/entrepreneur Praise Santos McKenna incorporated deadstock and upcycled fabrics from bridal powerhouse Vera Wang and, at the bride's request, included a tribute to her heritage in the raised shoulders that are typical for Filipino wedding dresses. The changes occurring in fashion are more than material, however: a new generation of contemporary designers is infusing fashion with thought-provoking narratives. Design house Ikiré Jones, whose work was featured in the 2018 blockbuster *Black Panther*, incorporates messages related to social justice into tailored suits made of textiles inspired by the African diaspora. Founded in Philadelphia by Nigerian American designer, writer, musician, and lawyer Walé Oyéjidé, the house works with tailor Sam Hubler to create, in their words, "clothing for a higher calling" that illuminates the lives of marginalized people and addresses issues related to migration and displacement.

Performers such as Rihanna and Viktoria Modesta are using their fame to disrupt commonly held conceptions of beauty. Rihanna's Savage X Fenty lingerie brand encourages body positivity by offering a broader range of sizes, and her make-up line Fenty Beauty focuses on inclusivity across skin tones and gender. Modesta turns what would traditionally be perceived as a "disability," her partial loss of a leg as a teen, into a powerful mode of self-expression that melds high-tech prostheses with fashion, art, and performance.

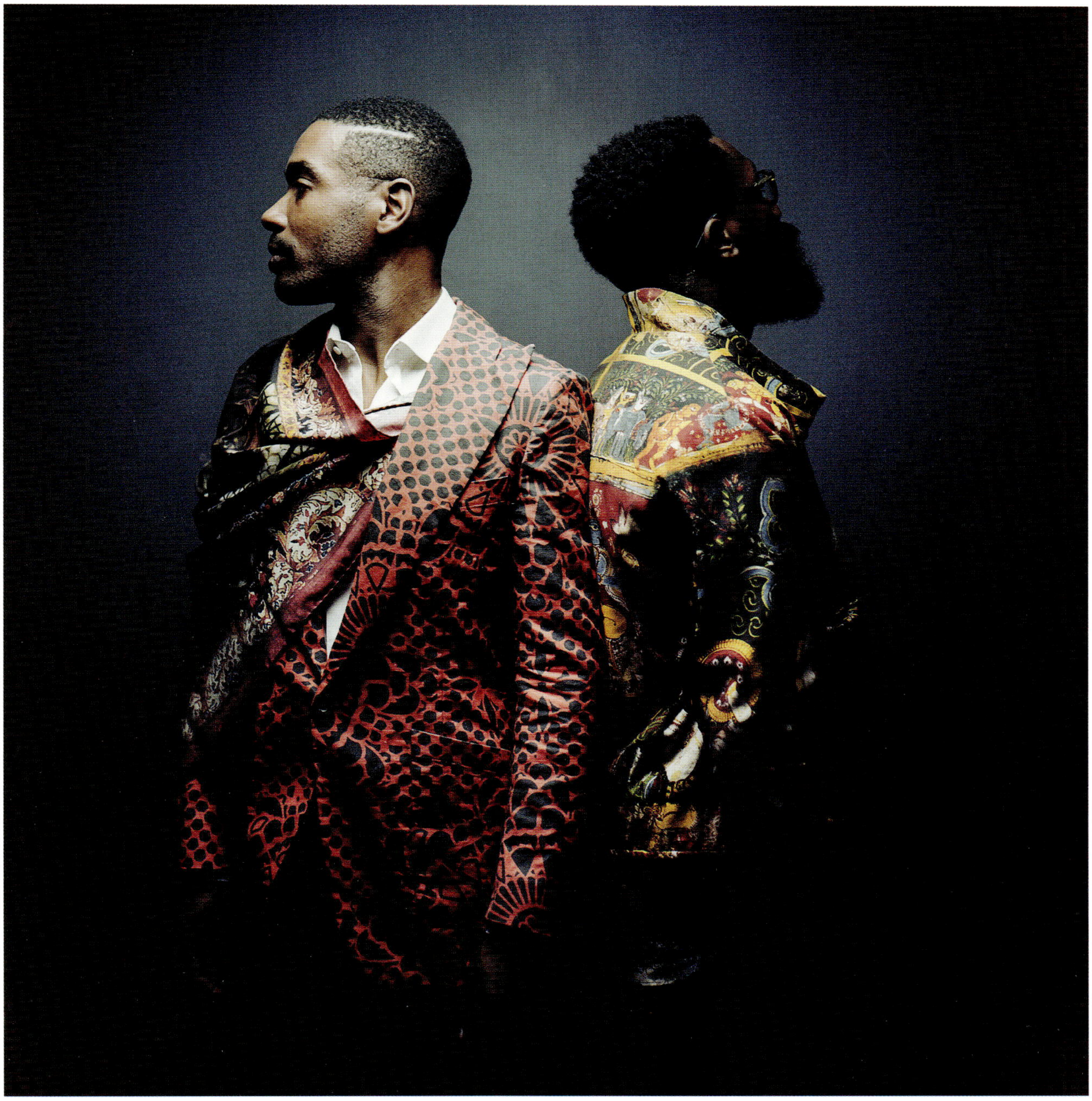

opposite Shelly Xu, "Three-Piece Zero Waste Wedding Design," 2021. Upcycled and deadstock fabrics from Vera Wang and Debs. Shelly Xu, SXD, for Praise Santos McKenna.

above Ikiré Jones, ensembles from "And Other Stories from Our Stolen Children" collection, Spring/Summer 2016.

Viktoria Modesta wearing an Elena Velez dress, prosthetic by Alex Freire, shoes by United Nude, and belt by Bond Hardware, 2020.

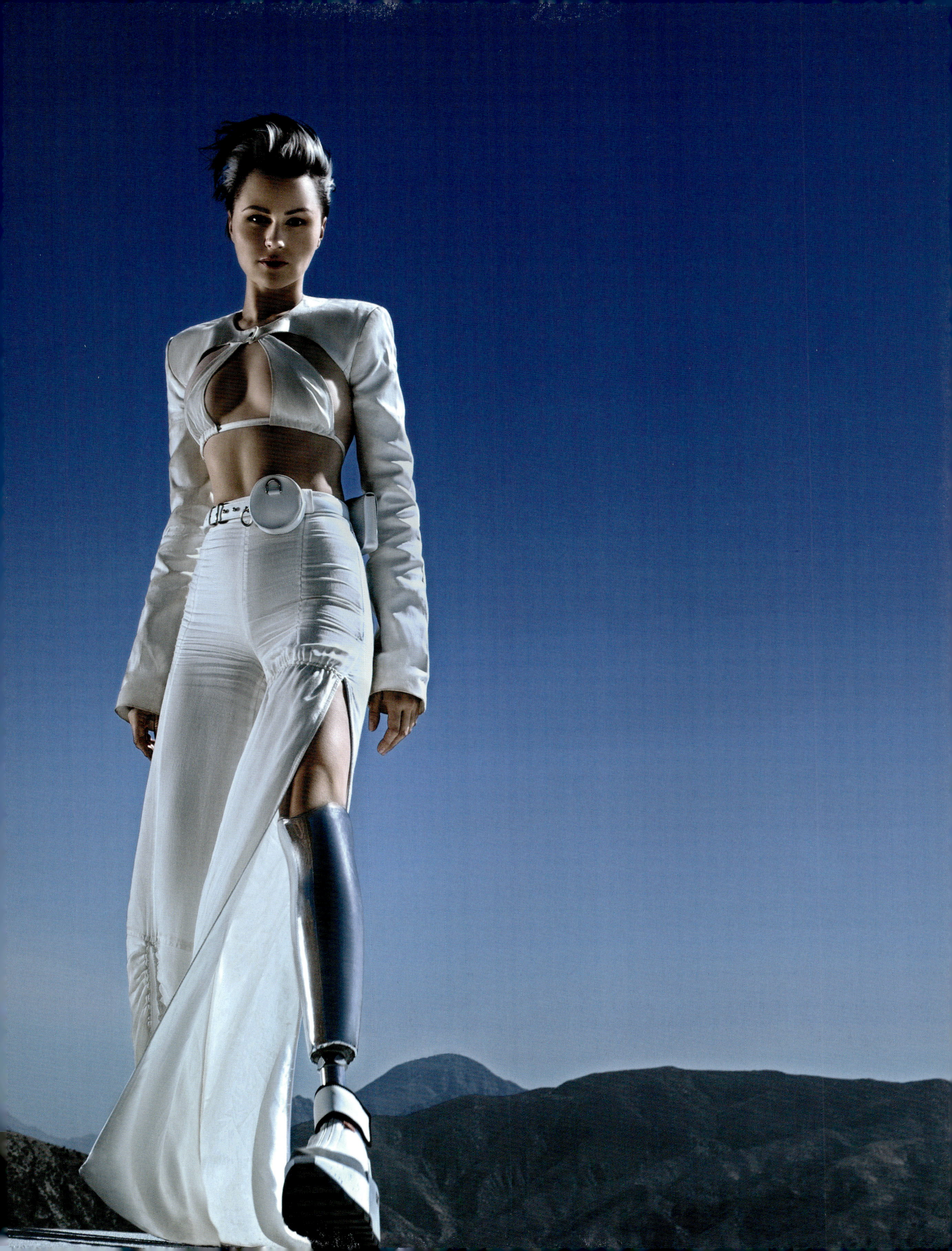

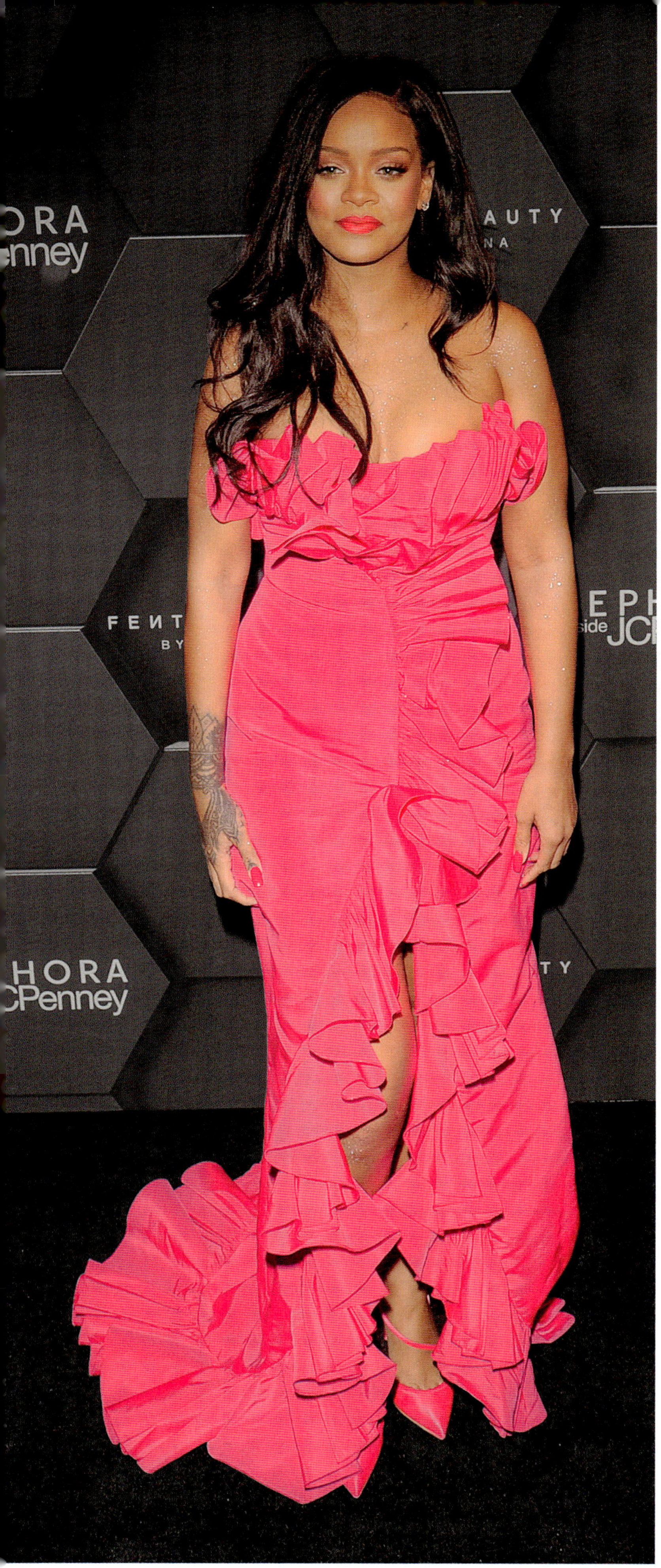

Calvin Klein, "Hot Pink Evening Dress for Rihanna," 2018. Silk faille. PVH Archives.

Fashioning America takes place at a moment when scholarly hierarchies are being toppled and new research surfaces every day. Within a month of fashion historian Elizabeth Way submitting her essay on an early twentieth-century Black designer based in Charleston, South Carolina, who is known to history only as Phoebe, for example, Charleston Museum staff announced that they believe they have discovered Phoebe's last name. This addition of a new narrative layer to Phoebe's story resonates with Native American author and naturalist Robin Wall Kimmerer's description of Indigenous time as nonlinear:

> We are told that stories are living beings, they grow, they develop, they remember, they change not in their essence, but sometimes in their dress. They are shared and shaped by the land and the culture and the teller, so that one story may be told widely and differently.[28]

Fashioning America is an attempt to change the story's dress, embracing the interconnectedness and great diversity of stories and storytellers past, present, and future in a country shaped by many cultures and many voices.

NOTES

1 Virgil Abloh, quoted in Thom Bettridge, "Virgil Abloh: Duchamp Is My Lawyer," *032c Magazine*, March 26, 2018, https://032c.com/magazine/duchamp-is-my-lawyer-virgil-abloh; and Abloh (@virgilabloh), " 'Why Nebraska?' My premise as a designer is rooted in merging different worlds together. The spirit of Aaron Bondaroff and the era in streetwear that birthed the likes of brands like Nom de Guerre," Instagram, September 30, 2014, https://www.instagram.com/p/tkW7A9GgZu/.

2 Marian Christy, "After a Fashion: Barefoot Brides Pleased," *Beaver County (Pa.) Times*, December 7, 1971.

3 Isabel Toledo, *Roots of Style: Weaving Together Life, Love, and Fashion* (New York: Penguin/Celebra, 2012), 5.

4 "The Native American and Indigenous Design Communities' Contribution to the American Fashion Industry, Council of the Fashion Designers of America," virtual conversation with Christian Allaire, June 21 and June 23, 2021, https://cfda.com/professional/industry-insights/industry-insight/the-native-american-and-indigenous-design-communities-contribution-to-american-fashion.

5 Ruth B. Phillips, *Identities: The Souvenir in Native American Art in the Northeast, 1700–1900* (Montreal: McGill-Queens University Press; Kingston: University of Washington Press, 1998), 218.

6 Blaire Sabol, "Bridge over Troubled Waters: The Institute of American Indian Arts," *Rags*, August 3, 1970, 37.

7 Tim Blanks, *The World of Anna Sui* (New York: Abrams, 2017), 128.

8 Susan S. Bean, *Yankee India: American Commercial and Cultural Encounters with India in the Age of Sail, 1784–1860* (Salem, MA: Peabody Essex Museum; Chidambaram, India: Mapin Publishing, 2001), 124.

9 "Alexander Hamilton's Final Version of the Report on the Subject of Manufactures," December 5, 1791, National Archives, https://founders.archives.gov/documents/Hamilton/01-10-02-0001-0007.

10 "Alexander Hamilton's Final Version of the Report on the Subject of Manufactures."

11 See Jessica Daves, *Ready-Made Miracle: The Story of American Fashion for the Millions* (New York: G. P. Putnam's Sons, 1967), 29, and Florence S. Richards, *The Ready-to-Wear Industry, 1900–1950* (New York: Fairchild Publications, 1951), 7.

12 Daves, *Ready-Made Miracle*, 29.

13 City of New York, "1898–1948: Fifty Years of Fashion," in *Golden Anniversary of Fashion: 1898–1948*, Official Jubilee Edition (New York: Mayor's Committee for the Commemoration of the Golden Anniversary of the City of New York, 1948), n.p.

14 Bernhard Kux, "Historian Jonathan Square and the Relationships Between Fashion and Slavery," CR Fashion Book, August 11, 2020, https://crfashionbook.com/testpages/pgslug-11b3fa5f-4c29-493e-9ab5-ead721f968a0/.

15 "The Ford Signed Chanel," *Vogue*, October 1, 1926, 165.

16 Daves, *Ready-Made Miracle*, 11.

17 Daniel R. Day, *Dapper Dan: Made in Harlem; A Memoir* (New York: Random House, 2019), 189.

18 Day, *Dapper Dan*, 210.

19 Tommy Hilfiger with Peter Knobler, *American Dreamer: My Life in Fashion and Business* (New York: Ballantine Books, 2016), 217.

20 Day, *Dapper Dan*, 259.

21 George Orwell, *The Road to Wigan Pier* (London: Victor Gollancz, 1937).

22 Rachel Tashjian, "The Battle for the Heart of the Great American Nudie Suit," *GQ*, April 19, 2019, www.gq.com/story/nudie-suit-legacy.

23 Fort Lonesome, artist statement sent via email to author, February 8, 2022.

24 Fort Lonesome, artist statement.

25 Amy Henderson, "What Is the Origin of Hollywood's Red Carpet?" *Smithsonian Magazine*, October 25, 2013, https://www.smithsonianmag.com/smithsonian-institution/what-is-the-origin-of-hollywoods-red-carpet-180949038/.

26 Tanisha Ford, *Dressed in Dreams: A Black Girl's Love Letter to the Power of Fashion* (New York: St. Martin's Press, 2019), 173–74.

27 The last selvedge denim maker in the United States, White Oak/Cone Mills in Greensboro, North Carolina, which supplied fabric for Wrangler, Levi Strauss, and Lee, closed in 2017. For more on the subject, see Sonya Abrego, "Cone Mills Denim: An Investigation into Fabrication, Tradition, and Quality," *Fashion Theory* 23, January 22, 2018, https://doi.org/10.1080/1362704X.2017.1420540.

28 Robin Wall Kimmerer, *Braiding Sweetgrass: Indigenous Wisdom, Scientific Knowledge, and the Teachings of Plants* (Minneapolis, MN: Milkweed Editions, 2013), 386.

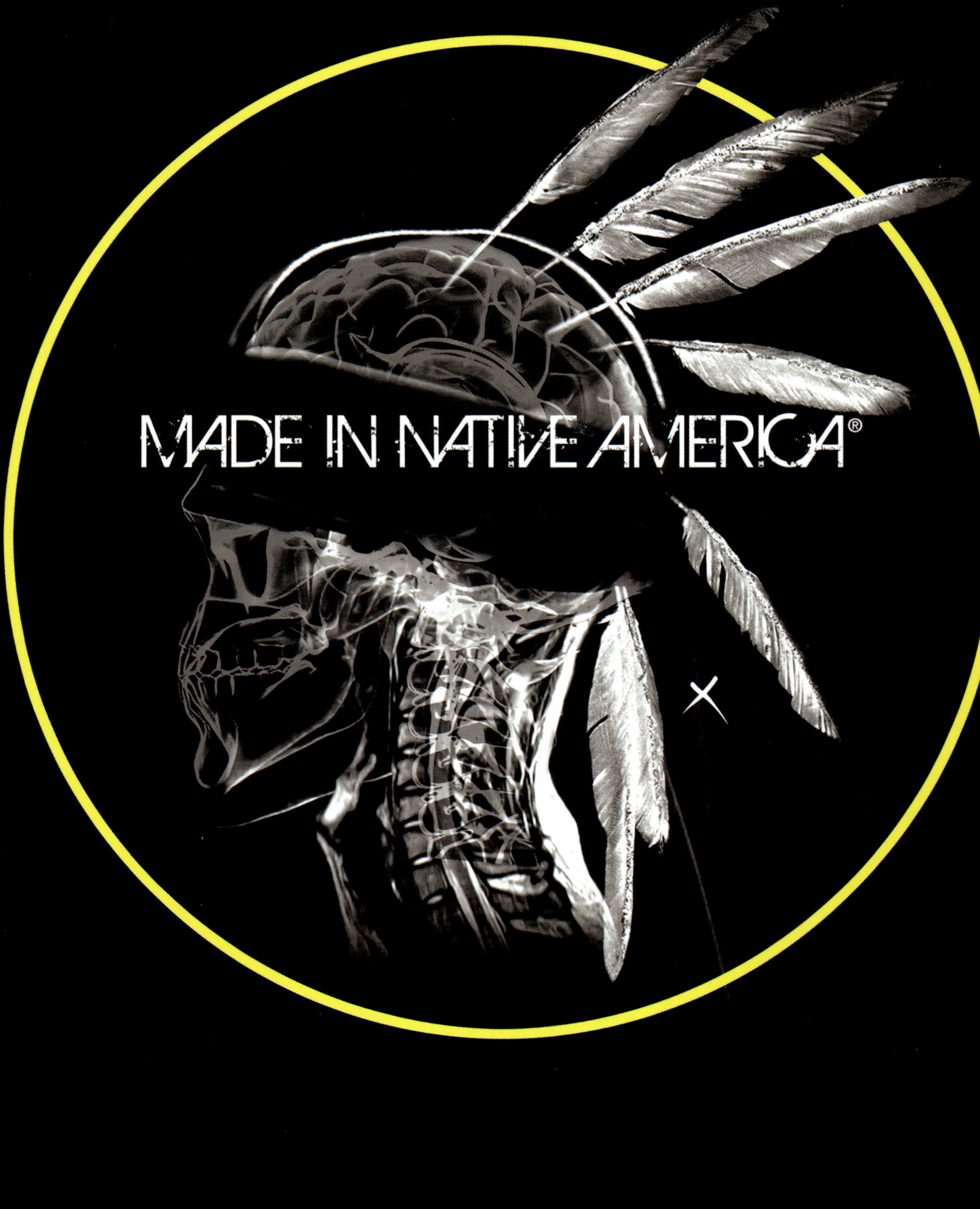
MADE IN NATIVE AMERICA®

Indigenous Fashion

EVERY GARMENT HAS A STORY

Amber-Dawn Bear Robe

Indigenous fashion has in recent years caught the eye of Native art enthusiasts, curators, and a niche general public. Despite this increased interest in the original design language of America, Native designers are neither new nor an anomaly. Whitewashed interpretations of Native dress have surfaced regularly in American style over the years, such as the "Squaw dress" of the 1950s, the free-flowing hippie style of the 1970s, the vogue for a Santa Fe / Southwestern aesthetic in the 1980s, and the turquoise phase of the early 2000s. Today, however, it is not a generic "Indian" style garnering attention but actual Indigenous designers.

Part of what fueled interest in Native design in the early part of the twentieth century was anxiety. During that period, America was consciously trying to untether itself from European traditions and forge its own culture. In this environment, there arose the realization that, as a proverbial melting pot, the United States "lacked a singular cultural heritage from which a distinctly American aesthetic might naturally arise."[1] A considered effort was put forth to generate an American design language that was fresh, original, and most important, non-European. Those spearheading this move turned with some irony to the work of the continent's original peoples on which to base their new ways of thinking.[2] A wave of interest in work made by Indigenous artists of all sorts was the result.

Leading this call to action was a group of white male curators, largely from the American Museum of Natural History (AMNH) in New York, who encouraged museums to open their doors for designers to study their collections of "primitive" and Native-made objects—Navajo textiles, Pueblo pottery, "Indian" artifacts—to help inform a new national design identity.[3] A prominent example was Morris De Camp Crawford, a textile scholar and editor at *Women's Wear Daily*, who initiated the "Designed in America" campaign of 1916 to 1922.[4] Crawford's effort included a series of lectures, special exhibitions, technical classes for artists and textile manufacturers, and a textile design contest. Hundreds of artists and silk manufacturers became involved in producing textiles based on museum artifacts,[5] with study rooms for designers set up in both the AMNH and the Brooklyn Museum. Regulars at the latter study room included leading designers of the day such as Harry Collins, Ruth Reeves, and Jessie Franklin Turner.[6]

Meanwhile, Crawford organized an expansive media campaign, writing more than two hundred articles and one hundred "design features" for *Women's Wear* and publishing two books between 1915 and 1922. Crawford's writings emphasized the importance of South and Central American textile art and the arts of Native North Americans. "The American designers of the pre-Columbian times had no Paris to refer to for their ideas," he wrote in 1916, stressing how "they" created "loveliness" from their own inherent beauty.[7] The guidelines he proffered through writings and lectures called for designers to use *Indian* works as inspiration rather than exactly replicate them, to lift and transform the *Indian* design of museum artifacts into an original American look.

Bead by bead, stitch by stitch, quill by quill, from honoring the life of the animal to the processing of every animal part, Indigenous clothing is one of a kind, hand-tailored and handcrafted with exceptional skill.

In essence, then, the initiative trained a generation of non-Native artists to appropriate Indigenous art, oblivious to the works' specific cultural meanings and diminishing Native art by viewing it as solely a design resource to be mined. Art made by Native artists was seen as curiosities and artifacts, disconnected from their individual makers. Fashion influencers such as Crawford made no attempt to humanize the cultures or artists behind the objects being studied. This type of thinking has persisted through the present in museum collections, which often position Indigenous work not as art but as artifacts and as divorced from particular Native groups in America. Founding an American design language on Native design principles expedited the widespread appropriation of American Indian art and design. The style known as "Southwestern," for example, highlights garments reflecting the New Mexico desert landscape, geometric patterns inspired by Navajo weavings and Pueblo pottery, and other generic references such as buckskin fringe and beadwork. In so doing, it robs the originals of their connections to the innovative work done by individual Indigenous artists and dehumanizes its original creators.

Another force in this appropriative effort was the influential arts educator, designer, and theorist Arthur Wesley Dow. He taught at significant art schools such as Pratt Institute in Brooklyn, published the seminal 1899 formalist instructional *Composition: Understanding Line, Notan and Color*, and helped shape the first generation of American modernist painters while head of the art department at New York's Columbia University Teachers College beginning in 1903.[8] Articles such as "Designs from Primitive American Motifs," which appeared in the *Teachers College Record* in 1915, called specifically for the creation of a national design language built on the forms of Indigenous "artifacts."[9] Dow believed that Euro-Americans could create an evocative style and a genuine American art form based on the material culture of "primitive" Americans.[10] Native American art, at that time labeled "ethnographic," was seen by Dow as "unspoiled" and autonomous from Europe, and so would be useful in generating a distinctly American art.[11] Americans now *needed* the original art and design of this land after previously shunning it. Following decades of genocide, forced assimilation, and legislation that crippled Native Americans and their way of life, Indigenous cultures were nominated as a hybrid icon of American identity. Stripped of individuality, Native Americans were no longer hostile combatants but innocuous fascinations, the defeated relics of the past. In the early 1900s, Indigenous people could not vote and were not considered citizens,[12] were subject to racist mistreatment, and were pushed onto reservations away from urban settings. The position embraced by nascent American modernists was contradictory: it construed Indian art as a representation of a "preindustrial" past connected to nature and pioneer history, only to then claim *Indian* art and design to symbolize America to the world—without Native consent.[13]

Appropriation of Native design is not consigned only to the past, of course. The exploitation of Native culture continues, without the appropriator understanding or even aware that Native people still exist and are very much engaged in all forms of contemporary artistic practice. Generically lifted Native design can be seen for sale in most North American tourist gift shops, airports, and department stores. Contemporary American and European designers routinely capitalize on Native culture by co-opting Indigenous imagery and culture in fashion and media campaigns. Victoria's Secret repeatedly and infamously used "Indigenous-inspired" garments on their runway, including Native American headdresses. In the "Wild Things" segment of a 2010 Victoria's Secret show, models wore animal-print lingerie and were painted with a grab bag of tribal tattoos from various groups around the world. Model Karlie Kloss, representing the Thanksgiving holiday, graced the runway wearing a long feather headdress, fringe, turquoise jewelry, and tiny, leopard-print lingerie. The company's "Exotic Traveler" theme in 2014 clad models in generic tribal-inspired designs, and in 2017, their "Nomadic Adventures" presentation included models showcasing Native American–inspired dress and at least one white-feather war bonnet.[14]

Other examples abound: Ralph Lauren's Santa Fe collection debuted in 1981; Isaac Mizrahi's 1991 "Tee Pee" series featured a "Totem Pole Gown" and a Native-inspired red coat embellished with colorful beaded geometric designs and fringe. Kermit Oliver, the only American ever to design for the French fashion house Hermès, used kachinas and generic "Plains Indian" imagery for many of his scarf patterns in the 1980s. More recently, high-end designers from Europe and America, including Karl Lagerfeld of Chanel, Proenza Schouler, KTZ, and Isabel Marant, have incorporated distinctly Native design elements into their garments. Retailers such as Urban Outfitters and Forever 21 often similarly embellish clothing. Fashion brand Dsquared2, which uses the motto of "Born in Canada, Made in Italy"[15] to justify their use of First Nations and Inuit imagery, originally titled their Fall/Winter 2015–16 collection "#Dsquaw."[16] Buckskin, beads, leather, fringe, moccasins, turquoise, and feathers have all come to symbolize *Indian* style, divorced from the original techniques, intent, and meaning.

Of course, the impresarios of the AMNH were not incorrect in a fundamental respect: Indigenous design is the original American design language. Bead by bead, stitch by stitch, quill by quill, from honoring the life of the animal to the processing of every animal part, Indigenous clothing is one of a kind, hand-tailored and handcrafted with exceptional skill. Indigenous design is extremely diverse and cannot be arranged into orderly categories or presented in one neat package. From the water-proof seal-gut capes created by Aleut artists to the fish-skin boots made by Athabascan artists, from the moose-hair-tuft adornments crafted by Cree and Dene people to the dispersive formline design of the Chilkat robes woven by Tsimshian and Tlingit artists, Indigenous design *is* couture.

Native nations and European visitors have continuously exchanged new materials, ideas, techniques, and technologies over the centuries. Creative output is a living entity, in tune with customs, attitudes, and beliefs that reflect its social environment. A poignant example is American fashion's response to the Civil War, which took the form of an attempt to create a more convenient clothing style using materials that were available amid the resource drain caused by the conflict. The need for clothing to be functional gave rise to the first ready-to-wear clothing manufactured and mass-produced in bulk. Indigenous clothing, by contrast, endured a much different outcome during the harrowing times of its wars with the inhabitants of the United

States, especially during the Reservation and Assimilation eras. In these periods, Indigenous clothing was not admired but was regarded—like the entire Native population—as a barrier and threat to western expansion. In the late nineteenth and early twentieth centuries, the government forced thousands of Native children from their families and homes, imprisoning them in boarding schools run by the federal government and churches. Living under severe rules, these children were forced to wear the accepted apparel of the time, a basic cotton dress and wool trousers.[17] Native style, adornment, and clothing were prohibited, and generations of Native society were forbidden to openly create in ways related to their own cultural backgrounds.[18]

Typical justifications by those appropriating Indigenous art and design include "we are honoring Indian culture," "all cultures are appropriated," and "don't be so sensitive," all offered without any awareness of the harm caused by decades of appropriation. Yes, it is undeniable that the First World may be seen as being built on a vibrant exchange of ideas and goods. And trade is obviously not an exclusively Western phenomenon: considerably before Spanish and European contact, between the ninth and twelfth centuries (850–1150 CE), Chaco Canyon in New Mexico was a bustling trade center of the ancestral Pueblo people. That site was one of many such historic locations in North America that fostered the exchange of ideas, materials, and foods and the intermingling of languages, songs, and dance. Organically evolving trade with all its interaction and associated experiences led to connections between individual creators and artists. That scenario is starkly different from the appropriation of Indigenous cultures. Contemporary ceramic artist and designer Virgil Ortiz points out that even Native artists themselves must take great care when working with material from their cultural history:

> It is incumbent upon each of us to know our own histories and speak with Elders if there are designs or symbols we should not be using, lest we end up following the pathway we are trying to correct. For me, that means researching traditional Cochiti Pueblo pottery designs on historic vessels and figures but modifying them for fashion and not just copying them. I remain sensitive to my Pueblo culture but aspire to advance our art as my ancestors did as they reacted to the changing world around them.[19]

In recent years, fashion and apparel entities have increasingly sought to collaborate with Native designers but have often done so in ways that generally do not always benefit those artists and do not represent a true collaboration or a long-term commitment to make change in the fashion industry.[20] Such actions do not reflect a commitment to the real inclusion of and representation for Indigenous artists and designers. Instead, these alliances are often used merely to validate the non-Native partner. And exceptions where more positive interactions have occurred sometimes have negative beginnings. In 2013, the designer Paul Frank, in partnership with the Museum of Contemporary Native Arts of the Institute of American Indian Arts (IAIA), debuted the company's first collaboration on a limited-edition clothing and accessories line with four Native American designers—Louie Gong, Autumn Dawn Gomez, Candace Halcro, and Dustin Martin. But the project was born out of controversy rather than via the corporation's initiative. In 2012, Frank hosted an event in West Hollywood dubbed "Dream Catchin' with Paul Frank: A Pow Wow Celebrating Fashion's Night Out." The party included guests dressed in fake feather and neon headbands who posed with plastic tomahawks in a room decorated with kitschy dream catchers, and a backdrop with the Paul Frank monkey-face logo wearing a feather headdress and striped face paint. The event met with the outrage it deserved; fashion scholar Jessica Metcalfe was central in calling out Frank's blatant misappropriation of Native culture and design for entertainment and commercial gain.[21]

A crucial figure in conscientious, responsible, and innovative American Native fashion history is designer Lloyd Henri "Kiva" New. In the words of Metcalfe, author of one of the first critical studies exploring Native American high-fashion designers,[22] "New played an important role in revolutionizing Native customary clothing design by celebrating Indianness and its ability to create a truly unique 'American' image. . . . He explained that there wasn't anything more American than the Native American, and he encouraged people to express this sentiment on their clothing."[23] New saw the power of fashion and the positive effect it could have for Native artists, becoming one of the first Native designers to create a successful high-fashion brand. He launched Lloyd Kiva Design Associates in Scottsdale, Arizona, in the 1950s, helping to establish the city as a high-end art and fashion destination. New sold his designs to Neiman Marcus and other luxury fashion retailers; his best-known works include purses and the color-clashing textiles he created and printed in his studio.[24] The Kiva style revolved around hand-colored and silk-screened fabrics patterned with distinctive Native motifs, and abstracted western landscapes became one of New's signatures. Designing for both men and women, he brought

opposite Lloyd Henri "Kiva" New, day dress, late 1950s. Screen-printed cotton. Courtesy of Danielle Picerne and Robert Black.

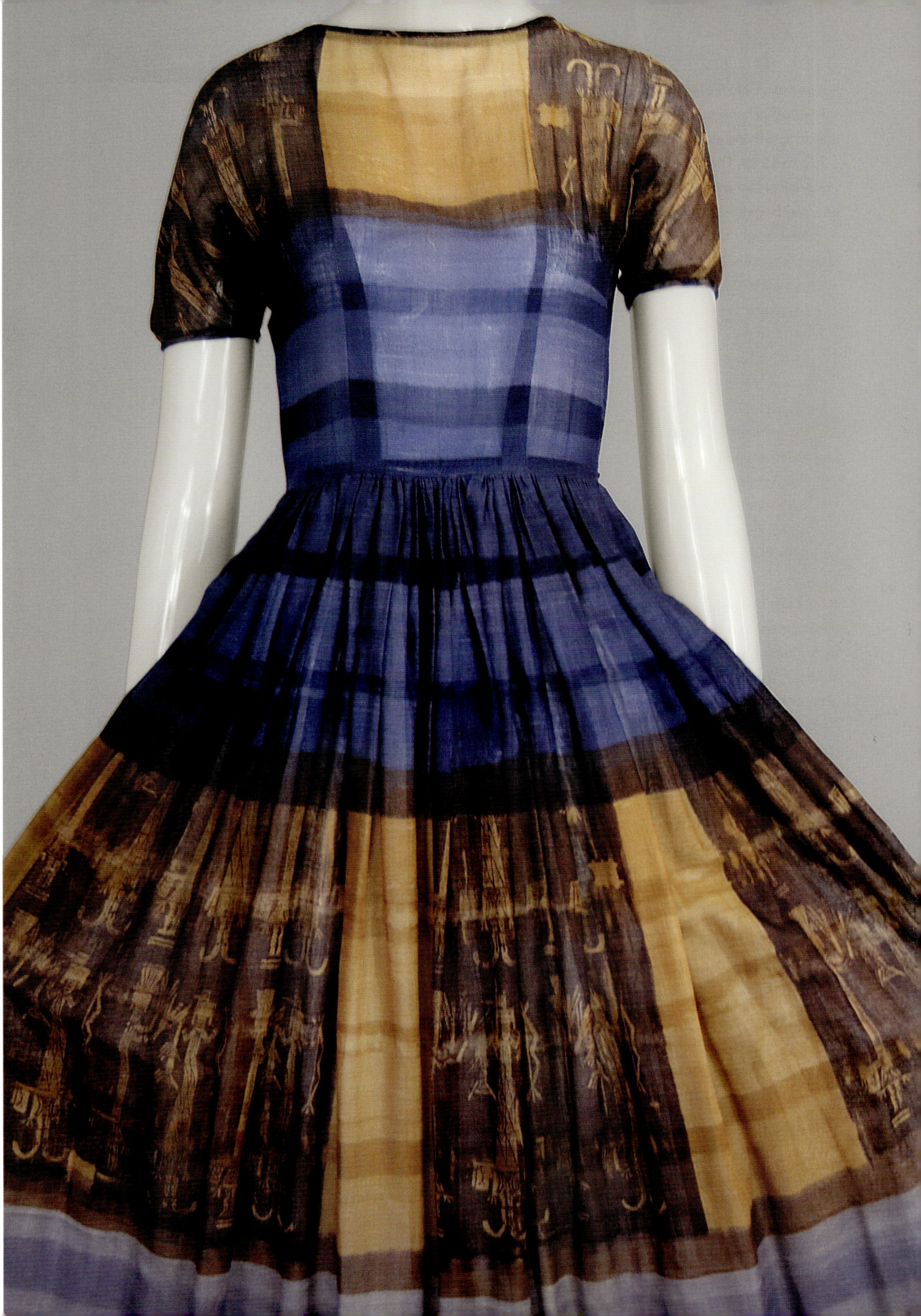

Native design into the larger fashion and style discourse, threading Native culture into each conception. New was also an important educator, serving as art director at the newly formed IAIA from 1967 to 1978. There, he impacted generations of students, fostering Native artists and helping their work be taken seriously, as something dignified and beyond tourist art.[25]

New taught his textile design process and techniques to students and encouraged them to experiment. In the influential alternative 1970s fashion magazine *Rags*, he described his aims as an instructor in this way:

> It will not be the intent of the Institute of American Indian Arts to "ram anyone's culture down his own throat." But it will be the intent of the Institute to make special deference to the fact that the (Indian) students are of a different cultural group and, in being so, have unique and valuable contributions to make, thereby making great use of traditions as spring-boards for personal creative action. The institute will assume from the beginning that it is not the business of an artist to attempt to recreate a tradition. Rather he is constantly in the process of creating a new one.[26]

To cite just one example, New's role can be seen in the development of IAIA alumni Patricia Michaels, class of 1989, who is known for her hand-dyed, painted, and silk-screened fabrics.[27] Michaels first became nationally recognized in 2013 with her success on season twelve of the reality television series *Project Runway*. Her student years at IAIA came after New's retirement, but he remained a presence among students beyond the classroom well after his official role ended. "Lloyd used to come to my studio in Santa Fe," she told me. "He was a mentor to me."[28] Michaels creates one-of-a-kind haute couture ensembles with hand-painted and printed textiles, drawing inspiration from nature and her Taos Pueblo roots. Her "Berries at Moonlight Kiss" collection was an attempt to debunk stereotypes. "Outside Native country," Michaels says, "the imagery [of Native Americans] takes our romances to a teepee on a buffalo robe, or rowing bare-breasted on a canoe." By contrast, the collection "lets [her] explore draping, felting, beadwork, and hand-painted textiles to bring that special memory of a kiss by our sacred wild berries."[29] With this body of work, Michaels is reclaiming what "romantic" means in a contemporary Indian context.

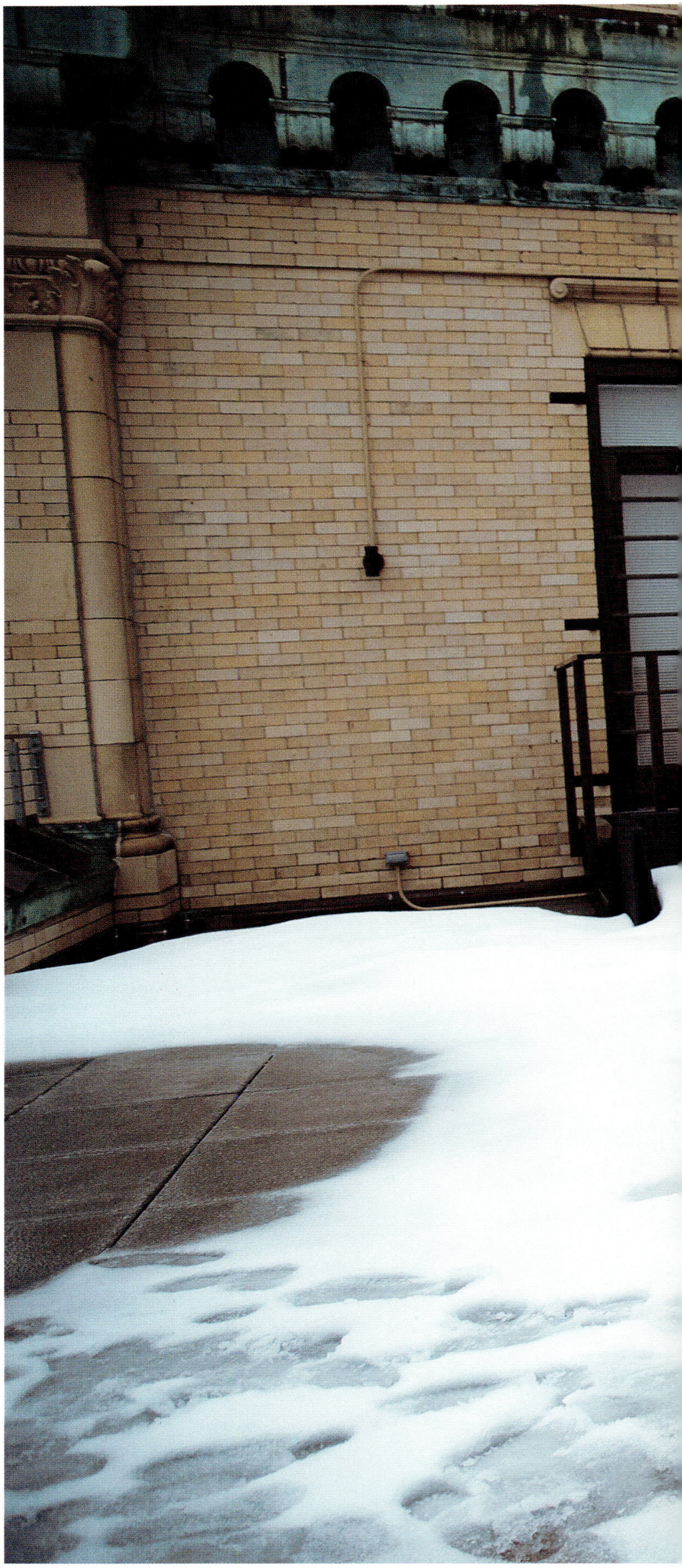

right Patricia Michaels, Moonlight Berries dress, Winter 2018. Felted wool, crinkled silk chiffon, antique glass beads, dyes, and jersey Lycra. Courtesy of Patricia Michaels.

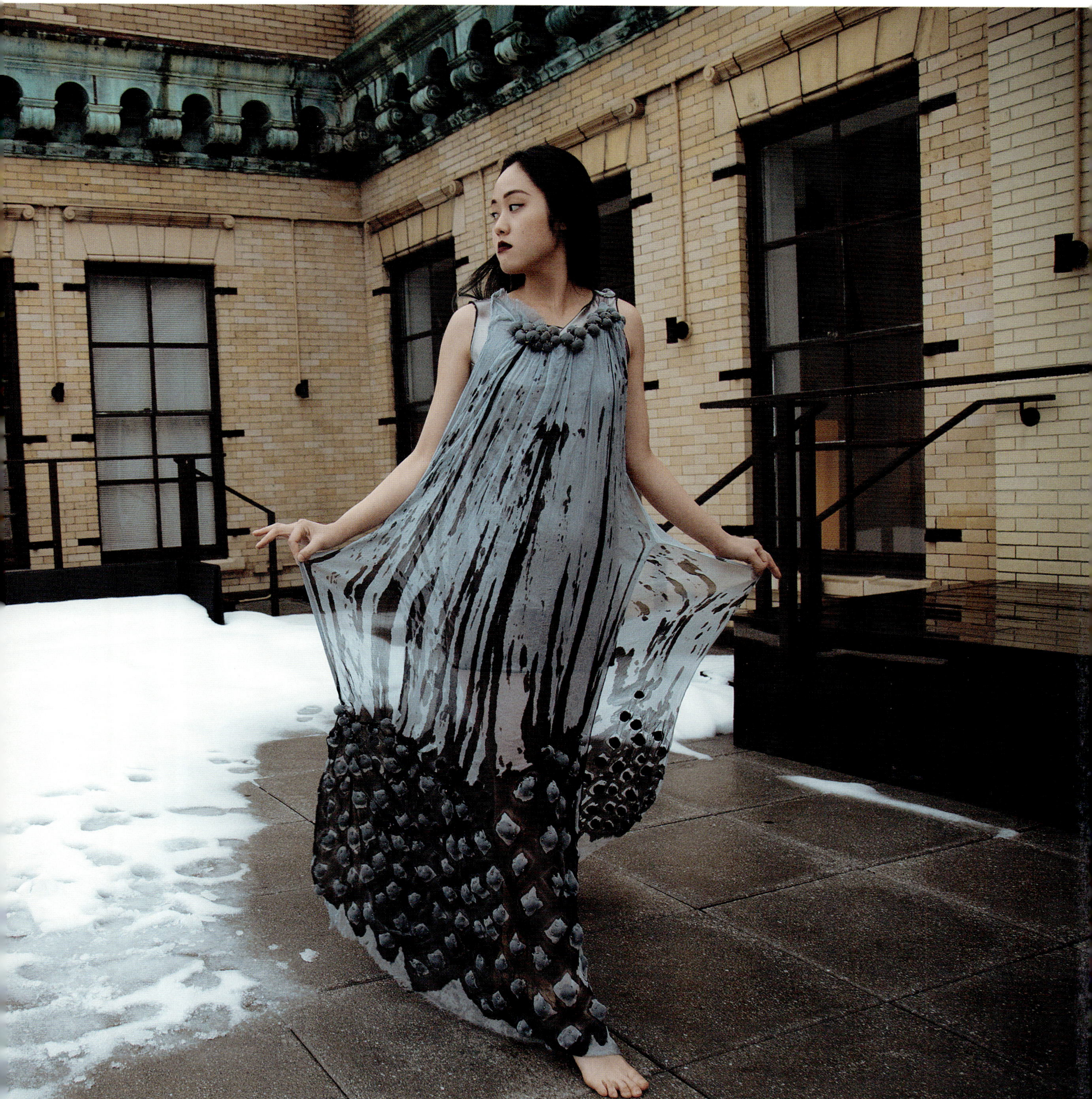

Whether walking in New York City or wandering in nature, Michaels allows her surrounding environment to infuse her fashion work. Her first Pottery Shard dress, made in 2018 with silk, leather, and mica crystals, is a direct response to looking at pottery shards when walking in the Taos foothills. Pueblo pottery, when broken, is meant to go back to the earth, and is not to be collected or taken from its place. Virgil Ortiz works similarly to Michaels, using pottery design, history, and techniques to create a visual language rooted in his Cochiti Pueblo culture, using apocalyptic concepts, fantasy, and futuristic storytelling centered around the Pueblo Revolt of 1680 and a posited future one in 2180, with nineteen characters representing the nineteen Pueblos.[30] Ortiz makes fashion, ceramics, and multimedia artworks, with each practice informing the other. All of his work, both one-of-a-kind and ready-to-wear, from zippers to the final execution, is made in Native America. "For Native designers, it is imperative that we understand the importance of ownership of our cultures, tribes, art, and designs," Ortiz notes. "Not ownership in a financial sense but in the sense that we can speak out with an authentic and authoritative voice to those who take designs without recognition or recompense."[31]

In the years after New emerged and began teaching, pockets of Indigenous designers and artists grew across Canada and the United States, creating innovative platforms for their work.[32] Native designers had to get exposure for their work on alternative runways, including guerilla-style fashion shows during annual Native art fairs such as Santa Fe's Southwestern Association for Indian Arts (SWAIA) Market and the Heard Museum's art market in Phoenix, Native art establishments, and more unexpected venues.[33] (Ortiz told me recently that the only places to create a makeshift runway in Santa Fe during the 1990s were nightclubs.[34]) Around a decade later, in 2002, he opened a boutique in Santa Fe with fellow artists Pilar Agoyo and Cody Sanderson called Heat: A Freak Boutique.[35] The same year, Ortiz was approached at the boutique during the SWAIA Indian Market by designer Donna Karan to collaborate on her Spring 2003 collection.[36] The result was a dress and skirt that fused Ortiz's pottery designs with Karan's garments.

In 2012, Jessica Metcalfe launched Beyond Buckskin Boutique, an online shop dedicated to promoting and representing Indigenous fashion and accessories artists. Around this time, Indigenous fashion, particularly contemporary collections, started to see a surge in public interest. The Peabody Essex Museum in Salem, Massachusetts, developed a successful exhibition, *Native Fashion Now*, that traveled to venues across the country between 2015 and 2017. Special-interest magazines, such as *Native American Art, Cowboys & Indians, American Indian Art,* and *Native Peoples*, began commissioning articles on Native designers.[37] Vancouver Indigenous Fashion Week began in 2017, Toronto launched its first Indigenous Fashion Week in 2018, and the Supernaturals agency representing Indigenous models formed in Vancouver in 2021. The SWAIA premiered its now-annual August fashion show in Santa Fe in 2014. All of these initiatives were started by Indigenous people who saw a void in platforms and representation for Indigenous designers who created work beyond regalia.

Ownership of "our" cultures, art, and designs is a common thread for Indigenous designers, whose work is frequently rooted in their unique histories. The husband-and-wife team Erik Brodt and Amanda Bruegl created a denim line called Ginew, which is part of Brodt's Ojibwe name (it translates as "Brown Eagle"). *Minobimaadiziiwin*, which means "Walk the good path," is an Ojibwe philosophy that guides the duo. Part of this philosophy is an environmental awareness, which many Native designers share. "The cost of fast fashion is out of sight, out of mind for most of the developed world," Brodt notes.[38] His and Bruegl's designs and concepts are rooted in Ojibwe and Oneida symbols and stories that they interpret into contemporary designs. The couple did not see clothes that represented who they are as Indigenous people. Using American-sourced materials, Ginew fuses elements of the pair's Ojibwe, Oneida, and Mohican heritage to create a contemporary Native American voice in an enduring American form, with the goal of making their apparel embody the values of courage, honesty, hard work, and loyalty.[39] "Every garment has a story," Brodt notes as well. Their Crow Wing Jeans and Heritage Coat are the first sew-by samples made by the company and are still worn and prized by Brodt.[40] The Heritage Coat is an homage to Bruegl's great-grandfather, who experienced a forcefully abrupt change in his life at the hands of the United States government during the Assimilation period.

Indigenous designers make fashion that fuses their specific cultural history to the present. Artist and designer Jamie Okuma stresses, "All of my pieces are culturally based on where I am from." Luiseño, Shoshone-Bannock, Wailaki, La Jolla, and Okinawan cultures are "threaded," as she puts it, through all of her collections.[41] But her highly sought-after beaded heels reflect

opposite Erik Brodt and Amanda Breugl for Ginew Jeans, Heritage Coat with fabric pattern created in collaboration with Dyani White Hawk, "We Walk Together" collection, 2019. Cotton, silk, and wool. Courtesy of Ginew Jeans.

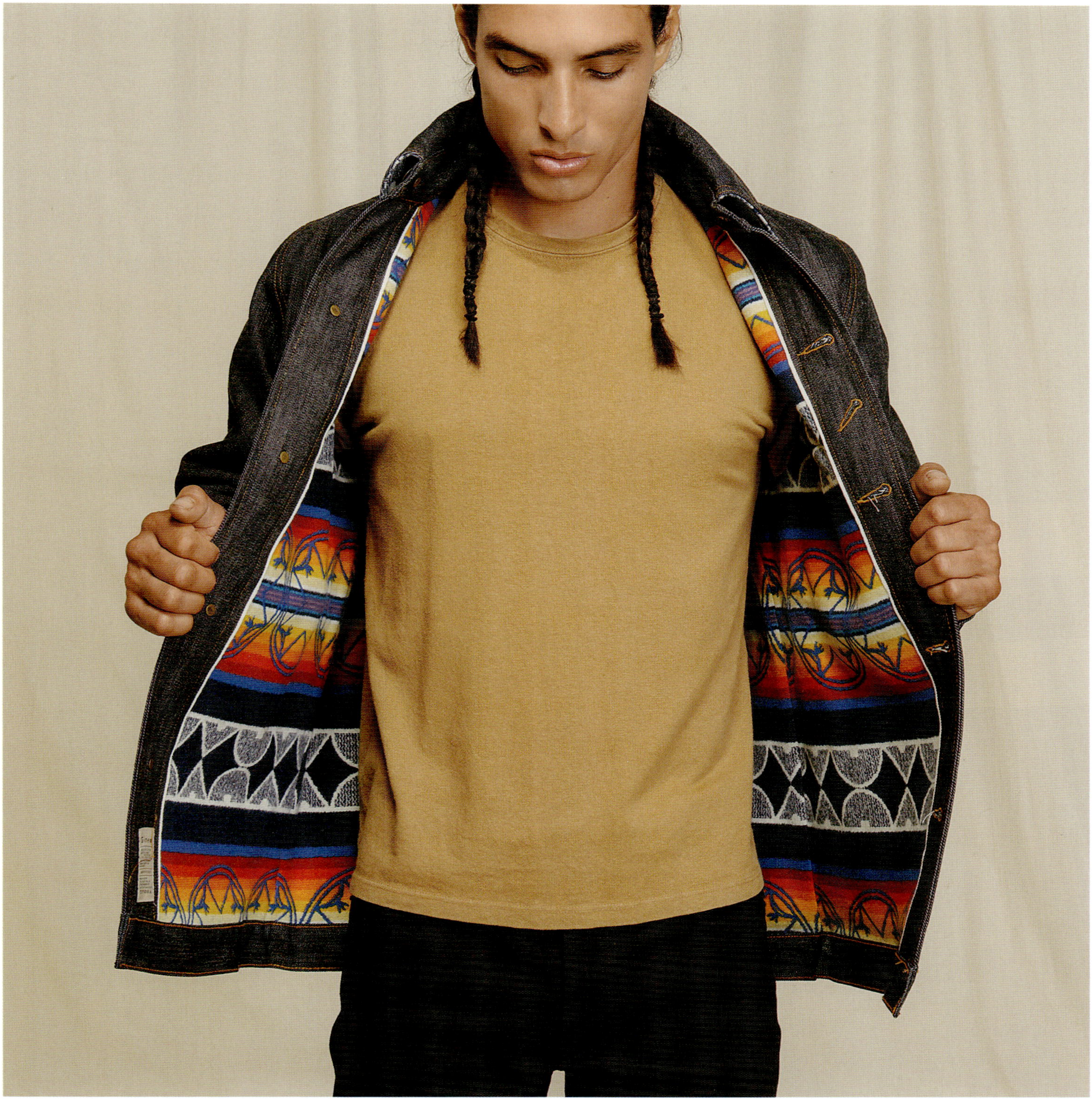

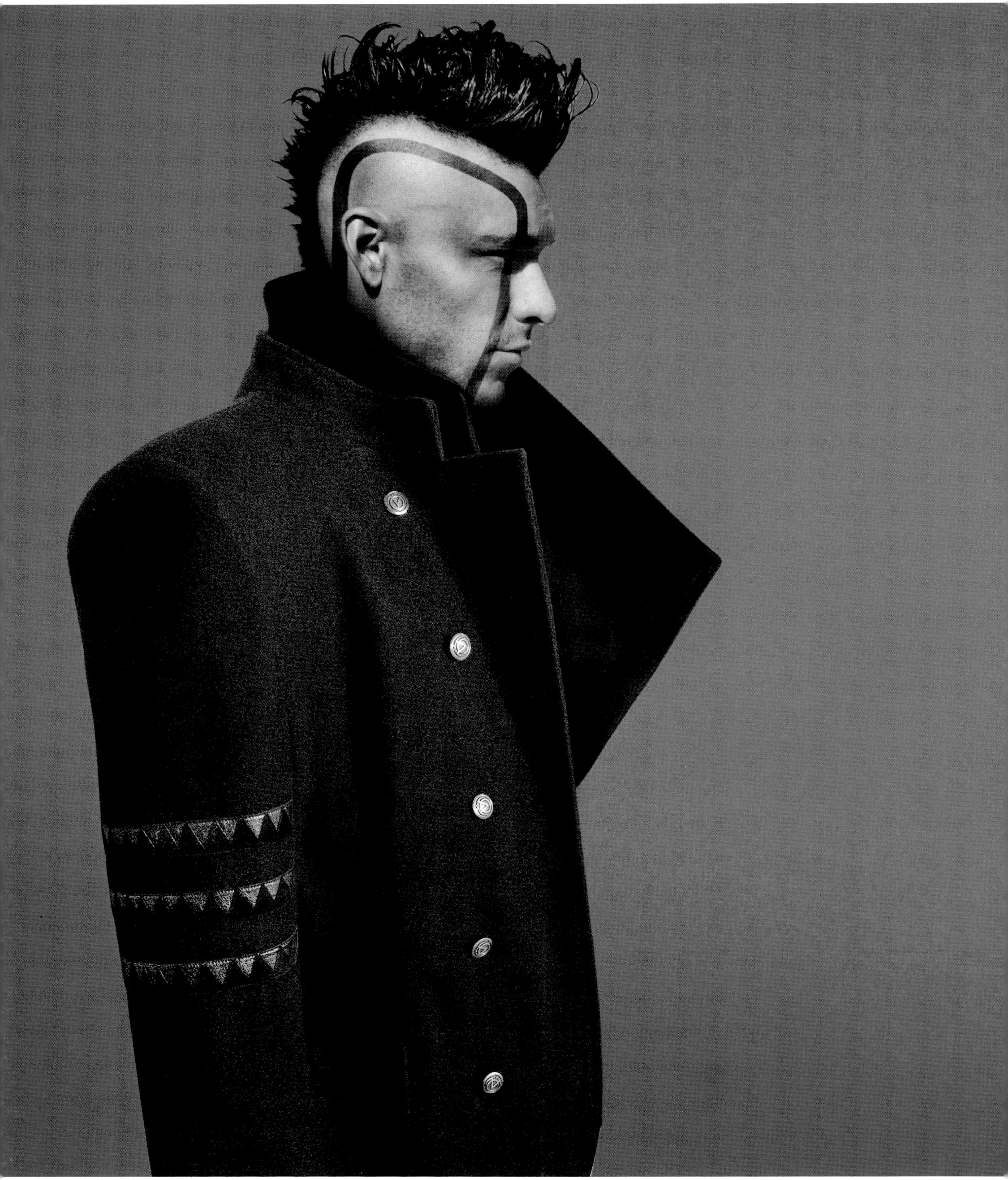

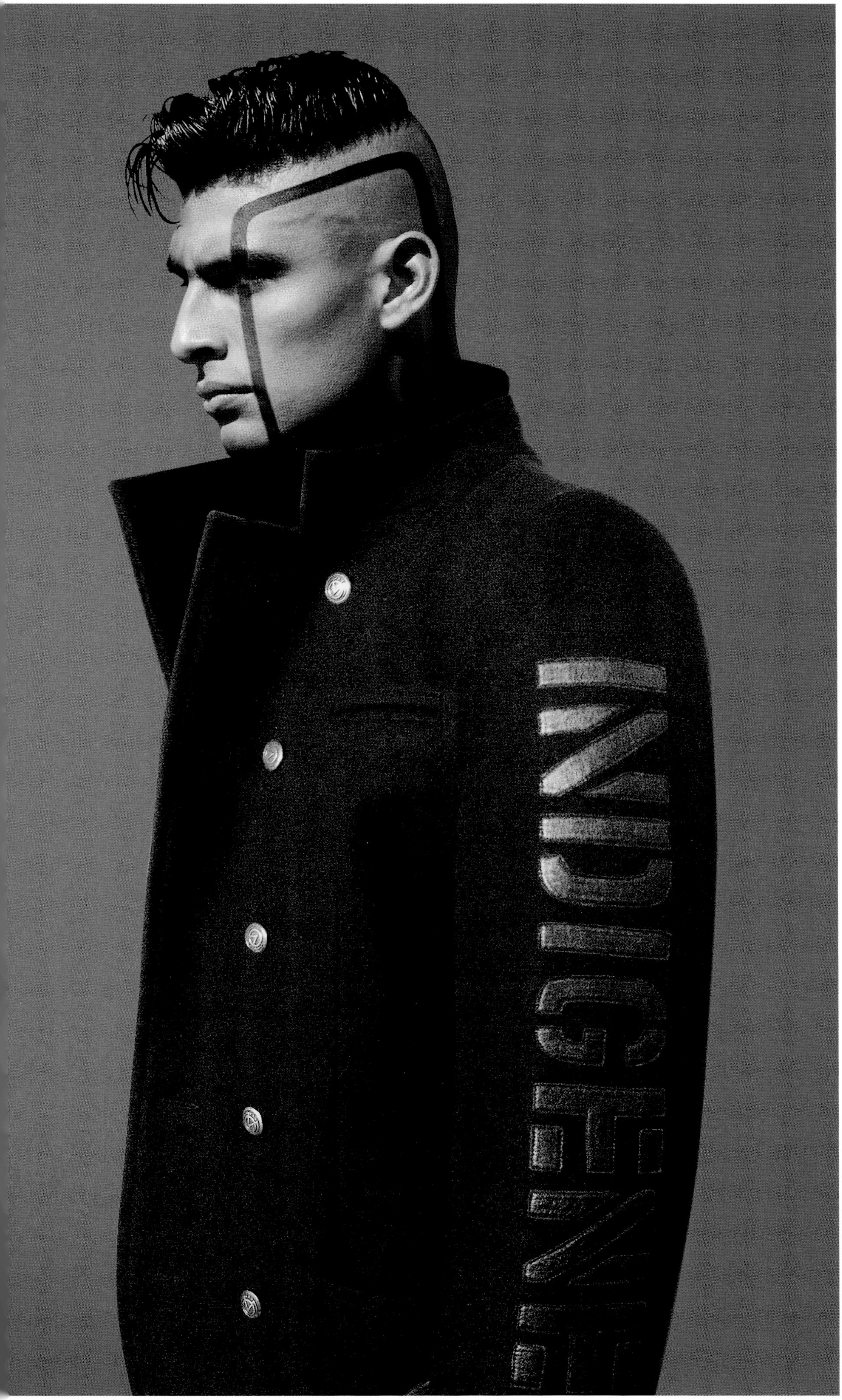

Virgil Ortiz, "Indigene" peacoat, 2014. Wool shell, leather appliqué, and sterling silver VO logo buttons. Photo and styling by Virgil Ortiz.

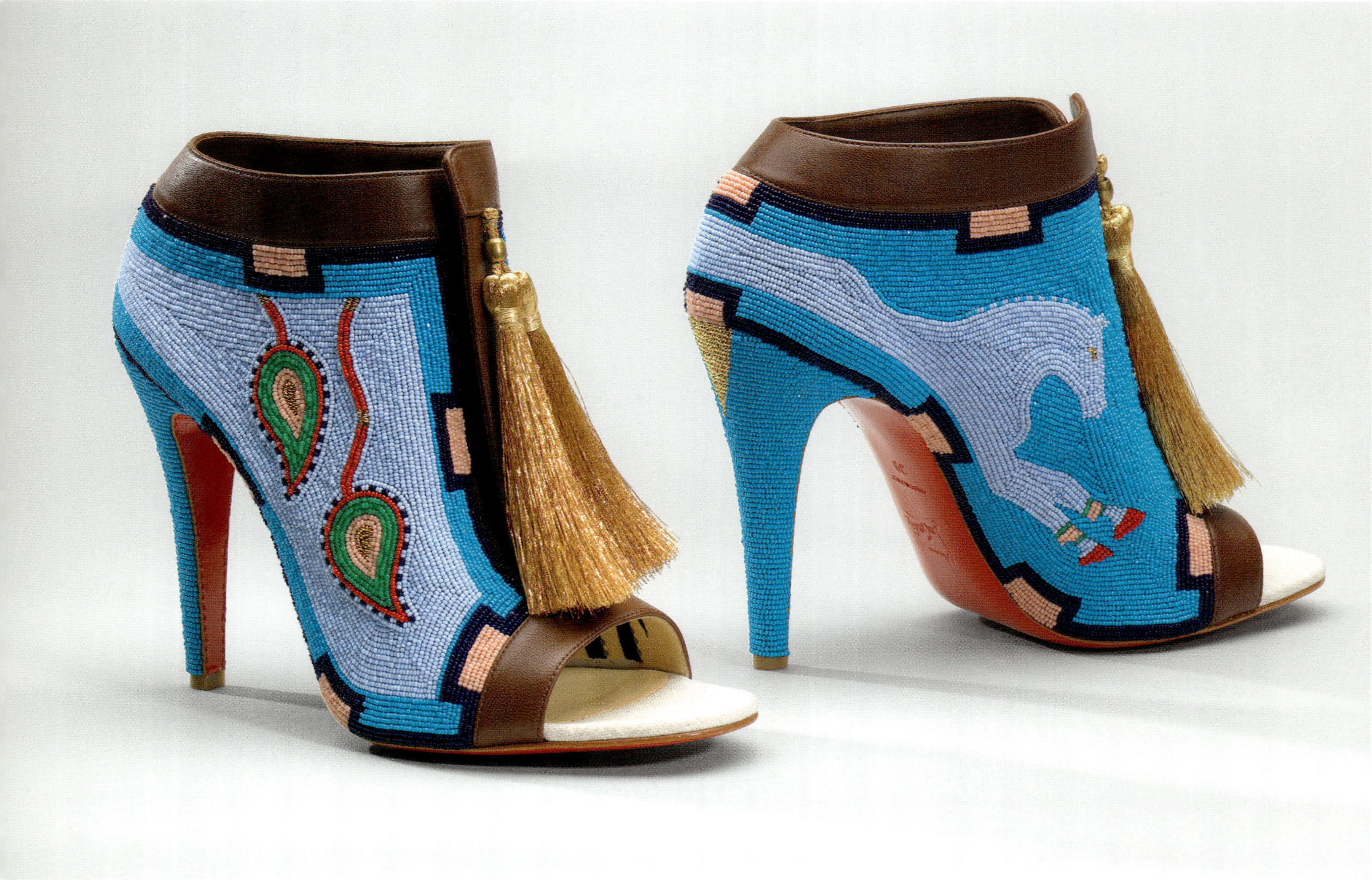

contemporary life as well. Her first, a pair of Christian Louboutin Chaotic 100 ankle boots hand-stitched with colored glass and twenty-four-karat-gold-plated beads forming abstract designs and a stylized leaping horse, grew out of a random conversation between herself, her mother, and her husband where she fretted over her "shopping problem" while considering purchasing some designer heels. "How can I justify buying these?!" she asked herself. Her answer was to transform them into high-fashion, work-of-art, one-of-a-kind footwear. Okuma's works, which take countless hours to make, are quickly snatched up by private collectors and museums. Despite their glamourous reach, each of the pairs contains a deeply personal narrative that she leaves undisclosed to the wearer.[42] This practice is manifest in creations by many Native designers, for whom collections may embody personal tales. "New objects become the storied object, the story container," writes scholar and artist Sherry Farrell Racette. Her description of contemporary Native art applies to contemporary Native fashion as well.[43]

The coming full circle to Native culture was devoid of self-awareness about the atrocities perpetrated by the United States on the original people of the land. *Indians* who were killed for their Indigenous identity are now seen as an inspiration for fashion, style, and a national identity. The individual artists who created the "*Indian* artifacts" that helped establish a new American design language were erased. A complete foundational history of America remains bypassed, providing a convenient path for the ongoing appropriation of Native art, design, fashion, and culture. The fashion industry needs to acknowledge that the approaches and perspectives of Indigenous designers exist beyond sheer visual and material qualities. Indigenous fashion can absolutely help differentiate American design on a global level—if Indigenous designers, artists, and creators are able to guide it.

above Jamie Okuma, *Adaptation*, 2011. Christian Louboutin Chaotic 100 ankle boots, glass and twenty-four-karat-gold-plated beads, and polyester tassels. Nelson-Atkins Museum, Kansas City, Missouri, A. Keith Brodkin Fund for the Acquisition of Contemporary American Indian Art.

NOTES

1 See Ann Tartsinis Marguerite, *An American Style: Global Sources for New York Textile and Fashion Design, 1915–1928* (New York: Bard Graduate Center for Decorative Arts, Design History, Material Culture, 2013), 26.

2 For more information on Native American art as the foundation to an American design language, see Marguerite, *An American Style*.

3 Marguerite, *An American Style*, 26–27.

4 From *Creating Textiles: Makers, Methods, Markets; Proceedings of the Sixth Biennial Symposium of the Textile Society of America, Inc. New York, NY, September 23–26, 1998* (Earleville, MD: Textile Society of America, Inc., 1999), 410.

5 Crawford's program was not limited to Native American collections; he was also extremely fond of Peruvian, Koryak, and Andean textiles.

6 Lauren D. Whitley, "Morris De Camp Crawford and the 'Designed in America' Campaign, 1916–1922," Textile Society of America Symposium Proceedings, 1998, 215.

7 Morris De Camp Crawford, "Embroidery Ideas from Stencils," *Women's Wear*, November 1916. Quoted in Whitley, "Morris De Camp Crawford," 412.

8 Arthur Wesley Dow biographical page, Smithsonian American Art Museum, https://americanart.si.edu/artist/arthur-wesley-dow-1325.

9 Arthur Wesley Dow, "Designs from Primitive American Motifs," *Teachers College Record* 16, no. 2 (March 1915): 31.

10 Dow, "Designs from Primitive American Motifs," 27.

11 Dow's theories are connected to the modernist primitive movement; see "Designs from Primitive American Motifs," 27.

12 Native Americans were granted citizenship in 1924 when President Calvin Coolidge signed into law the Indian Citizenship Act.

13 Promoters of Indian arts as "American" associated these qualities with "traditional" American values and identified the natural materials and motifs as reflections of the landscape of the United States.

14 Avery Matera, "5 Times Victoria's Secret Was Accused of Cultural Appropriation," *Teen Vogue*, November 7, 2018, https://www.teenvogue.com/gallery/victorias-secret-fashion-show-cultural-appropriation.

15 "The Beginnings," #D2Story, Dsquared2 website, September 3, 2018, https://www.dsquared2.com/experience/en/d2-life/the-beginnings/.

16 "Dsquared2 Under Fire for #Dsquaw Women's Fashion Collection," CBC, March 4, 2015, https://www.cbc.ca/news/indigenous/dsquared2-under-fire-for-dsquaw-women-s-fashion-collection-1.2980136.

17 A parallel history of forced education and assimilation for Indigenous children by the church and government took place in Canada.

18 Clothing was one aspect of assimilation programming that residential and boarding school systems imposed on Native children. For more information on the trauma of the experience and lasting impact experienced by Indigenous children, see Brenda Child, *Boarding School Seasons: American Indian Families, 1900–1940* (Lincoln: University of Nebraska Press, 1999); Tanya Talaga, *Seven Fallen Feathers: Racism, Death, and Hard Truths in a Northern City* (Toronto: House of Anansi Press, 2017); and the Legacy of Hope Foundation's online exhibition *Where Are the Children, Healing the Impacts of Residential School*, https://legacyofhope.ca/wherearethechildren/.

19 Virgil Ortiz, "Indigenizing Fashion: Reclaim Ownership of Our Cultural Imagery," Soundboard, Walker Art Center, June 6, 2019, https://walkerart.org/magazine/soundboard-indigenizing-fashion-virgil-ortiz.

20 Examples include Christie Belcourt and Versace, Virgil Ortiz and Donna Karan, Kent Monkman and Jean-Paul Gaultier, and Steven Paul Judd, Doug Good Feather, and B.Yellowtail and Faherty.

21 See, for example the post on Metcalfe's blog *Beyond Buckskin* titled "Paul Frank's Racist Powwow," September 9, 2012, http://www.beyondbuckskin.com/2012/09/paul-franks-racist-powwow.html.

22 Metcalfe's first academic, critical work on Indigenous fashion is her doctoral dissertation, "Native Designers of High Fashion: Expressing Identity, Creativity, and Tradition in Contemporary Customary Clothing Design" (PhD diss., University of Arizona, 2010).

23 Metcalfe, "Native Designers," 342.

24 Ryan Flahive, "Lloyd Kiva New: Art, Design, and Influence," in *Lloyd Kiva New: A New Century; The Life and Legacy of Cherokee Artist and Educator Lloyd Kiva New* (Santa Fe, NM: Art Guild Press, 2016), 24.

25 Flahive, "Lloyd Kiva New," 47.

26 Quoted in Blaire Sabol, "Bridge over Troubled Waters: The Institute of American Indian Arts," *Rags* 3 (August 1970), 36.

27 Patricia Michaels, telephone conversation with author, December 30, 2021.

28 Michaels, telephone conversation.

29 Patricia Michaels, Facebook message to author, December 20, 2021.

30 Virgil Ortiz, Zoom conversation, January 27, 2022.

31 Ortiz, "Indigenizing Fashion."

32 Until relatively recently, the late 1980s and early 1990s, contemporary Native art and design was excluded from major art institutions. One of the first curators to help change this was Lee-Ann Martin, who cocurated the major touring exhibition *Indigena: Contemporary Native Expression* in 1992 and *Land, Spirit, Power: First Nations at the National Gallery of Canada* the same year.

33 Jessica Metcalfe has written extensively about this topic in her dissertation "Native Designers of High Fashion," 263–79.

34 All closed now, these clubs included the Paramount, the Drama Club, SWIG, and Club West.

35 Metcalfe, "Native Designers," 301.

36 Metcalfe, "Native Designers," 304.

37 Metcalfe, "Native Designers," 40.

38 Erik Brodt, telephone conversation with author, December 23, 2021.

39 Brodt, telephone conversation.

40 A sew-by sample is used as a design prototype by the factory, with all the construction details needed to create a preproduction sample.

41 Jamie Okuma, telephone conversation with author, January 19, 2022.

42 Okuma, telephone conversation.

43 Sherry Farrell Racette, "Encoded Knowledge: Memory and Objects in Contemporary Native American Art," in *New Native Art Criticism: Manifestations*, ed. Nancy Mithlo (Santa Fe, NM: Museum of Contemporary Native Arts, 2011), 40.

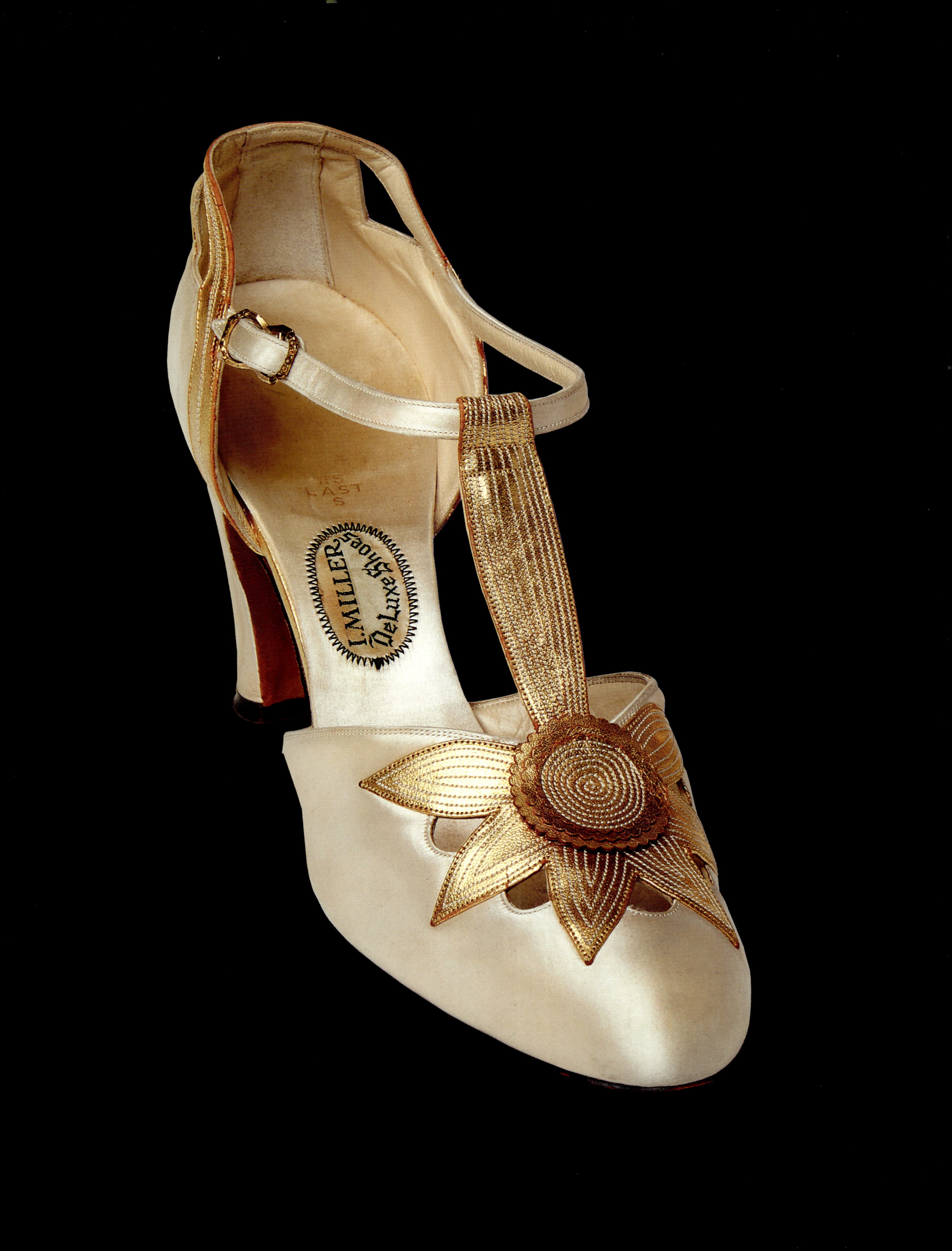
LAST
I. MILLER
DeLuxe Shoes

They Have Names

STORIES OF ERASURE

Michelle Tolini Finamore

The gaps in our histories make clear how people have been erased from them, particularly people of color, women, immigrants, and those of lower socioeconomic classes. These gaps appear at all levels. An account book covering the years 1727 to 1770, for example, tracks the clients of shoemakers James Fowler and Samuel Fowler Jr. of East Hartford, Connecticut, and is as significant for what it reveals as for what it conceals. One of their most active clients was Elizabeth Marshall; her name is always noted in the records, and she was almost certainly white. Black buyers, meanwhile, were not given names, identified only as "negro boy" or "negro woman."[1]

On the level of makers, the level we more commonly attend to in fashion history, information gaps based on structural biases likewise exist. For example, an early, important pair of shoes dating to the 1790s that resides in the collection of the Wadsworth Atheneum Museum of Art in Hartford, Connecticut, reflects the nature of the material preserved in museum collections. The shoes, by John J. White of Hartford, proudly bear a florid silk label calligraphed with "All kinds of Sandals, Silk & Stuff Shoes made & sold wholesale & retail at the Silk & Stuff Shoe Manufactory Hartford." The preservation of the shoes suggests that they were worn for a special occasion; the lore of the family who donated them connects them to the wedding day of Elizabeth Parson in Hartford in 1795.[2]

Compare this pair of shoes to a wedding dress from 1914 in the collection of The Charleston Museum in South Carolina, explored in detail in Elizabeth Way's essay in this volume. We know a good deal about the identity of the woman who wore it, Wilhelmine Dorothea Meyer; we know whom she married, the date of the wedding, and myriad other details related to Meyer's life. On the other hand, we know very little about Phoebe, the Black woman who made the dress, whose last name is unknown. When donating the dress to The Charleston Museum, Meyer's heirs described Phoebe as a seamstress.[3] She was far more than that, however; a seamstress is solely responsible for sewing. Phoebe was a dressmaker who both designed and constructed garments. Records tend to be kept when donations come from wealthy white donors, revealing the great disparity between the kind of information retained by and for different categories of people. Such seemingly small distinctions in record keeping create important, cumulative differences in our histories.

Three talented and entrepreneurial nineteenth-century couturiers with fascinating backgrounds who have been widely omitted from the traditional narrative of American fashion, likely for reasons of gender and race, are Madame Olympe, Elizabeth Keckley, and Mehitable Primus. An immigrant, an enslaved woman who attained her emancipation, and a free Black woman: these resilient and creative women reflect the difficulty of piecing together a unified narrative when American couture, unlike the professionalized and consolidated French *haute couture syndicale*, encompassed a wide geography and lacked an overarching story. Unlike the French, none of these designers had the benefit of formal training; in many cases, such as that of Keckley, they learned sewing from their mothers. By looking at the careers of Olympe, Keckley, and Primus, who hailed from three different cities—New Orleans; Washington, DC; and Hartford, Connecticut, respectively—we can expand the range of American fashion history beyond its familiar demographics and traditional centers of production.

These resilient and creative women reflect the difficulty of piecing together a unified narrative: American couture, unlike the professionalized and consolidated French *haute couture syndicale*, encompassed a wide geography and lacked an overarching story.

The genealogy of Euro-American fashion usually begins with the English-born, French-trained Charles Frederick Worth. The "Father of Haute Couture," as he is known, Worth is held up as the first designer to promote himself as an artist, the first to "sign" (label) his gowns, and the first to successfully secure royal patronage by clients such as Empress Eugenie. Worth was a key player in the 1868 establishment of the governing body of the French fashion industry, the Chambre Syndicale de la Haute Couture, which formalized the hegemony of the Paris couture industry. In America, there was no such national governing body or official documentation for fashion despite the hundreds, if not thousands, of designers who were as skilled as their French counterparts.

Where do the striking, custom-made creations of New Orleans designer Madame Olympe (Olympe Boisse) fit into this

opposite John J. White, shoes and detail of inner label, 1793–95. Silk, linen, and leather. Wadsworth Atheneum, Hartford, Connecticut, Gift of Charles B. Curtis.

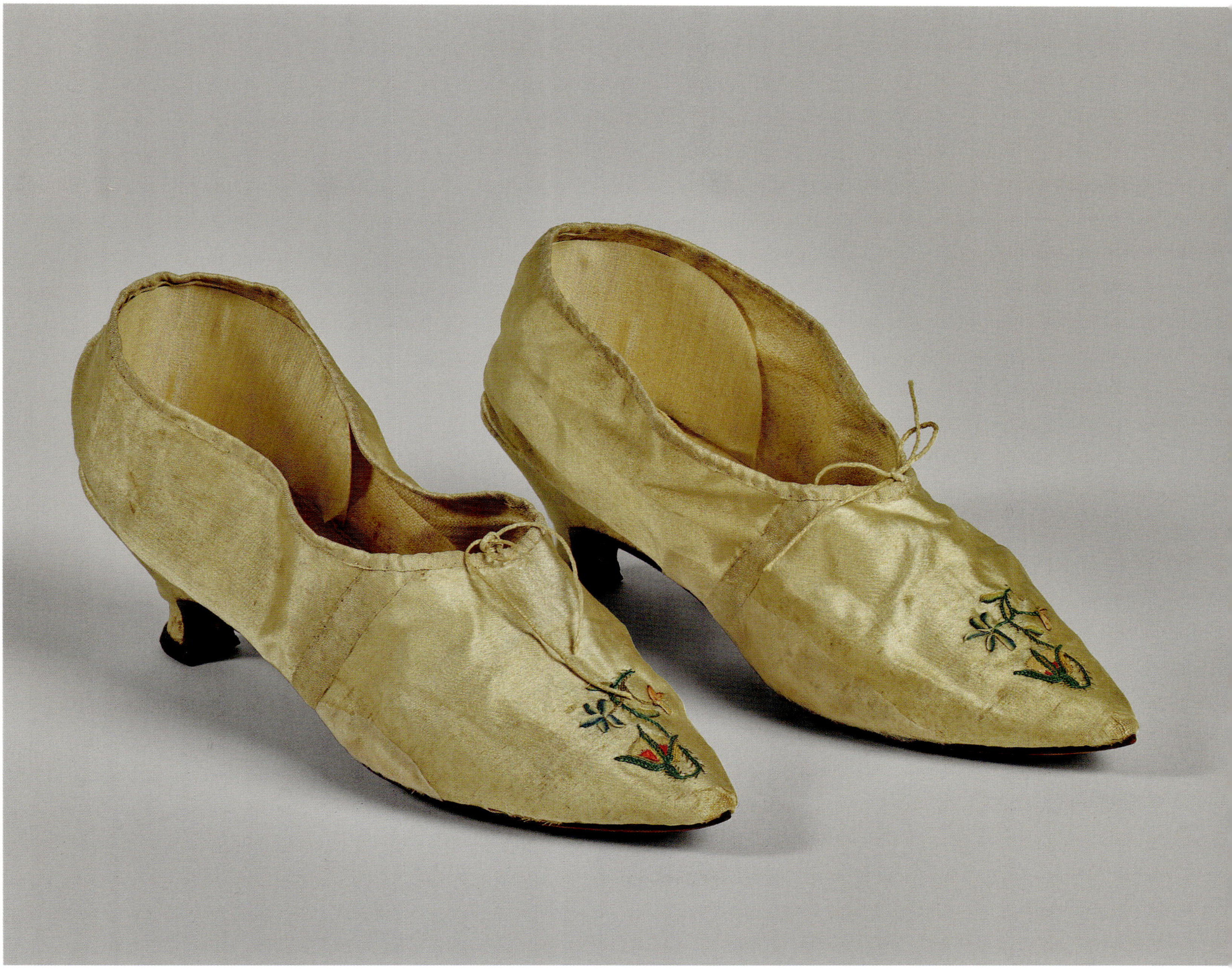

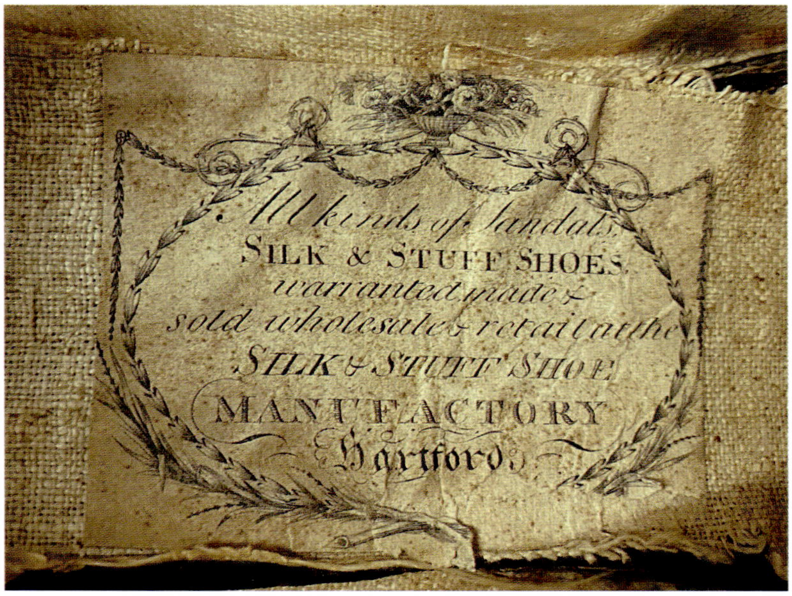
All kinds of Sandals,
SILK & STUFF SHOES
warranted made &
sold wholesale & retail at the
SILK & STUFF SHOE
MANUFACTORY
Hartford

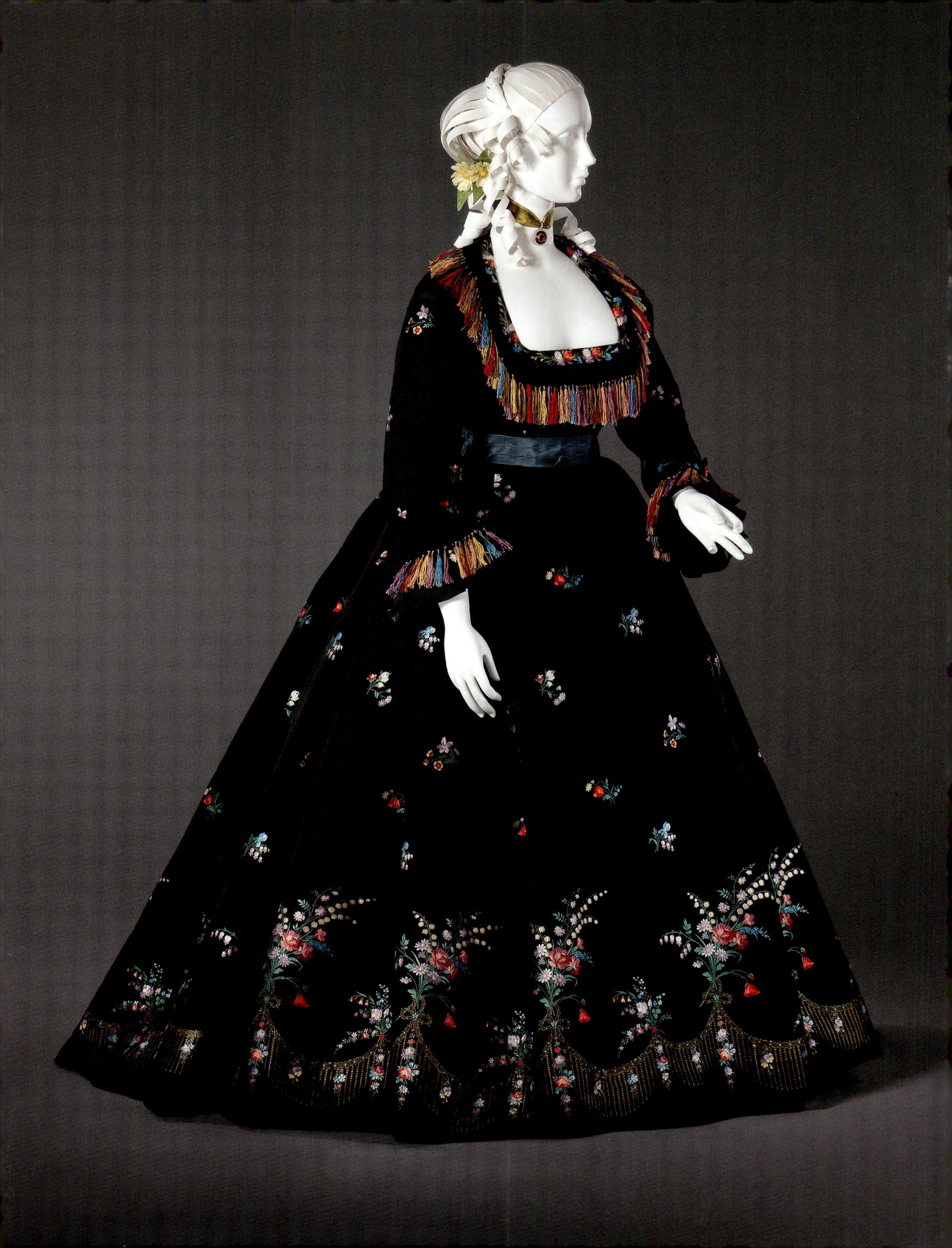

narrative? Madame Olympe's career paralleled that of Worth, and her gowns were as beautifully constructed and originally conceived as any Paris couture garment. And like Worth, Madame Olympe "signed" her dresses in the form of an interior label. It is believed Madame Olympe emigrated to the United States in the 1840s, starting her fashion career as a *modiste* and importer of French styles in New Orleans in 1851.[4] The term *modiste*, in common usage in the nineteenth century, referred to a maker and/or seller of fashion goods, including garments, hats, and fans. Madame Olympe's shop was a prime destination in New Orleans, a city with a thriving fashion industry. A vivid account from 1882 of a visit to her salon survives:

> *Modistes* and *Couturières*—French to the backbone—I mean to the staylace and back hair, abound in the French Quarter. . . . Bonnets are bonnets in New Orleans. I have been to the fountain head. In Canal-Street, nearly opposite the Grand Opera House . . . I have noticed a magasin [*sic*] of austerely splendid aspect. It has but two modestly-sized windows, in which are displayed, with studied carelessness, some parcels of rich tissues, some loosely floating lace, and a dainty fan and trailing feather or two. In the background I see some lace curtains and wire gauze blinds, with the single word "Olympe" inscribed in golden letters. Is Olympe the High Priestess of the Temple of Visiting Bonnets?[5]

Madame Olympe's location, across from the city's landmark French Opera House, was just one indication of her stature, which was perhaps enhanced by her connection to France. Her shop's elegance, as described, clearly approached that of any luxury fashion retailer in New York or Paris. Madame Olympe was also making dresses by at least the 1860s. One example from circa 1866 follows the fashionable silhouette of the day but is unique in contrasting vividly colored metallic passementerie and brightly embroidered flowers against black silk faille, perhaps in a nod to the bold color combinations of New Orleans style.

One designer whose story is integral to American history, and who worked at a marked disadvantage because of the color of her skin, was Mary Todd Lincoln's dressmaker, Elizabeth Keckley. Keckley was a formerly enslaved person whose couture abilities helped her purchase her hard-won freedom largely with income from her dressmaking. Her memoir, *Behind the Scenes: Or, Thirty Years a Slave, and Four Years in the White House* (1868), offers a remarkable account of the trials she faced throughout her life: she struggled with racism even after her notable success as Lincoln's *couturière*. Much as Empress Eugenie's patronage of Worth solidified his standing, Mary Todd Lincoln's status as American royalty bolstered Keckley's fame. Her dresses, custom made for her clients from the finest material possible, are undoubtedly couture but have suffered from a lack of scholarship because the canon has been so skewed toward the French. Extant examples of her work are few, and even for those in museum collections, attribution is not always certain. The circa 1861 strawberry-patterned black silk dress in the Abraham Lincoln Presidential Library and Museum is a magnificent example of dressmaking mastery. The dress was made at the time of Keckley's employment with the Lincoln family, and scholars believe it to be her handiwork, but there is no label identifying its maker.

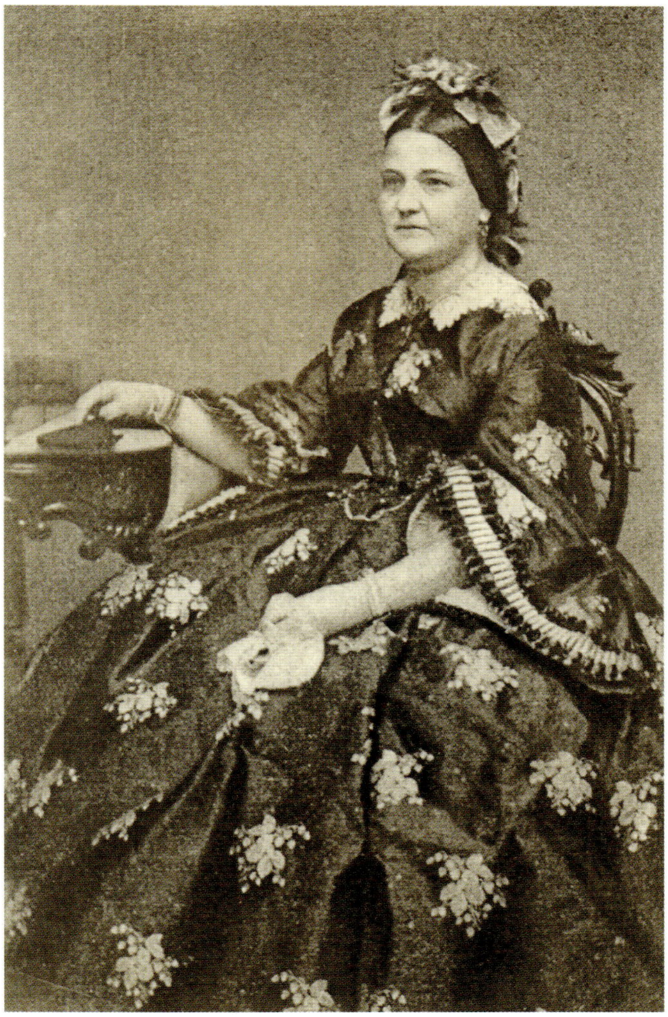

Mathew Brady, cabinet card depicting Mary Todd Lincoln wearing dress attributed to Elizabeth Keckley, ca. 1861. Abraham Lincoln Presidential Library and Museum, Springfield, Illinois.

opposite Madame Olympe Boisse, evening gown, 1866–67. Silk brocade, silk/metallic fringe, and silk ribbon. FIDM Museum Collection: Gift of Cathy Gordon. Courtesy of FIDM Museum at the Fashion Institute of Design & Merchandising, Los Angeles.

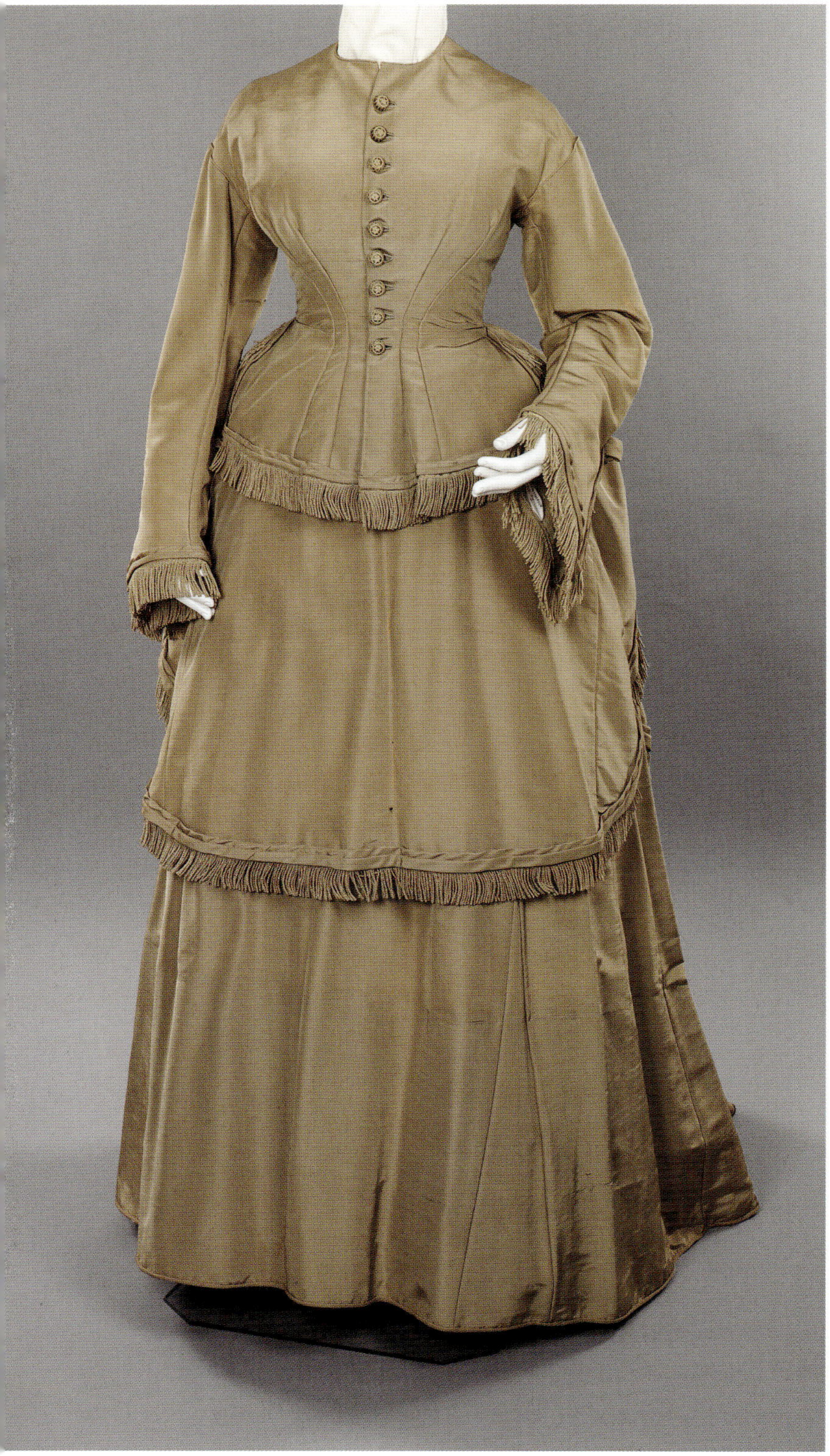

Attributed to Mehitable Primus, day dress, ca. 1870. Silk and linen. Wadsworth Atheneum, Gift of Edward A. Singleton.

While Keckley has gained scholarly notice over the years, dressmakers such as Mehitable Jacobs Primus, whose garments are also unlabeled, are only now garnering more research. Primus was one of a flourishing group of at least two dozen women of color who worked in the dressmaking trades in Hartford during the years 1840–99.[6] A respected member of the city's middle class, Primus ran a vibrant dressmaking business and trained numerous apprentices and seamstresses. Surviving letters from her daughter Rebecca provide a remarkable record of her life, but attribution of her dresses is rare. The Wadsworth Atheneum has one example, a meticulously constructed taupe faille dress that Primus likely made for her daughter around 1870,[7] when Rebecca moved back to Hartford after a job teaching newly emancipated people in the South.[8] Although quite simple in style (Rebecca was a self-professed "plain" dresser), the dress exhibits great skill in the form-fitting cut and the quality of the stitchwork; the only adornments are the matching crocheted buttons.[9] Its date, donation, and preservation indicate that it may have been her wedding dress.

Gender bias in the telling of history was not limited to the nineteenth century, however. Lithuanian immigrant Beth Levine, born in 1914, started her design career at the New York–based shoe company I. Miller before founding the Herbert Levine shoe company with her husband in 1948. While Herbert managed the factory, sales, and marketing, Beth was the creative force. Yet her name never appeared on the label because it was believed that a woman's name promoting the product would hurt sales. She was also an inventor, creating the novel "stocking boot" (a shoe with attached hosiery) and shoes called "Spring-o-lators" with devices that helped keep backless mules on one's feet. In her work, she experimented with unusual surfaces and textures and nontraditional materials such as vinyl and spandex, a creativity that resulted in works like a circa 1955 pair of pearl-encrusted high heels. Singer Nancy Sinatra famously wore Levine's handiwork when singing "These Boots Are Made for Walkin' " in 1966, a moment that helped popularize boots as high fashion.

Undergarments became a field in which many women worked because of its intimate association with the female body, sometimes achieving greater recognition. They contributed enormously to the hundreds, if not thousands, of corset patents filed in the nineteenth and early twentieth centuries. Emmeline W. Philbrook innovated important improvements for corsetry in the nineteenth-century. In 1881–82, she patented the Equipoise "underwaist," a garment that was eventually manufactured by George Frost of Boston as a more practical alternative to the norm of

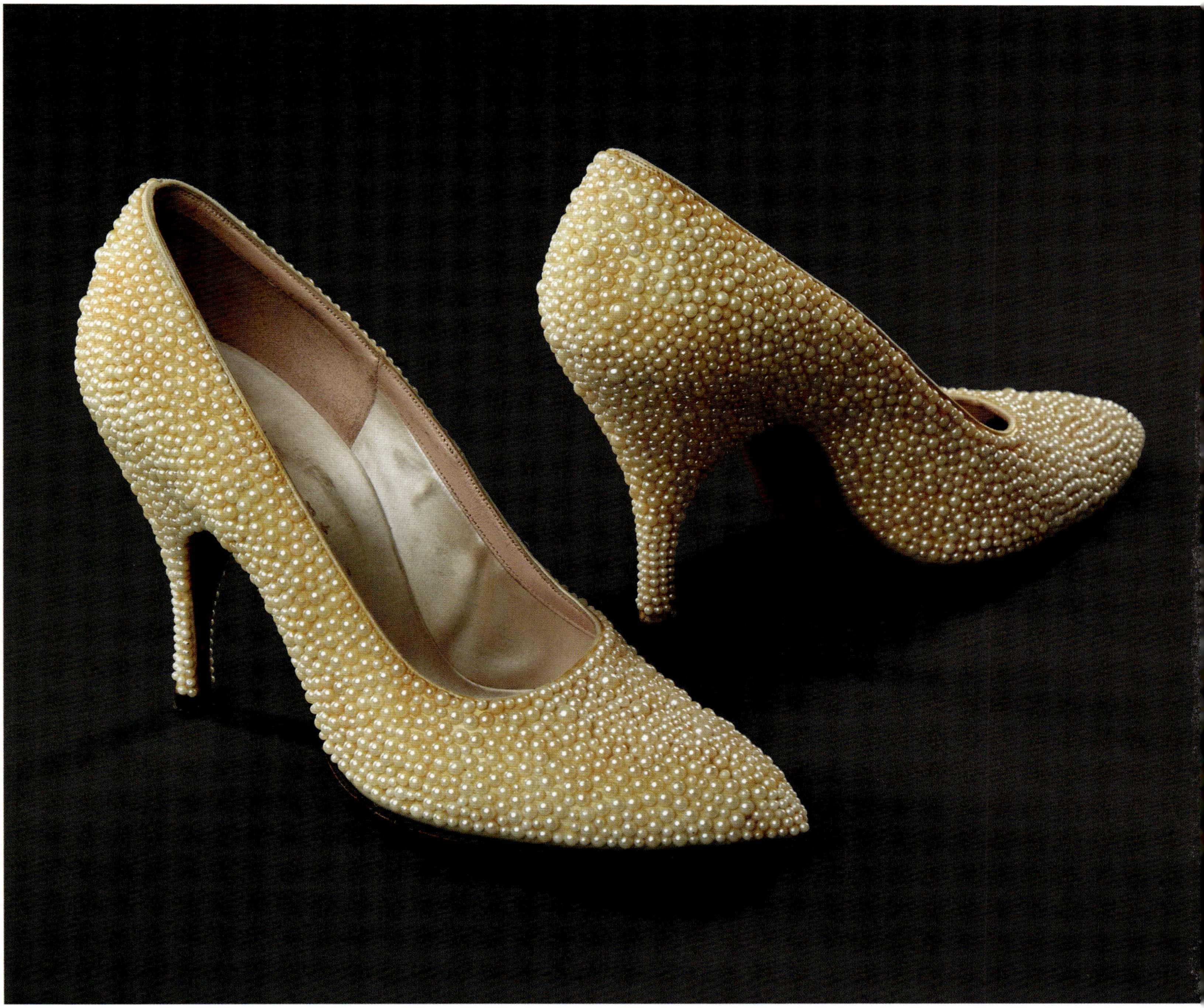

the day; to create it, she reconceived the corset to support undergarments from the shoulder via a two-layered design and wider shoulder straps.

New York–based Madame Griswold successfully filed patents for corsetry innovations, as did Mary Gifford, Elizabeth Gribbon, Aleatha H. Lockwood, Marie Southworth, and Ellen West. None of these women are household names today, but they pioneered more comfortable corsetry and, in the case of Lockwood, maternity corsets. In the twentieth century, Polish immigrant Olga Erteszek built underwear into a multimillion-dollar corporation. Erteszek pioneered more comfortable, "weightless" bras and the use of Lycra in her "panti-slips," colorfully printed undergarments, and tummy-trimming underwear that presaged today's Spanx. Unlike Beth Levine, who was kept from being publicly identified with her own company, Erteszek often featured in her Olga Company's public-relations campaigns. Today, contemporary firms such as pop star Rihanna's Savage X Fenty brand carry on the work of such women designing for women while attending to body inclusivity and positivity.

above Herbert and Beth Levine, shoes, 1950s. Leather and faux pearls. Jimmy Raye Collection, Salem, Massachusetts.

(Model.)

E. W. PHILBROOK.

UNDERWAIST.

No. 259,422. Patented June 13, 1882.

Fig. 1.

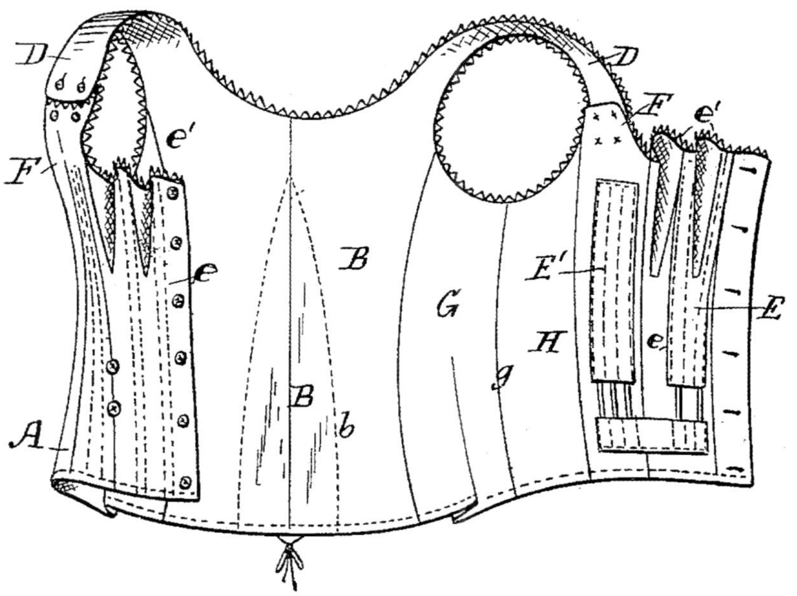

Fig. 2.

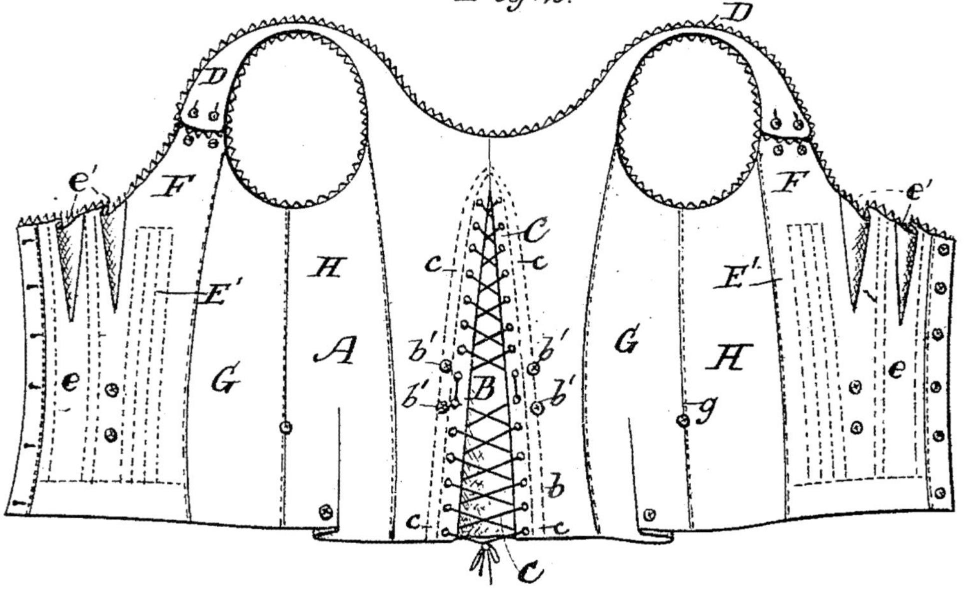

Fig. 3.

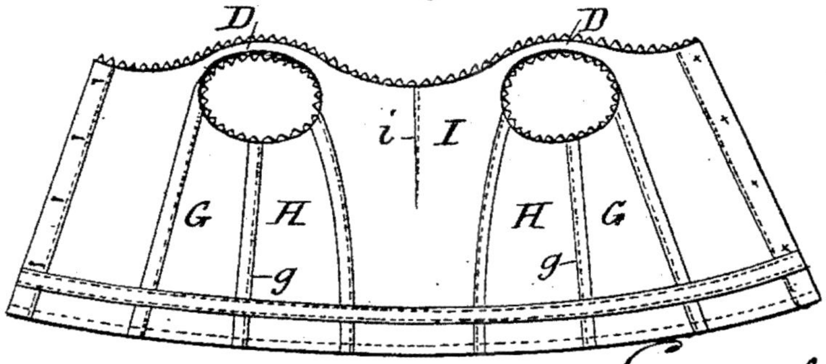

Witnesses:

E. E. Masson

Philip Mauro

Inventor:

Emmeline W. Philbrook

by A. Pollok

attorney

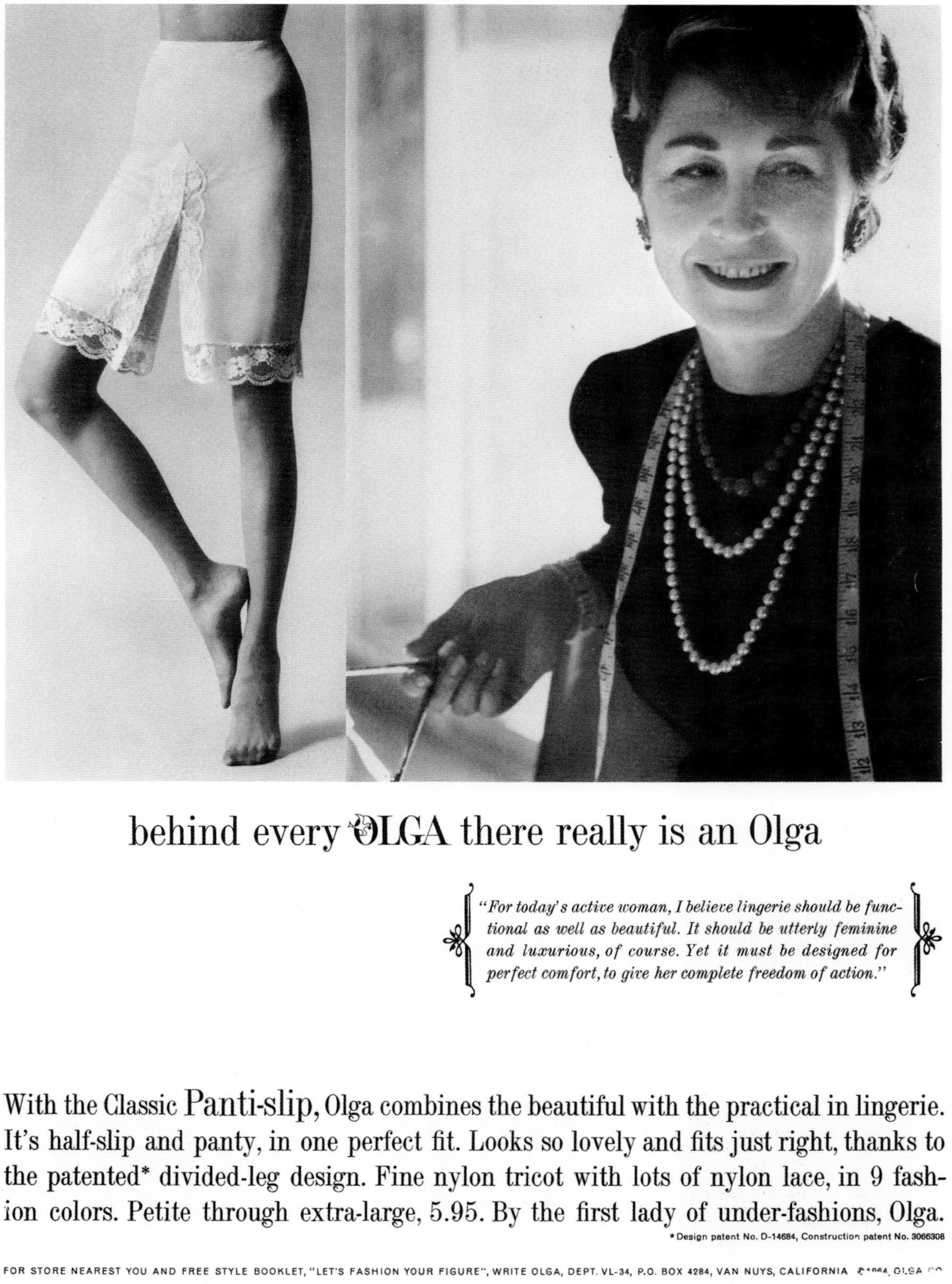

opposite Emmeline W. Philbrook, corset patent sketch, June 13, 1882 (no. 259,422).

above Olga advertisement, ca. 1968. Courtesy of Christina Erteszek.

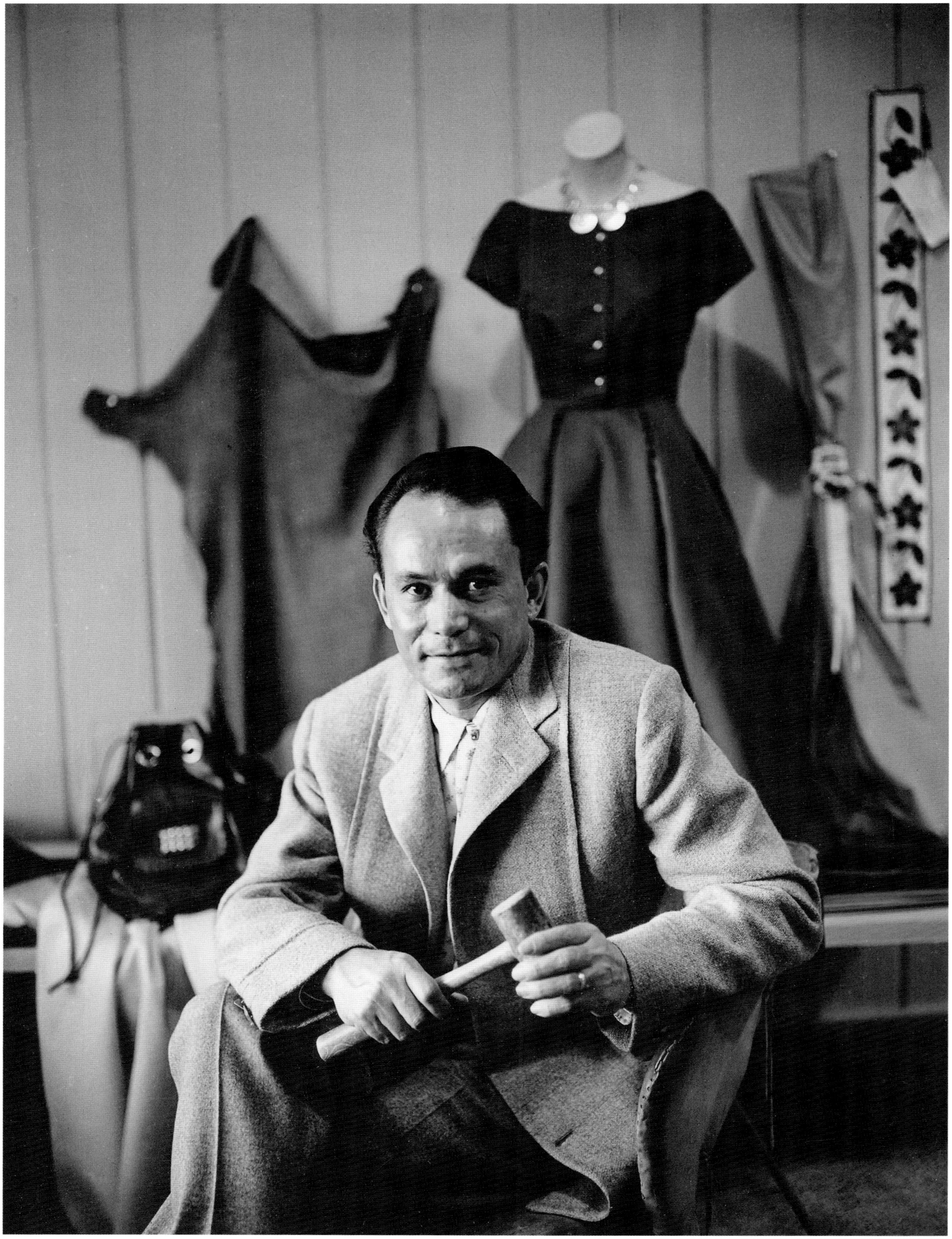

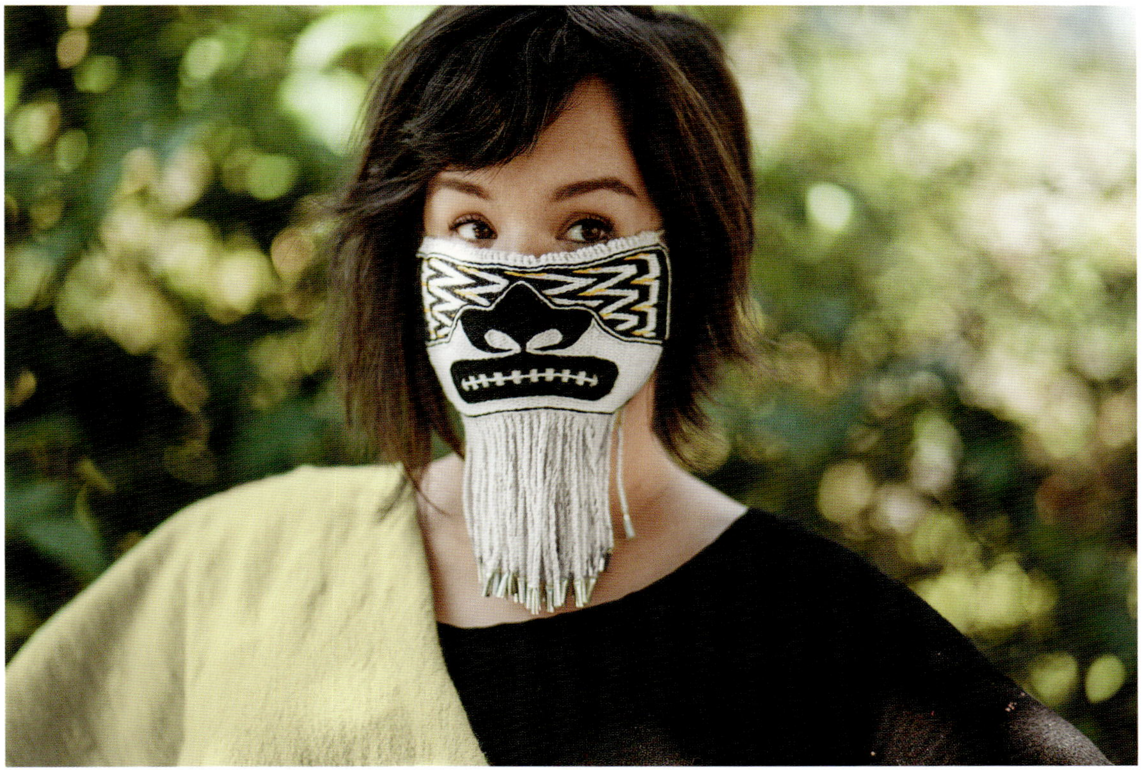

Cherokee designer Lloyd Henri "Kiva" New, a successful midcentury Indigenous designer and teacher, is well known in Native American design circles but has never been included in standard fashion histories. He deserves a place alongside American ready-to-wear designers Claire McCardell, Bonnie Cashin, and Norman Norell. New created innovative Native-inspired textiles and garments that were carried in luxury stores like Neiman Marcus; one was even worn by Miss Arizona in the 1957 Miss America pageant. At the height of his designing career, he left to lead the Institute of American Indian Arts (IAIA) in Santa Fe, New Mexico, solidifying his status as a crucial figure in contemporary Indigenous fashion.[10] During New's tenure at IAIA, which lasted from 1961 to 1978, he trained multiple generations of Native designers, including Kimberly "Wendy" Ponca and Clarissa Hudson Rizal, who were instructors when future designers of note Lily Hope, Ursala Hudson, and Patricia Michaels attended the school.

opposite Lloyd Henri "Kiva" New, Scottsdale, Arizona, 1956. IAIA MS015, Lloyd Henri New Papers, Institute of American Indian Arts, Santa Fe.

above Lily Hope, All Our Ancestors Chilkat Protector Mask, 2020. Merino wool, cedar bark, ermine, and tin. Wooshkindein Da.aat. Modeled by Lily Hope (Tlingit/Filipino).

Immigration has played a key role in American fashion, with designers both leaving the country and coming to it to achieve recognition—though in some cases, barriers against immigrants worked against them as well. Jan Matzeliger dramatically transformed the shoe industry. Born in Dutch Guiana (now Suriname) in 1852 to a white Dutch father and Black Surinamer mother, Matzeliger first became a sailor. After settling in the United States, in 1876 he started working in a shoe factory in Lynn, Massachusetts, in a region where the great majority of American ready-to-wear shoes were being produced. In 1883, Matzeliger patented a device that mechanized the attachment of a shoe's upper to its sole. The resulting invention allowed factories to make up to seven hundred pairs of shoes a day and cut their price in half. Matzeliger died of tuberculosis at age thirty-seven. Though his investors made millions, and his shares transferred to friends, loved ones, and his church at his death, he himself saw little profit from an invention that continues to have a long-lasting impact on shoemaking in America.[11]

Some American designers took the opposite route, leaving the United States to escape racial exclusion and find success. In the 1980s, Patrick Kelly moved to France to pursue his craft because, as a Black designer, he had difficulty gaining a foothold

Sorosis for A. E. Little Co., boots made ca. 1900 in Lynn, Massachusetts, when the city was one of the top three shoe-producing cities in the country. Metallic leather, wood, and metal. Jimmy Raye Collection, Salem, Massachusetts.

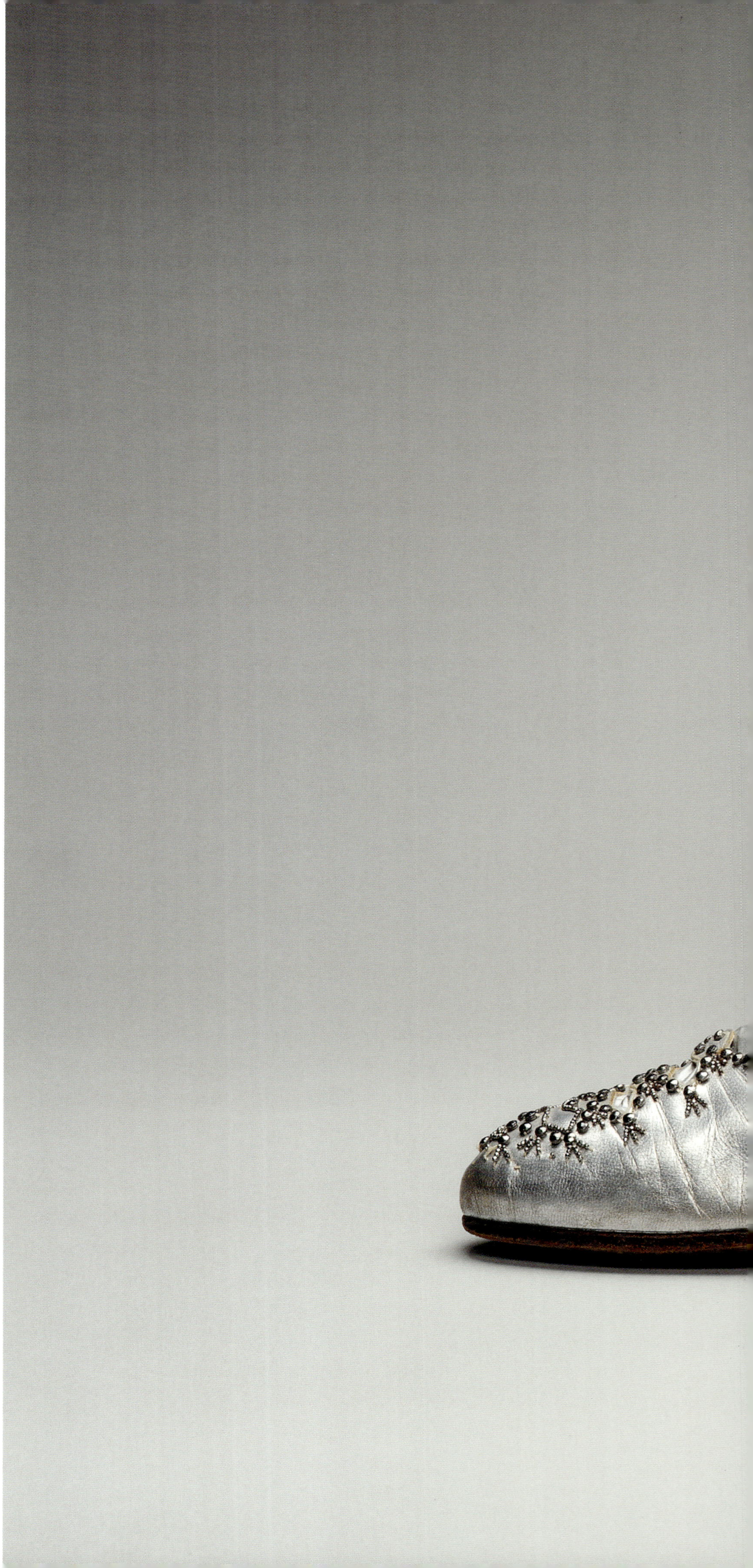

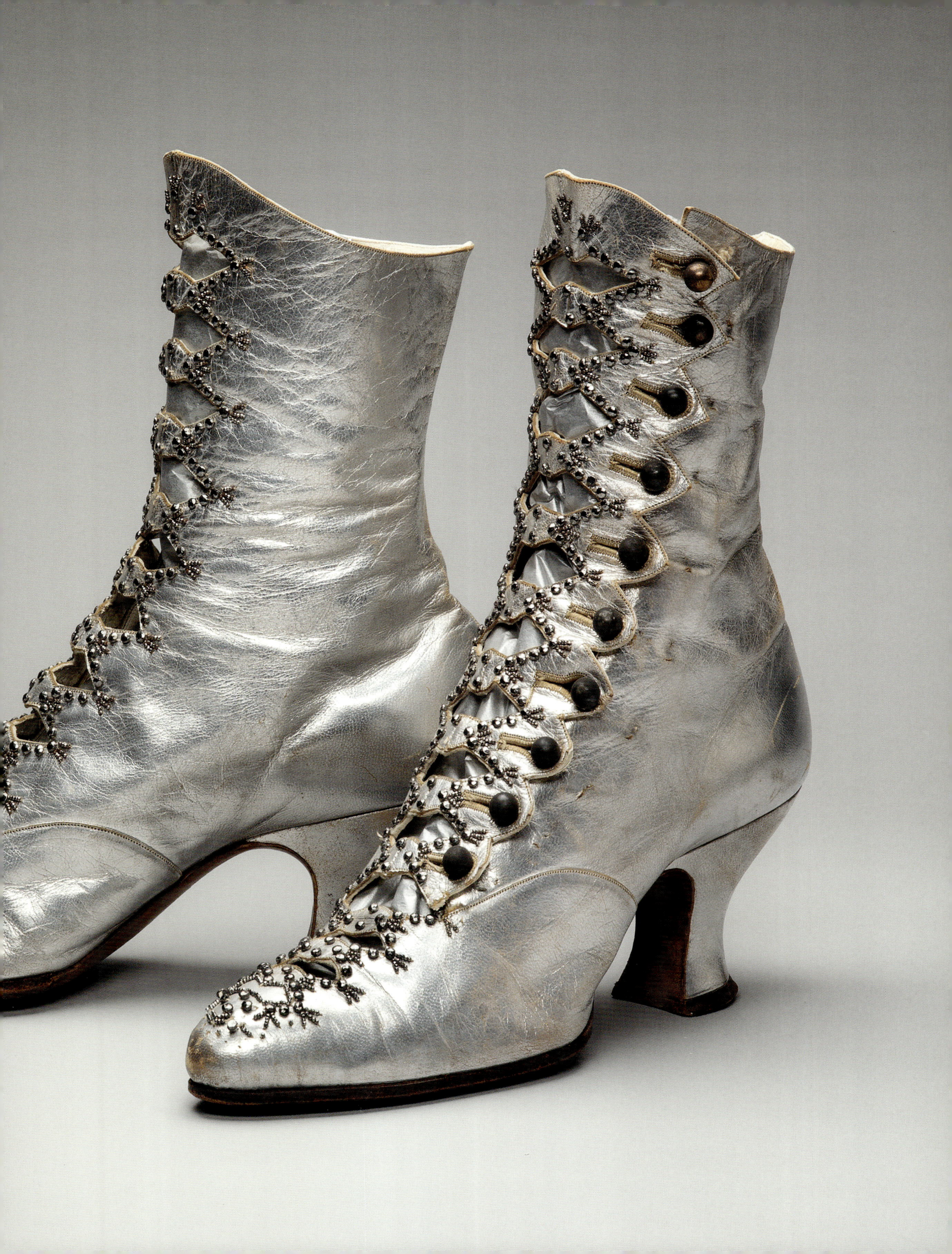

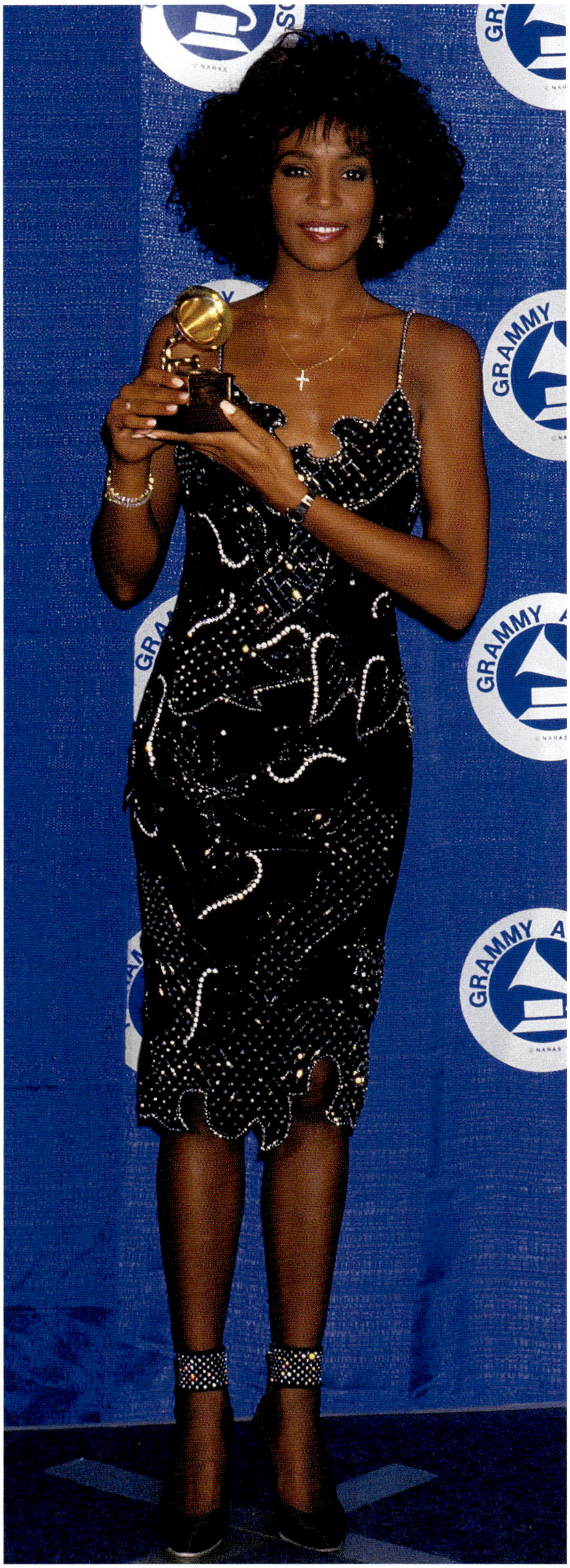

in the white-dominated American fashion industry. In France, his exuberant designs found a ready following, and in 1988 he became the first American, and first Black person of any nationality, to be appointed to the Chambre Syndicale du Prêt-à-Porter. Kelly's designs, such as his button-encrusted heart dress, reflected his Black heritage and southern upbringing, celebrating the tradition of exuberant churchgoing attire; others wove in subversive references to Josephine Baker and controversial racist imagery. Kelly died at a young age of AIDS in 1990 but is now proudly recognized as an American success story.

Kelly's contemporary Fabrice Simon also died of AIDS, in 1998, as part of the decimation it wrought on the fashion industry. Unlike Kelly, however, Fabrice's star has faded outside fashion circles. Fabrice was born in 1951 in Port-au-Prince and moved to New York in 1964 at age thirteen. In the late 1970s and 1980s, he created beaded party dresses that were all the rage on the New York City party circuit, worn by stars like Natalie Cole, Rita Moreno, and Whitney Houston and carried in department stores across America. Fabrice designed his dresses in New York, then sent the fabric to Haiti, where embroiderers turned the textiles into finely beaded works of art. His dresses represent the ultimate in hybridity: 1980s silhouettes with postmodern patterns that referred to his Caribbean heritage and Haitian beadwork traditions.

Connections to the entertainment industry such as those Simon possessed have always been good business for designers—and have been actively sought by other immigrants seeking to make their way in the United States. Although not a household name, the shoe designer Israel Miller had a presence that loomed large in the early days of New York cinema and theater. Originally from Russia, Miller came to New York City in 1892 and began producing beautiful, distinctive footwear. In 1895, he opened a store with a lengthy moniker: the Show Folks Shoe Shop Dedicated to Beauty in Footwear. His flagship at Broadway and West Forty-Sixth Street, operating under the more commercially nimble name I. Miller, made explicit tribute to its star clients. In an early kind of crowdsourcing, he asked his customers to vote on their favorite actors and commissioned artist Alexander Stirling Calder (the father of artist Alexander Calder) to carve

left Whitney Houston wearing a Fabrice Simon dress at the 1988 Grammy Awards.

opposite Patrick Kelly, day dress with matching gloves, Fall/Winter 1986–87. Wool, plastic, and glass. FIDM Museum Collection: Gift of Linda and Steve Plochocki. Courtesy of FIDM Museum at the Fashion Institute of Design & Merchandising, Los Angeles.

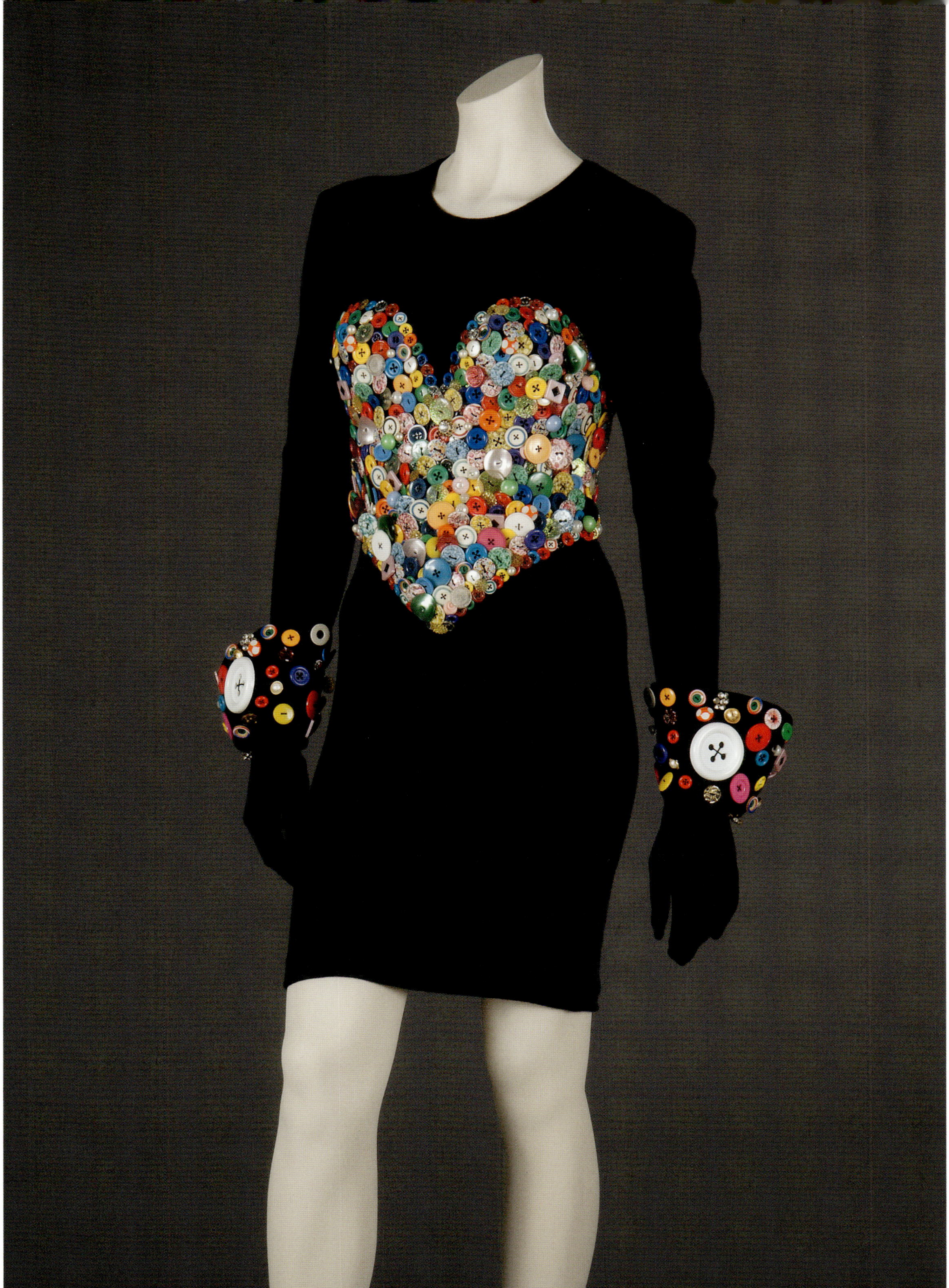

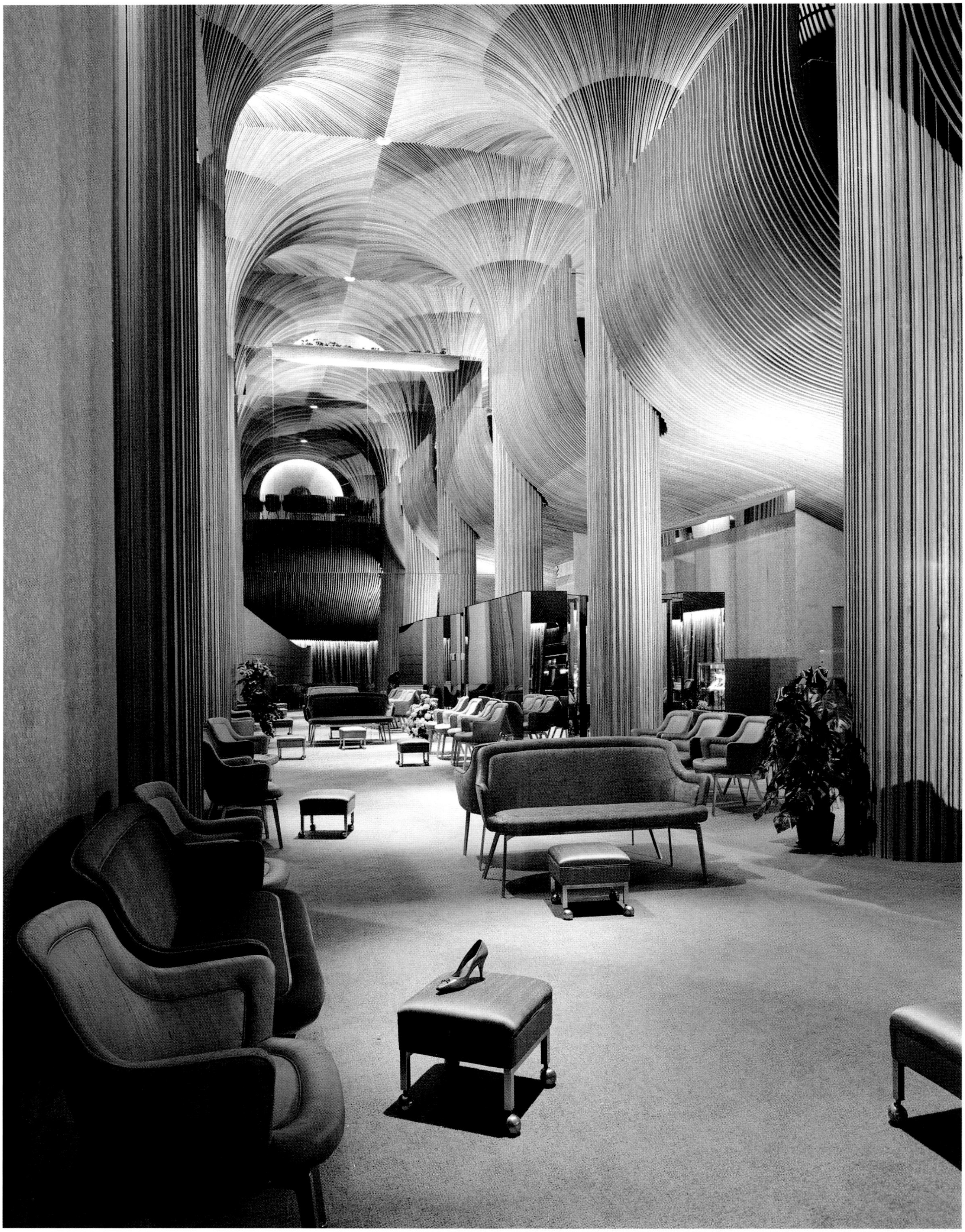

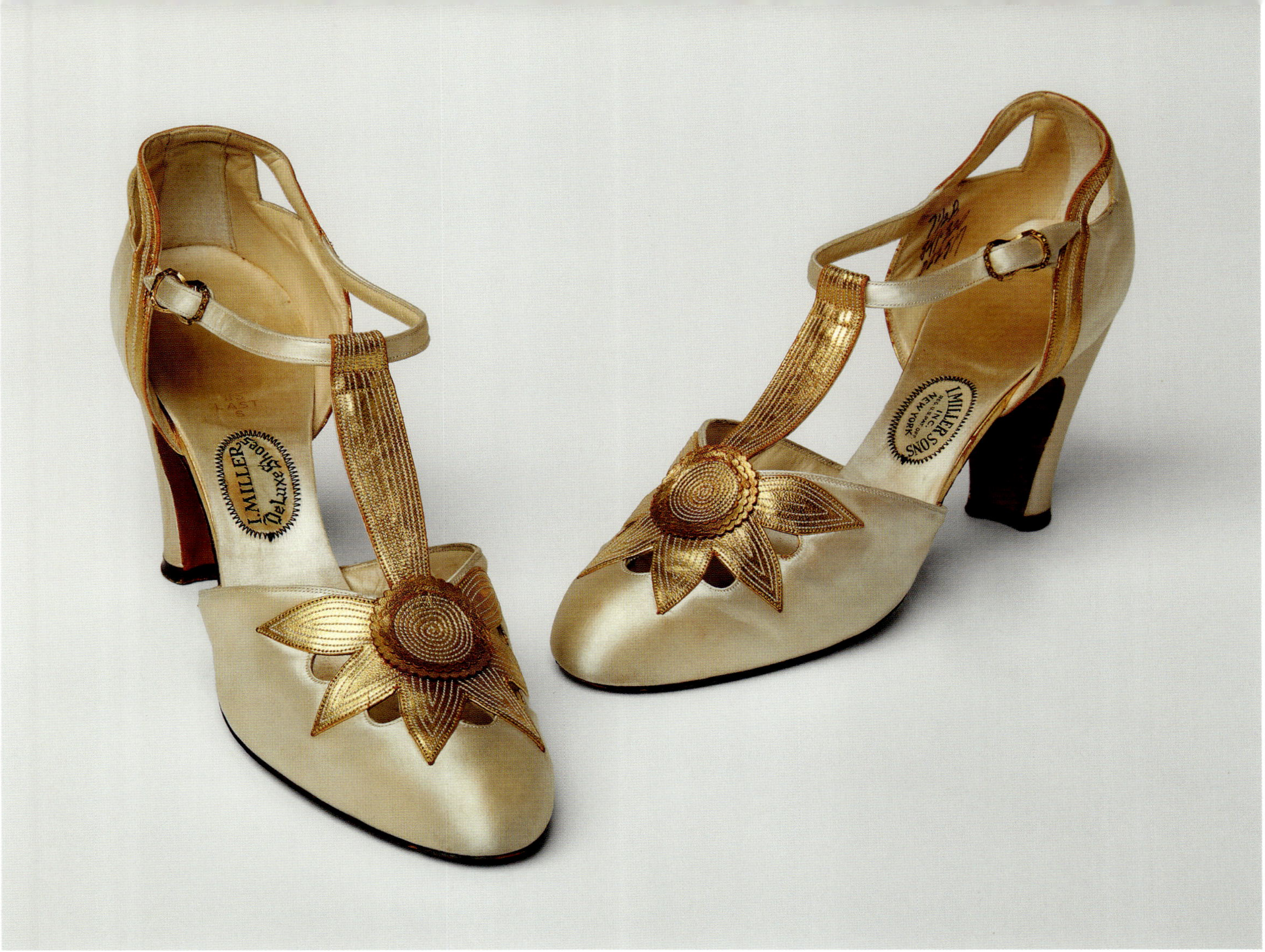

their likenesses. Sculptures of stage actress Ethel Barrymore, comedian Marilyn Miller, film actress Mary Pickford, and opera singer Rosa Ponselle were set into niches at the top of the building. At its zenith, I. Miller had two hundred twenty-eight retail outlets; the company also had factories in Brooklyn, Long Island City, and Haverhill, Massachusetts.[12] Miller maintained a high profile late into the twentieth century, receiving a tribute in singer Betty Davis's 1973 hard-rocking funk single "Steppin in Her I. Miller Shoes."

A similar business strategy was sought out by fashion entrepreneur Henriette Kanengeiser, who took the "stage name" Hattie Carnegie because of the surname's association with wealth and power. An Austrian émigré, Carnegie came to the United States in 1892, opened her eponymous fashion house in 1918,

opposite Interior, I. Miller shoe salon, New York, 1962.

above I. Miller, shoes, mid-1920s. Leather, silk satin, metal, and rhinestones. Jimmy Raye Collection, Salem, Massachusetts.

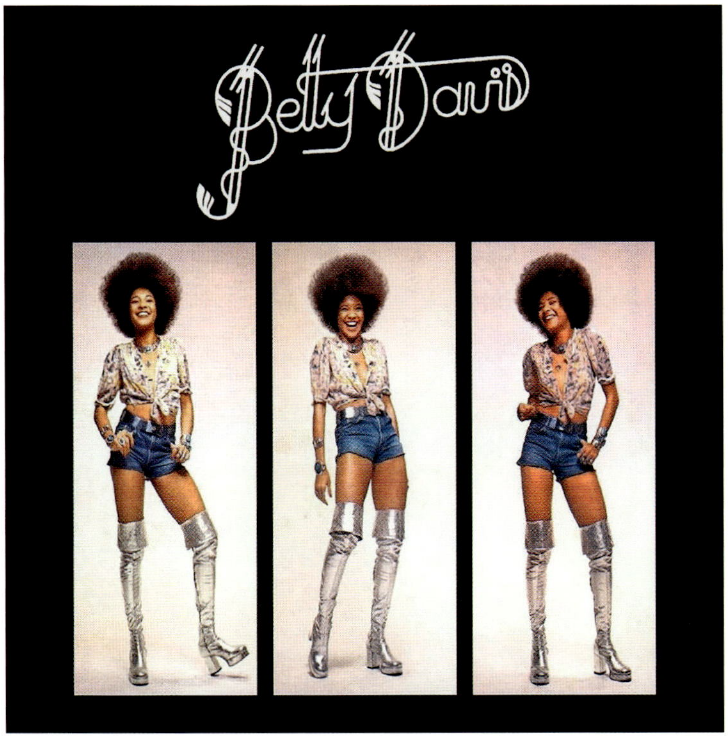

Cover of Betty Davis's "Steppin in Her I. Miller Shoes" single, 1973.

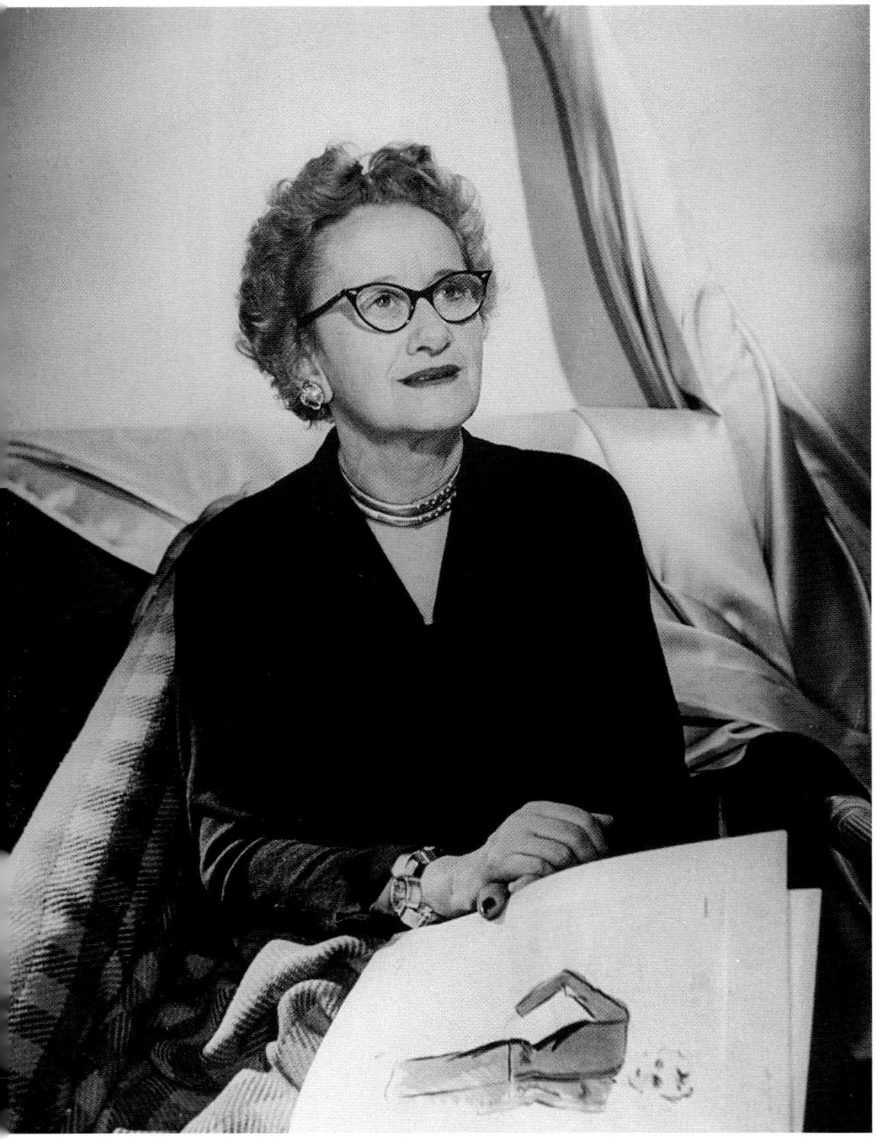

Dress designer Hattie Carnegie holding sketches amid bolts of material, 1947.

and recognized early on that associations with the star industry were good business. Carnegie is acknowledged in standard American fashion histories but has yet to be the subject of deep research because her work has been considered derivative of French design. Yet, at the height of her career, her salon at 42 East Forty-Ninth Street in New York had over one thousand employees. Actor Lucille Ball worked as a model for Carnegie before her career in television. Of the experience, she recalled:

> Hattie was a tiny dynamo, direct and outspoken. She wouldn't let anyone buy a dress she considered unbecoming. . . . Hattie taught me how to slouch properly in a $1,000 hand-sewn sequin dress and how to wear a $40,000 sable coat as casually as a rabbit. . . . Connie and Joan Bennett were frequent customers. . . . . Joan Crawford, Gloria Swanson, and Ina Claire also came to Hattie's.[13]

One of Carnegie's many successful acolytes was the designer Norman Norell, who began his career costuming stage and film stars and remained connected to the entertainment industry throughout his long career.

Countless other designers who went on to have a major impact on the fashion industry worked at Hattie Carnegie at some point in their careers, including Adrian, Pauline Trigère, James Galanos, and Claire McCardell. Firms like hers and department stores served as incubators for countless, mostly anonymous dressmakers and couturiers. African American designer Ann Lowe, the under-appreciated architect of Jacqueline Kennedy's wedding dress, worked at Hattie Carnegie and the luxury department store Bergdorf Goodman, but, per standard practice at the time, was never named as a designer. For all her accomplishments, Lowe was famously sent to the service entrance when she arrived with Kennedy's wedding dress at Auchincloss Farm in Rhode Island in 1953.

Lack of access to fashion is itself a form of structural bias. Although by the later twentieth century, much of the world could follow the latest trends via film, television, and print media, luxury fashion shows have been mostly inaccessible, particularly for people of color. The *Ebony* Fashion Fair, pioneered by Eunice Walker Johnson, brought exclusive international and American luxury fashion to a broad and diverse audience. Johnson was the

opposite Hattie Carnegie, *robe de style* evening gown, 1920s. Silk, Chantilly lace, tulle, and organza. Jimmy Raye Collection, Salem, Massachusetts.

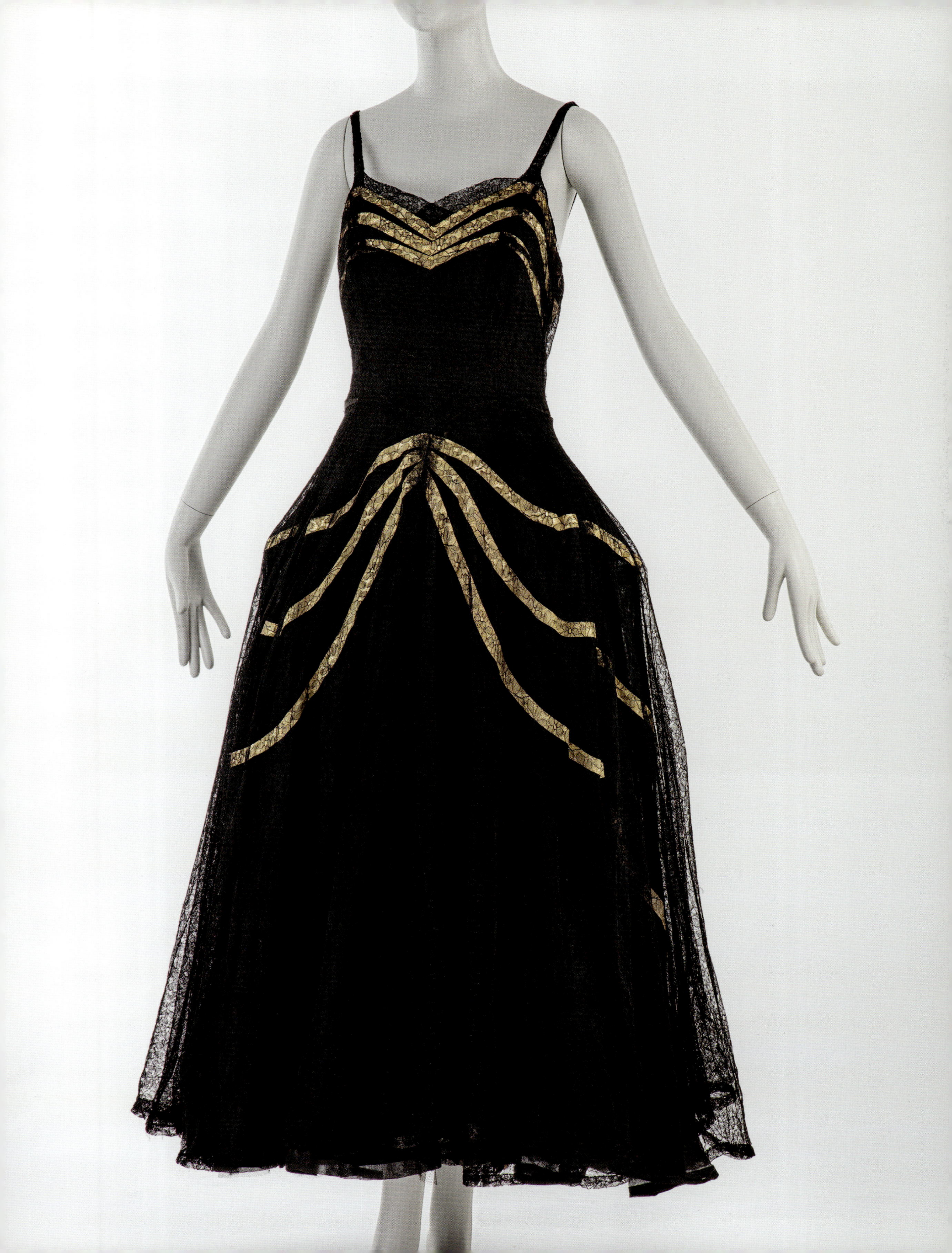

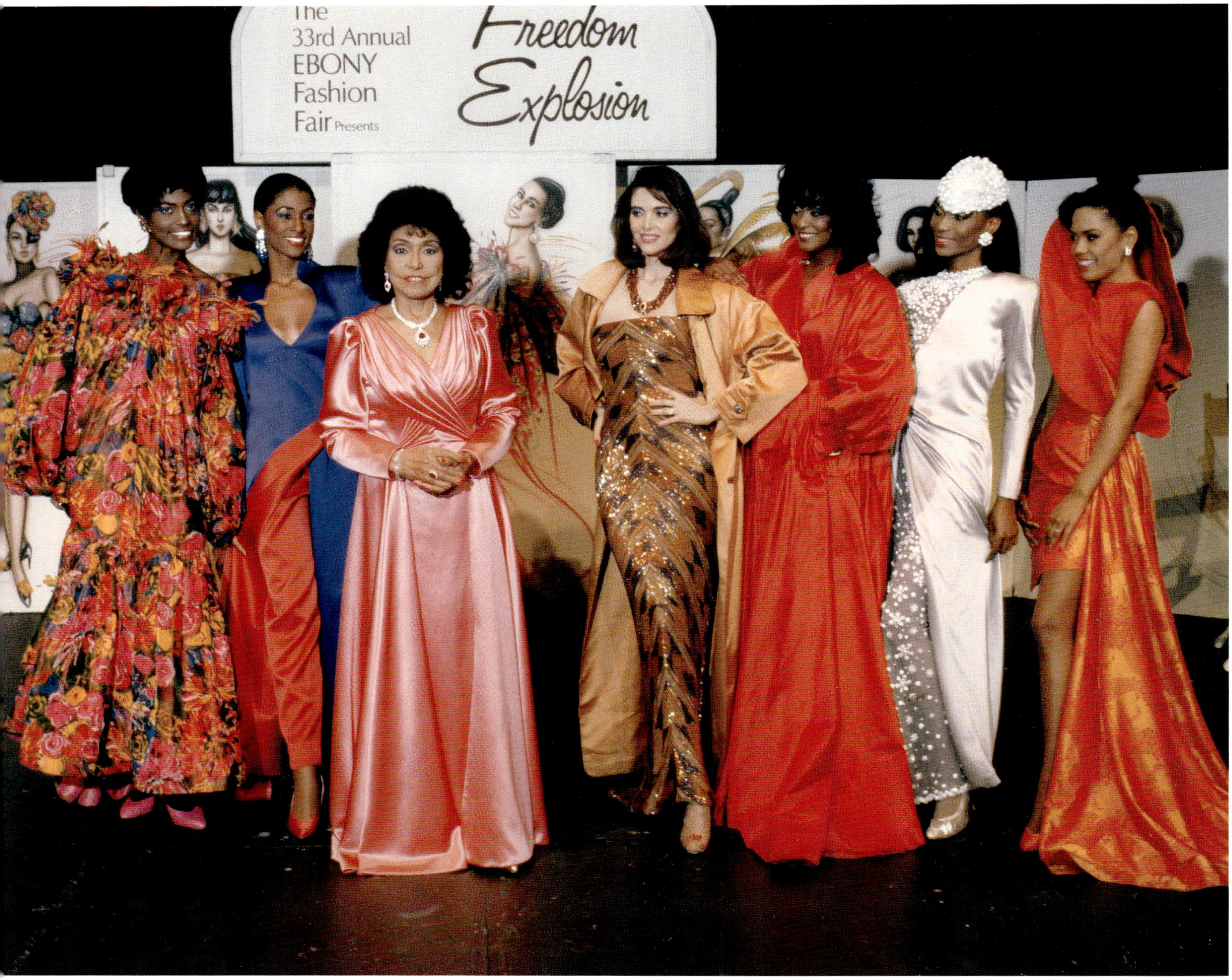

Eunice Walker Johnson (third from left) pictured with models at the 1991 Ebony Fashion Fair. Johnson started the Ebony Fashion Fair to help charities. Johnson Publishing Company Archive.

wife of entrepreneur John Johnson of the Johnson Publishing Company, which published the highly successful *Ebony* and *Jet* magazines. She regularly showed fashion on Black models in the pages of *Ebony*, and the annual Fashion Fairs went even further, bringing the excitement of live runway shows to Black audiences. Initiated in 1958, the shows traveled to large and small cities in the United States, Canada, and the Caribbean. The program was so successful that it ran for more than forty years, ending in 2009. Johnson showcased Black designers such as Fabrice Simon and Stephen Burrows alongside internationally recognized couturiers like Karl Lagerfeld, Christian Dior, Bob Mackie, and Yves Saint Laurent. A young and impressionable Patrick Kelly attended the *Ebony* Fashion Fair in 1970 and was transformed: "I was really impressed, and excited and mad. Even if you had money in Mississippi, who went to see a fashion show?"[14] Kelly's ultimate success meant that, sixteen years later, his work was featured on the runway at the 1986 *Ebony* Fashion Fair. The irony, however, is that Kelly may not have found that success had he remained in the United States. For future fashion historians confronting these stories of erasure, Kelly's words ring true: "If we can't deal with where we've been, it's gon' be hard to go somewhere."[15]

NOTES

1 Account book of James Fowler and Samuel Fowler Jr.—Shoemakers of Newport RI, 1727–1770, 44.160C, Wadsworth Atheneum, Hartford, Connecticut.

2 Gerald W. R. Ward and William N. Hosely, *The Great River: Art and Society of the Connecticut Valley, 1635–1820* (Hartford, CT: Wadsworth Atheneum, 1985), cat. no. 262, n.p.

3 For more information on Phoebe, see Elizabeth Way's essay in this volume, "Fashion as History / History as Fashion: Phoebe and Pyer Moss."

4 Kevin Jones, email to author, February 18, 2022. Jones is curator at the Fashion Institute of Design and Merchandising Museum, Los Angeles, and has done extensive research on Madame Olympe.

5 George Augustus Sala, *America Revisited: From the Bay of New York to the Gulf of Mexico and From Lake Michigan to the Pacific*, 6th ed. (London: Vizetelly & Co, 1886), 300.

6 Marla R. Miller, "Mehitable Primus and Addie Brown: Women of Color and Hartford's Nineteenth-Century Dressmaking Trades," in *Dressing New England: Clothing, Fashion and Identity* (Deerfield, MA: Dublin Seminar for New England Folk Life, 2010), 65.

7 Miller, "Mehitable Primus," 75.

8 Barbara J. Beeching, "The Primus Papers: An Introduction to Hartford's Nineteenth Century Black Community" (master's thesis, Trinity College, 1995), *Hartford Studies Collection: Papers by Students and Faculty*, 119, https://digitalrepository.trincoll.edu/hartford_papers/8.

9 Beeching, "The Primus Papers," 163.

10 For further exploration of New's role in fashion history, see the essay by Amber-Dawn Bear Robe in this volume, "Indigenous Fashion: Every Garment Has a Story."

11 Doneeca Thurston, email to author, January 3, 2022. Thurston is Executive Director of the Lynn Museum in Lynn, Massachusetts.

12 Landmarks Preservation Commission, June 29, 1999; Designation List 308 LP-2033, I. Miller Building, 1552–1554 Broadway (aka 167 West 46th Street), Manhattan, http://s-media.nyc.gov/agencies/lpc/lp/2023.pdf.

13 Lucille Ball, *Love, Lucy* (New York: Berkeley, 1997), 54.

14 Dilys Blum, "Patrick Kelly and Paris Fashion," in Lauren Camerlengo, *Patrick Kelly: Runway of Love* (San Francisco: Fine Arts Museums of San Francisco; New Haven: Yale University Press, 2021), 16.

15 Madison Moore, "Patrick Kelly's Seat at the Table," in Camerlengo, *Patrick Kelly*, 45.

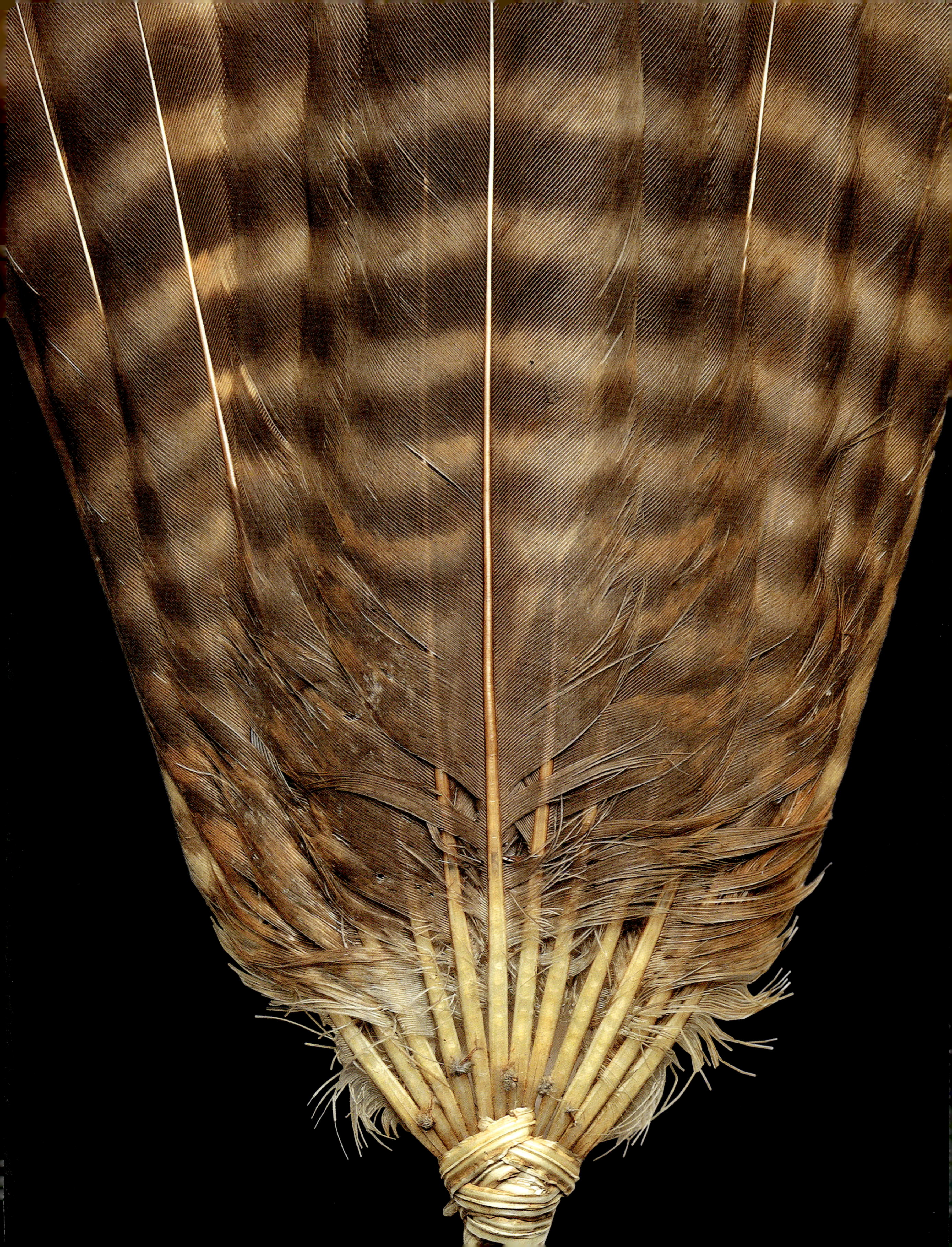

Woven into the American Fabric

BLACK CRAFTSPEOPLE AND THE CLOTHING TRADES IN PRE–CIVIL WAR CHARLESTON

Tiffany Momon and Torren Gatson

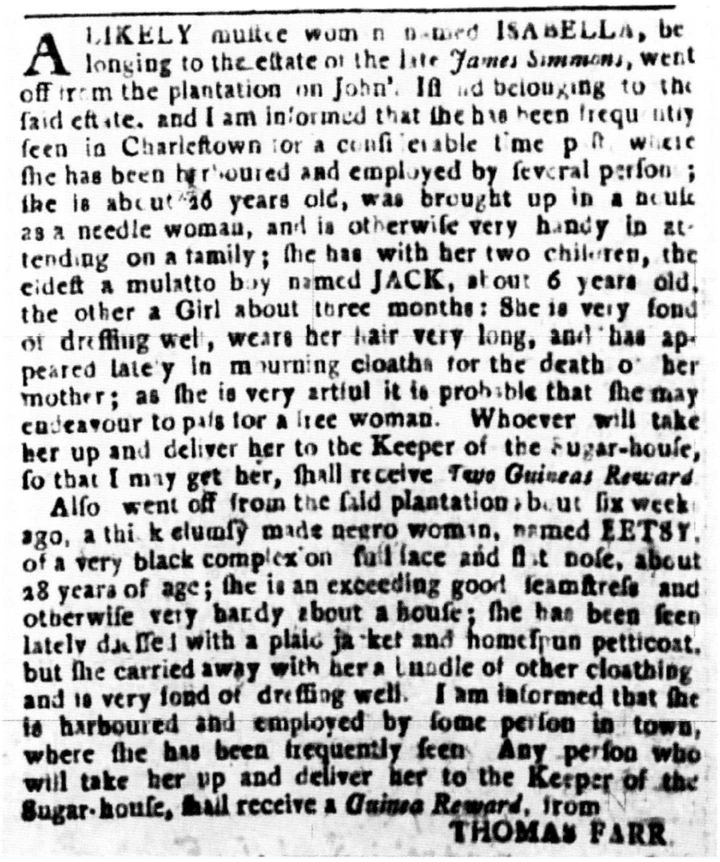

A LIKELY muſtee woman named ISABELLA, belonging to the eſtate of the late *James Simmons*, went off from the plantation on John's Iſland belonging to the ſaid eſtate, and I am informed that ſhe has been frequently ſeen in Charleſtown for a conſiderable time paſt, where ſhe has been harboured and employed by ſeveral perſons; ſhe is about 26 years old, was brought up in a houſe as a needle woman, and is otherwiſe very handy in attending on a family; ſhe has with her two children, the eldeſt a mulatto boy named JACK, about 6 years old, the other a Girl about three months: She is very fond of dreſſing well, wears her hair very long, and has appeared lately in mourning cloaths for the death of her mother; as ſhe is very artful it is probable that ſhe may endeavour to paſs for a free woman. Whoever will take her up and deliver her to the Keeper of the Sugar-houſe, ſo that I may get her, ſhall receive *Two Guineas Reward*.

Alſo went off from the ſaid plantation about ſix weeks ago, a thick clumſy made negro woman, named BETSY, of a very black complexion full face and flat noſe, about 28 years of age; ſhe is an exceeding good ſeamſtreſs and otherwiſe very handy about a houſe; ſhe has been ſeen lately dreſſed with a plaid jacket and homeſpun petticoat, but ſhe carried away with her a bundle of other cloathing and is very fond of dreſſing well. I am informed that ſhe is harboured and employed by ſome perſon in town, where ſhe has been frequently ſeen. Any perſon who will take her up and deliver her to the Keeper of the Sugar-houſe, ſhall receive a *Guinea Reward*, from

THOMAS FARR.

Advertisement placed by Thomas Farr in the *South Carolina Gazette* seeking the return of Isabella, an enslaved needleworker; her two children; and Betsy, an enslaved seamstress, November 4, 1780. Black Craftspeople Digital Archive.

While most popular histories of Charleston, South Carolina, are nostalgic reminiscences of the Old South, other stories remain dormant. Those stories illuminate the lives and experiences of African American craftspeople in Charleston, among them dressmakers, fan makers, seamstresses, glovemakers, shoemakers, and more. Despite the availability of sources, these histories are often missing from museum presentations of material culture due to a lack of available objects that can be directly connected to specific African American makers. In most museum collections, objects thought to be made by African Americans are considered anonymous. Nevertheless, the tales behind these objects deserve attention, and future institutional interpretations must include such accounts and recognize these makers even though many are unnamed. A lack of attributable objects does not absolve museum interpreters, curators, and others from telling these stories, which highlight the creativity and complexity of Black life prior to the end of the Civil War.

In the colonial period, Charleston-area enslavers not only depended on the labor of enslaved people to support their own enterprises; they also sold the labor of these individuals by hiring them out to work in various craft shops and industries. With this marketable commodity at hand, there was plenty of money to be made. As one visitor to Charleston noted in 1785, "Many idlers place their capital in negroes and, in the strict sense, are by them supported, living careless on the bitter sweat of the hired."[1] Historian Philip Morgan's research into the labor of enslaved artisans in Charleston revealed that at least one-third of enslaved women had a specialized skill.[2] Many of them practiced crafts thought to be appropriate for women, such as the clothing trades. In their research, historians James Newton and Ronald Lewis uncovered evidence of enslaved people working in more than two hundred fifty specific trades, including as bootmaker, cloak maker, clothmaker, clothes cleaner, clothier, dressmaker, embroiderer, fabric dyer, garment cutter, glovemaker, hatter, knitter, laundress, mantua maker, milliner, parasol maker, regalia maker, seamstress, shirtmaker, shoemaker, spinner, tailor, textile manufacturer, vest maker, and weaver.[3] The documentary evidence found by Lewis, Newton, and others provides an antidote to those who fail to acknowledge the presence and production of skilled Black craftspeople in preference of outdated scholarship that favors one-sided accounts that recognize only white craftspeople and exclude the Black women and men they often enslaved as part of their businesses.

One of the most useful ways to identify Black artisans in eighteenth-century Charleston is by examining advertisements seeking the return of self-emancipated individuals. Written to aid in their capture, these ads often list individuals' associated trades and skills as well as physical descriptions, previous enslavers, and potential destinations. One such notice appeared in the *South Carolina Gazette* on November 4, 1780. That year, a woman named Isabella self-emancipated along with her two children from the plantation of the late James Simmons on Johns Island, about ten miles southwest of Charleston. "Brought up as a needlewoman" and "fond of dressing well," she had frequently been seen in Charleston, and it came as no surprise to her enslaver that she had been "harboured and employed by several persons" in the city.[4] Isabella's skill as a needleworker undoubtedly contributed to her ability to support herself and her children. The same advertisement also sought the return of a woman named Betsy, who, like Isabella, was "very fond of dressing well."[5] Betsy was described as "an exceeding good seamstress," had also been spotted out and about in Charleston, and was believed to have been employed by someone there.[6] Further details of their existences are scant. But we can use what we do know to shape a story that brings these women to life while highlighting the harsh reality of their existence. Simmons's 1775 will documented the presence of a "Yellow Wench Called Isabel," but beyond that, both Isabella and Betsy disappear from the documentary record.[7] What remains to be discovered are details about garments they might have made, their lives after they self-emancipated, and whether or not they ever found themselves enslaved once again by the Simmons family.

Despite the availability of sources, these histories are often missing from museum presentations of material culture due to a lack of available objects that can be directly connected to specific African American makers.

Isabella's and Betsy's stories are not unique; most sources about enslaved craftspeople lack details of their everyday lives or the objects they created. What we can determine about their lives is worth recognizing, however. Between 1776 and 1781, four enslaved tailors self-emancipated from Charleston resident John Ward. At various times, Ward described himself as a tailor, habit maker, and merchant, making "all sorts of gentleman's cloaths and ladies riding habits in the newest and neatest fashions."[8] A few years later, Ward would advertise that he "also [made] parsons and lawyers gowns."[9] Ward's descriptions of his work provide insight into the labor of the men he enslaved. When Caesar, Fortune, and Dick, all tailors, self-emancipated from Ward in 1776, Ward placed an advertisement seeking their return:

> RUN away from the Subscriber the middle of December last, a Negro Man named Caesar, about 5 feet 10 inches high, well made, of a very black complexion, has a large nose. Also run-away this day, two Negro Men named Fortune and Dick; Fortune is about 5 feet 3 inches high, well made, very black complexion; has a high foretop head of hair, had on a nankeen coat, and a pair of black breeches, stammers a little in his speech. Dick, a tall slim fellow, about 5 feet 10 inches high, a Guinea negro, with his country marks on his face, had on a black coatter. These three negroes are taylors by trade, and well known in town, where they are supposed to be harboured.[10]

It is unclear whether Caesar, Fortune, and Dick were ever captured and returned to enslavement; Ward offered "a reward of Twenty Pounds . . . for taking up of Caesar, and Five Pounds each for Fortune and Dick, and delivering them." What the advertisement does make clear is that Ward knew that the three tailors would be able to find work in their trade in Charleston: "Their Master . . . hereby forbids all persons from harbouring or employing said negroes, as they will be prosecuted with the utmost severity of the law."[11] By writing this, he hoped to discourage white Charlestonians from hiring his enslaved men.

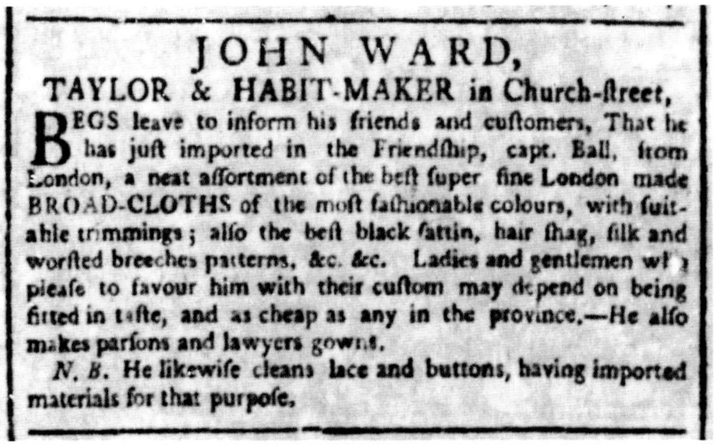
JOHN WARD,
TAYLOR & HABIT-MAKER in Church-ftreet,
BEGS leave to inform his friends and cuftomers, That he has juft imported in the Friendfhip, capt. Ball, from London, a neat affortment of the beft fuper fine London made BROAD-CLOTHS of the moft fafhionable colours, with fuitable trimmings; alfo the beft black fattin, hair fhag, filk and worfted breeches patterns, &c. &c. Ladies and gentlemen who pleafe to favour him with their cuftom may depend on being fitted in tafte, and as cheap as any in the province.—He alfo makes parfons and lawyers gowns.
N. B. He likewife cleans lace and buttons, having imported materials for that purpofe.

Advertisement placed by John Ward in the *South Carolina Gazette* describing his skills as a tailor and habit maker, January 16, 1762. Black Craftspeople Digital Archive.

In February 1781, about five years after Caesar, Fortune, and Dick freed themselves, a man named Waterford, an enslaved tailor, self-emancipated from the same John Ward. Ward placed an advertisement seeking his return:

> RUN away from the subscriber last Saturday night, a negro fellow named Waterford, a Taylor by trade, had on when he went away, a grey cloth surtout coat and a Bath coating waistcoat; he is a tall slim fellow, with a scar over his left eye, and has an iron on his leg. Whoever delivers him to me at No. 17 Broad street, shall have Two Dollars rewards; and whoever harbours or employs him will be prosecuted according to law.[12]

As in the cases of Caesar, Fortune, and Dick, Ward knew that Waterford would use his tailoring skills to find employment in Charleston because of the particular nature of enslavement there. Charlestonians were dependent on Black labor to support the clothing trades, and the threat of fines and potential prosecution for employing self-emancipated craftspeople was not enough to stop it from happening.

Examples abound of the self-emancipated finding work in the city outside the purview of their enslavers. When Frederick Grimke, brother to well-known Charleston jeweler John Paul Grimke, placed an advertisement in the August 7, 1777, edition of the *South Carolina and American General Gazette*, he wrote that not only had Jack, an enslaved tailor, self-emancipated, but also that he expected everyone who had employed Jack since he left Grimke's household to give Jack's earnings to him: "It is expected that those gentlemen he has been at work for, will call and settle with me; and I do hereby forbid all persons whatsoever from employing him hereafter, without a written order from me, and an arrangement on their part to pay his wages."[13] Grimke's demanding Jack's wages further evidences the role of hired-out enslaved persons in keeping the local economy running.

Like Jack, many self-emancipated individuals used their trades to support themselves as they attempted to live free lives. By taking ownership of his labor as a tailor, Jack could live independently. In her research, historian Amani T. Marshall found several instances of enslaved women involved in the clothing trades who used their skills after they freed themselves to live independent lives. Marshall uncovered the story of Celia, for example, a self-emancipated tailor and seamstress who used her skill in creating men's clothing to costume herself as a man and disguise her identity, creating an avenue for her to remain in Charleston and pass for free.[14] In the labor market of 1850s Charleston, she would compete with both enslaved and free Black women and white women. Marshall found that the most popular employment field for free working women were the clothing trades: "they found jobs as seamstresses, mantua makers, tailors, and milliners."[15] Additionally, of the "401 women working in the sewing trades in 1848, free women made up 50 percent, while white women were 44 percent and enslaved women, just 6 percent."[16] The data makes clear that Black women held a significant position in the clothing trades in Charleston. Furthermore, it presents the possibility that a great deal—the majority?—of the clothing attributed to unknown makers dating to this period in Charleston was made by Black women. The presence of this community and its members' way of life may have encouraged Celia and countless others in her position to claim their freedom and work for themselves.

No Charleston story captures better the connection between craftwork and liberation than the story of Black fan maker Tobias Scott. Born into slavery on James Island in 1827, Scott learned the fan-making trade as an enslaved child and used his skill to purchase his freedom. By the end of the Civil War, he, his wife Christiana, and their children relocated to Charleston, where the Scotts built a home at 17 Water Street.[17] For the next fifty years, Scott made fans of bird feathers, some with ivory handles and some with handles made of quills. An unsigned letter in the *Hartford Times* newspaper in faraway Hartford, Connecticut, provided insight into Scott's work. The writer of the letter described how, on a trip to Charleston, he visited Scott's shop on Water Street and "was awed when Scott opened boxes to reveal fan after gorgeous fan, fabricated from the feathers of peacocks, herons, spoonbills, owls and dozens of other birds, in colors 'one would hardly think a natural bird could produce.' "[18] The writer clearly admired Scott's handiwork: "Pink, blue, rosette, brown, gray, white and iridescent," he wrote, "the plumes were mounted on carved ivory handles, some of them in a zigzag style suited to the latest artistic caprice."[19] Scott's fans were well known throughout the Charleston area, and in 1902, while his work was on display at the South Carolina Inter-State and West Indian Exposition, the Charleston *News and Courier* newspaper reported that Scott sold a fan to President Theodore Roosevelt.[20] The fact that President Roosevelt purchased a fan from him would have made Scott and his work synonymous with high style.

opposite and overleaf Tobias Scott, fans, ca. 1875. Feathers, metal, and silk. The Collections of The Charleston Museum, from the Estate of Miss May I'on Simons, through Mrs. Arthur R. Young, 1953.

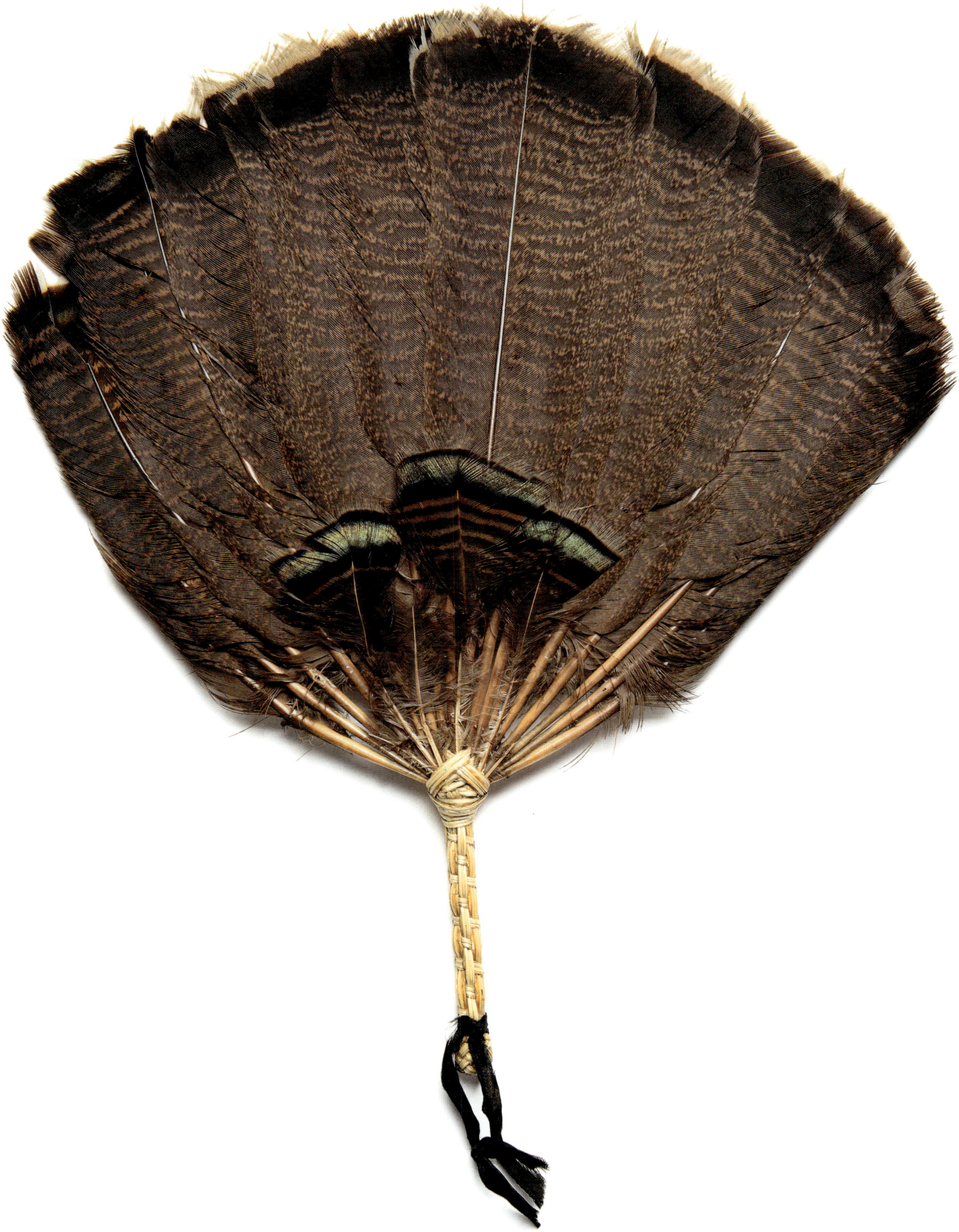

That association would have furthered Scott's success and provided his patrons with the opportunity to purchase a fan created by a Black man that was good enough for a United States president's wife.

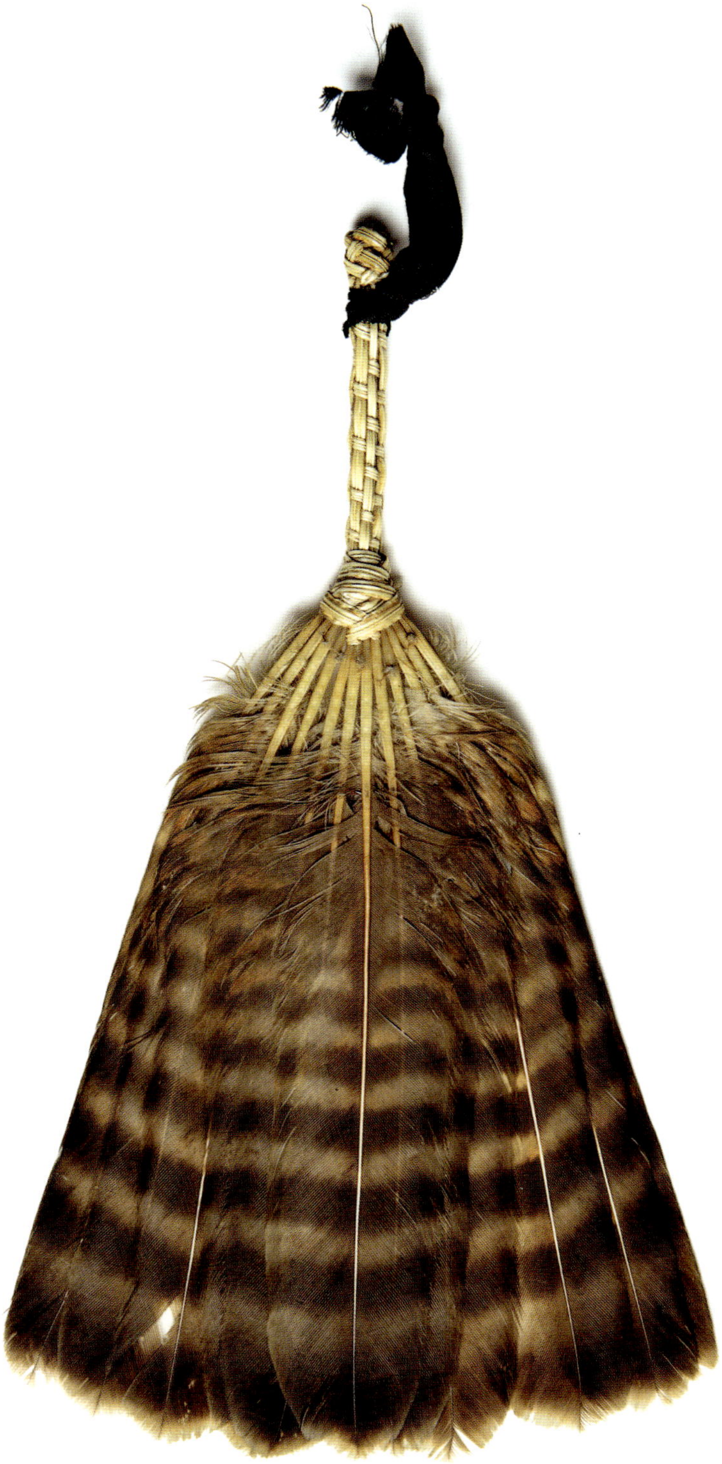

No Charleston story captures better the connection between craftwork and liberation than the story of Black fan maker Tobias Scott, who used the fan-making trade he learned as an enslaved child to purchase his freedom.

Tobias Scott's story is a perfect example of a Black craftsperson in the clothing trades securing both liberation and economic independence through their work. His story, like the others discussed, reveals that, despite the dehumanizing experience of slavery, Black people continuously demonstrated resilience and found autonomy through their execution of craftwork. Scott even achieved fame through his skill and exploitation of white adoration for his products. The Black craftspeople discussed in this essay represent merely a small fraction of those involved in the clothing trades at the time. Caesar, Fortune, and Dick, Betsy and Isabella, and Tobias Scott—all embody the spirit of those unknown artisans who used their abilities in fashioning apparel to craft avenues to freedom. The items they produced remain perhaps the best evidence of the true magnitude of their legacy on the southern cultural landscape. Their stories illuminate a world of high style and fashion trends both designed and materially created by Black craftspeople.

To understand the influence of Black craftspeople over the clothing trades and the steering of culture is also to understand the tremendously complex world of Charleston, from the colonial era through the end of the Civil War. Designed by Black minds and crafted by Black hands, the objects they made gave Black craftspeople an opportunity to gain economic independence amid the region's systemic racial oppression. The absence from museum collections of many objects created by Black craftspeople, often for white consumption, does not erase the sway that Black artisans had over the fashion world of the Lowcountry.

NOTES

1 Johann David Schöpf, *Travels in the Confederation (1783–1784)*, ed. Alfred J. Morrison (Baltimore: The Lord Baltimore Press, 1911), 201.

2 Mary Ferrari, " 'Obliged to Earn Subsistence for Themselves': Women Artisans in Charleston, South Carolina, 1763–1808," *South Carolina Historical Magazine* 106, no. 4 (October 2005): 240; Philip D. Morgan, *Slave Counterpoint: Black Culture in the Eighteenth-Century Chesapeake and Lowcountry* (Chapel Hill: University of North Carolina Press, 1998), 206.

3 James E. Newton and Ronald L. Lewis, "Appendix: Directory of Occupations Held by Black Artisans and Craftsmen Prior to 1865," in *The Other Slaves: Mechanics, Artisans, and Craftsmen*, ed. Newton and Lewis (Boston: G. K. Hall, 1978).

4 Thomas Farr, "Run Away," *South Carolina Gazette* (Charleston, SC), November 4, 1780.

5 Farr, "Run Away."

6 Farr, "Run Away."

7 James Simmons, "South Carolina, U.S., Wills and Probate Records, 1670–1980, Digital Image s.v. Will of James Simmons," Ancestry .com, March 9, 1775, https://www.ancestry .com/discoveryui-content/view/73001:9080?.

8 John Ward, "John Ward, Taylor from London," *South Carolina Gazette* (Charleston, SC), May 6, 1756.

9 John Ward, "John Ward, Taylor and Habit-Maker," *South Carolina Gazette* (Charleston, SC), January 16, 1762.

10 John Ward, "Run Away," *South Carolina and American General Gazette* (Charleston, SC), November 7, 1776.

11 Farr, "Run Away," 1776.

12 John Ward, "Run Away," *South Carolina and American General Gazette*, February 7, 1781.

13 Frederick Grimke, "Run Away," *South Carolina and American General Gazette*, August 7, 1777.

14 Amani T. Marshall, " 'They Are Supposed to Be Lurking about the City': Enslaved Women Runaways in Antebellum Charleston," *South Carolina Historical Magazine* 115, no. 3 (July 2014): 188.

15 Marshall, " 'They Are Supposed to Be Lurking about the City,' " 193.

16 Marshall, " 'They Are Supposed to Be Lurking about the City,' " 193.

17 Jennifer McCormick, "Tobias and Christiana Scott: The Road to Freedom," *Charleston Museum News and Events* (blog), accessed November 7, 2021, https://www.charlestonmuseum.org /news-events/tobias-and-christiana-scott-the -road-to-freedom/.

18 Susan Millar Williams, "The Fan Master," *Charleston Style and Design Magazine*, July 9, 2018, https://charlestonstyleanddesign.com /the-fan-master/.

19 Williams, "The Fan Master."

20 McCormick, "Tobias and Christiana Scott."

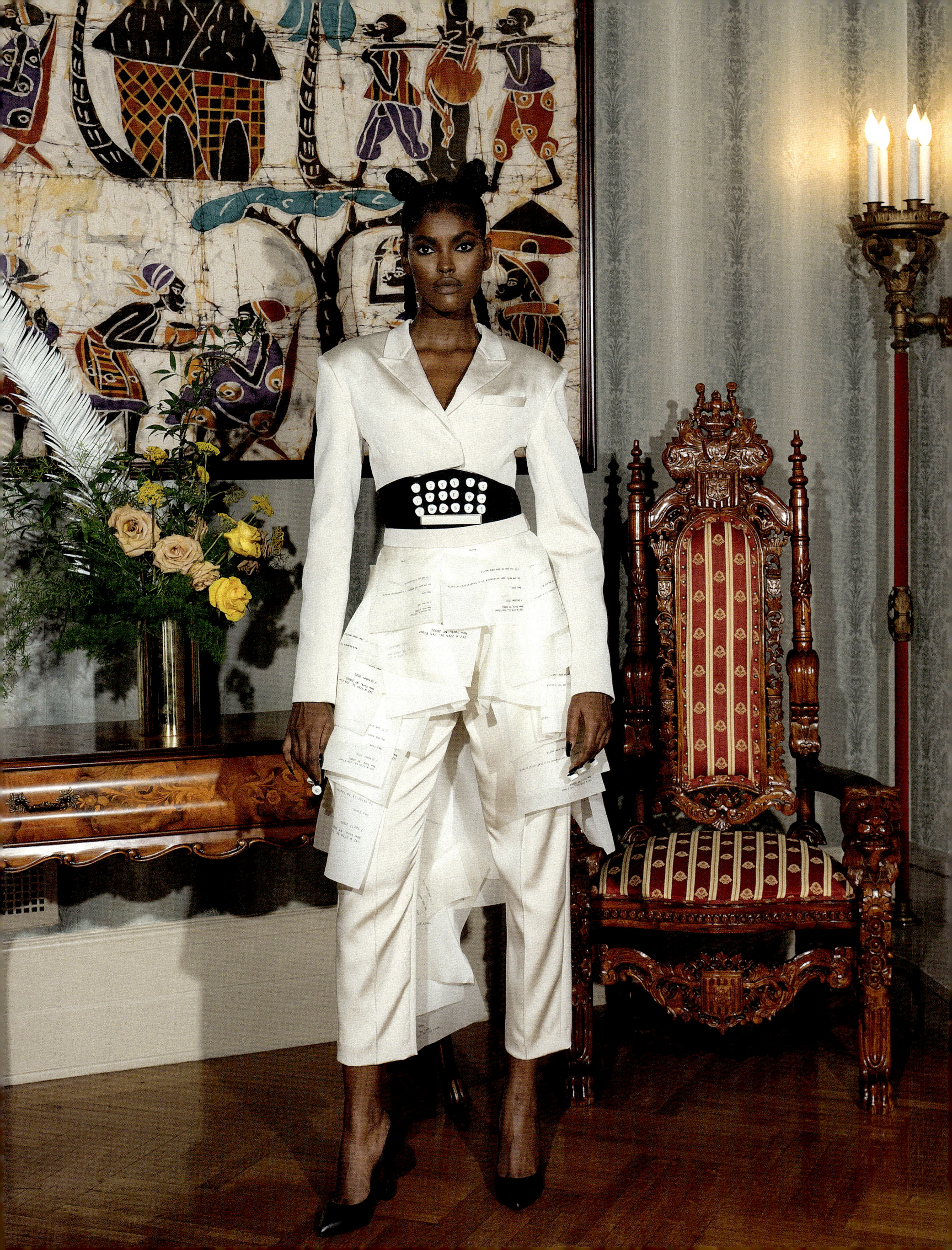

Fashion as History/ History as Fashion

PHOEBE AND PYER MOSS

Elizabeth Way

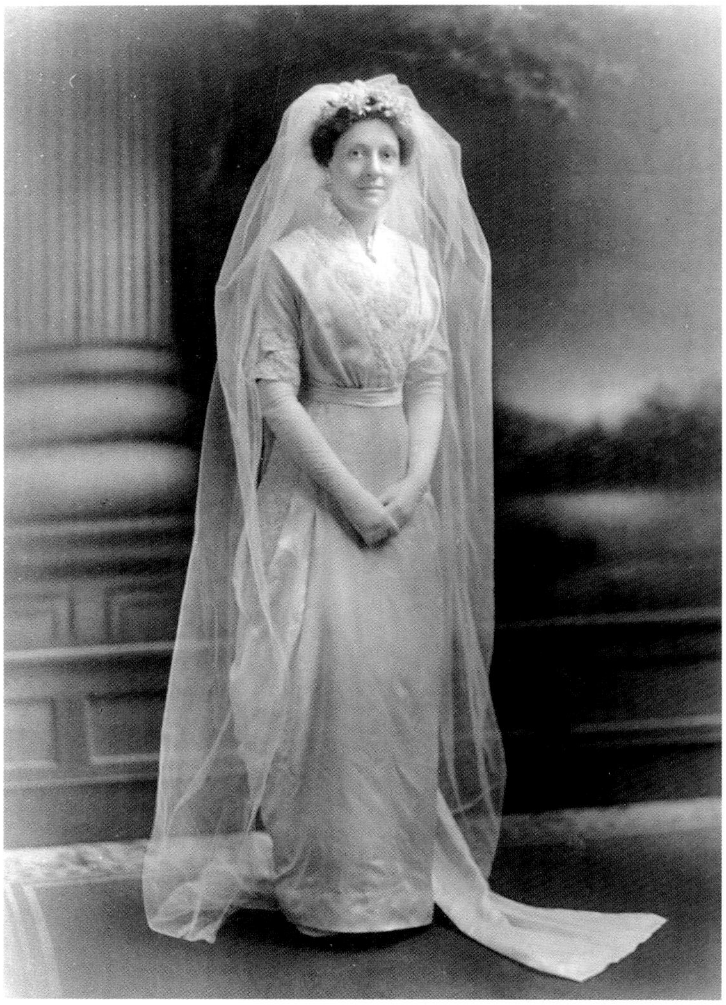

Wilhelmine Dorothea Meyer in her Phoebe wedding dress, January 7, 1914. Courtesy of The Charleston Museum, Charleston, South Carolina.

That fashion can reveal American history, from the biographies and aesthetics of the elite to the subcultures and innovations of the oppressed, should be no surprise. Garments survive with their stories, but these narratives differ wildly in what and how much they reveal. For Black Americans, both their history and their fashion can be fraught subjects—obscured, misunderstood, and dismissed while simultaneously appropriated and rebranded. With rare exceptions, the further back in time, the more elusive the evidence becomes. As Saidiya Hartman writes, "Every historian of the multitude, the dispossessed, the subaltern, and the enslaved is forced to grapple with the power and authority of the archive and the limits it sets on what can be known, whose perspective matters, and who is endowed with the gravity and authority of historical actor."[1]

Two makers presented in *Fashioning America* illuminate the ways in which Black history and fashion are intimate companions. Phoebe, a Black dressmaker working in the South during the early twentieth century, reaches across time and space to form a connection with Kerby Jean-Raymond, a contemporary New York-based Haitian American designer. Their relationship is inverse: what can be known of Phoebe's history begins with a fashion object, while Jean-Raymond starts with Black history and spins it into fashion. The wedding dress Phoebe left behind can only provide tantalizing speculations, leaving us to consider the lives and practices of the Black dressmakers who created American fashion over a century ago. But where she leaves off, Jean-Raymond picks up. Through his collections and presentations, he rescues the narratives of Black people and reinserts them into the evolving popular culture of American history.

PHOEBE, LAST NAME UNKNOWN

On January 7, 1914, Wilhelmine Dorothea Meyer married Adolf Hollings in Charleston, South Carolina. She was the well-educated, twenty-five-year-old daughter of a retired merchant and a first-generation German American on her father's side, second-generation on her mother's. Her wedding portrait shows her standing serenely against a painted backdrop wearing a white, silk satin gown with a full-length veil. At the time this gown was acquired by The Charleston Museum in 1986, four years after Wilhelmine's death, family lore preserved only the first name of the dressmaker, Phoebe, and that she was a Black "seamstress" working in Charleston. With this scant description, more questions about Phoebe, her life and business, her design aesthetic, and her relationship to Wilhelmine are raised than can be answered. Her gown, however, exists as an important piece of material culture representing a Black fashion maker who contributed it, among other works known and unknown, to a larger history of American fashion.[2]

The wedding dress Phoebe designed was very much in fashion in 1914, with its elongated silhouette and slim skirt, surplice bodice and V neckline, elbow-length sleeves worn with long gloves, and squared-off train. She embellished the gown opulently, using Brussels lace, faux pearls, net trim, glass beads, and brilliants. Her design stands in dialogue with fashions created across the Eurocentric world: illustrations of fashionable bridal wear from the early 1910s show similar features and details.[3]

opposite Phoebe, wedding dress, 1914. Silk, cotton, glass, metal, and sand. The Collections of The Charleston Museum, Gift of Wilhelmine Dorothea Meyer Hollings, 1986.

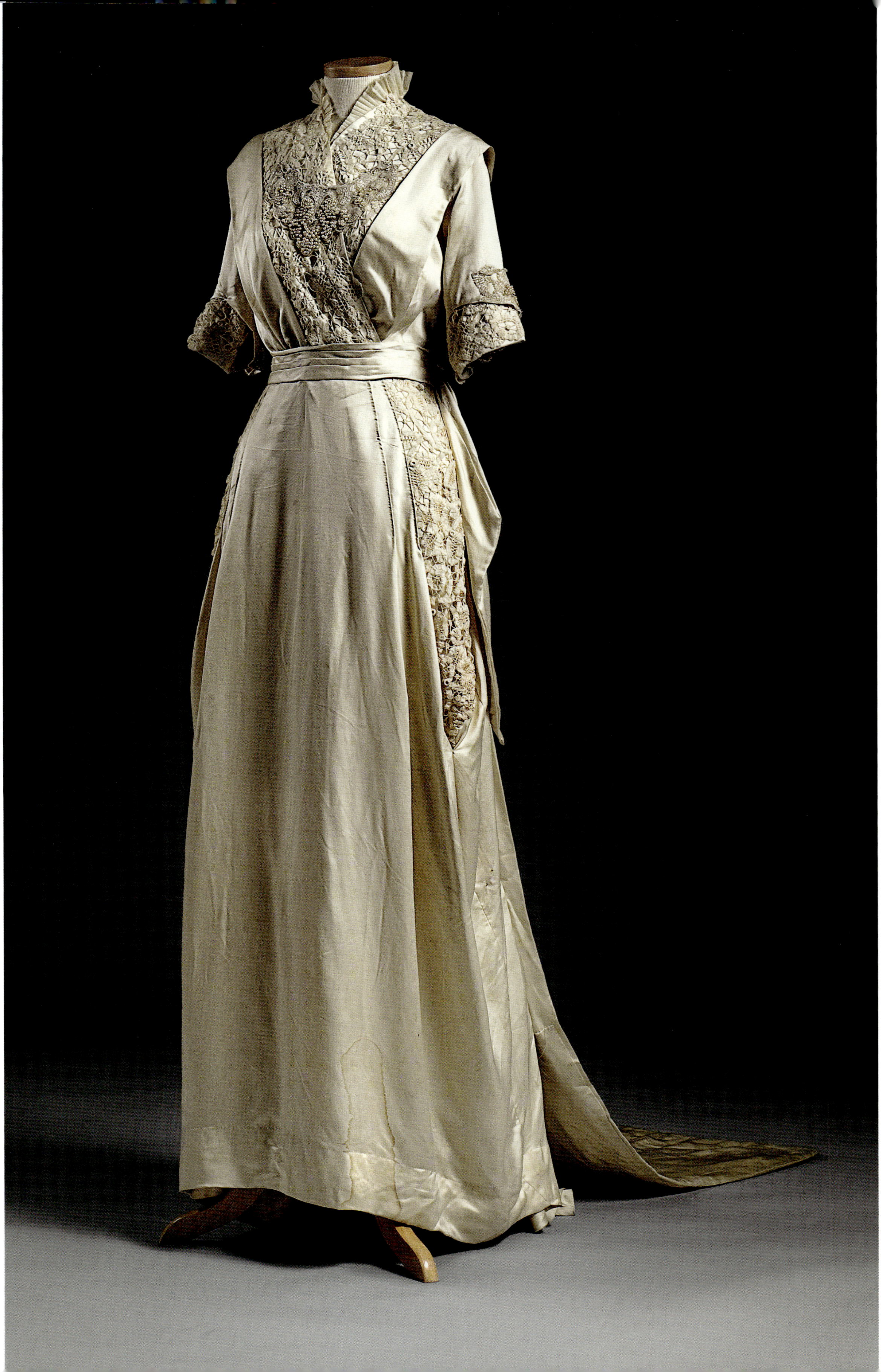

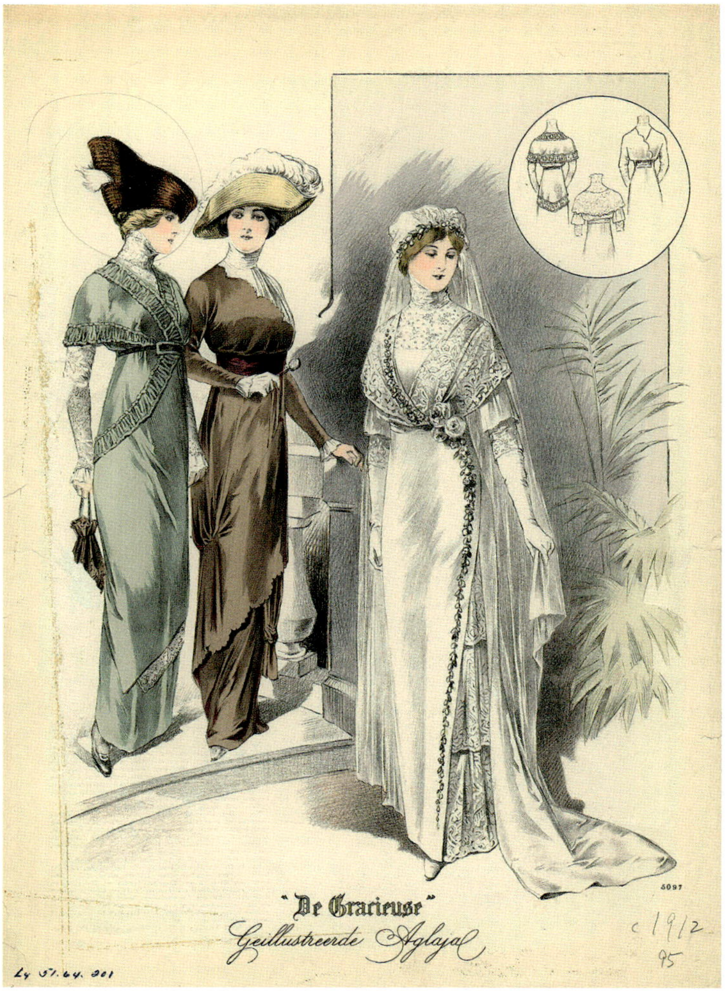

Wedding dress illustrated in *De Gracieuse* magazine (The Memory), 1912. Costume Institute Fashion Plates, Weddings 1860–1915, Plate 065. Metropolitan Museum of Art, Gift of Woodman Thompson.

The dress was modern in its shape—portending the straightening silhouette of the 1920s—though traditional in its materials, as befits a wedding gown. It shows that as a dressmaker (not simply a seamstress), Phoebe was aware of fashion trends emanating from Europe, perhaps through fashion periodicals, her clients' knowledge, and the work of fellow dressmakers in Charleston. The construction shows technical expertise and a sophisticated design sensibility that favored elegance over the more exoticized and eccentric design elements also popular at the time, best illustrated by the Orientalist fantasies of lampshade tunics and "harem" pantaloons created by Parisian couturier Paul Poiret.[4]

Phoebe was a part of Charleston's long history of Black craftspeople. Before the Civil War, the urban environment fostered a large population of both free Black and enslaved skilled artisans who catered mostly to white clients. Historian Amrita Chakrabarti Myers notes that low wages and occupational restrictions faced by free Black men and women meant that more Black women needed to work to support their households compared to white women. Women were even more limited in professional choices than men, but dressmaking and sewing offered flexibility and relatively high pay and attracted Black women in large numbers. For example, in 1860 and 1861 nearly 60 percent of employed Black women in Charleston worked as seamstresses, mantua makers, or dressmakers.[5] There is a well-established history of Black women from all over the United States empowering their daughters and granddaughters with professional-level sewing and dressmaking skills, an inheritance that gave them a means of supporting them and their families. Both Elizabeth Keckley, a mid-nineteenth-century dressmaker to Washington, DC's political elite, and Ann Lowe, who designed evening gowns for wealthy white women in Alabama, Florida, and New York from the 1910s through the 1960s, learned their skills from their mothers and transformed their families' enslaved labor into thriving businesses.[6] It is possible that Phoebe did the same and that her mother was among antebellum Charleston's free Black dressmakers, or that she descended from a line of enslaved and highly skilled fashion makers.

There were various other ways women learned dressmaking during the early twentieth century. Phoebe could have been apprenticed to a dressmaker as a young woman or might have learned through a college course, such as the sewing class offered at Howard University. Phoebe also could have taught herself dressmaking through the increasing number of how-to manuals and drafting systems being sold at the turn of the twentieth century. The historian Wendy Gamber notes that *Dressmaking Self Taught in Twenty Complete Lessons*, published in 1911 by Madam Edith Marie Carens, was one such book among others that "presented themselves as effective substitutes for apprenticeship."[7] Phoebe's dress for Wilhelmine exhibits a high level of professionalism for a self-taught dressmaker, but no possibility can be ruled out.

With nothing more than a first name and city of residence, it is difficult to know the details of Phoebe's professional and personal life. Carole Bennett, a researcher with The Charleston Museum, and Virginia Theerman, the museum's curator of historic textiles, suspect Phoebe might be Phoebe Lawrence, a seamstress and dressmaker listed in the Charleston City Directory from 1905 to 1930.[8] Lawrence also worked as a laundress, music teacher, and domestic during this period. Or, Phoebe may have been Phoebe White, a thirty-nine-year-old mulatto dressmaker living in Charleston's Sixth Ward in 1910, close to Wilhelmine's home in the Fifth Ward. White ran her dressmaking business from her home, which she shared with her cousin Georgie, also a dressmaker; her mother Martha, the homeowner; her brother John, a carpenter; and her cousins Minnie and Virginia, a bookkeeper and teacher, respectively.[9] Or perhaps she was Phoebe A. Owens, a Black dressmaker who lived farther north and west in Ward Twelve in 1910. At that time, Owens was forty-five and had been married to William A. Owens for twenty years. William worked in a cotton mill, and they rented the home that they shared with their three children. Their twenty-year-old daughter Margaret was also a dressmaker—likely taught by her mother and working as her assistant. Phoebe's other two children, fifteen-year-old Ester and eighteen-year-old William, were recorded as having attended school.[10]

So much cannot be known about Phoebe, but it is probable that, as a Black woman, she felt the social environment becoming increasingly hostile in Jim Crow–era Charleston. In 1913, perhaps while Phoebe began work on Wilhelmine's dress, the Woodrow Wilson administration enacted federal segregation in workplaces, restrooms, and lunchrooms. This step further codified the state and local laws and unspoken rules that restricted Black life in Charleston. Fifty-one Black Americans were lynched both that year and the next, and though the Great Migration was not yet in full motion, South Carolina's Black population was decreasing. Black people made up 55 percent of South Carolinians in 1910, down from 58.4 percent in 1900 and 59.8 percent in 1890.[11]

Increasing racial tensions could be why Phoebe A. Owens left Charleston with her husband and two of her children. The 1920 census finds them in New York City and Owens continuing her work as a dressmaker.[12]

There is a well-established history of Black women from all over the United States empowering their daughters and granddaughters with professional-level sewing and dressmaking skills, an inheritance that gave them a means of supporting them and their families.

Much more can be determined about Wilhelmine's personal history than Phoebe's. For instance, her father John Meyer immigrated to the United States in 1870 and by 1910 owned his home on Hasell Street, supporting his wife and daughter.[13] Their neighbors included Abram Morgan, identified as a mulatto coachman, his wife Elizabeth, a servant, and their four children; Frederick Stender, another first-generation German American who was a retired merchant living with his six children; and Flora Hamilton, a single Black laundress. Wilhelmine attended both Mrs. Smith's School and Memminger Normal School and, remarkable for her times, went on to work as a legal secretary.[14] But what about Phoebe can be gleaned from Wilhelmine's story? Unfortunately, only generalities. Historian Jeffrey Strickland notes that German immigrants and Black Charlestonians maintained a somewhat amicable relationship before and after the Civil War. German newcomers to the southern city filled a middle-class merchant sector left open by the intense social

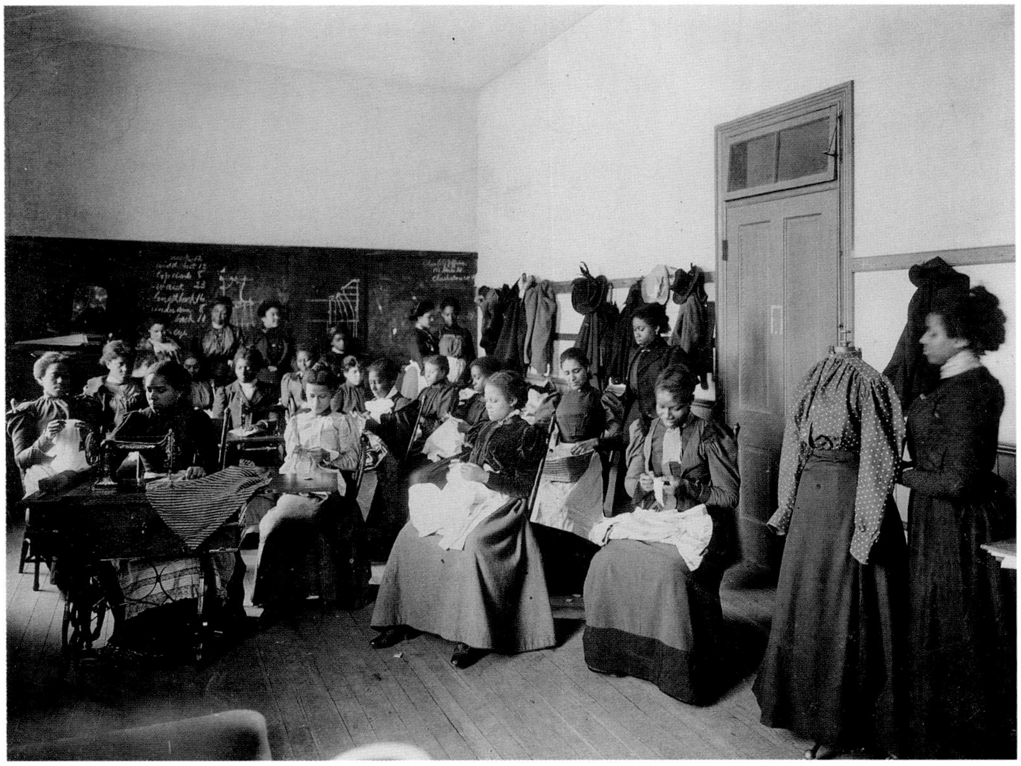

W. E. B. Du Bois, Sewing class, Howard University, Washington, DC, ca. 1900. Library of Congress, Washington, DC.

disparities driven by racism and enslavement in Charleston. German merchants sold goods to Black customers, both enslaved and free, though increasing opposition to this practice by white Charlestonians led to a restriction on credit offered to Black customers and a subsequent protest by Black Charlestonians against German merchants in 1871.[15] Black-German relations in Charleston were at a peak in 1870 when Wilhelmine's father first came to the city and declined afterwards: "The second-generation German Americans would identify with white Southern ethnics and demonstrate a greater commitment to Jim Crow policies."[16] Yet in 1910, Wilhelmine's street looked more like what Strickland described as Charleston in 1870: "The economic ties between blacks and Germans were reflected in Charleston's social geography, as employers and employees, buyers and sellers, resided in the same households, streets, and neighborhoods."[17]

Considering Wilhelmine's proximity to and possible familiarity with Black neighbors, it is not surprising that she might choose a Black dressmaker for her wedding gown. It is also possible that Jim Crow discrimination forced Black dressmakers like Phoebe to charge lower prices to attract customers. In line with the increasing segregation in the city, by 1920 Wilhelmine and her husband Adolf, a paper dealer, lived on a street populated by white families, and their neighbors included upper-middle-class professionals: a dentist, an engineer, a stenographer, and a dressmaker.[18] While we have not uncovered the course of Phoebe's life, the Hollings were increasingly upwardly mobile—Wilhelmine's son went on to serve as South Carolina's governor and a United States senator. His prominence is a likely reason that Wilhelmine's dress resides in The Charleston Museum.

PYER MOSS

Phoebe was one of multiple generations of Black Americans who, despite their vital roles in creating and maintaining American culture, were shut out of mainstream society. A century later, Kerby Jean-Raymond articulated the continuation of this experience. He pinpointed the impetus behind his "American, Also." fashion collections (2018–20) to an incident in which he and some friends, all Brooklyn-born Black Americans, felt a sense of threat emanating from a white body in an American flag: "We crossed the street when we saw this old dude had on an American flag tracksuit and all of us felt threatened and we crossed the street. We didn't even talk about it, it was just reflex." On later reflecting, his friend expressed, "I don't know; I just never really felt American like that."[19]

The creative result of this encounter was three collections for Jean-Raymond's brand Pyer Moss dedicated to accepting "the outsider" in American culture, namely, Black people. "My purpose of doing this specific thesis, 'American, Also.' Jean-Raymond noted, "was to take elements of popular American society and show how black people have a hand in it, like rock 'n' roll, the standard family values, the American cowboy, things that are so stereotypical White American and show, hey, this is actually black."[20] That Jean-Raymond uses fashion to create a more accurate and inclusive historical narrative subtly illuminates figures like Phoebe; he extends her legacy as a Black fashion maker while reasserting Black Americans' significance as a whole in the nation's history.

> "My purpose of doing this specific thesis, 'American, Also.' was to take elements of popular American society and show how black people have a hand in it, like rock 'n' roll . . . the American cowboy, things that are so stereotypical White American and show, hey, this is actually black."—*Kerby Jean-Raymond*

The second collection of the "American, Also." series, called "American, Also. Lesson 2," was inspired by "the common black family experience" and shown at the Weeksville Heritage Center in Crown Heights, Brooklyn, in 2018.[21] Jean-Raymond drew the fashion community away from Manhattan and to the site of one of the largest antebellum free Black communities: the town of Weeksville was established after New York state abolished slavery in 1827, becoming a thriving Black community of seven hundred families where Black people could establish lives away from violence and discrimination. The town took in refugees of the 1863 Draft Riots in Manhattan and maintained a school, church, and newspaper.[22] Weeksville's significance to Jean-Raymond was based both on its nineteenth-century past and its present. "I grew up five minutes away from here," he told a fashion journalist in 2018. "It's a really meaningful spot." His implication was not only historical but related to the way it might affect those living nearby today: by having the

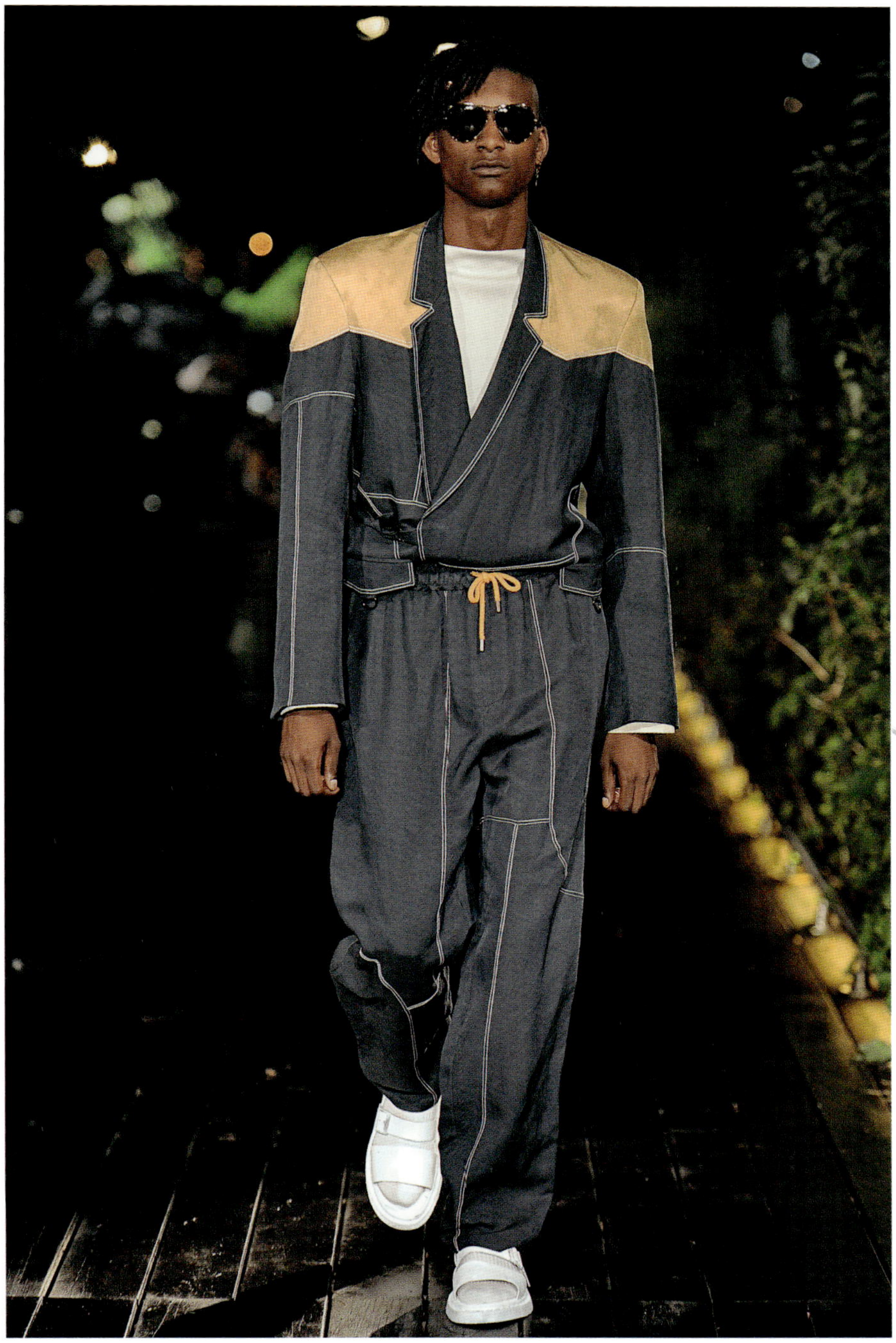

show at a location in the middle of public housing projects, he said, "It lets people know what they can do on their own."[23]

The garments in the Weeksville collection celebrated the normality of Black life: "I want to show that black can be beautiful and not just sensationalized," Jean-Raymond explained at the time. "Not always tragic, not always 'for your entertainment.' It can exist on the sole purpose of us being us."[24] The designs showed the more consistent aesthetic that he began to develop around 2018, a style he dubbed "spiritual sportswear."[25] The collection remixed elements of American sportwear into fashion that spoke in a twenty-first century vernacular. For example, a man's suit is rendered in pliable denim with a leather yoke and a drawstring waistband. Worn with a collarless shirt, socks, and athletic slides, the piece merges streetwear and westernwear influences into a sense of luxury that speaks to modern leisure. Jean-Raymond enlisted artist Derrick Adams to create intimate portraits of Black people that were printed and beaded on the clothing. The presentation, titled "Normal," also included a capsule collection with the brand

above Kerby Jean-Raymond for Pyer Moss, man's suit, "American, Also. Lesson 2—Normal" collection, 2018. Denim and leather. Courtesy of the Hinton Group.

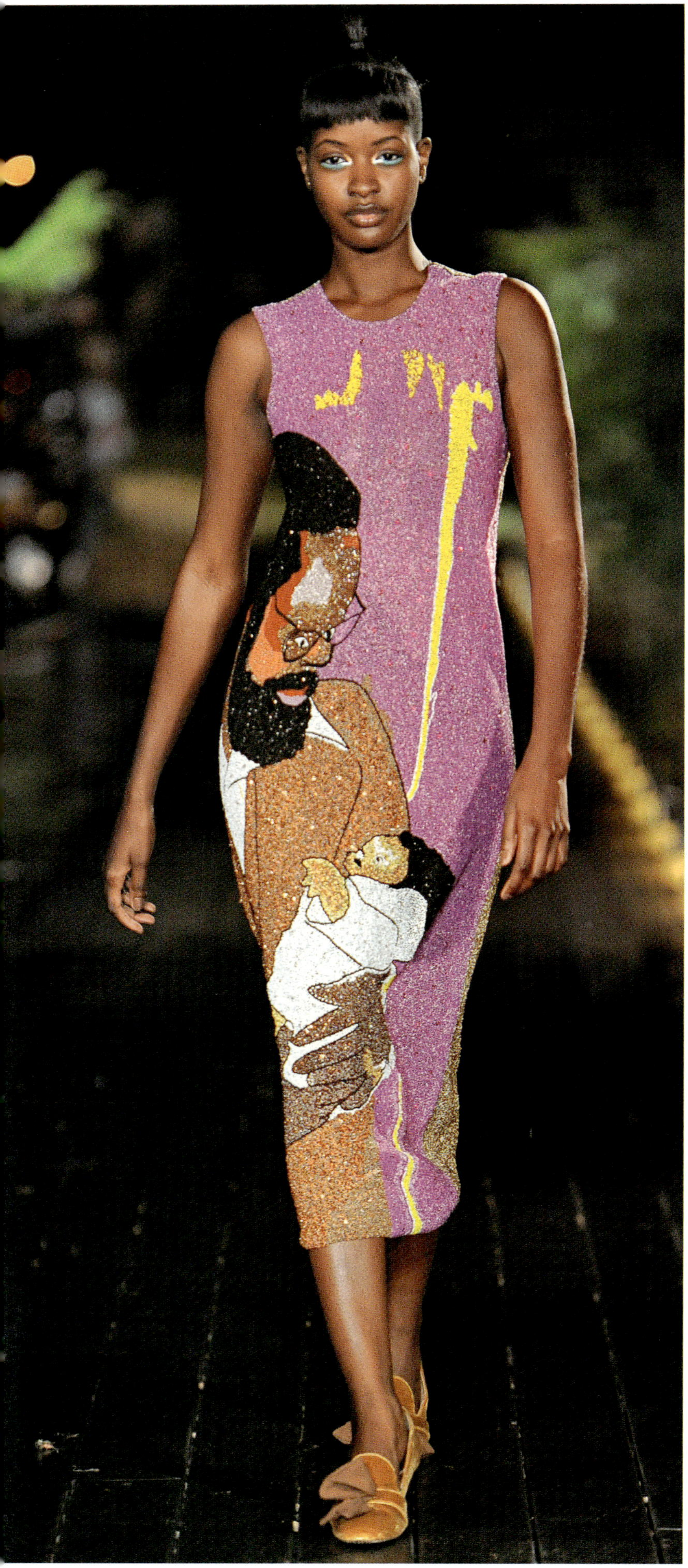

FUBU, a hip-hop apparel company founded in 1992 whose name stands for "For Us By Us." The previous season, Pyer Moss had collaborated with Cross Colours, another streetwear brand that creates, per their slogan, "clothing without prejudice." Both were successful, influential Black-owned brands during the 1990s, yet as Jean-Raymond has pointed out, they were "never considered in that same realm as [other] American designers because they were considered 'urban.' "[26] The presentation at Weeksville, with its collaborations with other Black creators, encompassed Jean-Raymond's philosophy that, more so even than the clothing, genuine experiences are what drive and will continue to drive fashion: "The experience has to be authentic to the designer because at the end of the day people want to align to you. They want to know who you are as a person."[27]

Jean-Raymond has been able to take control of his business in ways that dressmakers like Phoebe could have never imagined, using his design practice to redress Black erasure.

Kerby Jean-Raymond may be the most influential and significant fashion designer working in America. This is a bold statement, but he stands at the forefront of the changing American fashion industry. Pyer Moss has evolved significantly since its founding in 2013. Jean-Raymond's first collections lacked focus and a design identity until he began infusing his own experiences into the clothing. Elements of his collections—like the 2014 They Have Names T-shirt that listed thirteen unarmed Black men killed by police and the film on police brutality accompanying his spring 2016 show—made unapologetic commentary on Black life in America, recording history as it occurred. They led retailers to drop his line and fashion editors to rebuke him for his "negativity."[28] Yet his radical design statements, experiential shows, and soon-to-be-revised business model would prove prescient. Jean-Raymond began by following

Kerby Jean-Raymond for Pyer Moss, dress, "American, Also. Lesson 2—Normal" collection, 2018. Silk and sequins. Courtesy of the Hinton Group.

a traditional wholesale model for Pyer Moss, and he sold a majority stake in his company in 2014, only to find himself underfunded and unprofitable. With the brand on the verge of collapse, his audacity and innovative design attracted Reebok in 2017, and their partnership allowed him to buy Pyer Moss back, reestablishing it as one of the few Black-owned luxury companies.[29] Jean-Raymond reconfigured his business, cutting down on fashion shows and focusing on direct-to-consumer sales and retailers willing to market the Pyer Moss brand in full.[30]

Nineteenth- and early twentieth-century Black dressmakers such as Phoebe, Elizabeth Keckley, and Ann Lowe used fashion to take control of their lives; they used their skills and creativity to support themselves and others, and their surviving material culture reveals not only the history of American fashion but also the contributions of Black designers to American history. Jean-Raymond builds on their work and has been able to take control of his business in ways that dressmakers like Phoebe could have never imagined, using his design practice to redress Black erasure. When he won the prestigious Council of Fashion Designers of America / Vogue Fashion Fund Award in 2018, *Washington Post* writer Robin Givhan noted, "His victory . . . speaks not only to his success as a designer but also to his ability to nudge fashion toward a place of great social engagement and responsibility."[31] In the wake of the resurgence of Black Lives Matter in 2020—a very different moment from 2016 when he lost retailers over his support of the movement—he asked fellow Black designers:

> Do we want to continue to buy into and ask for help from a system that doesn't represent us? . . . We have a lot of creative resources, and they take those resources and sell them abroad. . . . So we've run into this weird conundrum. Do we play in, or do we play out? The obvious answer is we play out, but we don't have the resources to start businesses.[32]

In response, he extended his activist design practice and created opportunities for other unrepresented creatives within Pyer Moss, as well as with Reebok—he serves as vice president of creative direction and artistic director of Reebok Studios, a division that supports emerging designers—and through Your Friends in New York, his partnership with the French luxury corporation Kering. The project serves as an incubation space for designers, artists, and philanthropists. Jean-Raymond is committed to supporting designers like himself: those with talent, innovative ideas, and fresh perspectives to add to American fashion, but who are also unlikely to attract investment and mentorship as a result of institutional biases.[33] In doing so, he is helping to shape the future of American fashion.

In 2021, Jean-Raymond became the first Black designer invited to show on the Chambre Syndicale de la Haute Couture's official schedule. Instead of staging a couture show in Paris, Jean-Raymond chose Villa Lewaro, the Hudson Valley estate of Madam C. J. Walker, a prominent and wealthy Black American hair-care entrepreneur, as the venue for a collection dedicated to Black inventors. Black Panther leader Elaine Brown spoke on the history of the party, and the larger-than-life looks included a hooded cape of hot rollers in tribute to Solomon Harper, the inventor of electrically heated hair rollers, and "a gold T-shirt minidress pieced together from hundreds of metallic discs beneath a lock headpiece" in a reference to Black inventor W. A. Martin, who patented the precursor of the modern door lock.[34] *New York Times* fashion writer Vanessa Friedman wrote of the occasion, "Mr. Jean-Raymond is part of a new generation of designers that plays by the rules of the most traditional, elitist form of fashion while at the same time reinventing them in their own image."[35] That image is not only one of Black pride but also historical discovery. As much as Phoebe's wedding gown, and on a much larger platform, Pyer Moss's collections harness fashion to create a bridge to a Black past.

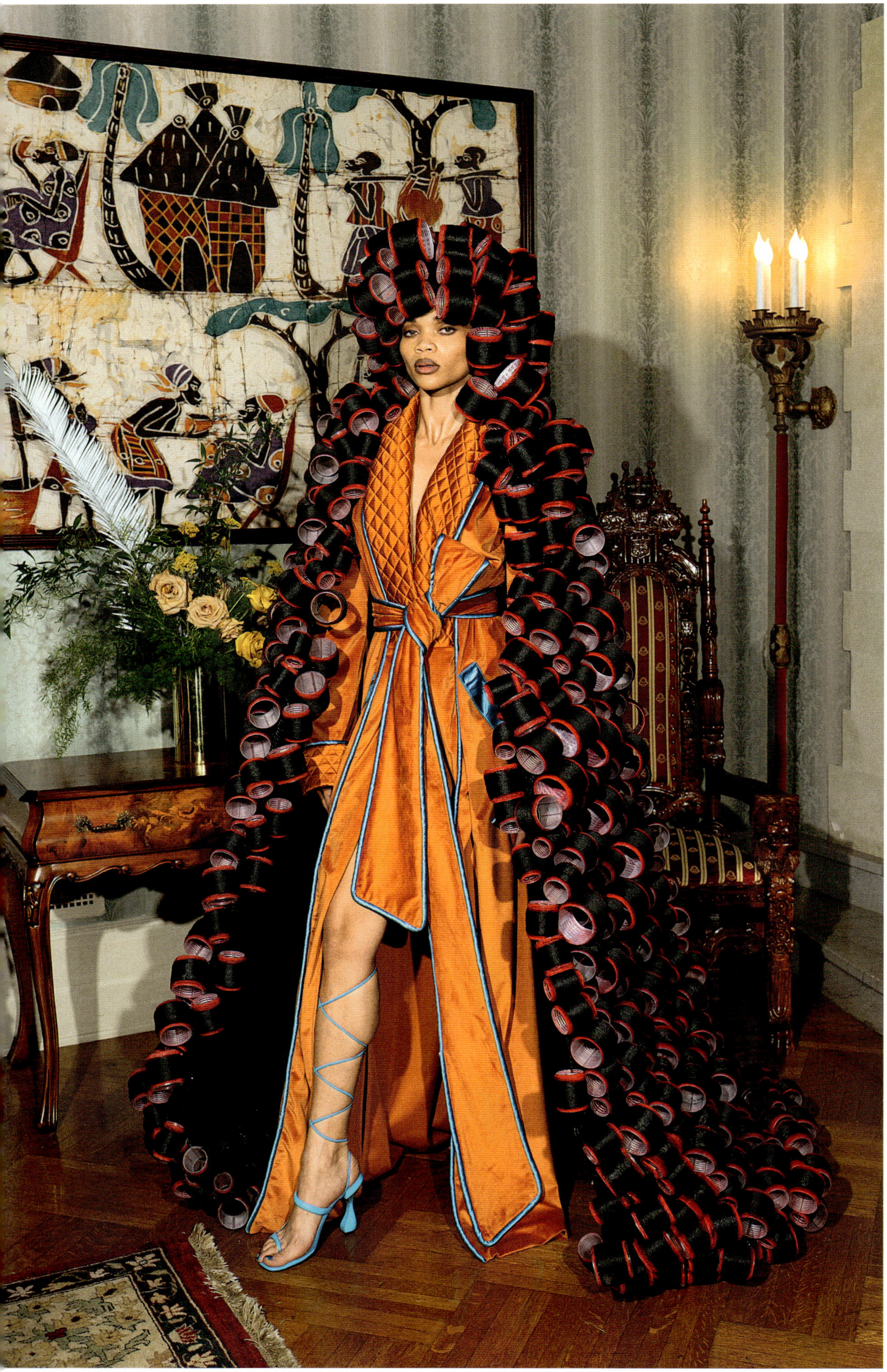

Kerby Jean-Raymond for Pyer Moss, dress and hair curler headdress, "Couture 1—Wat U Iz" collection, 2021. Velvet, satin, and hair curlers. Courtesy of the Hinton Group.

NOTES

1 Saidiya Hartman, *Wayward Lives, Beautiful Experiments: The Intimate Lives of Riotous Black Girls, Troublesome Women, and Queer Radicals* (New York: W. W. Norton, 2019), xiii.

2 The Charleston Museum also holds a grey wool coat that Phoebe made for Wilhelmine Meyer Hollings's trousseau, 1914, accession number 2010.019.

3 John Peacock, *20th-Century Fashion: The Complete Sourcebook* (London: Thames & Hudson, 1993), 39, 47.

4 Harold Koda and Andrew Bolton, "Paul Poiret (1879–1944)," in Heilbrunn Timeline of Art History, Metropolitan Museum of Art, New York, September 2008, http://www.metmuseum.org/toah/hd/poir/hd_poir.htm.

5 Amrita Chakrabarti Myers, *Forging Freedom: Black Women and the Pursuit of Liberty in Antebellum Charleston* (Chapel Hill: University of North Carolina Press, 2011), 31, 48, 83, 92.

6 Jonathan Michael Square, "Slavery's Warp, Liberty's Weft: A Look at the Work of Eighteenth- and Nineteenth-Century Enslaved Fashion Makers and Their Legacies," in *Black Designers in American Fashion*, ed. Elizabeth Way (London: Bloomsbury, 2021), 29–46.

7 Wendy Gamber, " 'Reduced to Science': Gender, Technology, and Power in the American Dressmaking Trade, 1860–1910," *Technology and Culture* 36, no. 3 (July 1995): 465–66.

8 Carole Bennett and Virginia Theerman, internal document, undated, the Charleston Museum.

9 United States Census Bureau, "1910 United States Census for Phoebe White, South Carolina, Charleston Ward 6 District 0036."

10 The 1910 census incorrectly lists Phoebe A. Owens as Phoebe A. Oakes. United States Census Bureau, "1910 United States Census for Phoebe A. Oakes, South Carolina, Charleston Ward 12 District 0063."

11 Department of Commerce and Labor Bureau of the Census, *Thirteenth Census of the United States Taken in the Year 1910: Statistics for South Carolina* (Washington, DC: Government Printing Office, 1913), 585, Table 1—Color, Nativity, and Parentage.

12 United States Census Bureau, "1920 United States Census for Phoebe H. Owens, New York, Manhattan Assembly District 21 District 1440."

13 United States Census Bureau, "1910 United State Census for John A. D. Meyer, South Carolina, Charleston Ward 5 District 0030."

14 "Mrs. Wilhelmine Hollings, Senator's Mother, Dies," *State* (Columbia, SC), August 22, 1982, 42.

15 Jeffrey Strickland, "How the Germans Became White Southerners: German Immigration and African Americans in Charleston, South Carolina, 1860–1880," *Journal of American Ethnic History* 28, no. 1 (Fall 2008): 54–55.

16 Strickland, "How the Germans Became White Southerners," 66.

17 Strickland, "How the Germans Became White Southerners," 56.

18 United States Census Bureau, "1920 United Stated federal Census for Adolf Hollings, South Carolina, Charleston Ward 12 District 0067."

19 Quoted in Obi Anayanwu, "Kerby Jean-Raymond on Reinventing the System," *Women's Wear Daily*, November 5, 2019, https://wwd.com/fashion-news/designer-luxury/kerby-jean-raymond-on-reinventing-the-system-1203360152/.

20 Anayanwu, "Kerby Jean-Raymond on Reinventing the System."

21 "Collection 2," Pyer Moss website, accessed September 18, 2021, https://www.pyermoss.com/blogs/runway/collection-2.

22 Julia Jacobs, "How Weeksville, a Center of Black History, Fought to Survive," *New York Times*, April 6, 2021, https://www.nytimes.com/2021/04/06/arts/design/save-weeksville-cig.html; and Corina Knoll and Morgan Jerkins, "Weeksville, a Haven for Free African-Americans Before the Civil War, Is Fighting for Survival," *New York Times*, March 19, 2019, https://www.nytimes.com/2019/05/10/nyregion/weeksville-brooklyn-crowdfunding-campaign.html.

23 Quoted in Rachel Tashjian, "Pyer Moss Deserves All Your Attention, Love, Money, and Brainpower," *Garage Magazine*, September 9, 2018, https://garage.vice.com/en_us/article/zm5b8a/pyer-moss-ss-19-review.

24 Quoted in Tashjian, "Pyer Moss Deserves All Your Attention."

25 Quoted in Rachel Tashjian, "King Kerby: Inside the World of Pyer Moss," *Garage Magazine*, February 5, 2019, https://garage.vice.com/en_us/article/vbwe7x/pyer-moss-kerby-jean-raymond.

26 Quoted in Tashjian, "Pyer Moss Deserves All Your Attention."

27 Quoted in Anayanwu, "Kerby Jean-Raymond on Reinventing the System."

28 Aria Hughes, "40 of Tomorrow: Kerby Jean-Raymond of Pyer Moss," *Women's Wear Daily*, November 29, 2018, https://wwd.com/fashion-news/fashion-features/40-of-tomorrow-kerby-jean-raymond-of-pyer-moss-1202914551/; Robin Givhan, "Pyer Moss Designer Steps outside Fashion and into the Conversation about Race," *Washington Post*, August 21, 2015, https://www.washingtonpost.com/news/arts-and-entertainment/wp/2015/08/21/pyer-moss-designer-steps-outside-fashion-and-into-the-conversation-about-race/; Tashjian, "King Kerby"; and Anayanwu, "Kerby Jean-Raymond on Reinventing the System."

29 Cathy Horyn, "The Lost Season," *The Cut*, September 1, 2020, https://www.thecut.com/2020/09/pyer-moss-cathy-horyn-the-lost-season.html; Anayanwu, "Kerby Jean-Raymond on Reinventing the System"; and Tashjian, "King Kerby."

30 Anayanwu, "Kerby Jean-Raymond on Reinventing the System."

31 Robin Givhan, "Fashion Finally Crowns a New Prince Who's Determined to Make the Industry More Relevant," *Washington Post*, November 6, 2018, https://www.washingtonpost.com/arts-entertainment/2018/11/06/fashion-finally-crowns-new-prince-whos-determined-make-industry-more-relevant/.

32 Quoted in Horyn, "The Lost Season."

33 Joelle Didrerich and Obi Anyanwu, "Kerby Jean-Raymond Partners with Kering on New Creative Platform," *Women's Wear Daily*, September 10, 2020, https://wwd.com/fashion-news/fashion-features/kering-partners-with-kerby-jean-raymond-on-new-creative-platform-1234578648/.

34 Vanessa Friedman, "A Black American Designer Disrupts the French Couture," *New York Times*, July 11, 2021, https://www.nytimes.com/2021/07/11/style/pyer-moss-couture.html.

35 Friedman, "A Black American Designer Disrupts the French Couture."

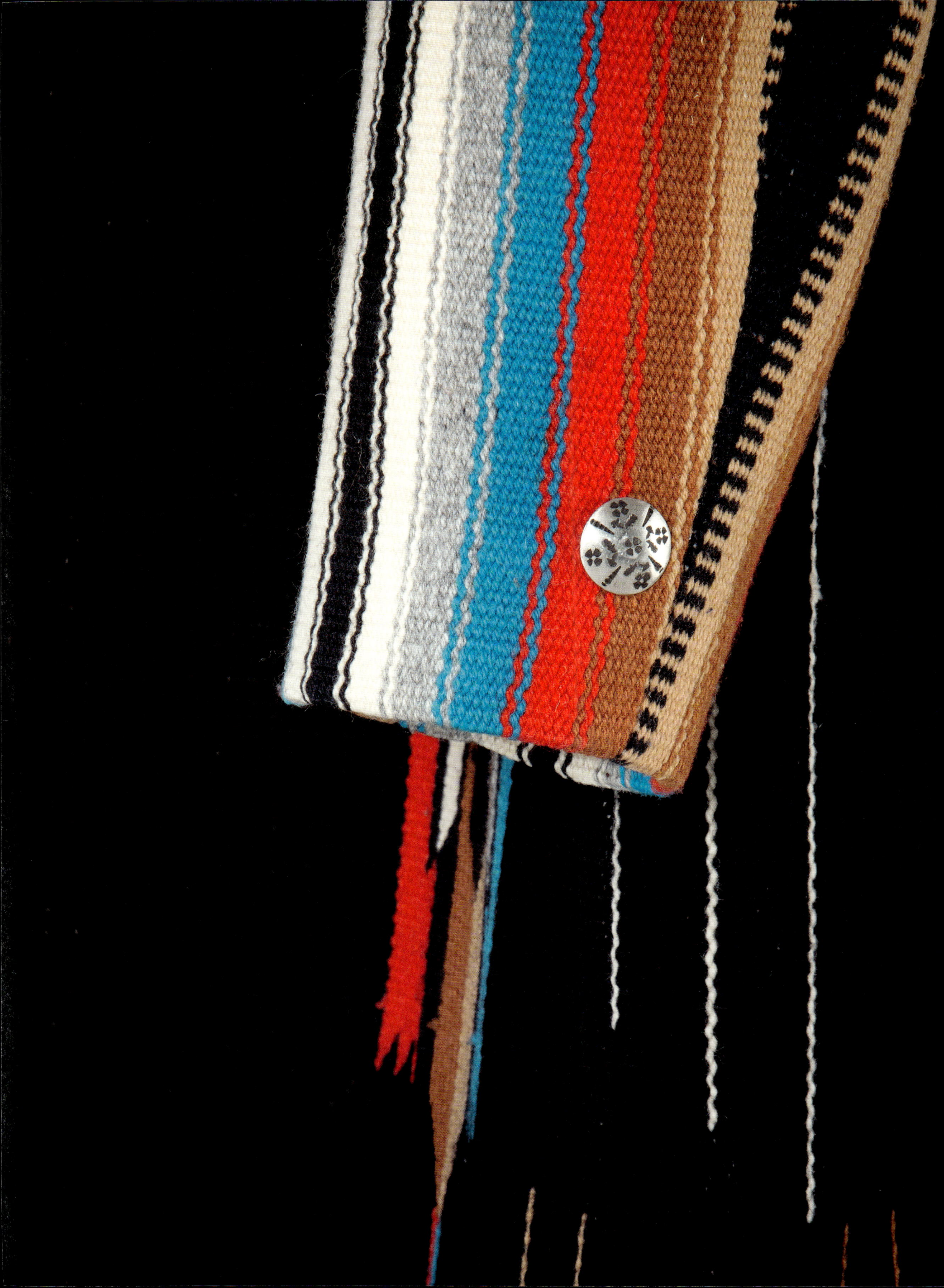

Westernwear

COMPLICATING AMERICAN ICONS

Sonya Abrego

Blue jeans, bandanas, cowboy boots, embroidered shirts, cowboy hats: westernwear is the most iconic American style regardless of era or convergence with the fashion trend of the day. Some of the first recognizable American brands were makers of westernwear—Levi Strauss & Co., est. 1853; Justin Boots, est. 1879; Stetson, est. 1865. Yet, in our present moment, when the word *iconic* is used for any garment or fashion that has successfully endured more than a season or two, another term might be in order. A similar reassessment of westernwear's Americanness, one that offers a more inclusive and nuanced perspective on the style's connection to national identity, is also overdue.

The instant, surface-level recognition that accompanies westernwear is the product of two centuries of literature, art, print culture, photography, film, and television. The romantic mythologizing of the Old West brought the aesthetic from its local origins to global audiences and helped define the United States' understanding of itself. The West as a place of freedom and adventure is a recurring theme that, vague as it may be, has resonated with countless generations of Americans. Understanding the western genre and the enduring success of westernwear demands, then, a slipping between the real and the imaginary.

As an amalgam of garments from different dress and craft traditions, westernwear constitutes a material index of the diversity of the American West.

Unfortunately, America's self-image is rife with omissions and fallacies. The facts of the history of the American West are often obscured or embellished in creative retellings and baldly false accounts, and historical figures have promoted their own mythologizing ever since Buffalo Bill turned his life story into a lucrative performance. The aspirations for and mythology of the West, however, emerged from a selective writing and reading of history in service of nationalistic goals. An honest reckoning exposes willful blind spots. Foremost among them is that the "adventure" of westward expansion was, in fact, a violent imperialist conquest that devastated Indigenous populations. Popular histories that focus on individuals like Davy Crockett or intrepid pioneers on the Oregon Trail have made the heroes of western movies, television, and comic books almost exclusively white males, ignoring the fact that the West boasted a multicultural, multilingual population that included Mexican, Black, Indigenous, and Chinese cowboys, cowgirls, rodeo riders, ranchers, and community leaders.

Representations of the West that successfully whitewashed its heterogeneous reality have not only done a disservice to history but also helped construct a media landscape primed to exclude those who do not reflect the image of the white cowboy hero. The blending of frontier facts and fictions in popular narratives buttressed a patriotic identification with a type of simplified Americana that has overshadowed what makes the West and westernwear significant, compelling, and truly American. Scratching the surface of these myths reveals a wide variety of cultural contributions, along with nuanced combinations of function and fashion, industry and craft, modernity and tradition.

Westernwear is a casual style identified with the western and southwestern United States and associated with the clothing and lifestyle of cowboys who raised cattle and horses in the late nineteenth century. American cowboy culture coalesced after the Civil War, its garb emerging from a set of materials and techniques adapted from Mexican rancheros and influenced by continuous technological development.[1] The familiar garment types have precedents in Spain—the continent's first imperialist power—and the first cowboys in what is now the United States wore garments brought north from Mexico. Cowboy attire maintained several conventions taken from the style of Mexican vaqueros, whose apparel was designed for horseback riding; these garments included tight-fitting pants, short jackets or boleros (outerwear that can be sleeveless or with sleeves, with front seams that curve away above waist level), boots with pointed toes and an angled heel, wide-brimmed hats, and *chapajeros*, known as "chaps" in English, that cover the legs.[2] At the same time, Native American design traditions such as colorful weaving, fringed buckskins, and fine silverwork were incorporated into cowboy apparel. These Indigenous materials and motifs, as varied and distinct as the populations that made them, were worn by the United States' original inhabitants and thus in their practical aspects were well adapted to the environment.[3] Indigenous and Mexican elements also combined with workwear of European American origin, such as sturdy wool trousers and shirts, which were some of the first clothes to be mass-produced in factories. As an amalgam of garments from different dress and craft traditions, westernwear thus constitutes a material index of the diversity of the American West.

Cowboys are defined by the work that they do, and their clothes speak to that connection. Westernwear was created for active, physically demanding labor where function and durability

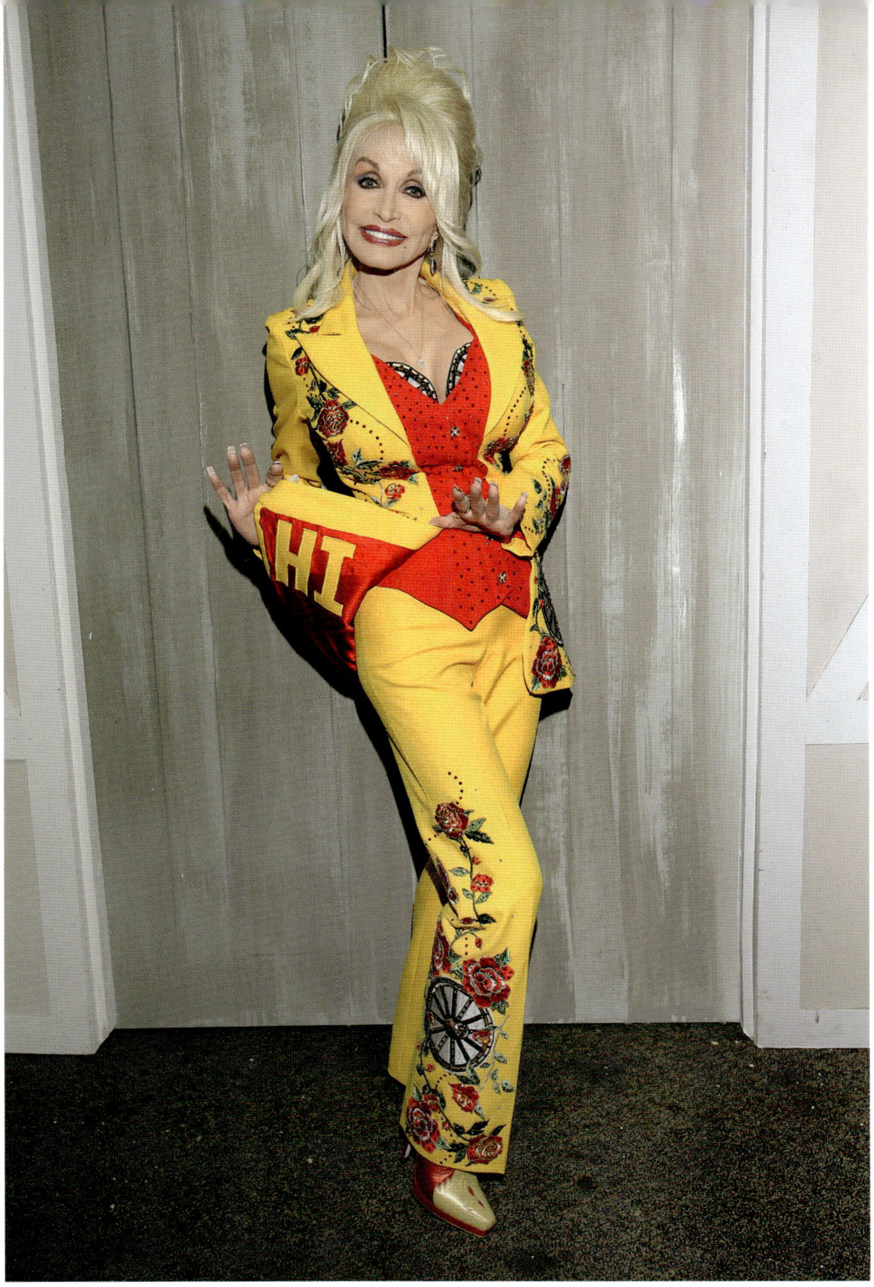

are key. Not unlike barbed wire and revolvers, the clothes are tools that help cowboys do their jobs. Boots with narrow toes and high heels help secure and protect the foot in a stirrup while riding, chaps shield legs from thorns and brush, hats shade the head but could also double as food or water receptacles for horses. Bandanas made from calico cotton or silk could serve as towels, handkerchiefs, or masks, and the reinforced sections of the yoke and cuffs on western shirts are made to withstand heavy wear. Historians have often celebrated this type of functionality as a hallmark of American fashion that has inspired generations of sportswear design.

Recently, however, Andrew Bolton, the Wendy Yu Curator in Charge at the Costume Institute at New York's Metropolitan Museum of Art, challenged the notion of defining American style in terms of "the language of sportswear and ready-to-wear, emphasizing the principles of simplicity, practicality, functionality, and egalitarianism," as opposed to more emotionally resonant attributes.[4] While functionality and creative expression are both aspects of American design, creating a binary between the two, as Bolton does, seems unnecessary. Westernwear is evidence that function and fashion coexist and that divisions between them might be irrelevant.

Westernwear ranges from the rough-hewn and simple to the flamboyant and expressive, depending on who is wearing it and the circumstances. For more than a century, westernwear has demonstrated that practical clothes can be colorful, stylish, and a means of personal expression. The combinations of color, embellishment, and customization—mixing fringe, leather work, silver conchos, embroidery, appliqué, and metal studs—are limitless. Individual instances of western style function much like western movies,

above Dolly Parton in Nudie Cohn suit during Dollywood's twenty-third annual grand opening, 2008.

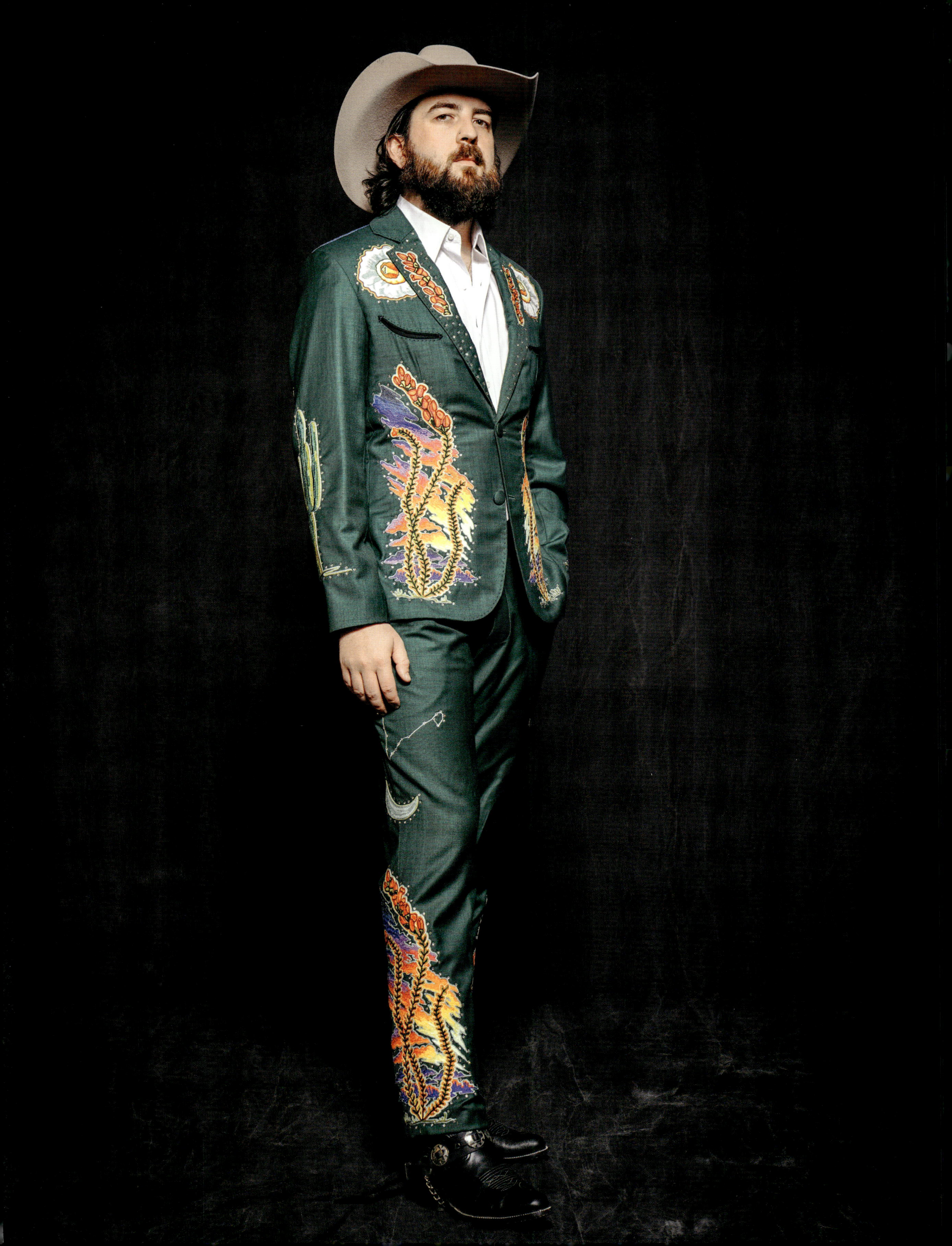

offering distinct interpretations within the same genre. The essential elements—yokes, piping, collar, snaps, arrow pocket stitching—might be the same, but the arrangements and details tell different stories. While westernwear is occupational dress, it is not a uniform.

On the contrary, taste, personal style, and attention to appearance have always been integral to this form of sartorial expression. In his account of ranching in Montana from the 1860s through the 1880s, pioneer rancher Granville Stuart described how the cowboys in his area "wore the best clothes that they could buy and took great pride in their personal appearance and trappings."[5] Cowboy memoirs and letters often recount the pride felt in being able to get the right clothes. In 1879 Nebraska, cowboy Teddy Blue Abbott spent his first paycheck on a new outfit, immediately had it photographed, and later recalled, "I thought that I was dressed just right for the first time in my life."[6] Looking good, wearing the same quality hat as "top hands," stirred palpable emotions. Retailers would come to understand this fact, and westernwear catalogues supplied chaps with decorative studs in fanciful patterns as early as 1900 and still offer bold, vibrant options into the present.[7] The creativity evident in these clothes at all levels, from the meticulously handcrafted to the industrially fabricated, is boundless.

Cinema has been perhaps the key disseminator of westernwear. Western movies offered highly styled heroes, such as the 1920s star Tom Mix in his Montana hat; the title character of *Shane*, played by Alan Ladd, pairing golden buckskins and a shining silver belt; and John Wayne in battered Levi's captured by John Ford. Hollywood cowboys inspired countless imitators, and costume designers were in turn inspired by working hands. Rodeo, for example, is a rugged and intensely physical sport, but flamboyant garb is not out of place in the rodeo ring. Early twentieth-century rodeo champion Vera McGinnis affectionately described her fellow riders' tastes as "loud" and "gaudy";[8] it wasn't uncommon to see riders mount a bucking bronco or take down a steer while wearing ornate tooled-leather chaps, multicolored satin shirts, and inlaid boots. Sparkling silver belt buckles could be part of a winner's prize, a wearable marker of their skill that could broadcast their acumen outside the ring. The more fanciful, ostentatious elements were not bound by traditional gender norms. Floral embroidery, sequins, and appliquéd butterflies could be seen on men as well as women, designed to be worn by anyone with the brio to adopt them. Expressive styles that challenge convention have always existed outside high fashion, notably, as in this case, among working-class people. Like zoot suits or punk looks, flashy western styles are worn by those who want to stand out, and stand out on their own terms.

opposite Fort Lonesome, chain-stitched western suit made to measure for country musician Andrew Howard, 2020. Silk/wool fabric, wool thread, and rhinestones.

Beginning in the mid-twentieth century, country-music performers were also instrumental in bringing westernwear to the public eye. The ultimate expression of western glamour can be found in the work of the tailors who dressed them, with Nathan Turk, Rodeo Ben, and Nudie (all Jewish émigrés from Eastern Europe) being among the most famous and the most frequently copied. Nudie Cohn, born Nuta Kotlyarenko in Kyiv, started Nudie's Rodeo Tailors in Los Angeles to cater to the entertainment industry and is credited with popularizing "rhinestone cowboy" styles.[9] The ensembles he created, known as Nudie suits, don't differ in form from more conventional western apparel, but every feature is heightened. Embroidery that might typically be found as a detail on cuffs, collar, or pockets spill over the whole of shirts, jackets, and pants. The colors are bold and the motifs big, with metallic thread, shimmering rhinestones, and sequins used in abundance. Nudie's designs foregrounded the individuality of performers who amplified their image or personal brand by sometimes incorporating visual tropes drawn from their names or hit songs, like Porter Wagoner's suit emblazoned with chain-stitched wagon wheels or Webb Pierce's spiderwebs. The 1950s Nudie suit made for Hank Snow, a singer born in Canada who became a Nashville star, features rich floral embroidery that beautifully recalls the needlework of Nudie's Eastern European origins. The suit is a seemingly incongruous combination of the varied identities and influences that the quintessential westernwear look embodies.

There is, however, more to a Nudie suit than visual flair. Historian Peter La Chapelle sees a deeper meaning of solidarity expressed through rhinestone cowboy suits. Like much of their audience, who appreciated the flamboyant attire, most country musicians in the early to mid-twentieth century were working people defined by personal histories rooted in manual labor and rural communities. The antithesis of the stereotype of the drably dressed laborer or farmer, the Nudie suit conveys opulence and individuality, celebrating ways of life that were often ignored or maligned in popular culture. The outfit was both part of the performance and a sign of respect for the audience. By exaggerating western motifs and styles, Nudie and other tailors like him celebrated regional lifestyles and traditions.[10] The rhinestone cowboy tradition is carried on today by performers as varied as Lil Nas X, Chris Isaac, and Orville

Peck, and by makers like Fort Lonesome, Union Western Clothing, Ashlyn Evans, and Manuel Cuevas.

Manuel Cuevas in particular is a living legend of western design. He worked for Nudie's Rodeo Tailors in the 1950s and went on to found his own bespoke westernwear shop, presently in Nashville, that caters to country and rock 'n' roll stars or anyone looking for distinctive westernwear. Manuel's unique pieces blend the glitter of Hollywood rhinestone cowboys with beads, fringe, and southwestern weaving like that seen in Chimayo blanket jackets. Chimayo is one of several weaving traditions from the Rio Grande Valley in northern New Mexico with origins in the late nineteenth century. Its distinctive motifs are the product of a dynamic interconnection between weavers who creatively combined stripes and variations on *saltillo* (diamond) shapes on the one hand and the changing tastes of consumers on the other. It remains a vibrant, ongoing craft tradition that is highly valued by collectors.[11]

Expressive styles that challenge convention have always existed outside high fashion, notably among working-class people. Like zoot suits or punk looks, flashy western styles are worn by those who want to stand out, and stand out on their own terms.

Another woven textile with a sustained presence in westernwear is the Pendleton blanket, the product of sheep raising and jacquard weaving technology imported from Europe to Oregon in the 1890s. Wool blankets produced in the town of Pendleton by the eponymous company bear dynamic, geometric designs inspired by local connections with the Indigenous communities of the neighboring Umatilla Valley—the Umatilla, Cayuse, and Walla Walla. The tribes also formed a base of enthusiastic consumers. In these communities, blankets had historically served both practical and ceremonial functions; they were worn as robes and exchanged as gifts, often as part of ceremonies or to mark significant events such as birth or marriage, and were passed down through generations.[12] In settler communities, Pendleton's wares also became popular, valued as contributions to domestic interiors, and their blanket jackets were colorful and sturdy options for colder months. While its origins may be mixed, the Pendleton blanket is part of the Native American design idiom and constitutes a definitive statement of Indigenous identity.[13] Its strong visual impact and historical resonance continues to play a part today in the designs of contemporary Indigenous designers such as Korina Emmerich (EMME Studio) and Ginew, both of whom combine classic Pendleton motifs and original patterns in their work.

Some elements of westernwear have become so embedded in day-to-day attire that they blend in unnoticed. Denim jeans are recognized as both an indisputably American item and a global commodity. The transition from a regional innovation to an international phenomenon evolved over the twentieth century, and with each reinterpretive subversion, jeans retained associations of versatility, egalitarianism, and unpretentiousness. Parisian designer Yves Saint Laurent famously wished he had invented them; Andy Warhol wore them under his tuxedo pants to feel comfortable at formal affairs; and Georgia O'Keeffe, who made jeans a regular part of her wardrobe, asserted: "I rather think they are our only national costumes."[14] Jeans are workwear with western roots, emerging from California. The first five-pocket, riveted, blue denim jean was created by Levi Strauss and Jacob Davis with gold and silver miners in mind, but San Francisco's location and connections to other western industries ensured cowboys and cowgirls quickly adopted them as standard attire. Relative proximity to Hollywood, the image-making capital that brought visions of the West to the world, also secured Levi's visibility.

Jeans were also some of the first ambassadors for American fashion. In 1947, San Francisco apparel manufacturers organized a unique publicity venture to showcase their designs in Paris. Known as the "Fashion Flight," the trip brought West Coast designers, models, and company representatives to France in the spirit of sharing American design and assuaging fears about makers in the United States copying Parisian fashion.[15] The goal was to show that West Coast styles were desirable in their own right while also courting new business partnerships with French companies. Levi Strauss & Co.'s 701 jeans, the first the company made for women, were paired with shimmering satin western shirts and cowboy hats. At a time when women wearing pants was still daring, these cowgirl styles couldn't

opposite Manuel Cuevas, Chimayo blanket coat, 1980s. Wool. FIDM Museum Collection: Gift of Patrick Duncan. Courtesy of FIDM Museum at the Fashion Institute of Design & Merchandising, Los Angeles.

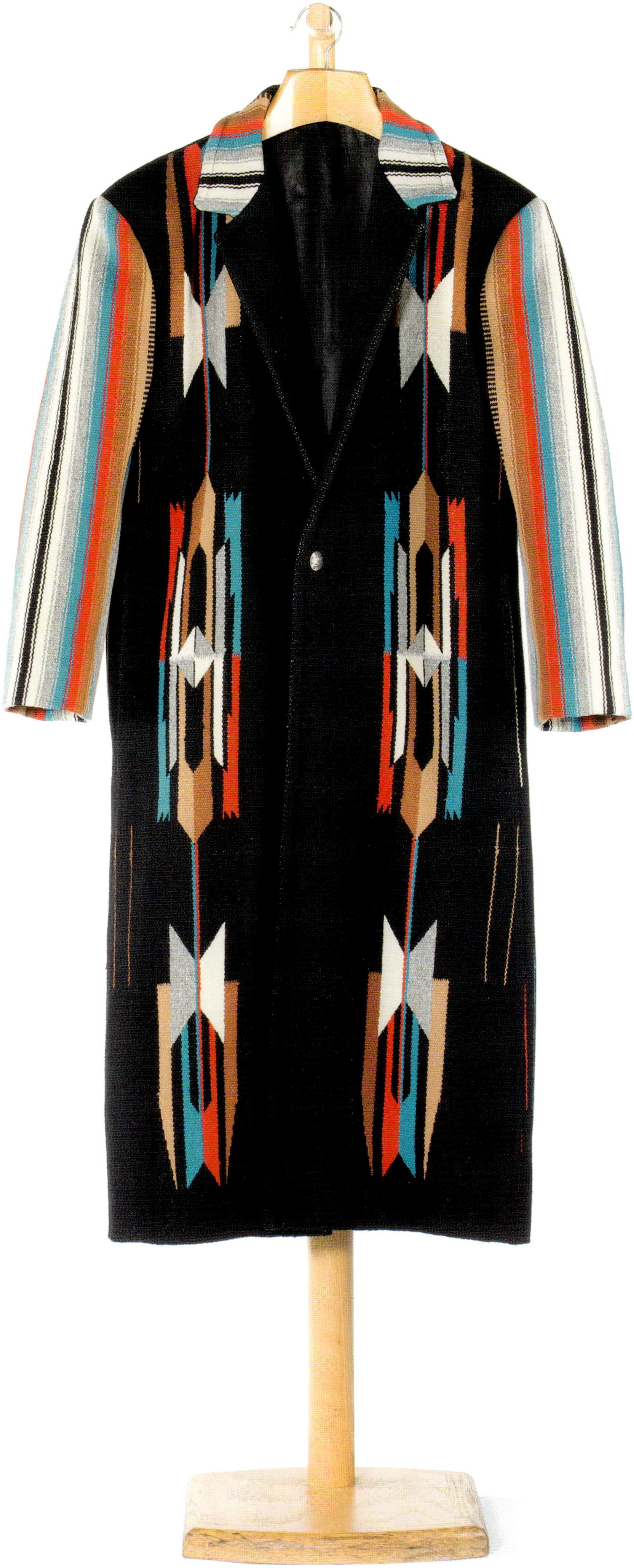

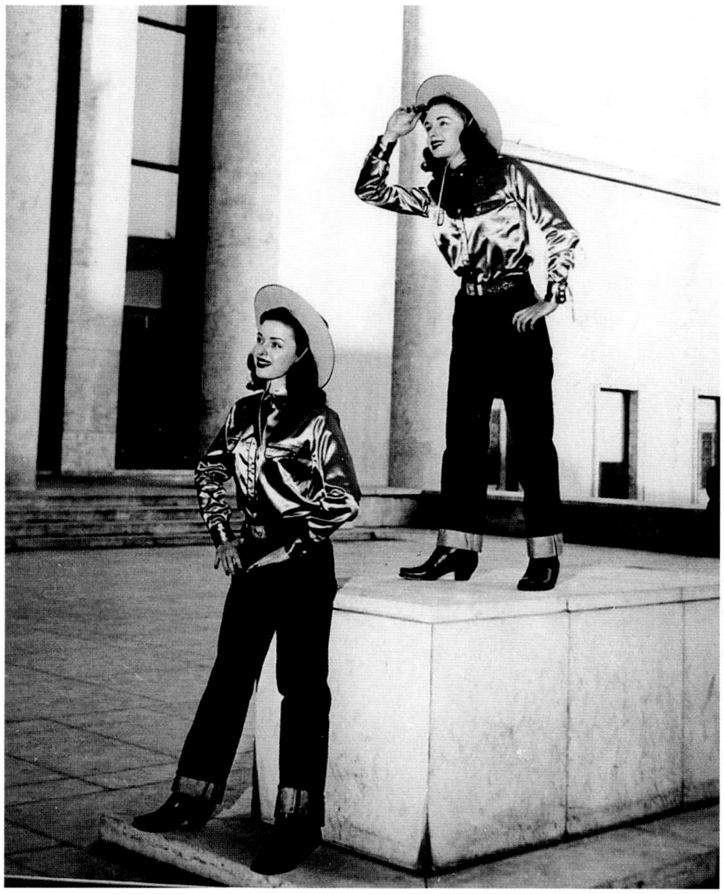

Pat and Priscilla Emery in Levi Strauss jeans and western shirts at the All American Fashion Show, Paris, 1947. Levi Strauss & Co. Archives, San Francisco, California.

have been more different from what Paris offered, or more representative of casual fashions to come.

Fabricating jeans requires large-scale mechanized weaving, rope-dying, cutting, and sewing with machines strong enough to handle the heavy cotton twill and industrially fabricated metal rivets. (It was, in fact, the novel application of rivets to strengthen the pockets that secured the original patent for the design for Jacob Davis and Levi Strauss in 1873.[16]) The cowboys and laborers who originally wore jeans were some of the first beneficiaries of these innovations in industrial apparel manufacture. The seeds of modern ready-to-wear, an industry synonymous with American fashion that dominates how clothing is made and consumed today, had been planted in the Old West.

At the time of their invention, jeans shared more in common with industrial design than fashionable attire. While avant-garde aesthetics are often attributed to European origins, some midcentury designers, architects, and critics—notably Sigfried Giedion and John Kouwenhoven—sought to locate the roots of the modern movement in American vernacular design and industry. Giedion framed innovations in the design of hand tools, machinery, and construction as essentially modern before their time.[17] In his 1948 tome *Made in America*, Kouwenhoven extended the nation's claim to modern design further still. He noted that nineteenth-century American products such as rifles and woodworking machines, even steam engines and sailing vessels, were marked by restraint and simplicity of form that characterized what he labeled "democratic-technological vernacular."[18] Although he didn't discuss clothing, the simple design, industrial fabrication, and accessibility of jeans epitomize this notion. This industrial functionality might explain why jeans simultaneously exist in and outside fashion. The five-pocket jean has changed surprisingly little since its invention nearly one hundred fifty years ago, but its component parts and denim itself have been reimagined by designers with visions as different as Isabel Toledo's sophisticated aesthetic and Junya Watanabe's deconstructed streetwear.

Fashion past and present offers direct, embodied access to imagined and overlooked possibilities. Designer Kerby Jean-Raymond's 2018 Pyer Moss collection includes western elements like bandanas, chaps, yoked shirts, rawhide leather, and denim and complicates the garments with variations in proportion and silhouette, as Elizabeth Way explores in here essay here. Jean-Raymond's interventions draw the richness of African American style into dialogue with some of the nation's most recognizable sartorial symbols. By placing this clothing on Black models on the runway, and in accompanying advertisements that featured contemporary Black cowboys and cowgirls from Compton and Baltimore, he invites us to consider why such apparel might look familiar on some people and unfamiliar on others, even though there have been Black cowboys for as long as there have been cowboys at all.[19]

Westernwear, like the American West itself, is both immediately familiar and strange. Its strangeness lies in the transformation of a regionally specific, working-class aesthetic into a celebrated national style. It is also unusual in that fashions originating from regions as diverse as Tennessee, Texas, New Mexico, California, and Oregon are all legitimately western. Representations of the Old West have now existed far longer than the historical moment that inspired them. Their merging of fact and myth, and the subsequent excavation of the truths behind them, remains fertile ground for imagination, revision, and debate. Westernwear is one form of this dialogue, embodying the West and its dynamic and conflicting nature, and offering a means of understanding the embeddedness of the West in American culture and the ways that it still resonates with us.

NOTES

1 Américo Paredes, *Folklore and Culture on the Texas-Mexican Border* (Austin: CMAS Books, Center for Mexican American Studies, University of Texas at Austin, 1993), 23.

2 Valerie Cumming, C. W. Cunnington, and P. E. Cunnington, "Bolero," in *The Dictionary of Fashion History* (Oxford: Berg Publishers, 2010), 25. For chaps, see Laurel Wilson, "American Cowboy Dress: Function to Fashion," *Dress* 28 (2001): 41.

3 See Josephine Paterek, *Encyclopedia of American Indian Costume* (Denver: ABC-CLIO, 1994), 461; and Holly George-Warren, *How the West Was Worn* (New York: Harry N. Abrams; Los Angeles: Autry Museum of the American West, 2001), 14.

4 Wall text for *In America: A Lexicon of Fashion*, Metropolitan Museum of Art, New York, 2021–22.

5 William Manns cites Stuart's *Forty Years on the Frontier* in William Manns et al., *Cowboys and the Trappings of the Old West* (Santa Fe, NM: Zon International, 1997), 11.

6 Manns et al., *Cowboys and the Trappings of the Old West*, 11.

7 Wilson, "American Cowboy Dress," 44.

8 Vera McGinnis, *Rodeo Road; My Life as a Pioneer Cowgirl* (New York: Hastings House, 1974), 23.

9 Jamie Lee Nudie and Mary Lynn Cabrall, *Nudie: The Rodeo Tailor* (Salt Lake City: Gibbs Smith, 2004).

10 Peter La Chapelle, "All That Glitters: Country Music, Taste, and the Politics of the Rhinestone 'Nudie' Suit," *Dress* 28 (2001): 6.

11 Helen R. Lucero, *Chimayó Weaving: The Transformation of a Tradition* (Albuquerque: University of New Mexico Press, 1999).

12 Robert W. Kapoun, *Language of the Robe: American Indian Trade Blankets*, 1st ed. (Salt Lake City: Peregrine Smith Books, 1992), 7.

13 Kimberly G. Wieser, *Back to the Blanket: Recovered Rhetorics and Literacies in American Indian Studies* (Norman: University of Oklahoma Press, 2017), 10.

14 Yves Saint Laurent: "I have often said that I wish I had invented blue jeans: the most spectacular, the most practical, the most relaxed and nonchalant. They have expression, modesty, sex appeal, simplicity—all I hope for in my clothes." *New York*, November 28, 1983, 53. Warhol was known to wear his Levi's 501s under formal attire, even when visiting the White House in 1975; see Simon Chilvers, " 'Hip, Rebellious, Even a Bit Sinister': How Andy Warhol Made Pop Art Fashion," *Guardian*, March 2, 2020. O'Keeffe's remark comes from an undated letter to the art critic Murdock Pemberton quoted in Wanda M. Corn, *Georgia O'Keeffe: Living Modern* (Munich: Prestel; New York; Brooklyn Museum, 2017), 117.

15 Katherine Jamison, "California: Paris Show Spurs Efforts of San Francisco Designers: 37 Manufacturers Participating in "World Preview" of San Francisco Fashions Taking Place in Paris on Oct. 17," *Women's Wear Daily*, September 3, 1947, 1.

16 Michael Harris, *Jeans of the Old West*, 1st ed. (Atglen, PA: Schiffer, 2010), 20.

17 S. [Sigfried] Giedion, *Space, Time, and Architecture: The Growth of a New Tradition* (Cambridge, MA: Harvard University Press, 1954), 348.

18 John A. Kouwenhoven, "What Is Vernacular?" in *Made in America: The Arts in Modern Civilization* (New York: Doubleday, 1948), 15–53.

19 Bruce A. Glasrud and Michael N. Searles, *Black Cowboys in the American West: On the Range, on the Stage, behind the Badge* (Norman: University of Oklahoma Press, 2016).

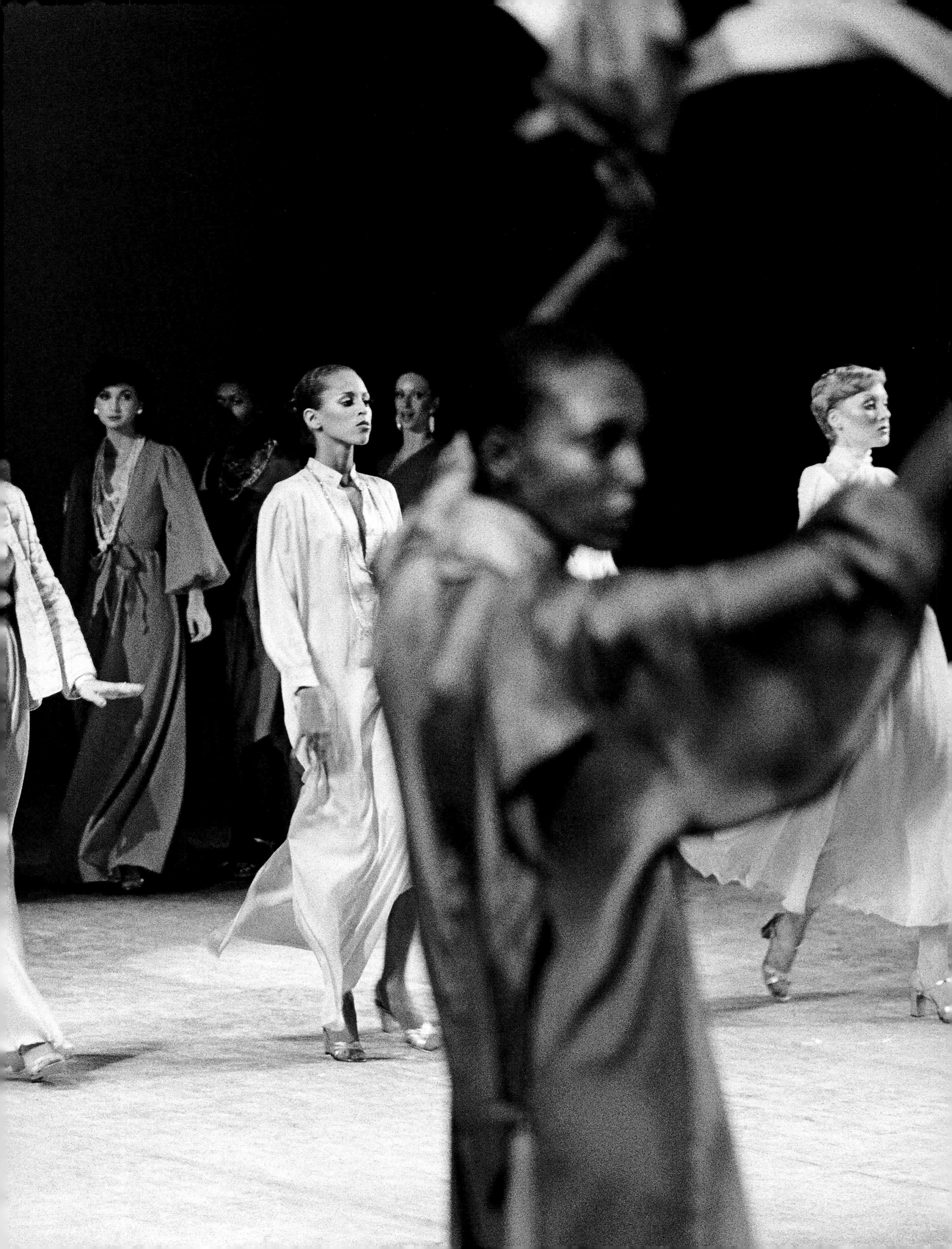

Paris Fashions Americanized

THE DEVELOPMENT OF AMERICAN STYLE

Michelle Tolini Finamore

In the midst of the Great Depression, Arkansas native Dorothy Shaver, merchandising strategist and eventual president of Lord & Taylor department store, started an "American Fashions for American Women" campaign; her goal was "to show the world, to show this country what American designers could do."[1] Shaver was unwavering in her belief that Americans had ample talent and a uniquely modern design sensibility that could compete with the titans of the industry in Paris. Yet Shaver was reproached by her contemporaries for spearheading a "deep dyed plot against the Parisian world of fashion, in which Lord & Taylor exploded the bomb."[2] Why was Shaver's campaign perceived as so radical? Her effort represented a challenge to over two hundred years of American fashion looking to Europe as its lodestar. It was only in the beginning of the early twentieth century that American style began to carve out the distinctive national identity it has today.

In the nineteenth century, American women got their information about fashion from periodicals such as *Godey's Lady's Book*. Published in Philadelphia, the magazine served as a fashion bible, especially for women who lived far away from urban centers. As early as 1830, its editor in chief questioned looking constantly to Europe for style: "Are we always to be indebted to Paris and London for our mode of dress? . . . Shall we never be fashionably independent—republicans in costume as well as character?"[3] Each issue of the magazine included hand-colored fashion plates that featured "Paris Fashions Americanized"—designs that were adapted to suit American tastes with "better, cleaner colors . . . and less ostentatious trimming than the foreign originals."[4] The idea of simpler lines and fewer frills and furbelows is a recurring theme in American design, speaking to the practicality that is often associated with the American look.

From the early twentieth century (and into the twenty-first), American *Vogue* has been the preeminent fashion magazine and key arbiter of taste. Founded in 1892, it originally positioned itself as an ambassador for elite European style, focusing on Paris couture houses and socialites and their designer clothes. The broader messaging went beyond fashion to include editorial content that touted anti-immigration and anti-mass-production perspectives.[5] By the 1910s, however, with World War I looming, limitations on imports from Europe forced Americans to look increasingly to their own shores for inspiration, and the magazine began to take a slightly more inclusive, populist stance. *Vogue* started showcasing more American designers and began to feature stars of the stage and screen for the first time. Other women's magazines followed suit, with *Ladies' Home Journal* starting an "American Fashions for American Women" campaign, and the *New York Times* conducting a contest for American design in 1913. Initiated by the jingoistic fashion editor Edward Bok, the contest was meant to provide an antidote to what he called the "freakish" designs of France and couture's hegemonic control over American fashion design.[6] The winning garments were those inspired by the flora and fauna of America's wilderness, James McNeill Whistler's *Nocturne* paintings, and Native American design, with prizewinning items including a hat featuring a cotton boll and a Quaker-inspired day frock. The contest did not include Native or Quaker designers, however; rather, it rewarded those who appropriated from those traditions, which mirrored developments in museum programming and art education at the time.[7] The language surrounding the *Times* contest is revealing in terms of how it signaled the different ways the French and American industries were perceived: Paris garments were made in "ateliers," while American clothing was made in "workrooms"; the French made garments for the "exclusive elect" or "limited class," while American designers created for the "average woman." The democratic nature of the American industry, particularly in the realm of ready-to-wear, was also presented as a foil to the "tyranny of haute couture."[8]

While many American fashion writers still traveled to Paris for inspiration—as did the many copyists who worked for ready-to-wear firms to reverse engineer couture designs—editorial coverage of American design continued its rise. Fashion critic Lois Long, who wrote under the pseudonym Lipstick, began chronicling American fashion for the *New Yorker* in the 1920s. She was one of many critics of the system of copying from the French. Fashion designer and social activist (and Long's fellow Vassar alum) Elizabeth Hawes likewise believed that American women should buy American design rather than be rabid followers of the French. Hawes began her fashion career working as an haute couture copyist, sharing the experience in her popular critique of the industry called *Fashion Is Spinach* (1938). In 1926, she noted, there were more than one hundred American fashion reporters in Paris. Echoing the pleas in *Godey's Lady's Book* to focus on American design and culture, Hawes observed, "Fashion is so shrouded in mystery, so far away and so foreign, so complicated and so boring when you understand its ways, that it has become a complete anachronism in modern life."[9]

opposite Pauline Trigère, Sketch for "Star Spangled Stripes" dress, Spring/Resort 1975. Courtesy of Kent State University, Ohio.

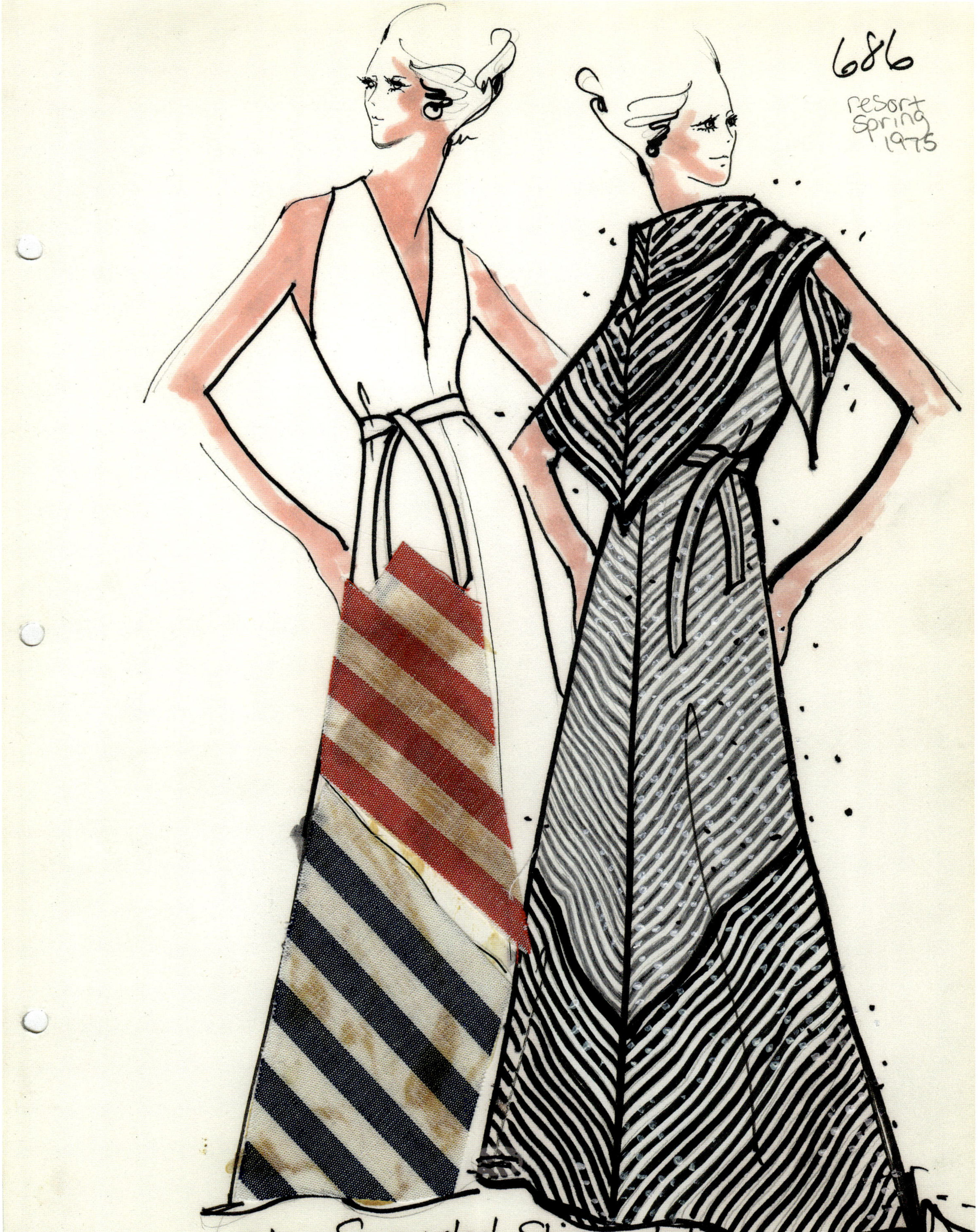
686
resort
Spring
1975
Star Spangled Stripes-fichu

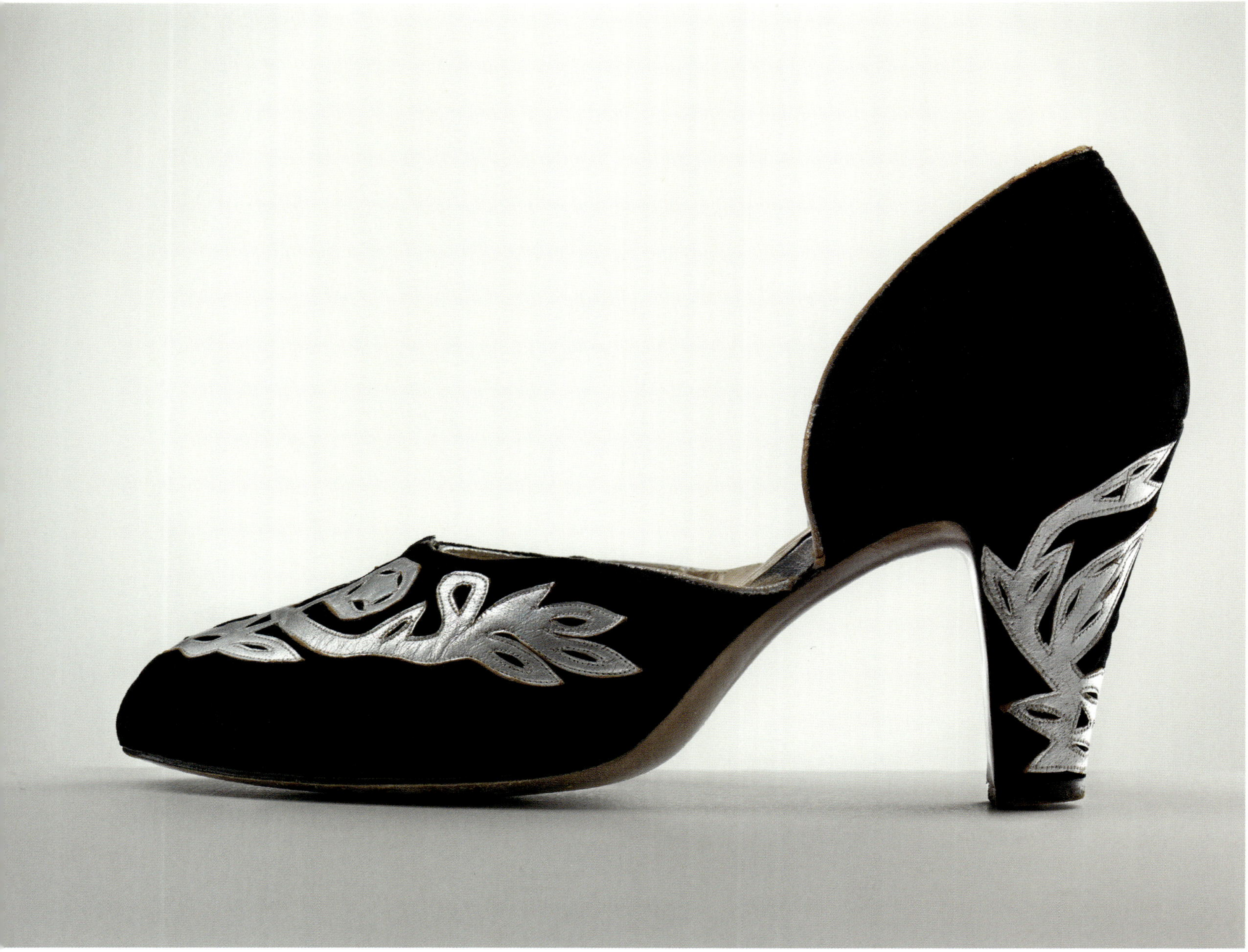

Salvatore Ferragamo, shoes, early 1920s. Suede, leather, metallic leather, and metal. Jimmy Raye Collection, Salem, Massachusetts.

In the material aspects of fashion, intriguing crossovers occurred that belied the idea of the United States as a mere receiver of European ideas. Although Italian shoe designer Salvatore Ferragamo is primarily associated with Italian luxury footwear, he cut his teeth in Hollywood and became known as the "shoemaker to the stars." In 1915, Ferragamo left Italy, where handcrafted shoes still reigned supreme, to learn the secrets of ready-made shoes, recalling in his memoirs, "I would go to America, and among the machines I would found my fortune."[10] He first worked at the mechanized Queen Quality Shoe Company in Boston, which turned out hundreds of shoes for every one he was making in Italy. Within a few weeks, he realized that his heart remained with the handmade. He set out for the West Coast to join his brothers, who were working as carpenters and tailors, and began working in the burgeoning film industry after he convinced the American Film Company's wardrobe director that he could create better cowboy boots than those they were currently making.[11] He eventually opened up his Hollywood Boot Shop, adorning the feet of movie stars such as Dolores del Río, Pola Negri, and Mary Pickford. Around 1927, he returned to Italy, bringing back what he had learned about ergonomic design and star promotion to his shoemaking atelier in Florence, where Ferragamo is based today.

> Paris garments were made in "ateliers," while American clothing was made in "workrooms"; the French made garments for the "exclusive elect" or "limited class," while American designers created for the "average woman."

While the reality of history is much more nuanced, the notion that haute couture ateliers are the sole wellspring of fashion has remained the standard narrative in fashion, particularly when it comes to the 1940s and 1950s. The first designer of the era to be mentioned is invariably Christian Dior. His post–World War II "New Look," introduced in 1947, clad his "women flowers" (as he called them) in dresses that were overtly "feminine," with cinched waists, soft shoulders, rounded busts, and lavishly full skirts. Dior's New Look garnered substantial press attention, but many other designers were experimenting with this silhouette prior to Dior, and some have posited that Hollywood's 1940s designs for historic dramas had an impact on the evolution of this style.[12] At the same time the New Look was taking hold, developments in the United States proceeded unabated. In the 1930s and 1940s, key figures of the period such as Dorothy Shaver at Lord & Taylor actively supported American designers such as Elizabeth Hawes, Clare Potter, Pauline Trigère, Sally Victor, and Lily Daché. The Second World War, like the First, cut the country off from Paris, resulting in more press attention on American design.

The same year the New Look was introduced, an American fashion show was held in Paris, featuring playclothes, ready-to-wear, bathing attire, and denim—all key exports that continued to be identified with American style for decades to come. The 1947 "Fashion Flight" brought West Coast design to Paris on two Matson DC-4 airplanes to promote Spring 1948 collections, including the work of San Francisco–based fashion makers Levi Strauss, Irene, and Lilli Ann. The show's timing was strategic, capitalizing on the increased interest in American style sparked by the presence of GIs in postliberation Paris who wore jeans and other casualwear when not in uniform. The models included movie star Joan Leslie and twins Priscilla and Pat Emery, with the latter two wearing the Levi's ensembles. "Parisians are looking at us queerly on the streets," Pat noted at the time. "They look at our clothes and spot us as Americans right away."[13] Ironically, although the Fashion Flight aimed to reinvigorate America's presence on the European fashion stage after wartime border closures, it only further cemented the idea of Paris as the font of style. The trip ultimately resulted in formalizing a system for American West Coast manufacturers to purchase Paris designs for a set fee, attend the Paris shows so they would have a six-month jump on marketing the latest styles, and bring Paris fashion shows to San Francisco. Various American press accounts quote Paris designers who specifically remarked on the style, practicality, and affordability of American fashion, yet the underlying message was that European design houses "create" while American design houses "produce." The Paris couture industry, which relied heavily upon the United States and South America for patronage, understood that they had to retain their status to ensure future business. Their efforts undoubtedly succeeded: even as American design continued to gain international recognition, Paris remained at the apex of high-style trends well into the 1960s. Fashion icon and first lady Jacqueline Kennedy famously commissioned American designers such as Chez Ninon and Oleg Cassini to make copies of gowns by Givenchy and Christian Dior for her official appearances.

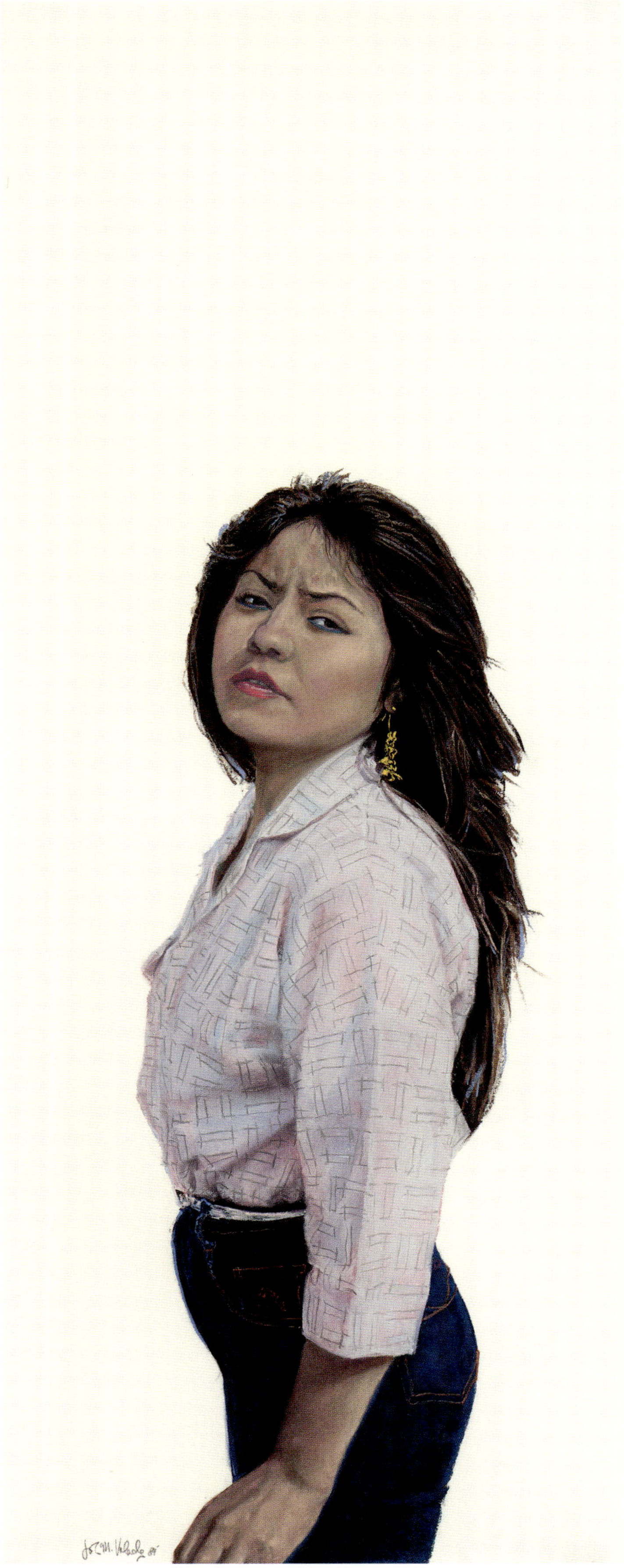

The great countercultural shake-ups of the later 1960s and the 1970s, with the hippie generation rejecting the "fashion fascism" associated with elitist couture, helped solidify the lasting impact of American fashion's global presence. The elevation of jeans from workwear to high fashion began in the early 1970s, when Levi Strauss won the fashion industry's annual Coty Award and European designers started to notice denim's style potential. Yves Saint Laurent freely admitted that he found inspiration in American teens who shopped at army/navy surplus stores, donning sailor's peacoats to wear with their jeans; such declarations prompted one reporter's headline "Levi Strauss with a French Accent Is Yves Saint Laurent."[14] In 1976, American fashion publicist and "Empress of Seventh Avenue" Eleanor Lambert observed, "The Levi look, perhaps more than any other fashion, helped to erase class distinction from modern dress."[15] Jeans remain quintessential workwear and casualwear, and one of the best examples of "democratic" design.

The great differences between European fashion and American style coalesced in one event—the November 28, 1973, Grand Divertissement à Versailles charity event, now referred to in fashion circles as "The Battle of Versailles." This fashion show, which helped raise funds for the restoration of the Palace of Versailles, pitted French high-fashion designers directly against their American counterparts. The haute couture houses opened the event with a conventional, subdued, two-and-a-half-hour-long presentation with fashions by Pierre Cardin, Christian Dior, Givenchy, Yves Saint Laurent, and Emanuel Ungaro.

In marked contrast to the formality of the French, the American show opened with Liza Minelli exuberantly singing and dancing, followed by an array of ethnically diverse models wearing brightly hued, flowing, body-conscious garments by New Jersey–born Stephen Burrows and Iowa native Halston. Although the fashion industry had been hiring Black models on a small scale, people of color still rarely appeared on the runway at the time.[16] Designs by Dominican immigrant Oscar de la Renta, Indiana's Bill Blass, and Brooklyn-bred Anne Klein rounded out the American presentations at the event. The sheer energy, color, and sexiness of the creations provided a welcome respite from the formality of the French couture and helped solidify America's place internationally.

left John Valadez, *The Jean Seller*, 1989. Pastel on paper, 42 × 18 ½ in. (106.7 × 47 cm). Crystal Bridges Museum of American Art, Bentonville, Arkansas, 2010.29.

opposite Stephen Burrows, day gown, ca. 1969. Wool blend. FIDM Museum Collection: Gift of Jo Holzman. Courtesy of FIDM Museum at the Fashion Institute of Design & Merchandising, Los Angeles.

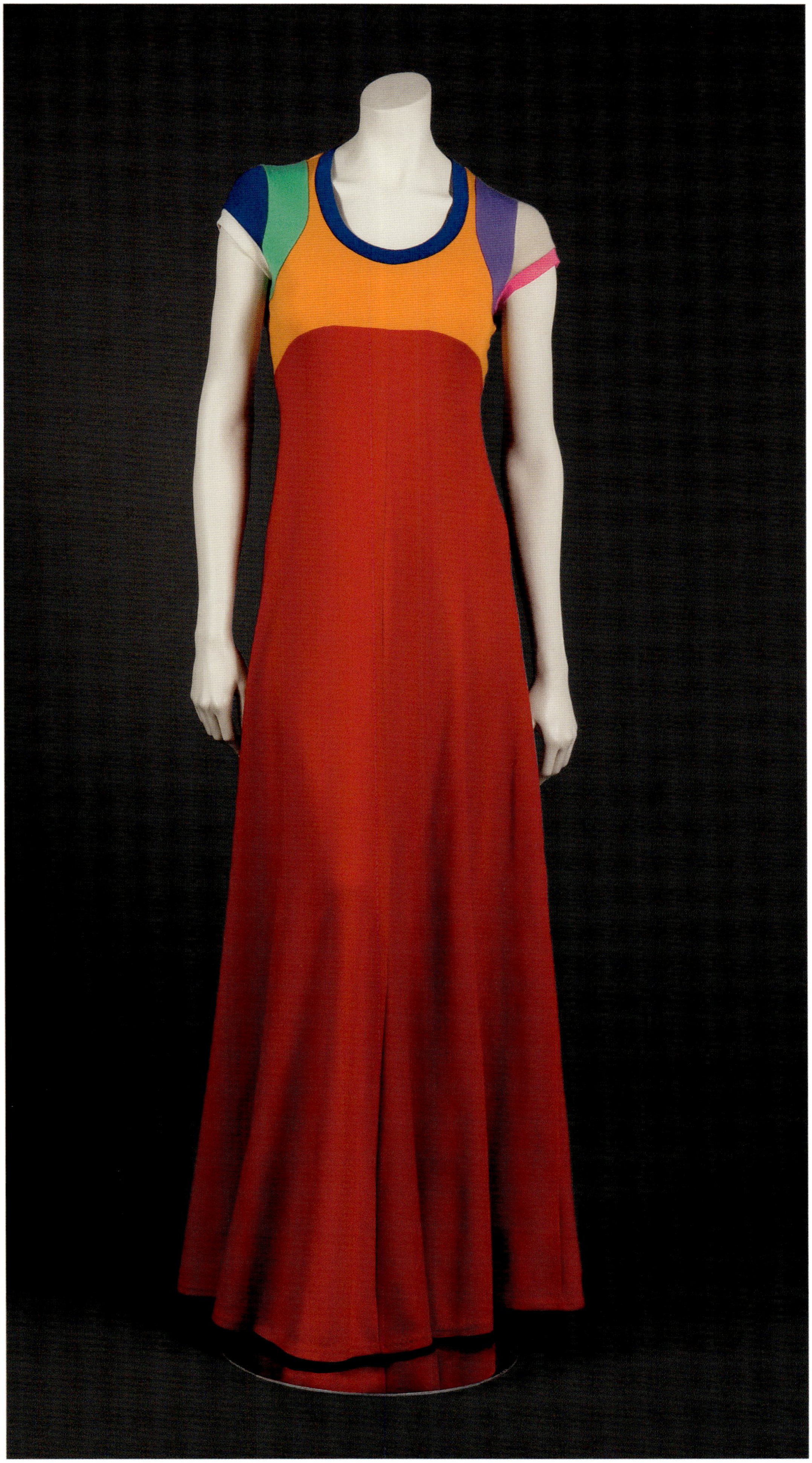

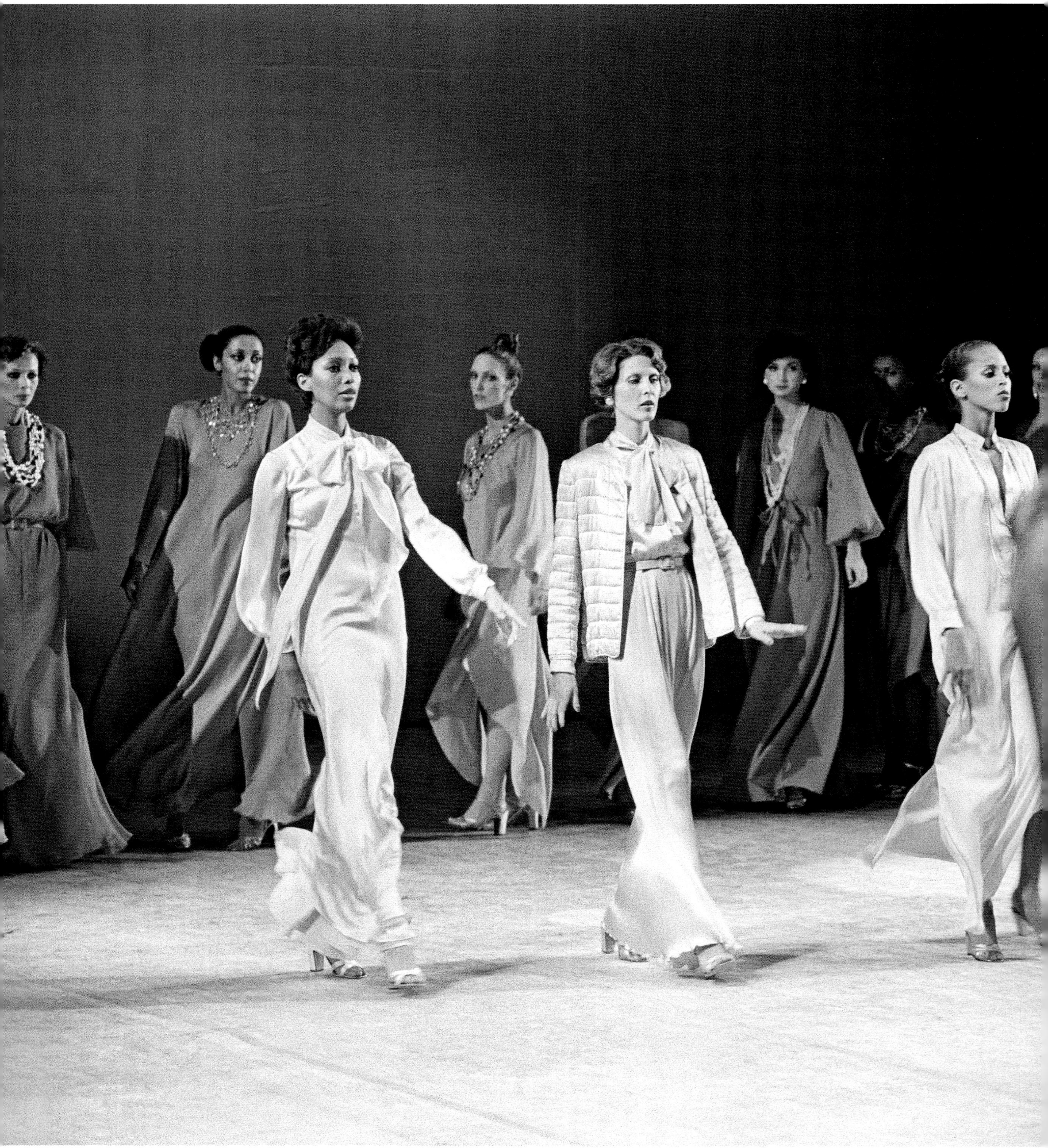

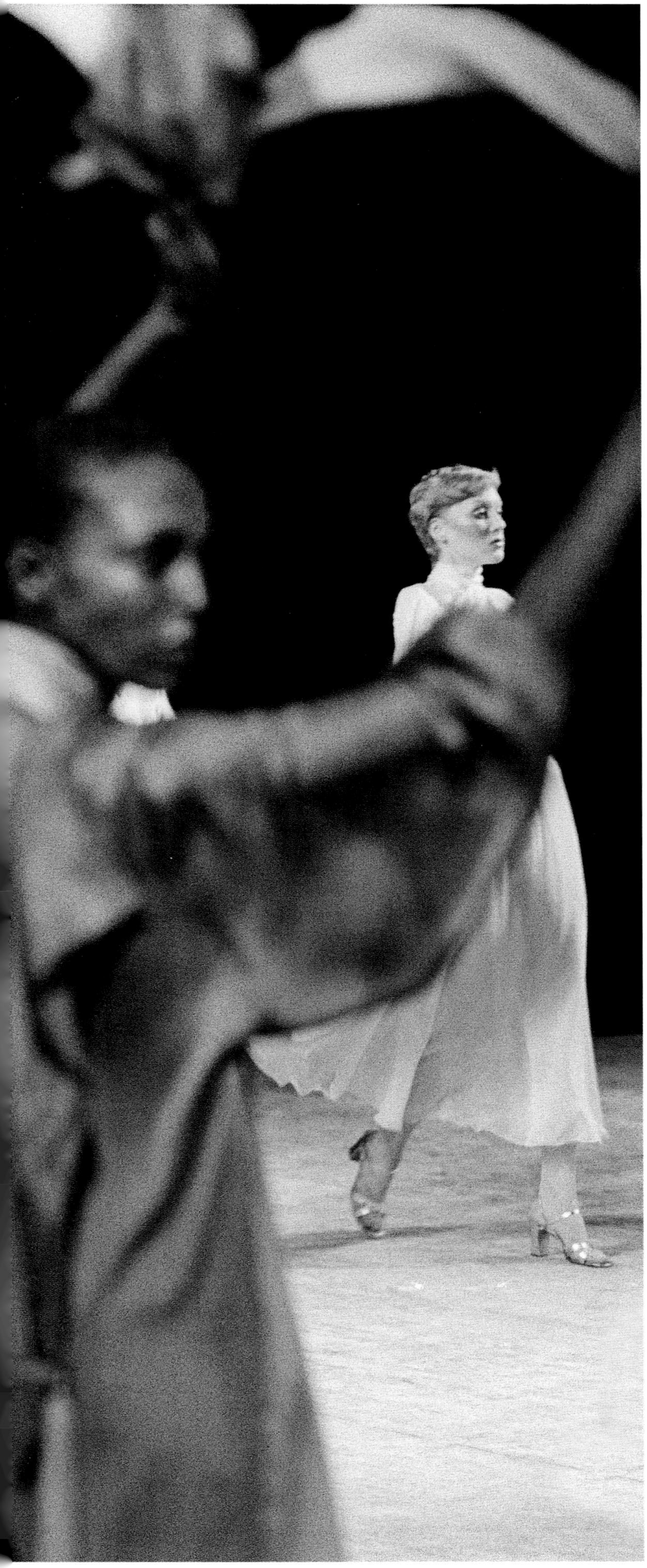

The vibrancy and significance of the Battle of Versailles was recently celebrated when the actress Zendaya paid homage to the event in her 2019 collection for Tommy Hilfiger. One typical color-blocked jersey dress reflected the body-skimming designs of Stephen Burrows, but Zendaya added a contemporary twist with runway models who reflected an American-inflected diversity of body size.

Today, as international boundaries continue to become ever more fluid, the notion of global style is on the rise. The American impact within that sphere is profound. Instead of showing his Spring 2022 collection in Milan, London-born designer Daniel Lee held his ready-to-wear show for Italian company Bottega Veneta in a Detroit movie palace turned parking garage. For the collection, he asked himself "What's American?" and answered by filling the runway with sportswear-inspired looks, Marilyn Monroe's *Seven Year Itch* halter dress paired with sneakers, and puffer coats with baggy pants. Another fabled French couture house, Balenciaga, recently eschewed Paris Fashion Week to premiere its 2022 collection by Demna Gvasalia, a native of the country of Georgia, via a specially commissioned twenty-minute episode of *The Simpsons* that revolved around Marge Simpson's fantasy of owning a couture dress. Paris couture house Balmain announced a collaboration with the toymaker Mattel involving the all-American Barbie doll in January 2022. Perhaps the ultimate tribute to global American influence is the 2021 collection designed by Alessandro Michele, who brought his "Gucci Love Parade" to Hollywood Boulevard. For an evening, Michele filled Hollywood—the "American Olympus," as he calls it—with his visions of Marilyn Monroe, Elizabeth Taylor, and cowboys.

left Battle of Versailles Fashion Show at the Palace of Versailles, 1973, featuring American designers Stephen Burrows, Halston, Oscar de la Renta, Bill Blass, and Anne Klein.

overleaf Tommy Hilfiger, Tommy X Zendaya ensemble, Runway Look 64, Spring 2019. Silk and polyester. PVH Archives.

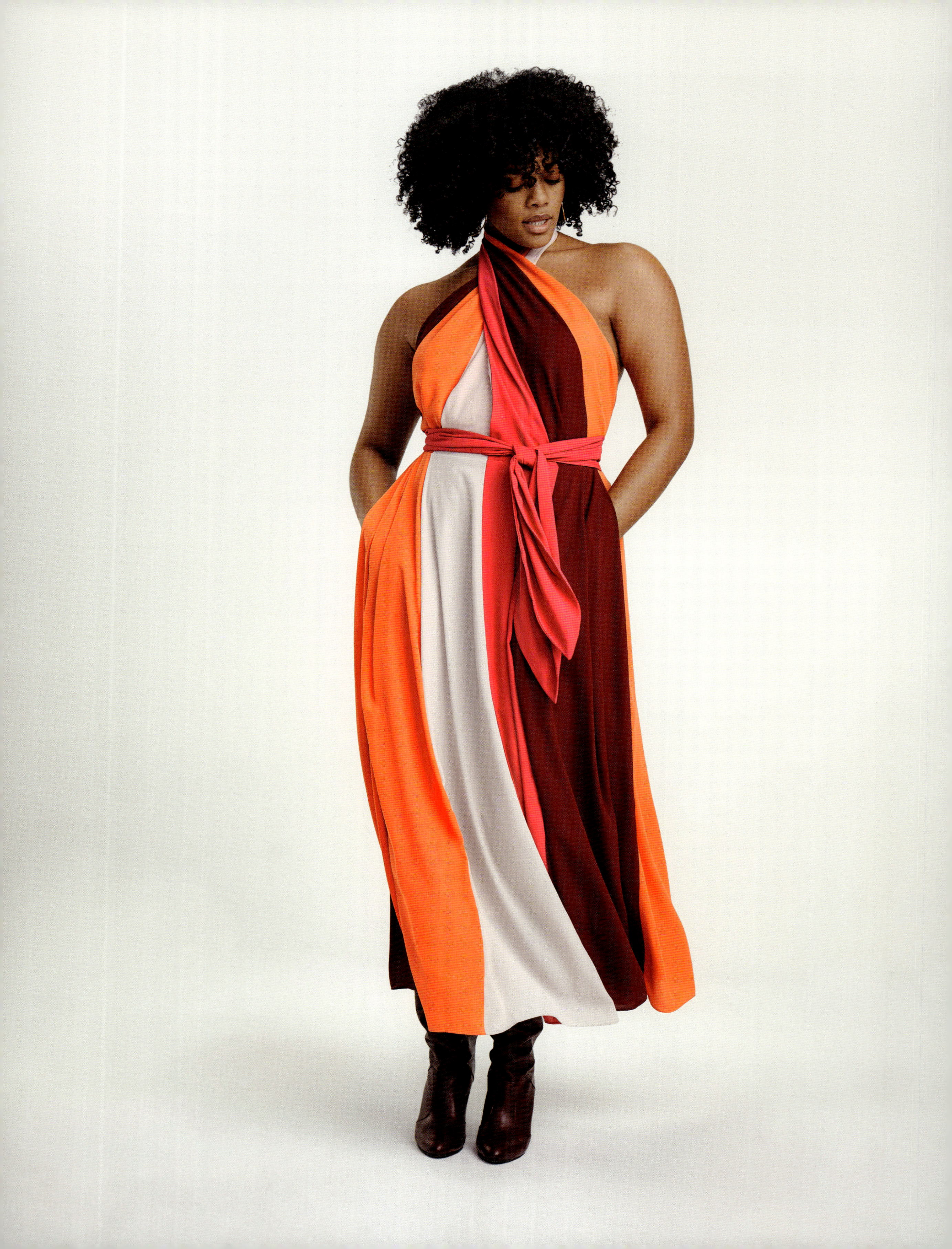

NOTES

1 Dorothy Shaver, "Speech to Members of the Fashion Group," ca. early 1950s. Dorothy Shaver Papers, Box 7, Folder 34, Archives Center, National Museum of American History, Smithsonian Institution, Washington, DC.

2 Tiffany Webber-Hanchett, "Dorothy Shaver: Promoter of 'The American Look,'" *Dress* 30 (2003): 85.

3 Sarah Josepha Hale, quoted in Melanie Kirkpatrick, *Lady Editor Sarah Josepha Hale and the Making of the American Modern Woman* (New York: Encounter Books, 2021), 47.

4 City of New York, "1898–1948: Fifty Years of Fashion," in *Golden Anniversary of Fashion: 1898–1948*, Official Jubilee Edition (New York: Mayor's Committee for the Commemoration of the Golden Anniversary of the City of New York, 1948), n.p.

5 Alison Matthews David, "*Vogue*'s New World: American Fashionability and the Politics of Style," *Fashion Theory* 3, no. 6 (2006): 13–14.

6 Michelle Tolini Finamore, *Hollywood before Glamour: Fashion in American Silent Film* (London: Palgrave Macmillan, 2013), 57.

7 For more on the movement in American art to look to Native design sources for "modern" approaches, see Amber-Dawn Bear Robe's essay in this volume, "Indigenous Fashion: Every Garment Has a Story."

8 Edward Bok, "Names of the Nine Prize Winners and Descriptions of Their Designs," *New York Times*, February 23, 1913.

9 Elizabeth Hawes, *Fashion Is Spinach* (New York: Random House, 1938), 13, 74.

10 Salvatore Ferragamo, *Shoemaker of Dreams: The Autobiography of Salvatore Ferragamo* (London: George G. Harrap & Co., 1957), 36.

11 Ferragamo, *Shoemaker of Dreams*, 47.

12 Maureen Turim, "Designing Women: The Emergence of the New Sweetheart Line," *Wide Angle* 6, no. 2 (1984): 4–11.

13 From a *San Francisco Chronicle* article quoted in "The Fashion Flight—California Comes to Paris," Aenigma, accessed February 19, 2022, https://www.aenigma-images.com/2017/02/fashion-flight/.

14 Mary Ann Crenshaw, "Levi Strauss with a French Accent Is Yves Saint Laurent," *Rags* 6 (November 1970): 26–28.

15 Eleanor Lambert, *World of Fashion: People, Places, Resources* (New York: R. R. Bowker, 1976), 237.

16 For more on ingrained racial bias in the fashion system, see Xuxa Rodríguez's essay in this volume, "Refashioning the World: Whiteness, Racial Plagiarism, and Diversifying the Future."

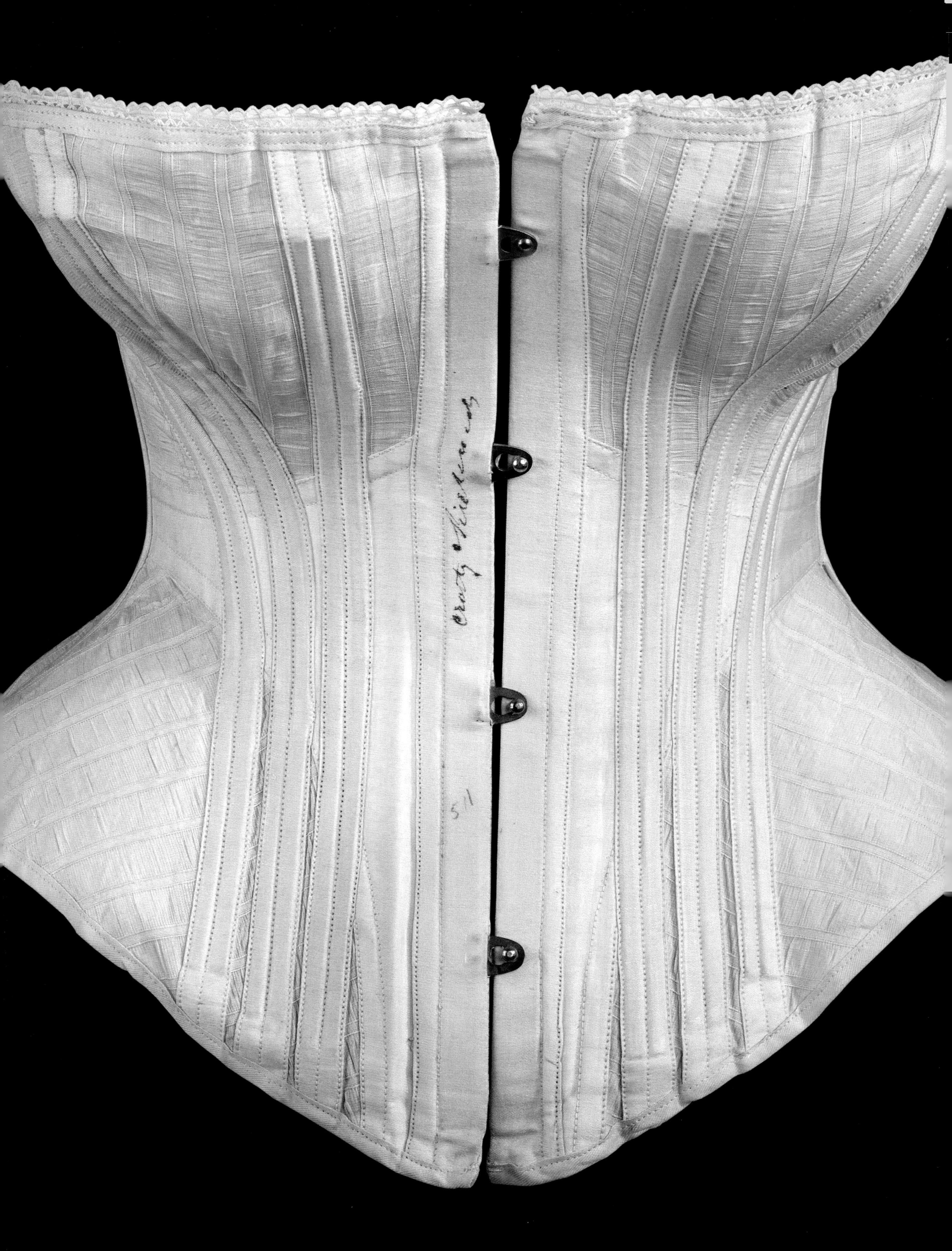

Shaping the Standard Body

SIZING IN AMERICAN FASHION

Emma McClendon
and Lauren Downing Peters

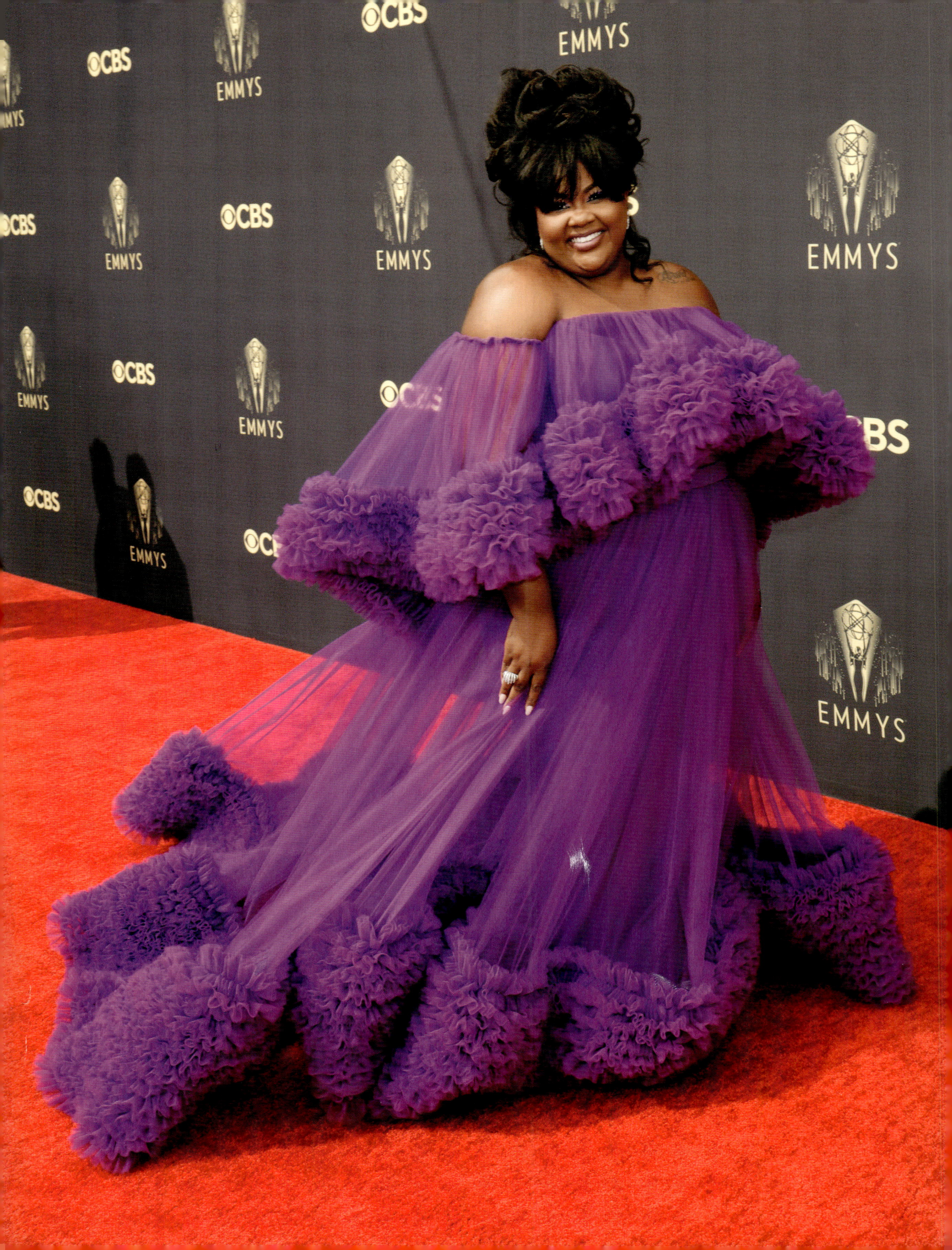
EMMYS
CBS

Over the last decade or so, American designers have led the charge in fashioning a more inclusive industry. In 2021, for instance, the actress and comedian Nicole Byer, who self-identifies as plus-size, took to the Emmys red carpet in a dramatic purple Christian Siriano gown that flouted the design edicts of figure flattery. Rather than hugging her curves and creating a conventional hourglass silhouette, Siriano's dress took up space and commanded attention. While the gown seemed to suggest that designers had finally cast aside the moralizing edicts of plus-size design, the gesture was a relative outlier. More often than not, both within high fashion and the mass market, size inclusivity has been met with resistance and even hostility. When model and activist Lauren Chan walked for Chromat in 2017, for example, angry netizens argued that her swimsuit-clad, size-sixteen body had no place in a fashion show. The social media backlash to Chan's presence on a New York Fashion Week runway—a space that, historically, has been the purview of slender bodies—could easily be written off as a byproduct of a particularly American brand of weight bias that has grown increasingly outmoded amid the rise of the body positivity movement. But such a reaction has deep roots: slenderness has, for a very long time, been upheld as the "norm" in American fashion. Fashion design practices affect which bodies get to participate in fashion, most pointedly in the way garments are sized.

Sizing should be understood as a medium that legitimized deeply ingrained biases about what constituted a "good" or "normal" body in American culture.

Sizing is too often glossed over in histories of American fashion. If mentioned, it is typically framed as a democratizing force that facilitated the mass manufacture and consumption of clothing in the United States. Yet, the cultural shift that occurred when consumers began to think of their bodies as *sized* is equally important. Prior to the advent of sizing, garment fit was a highly personal and intimate process that was either negotiated by the tailor or dressmaker in consultation with the wearer, or something that the wearer attempted to navigate themselves at home. The purportedly scientific sizing systems introduced during the nineteenth century alienated wearers from the process

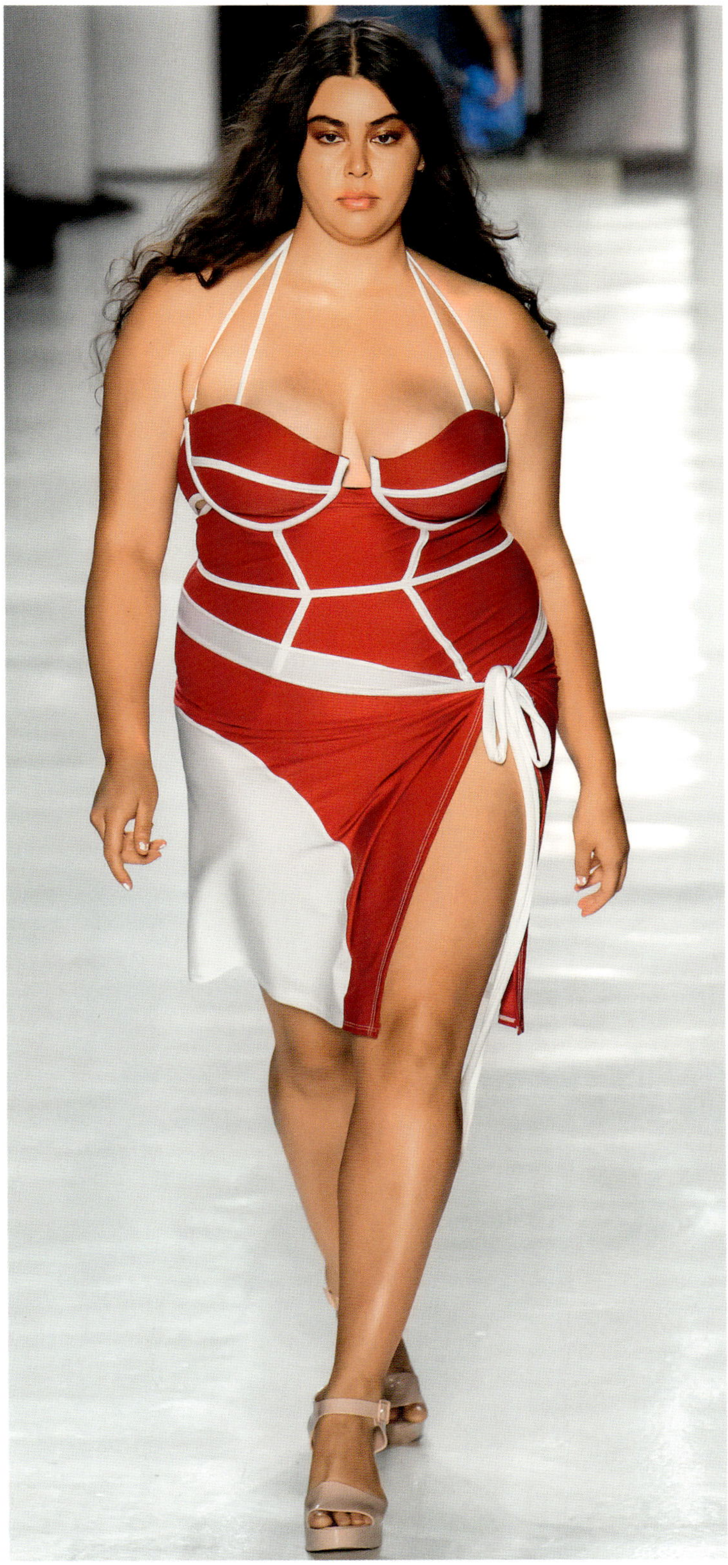

above Chromat, swimsuit worn by Lauren Chan, "Serenity" collection, Spring/Summer 2018.

opposite Christian Siriano, "Dress for Nicole Byer," Emmy Awards Red Carpet, 2021. Silk tulle. Courtesy of Christian Siriano.

while simultaneously establishing categories of bodies that set new parameters for normalcy. Despite the claims made to the scientific objectivity of the earliest sizing systems, however, most were based on a narrow range of body types. As a result, a perfect fit was out of reach for most Americans. Sizing should therefore be understood as a medium that legitimized deeply ingrained biases about what constituted a "good" or "normal" body in American culture.

THE NINETEENTH CENTURY PATTERNS PAVE THE WAY

Standardized sizing, as we know it, originated in the grading systems devised for mass-manufactured paper patterns throughout the nineteenth century. During this period, American women had very few options for where and how to obtain fashionable clothing. If you wanted something entirely new, you had to first purchase fabric and then either take it to a dressmaker or make your own clothes at home. If you were doing the latter, you would probably begin by deconstructing an old garment and then use the pieces both as stencils to mark and cut new pieces, and as a guide for assembling and sewing the new garment.

By the 1860s, a wide array of tools appeared on the American market that purported to simplify this process through a mathematical system based on "scientifically" determined proportions of the female body. The tools came in the form of large, perforated cards or paper diagrams, such as Justin Clavé's proportional tool from 1859. Periodicals like *Godey's Lady's Book* and *Harper's Bazaar* also included patterns in their issues, but these were miniaturized to fit within the magazine's pages and thus needed to be mathematically scaled up. Home sewing skills and knowledge varied widely, and these methods could be incredibly difficult to implement for the amateur home sewer.

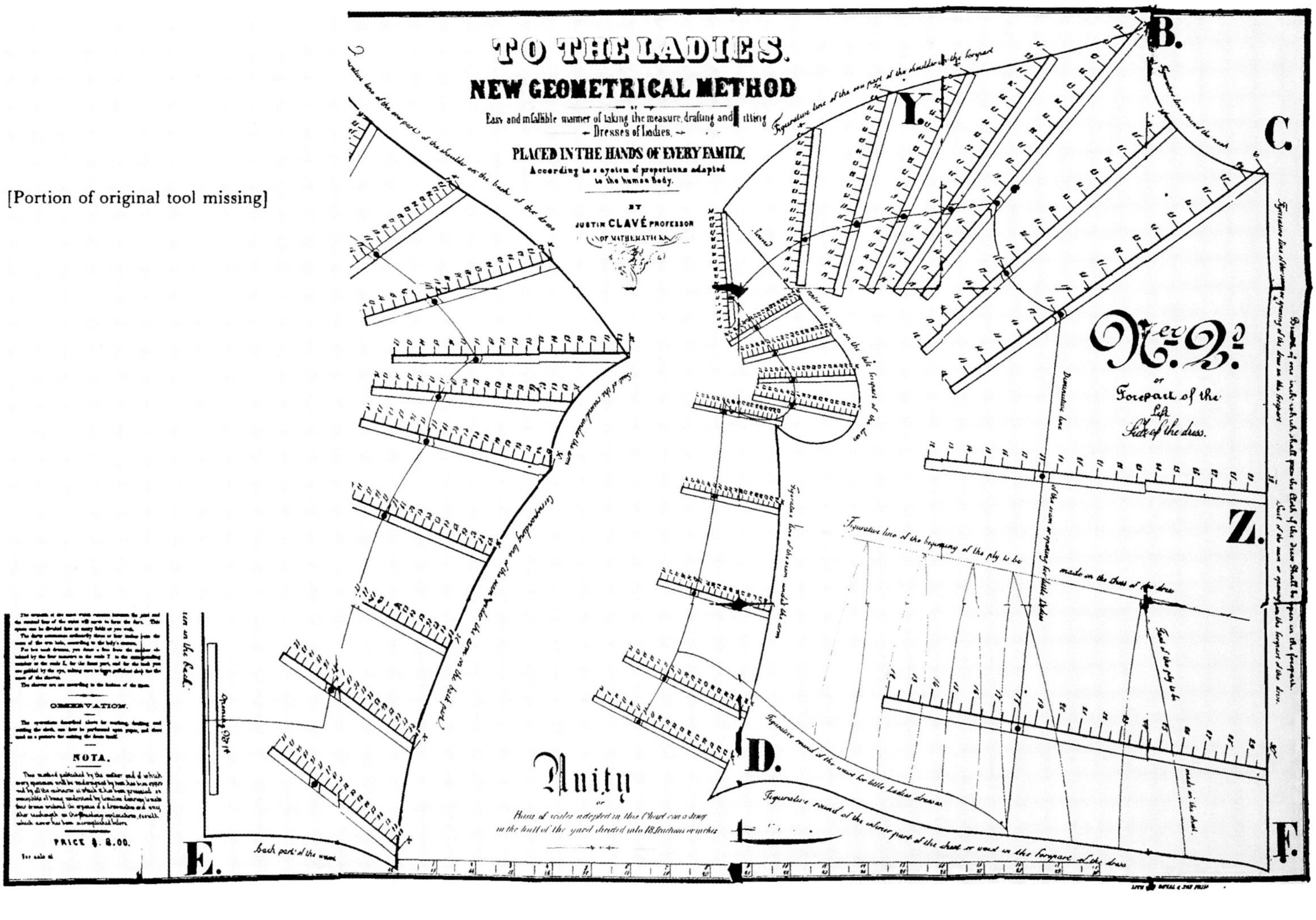

Instructions and tool for Justin Clavé's proportional system for garment making, printed in Philadelphia, 1859 (pictured in Kidwell, 1979, p. 26). Library of Congress.

Complicating matters further, this "proportional method" of sizing required a great deal of customization. It used only one measurement (e.g., the waist or bust) as a starting point, which then determined all of the other drafting points. For example, if a home sewer determined she had a thirty-six-inch bust, she would tick all the perforated spots that corresponded to a thirty-six, tracing a pattern that had a waist, length, shoulder, neckline, and sleeve in a size that the tool's maker had predetermined *should* fit a woman's body with a thirty-six-inch bust. Not surprisingly, this rarely worked. As historian Claudia Kidwell has noted, the "perforated proportional system worked well only for a few women . . . who conformed to the creator's notions regarding proportional figures."[1]

> **Proportional methods, rooted in Enlightenment-era notions of beauty, symmetry, and ratio drawn from fine art and sculpture, were based on theories of "correct" proportions rather than on real women's bodies.**

Proportional methods, rooted in Enlightenment-era notions of beauty, symmetry, and ratio drawn from fine art and sculpture, were based on theories of "correct" proportions rather than on real women's bodies.[2] Unlike the menswear industry, which could draw upon a large data set of male body measurements compiled during the Civil War to create a sizing system for menswear, there were no such data sets for women's bodies until the late 1880s. Even then, the sets were produced by elite women's colleges such as Vassar, Smith, and Pratt and were therefore highly biased toward the proportions of young, white, affluent women.[3] For all but the rare few, alterations were therefore necessary to make garments based on proportional sizing systems actually fit. Further complicating matters, it would not always be clear to the novice what aspect of the pattern needed to be tweaked or how to go about doing so. As a result, most women relied on someone with experience and training to get a precise fit.

Experiments with proportional sizing methods for home sewing occurred on both sides of the Atlantic in the nineteenth century, but a key shift took place during the 1860s when the New York-based companies Butterick and Madame Demorest began selling paper patterns that were mass-produced in graded (i.e., proportionally scaled) sizes. The patterns came precut and presized, so that there was no longer a need to trace pieces from a perforated card or scaled-down chart. All the home sewer had to do was measure her bust, waist, or hip, compare that to the company's chart, and order her numerical size. A few weeks later, the graded paper pattern appeared in her mailbox, ready to use. This innovation simplified the process of making the pattern itself, and, in doing so, did democratize fashion by making the latest shifts in silhouette more accessible to a wider public that included those outside urban centers who ordered the patterns by mail. These patterns, however, were still based on proportional systems and therefore did not fit the vast majority of women.

The schism between the ideal and the reality of the sizing technology is apparent in the many dressmaking guides and advice columns of the period. For example, in a March 1888 column for *Ladies' Home Journal*, the author Emma Hooper wrote that, despite the wealth of paper patterns on the market, a good fit was still difficult to achieve: "many a little thing about making a dress puzzles weary brains, and yet, these same little things are of vital importance."[4] Hooper gives several examples of these "little things," including a particular cut that a woman with a full bust will need to make under the arm, or a piece of wadding a woman with an asymmetrical shoulder line will need to add around the neck to fit a bodice correctly.[5] In other words, the mass-produced patterns were merely starting points, or rough guides to shape and silhouette, that were relatively well-fitting compared to whatever a completely untrained amateur home sewer might try to create alone. Expertise, advice, and intervention remained necessary to actually fit garments to an individual woman's body.

Some pattern companies, in rare bouts of introspection, did include caveats that alterations would be necessary. For example, when the *Ladies' Home Journal* launched its own sized patterns in 1905, the announcement explained, "Each pattern is cut in correct proportions taken from standard sizes of the majority of figures, but in very many cases you will find it absolutely essential to alter it to your own figure."[6] Notably, this disclaimer disappeared after the initial announcement. In later issues, the journal instead warned, "In ordering patterns it is most important that the measurements should be taken according to our method, to secure a good fit."[7] This phrasing placed the onus of the promised "good fit" firmly on the customer's ability to take "correct" measurements according to the magazine's instructions. The instructions explained exactly how to place the tape

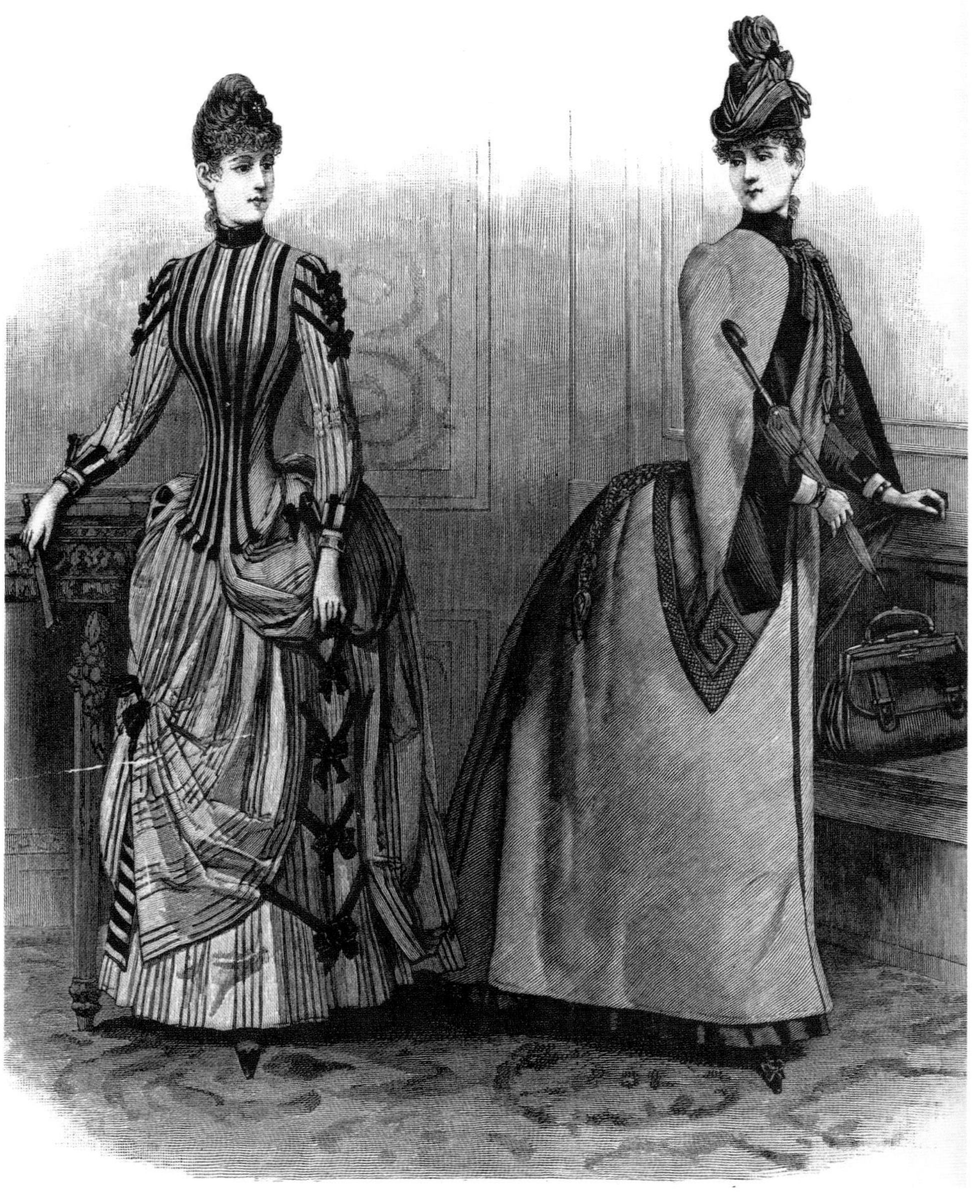

measure and whether to leave it slightly loose or tight in various places. Thus, if a customer complained about an ill-fitting result, the magazine could claim that the customer was inexact in her measuring and did not follow the directions properly. The sizing system wasn't at fault; the consumer was.

Part of the issue facing both at-home sewers and pattern makers of the period was the intricacy of the fashionable silhouette itself. Dresses of the time consisted of a tightly tailored bodice that flowed into a skirt, which cascaded over an equally rigid bustle into a complex arrangement of decorative gathers and folds. The desired fit of the bodice was ideally so tight that it would create a look, in the words of the time, "as though [the wearer] had been melted and poured into it."[8] Crucially, this silhouette was also fitted around a corset. The hard, boned undergarment sculpted the wearer's torso into an exaggerated hourglass, and the bodice was supposed to tightly adhere to these same lines, which required a complex negotiation of darts, seaming, cutting, and wadding that were outside the capacities of some home sewers. With mass-produced patterns, the moment of misfitting (or the moment when the consumer confronted the flaws of the product in how it interacted with her body) took place at home, away from the space of sale. Patterns sold a dream. It was the promise of endless, cheap access to fashion rooted in science and technology. But the promise was a lie—a marketing tool disguised as a technological breakthrough.

above Illustration from "Winter Day and Evening Toilettes," *Harper's Bazaar*, December 15, 1888 (cover).

opposite Dr. Warner's Coraline Corset Trade Card, 1890s. Private Collection.

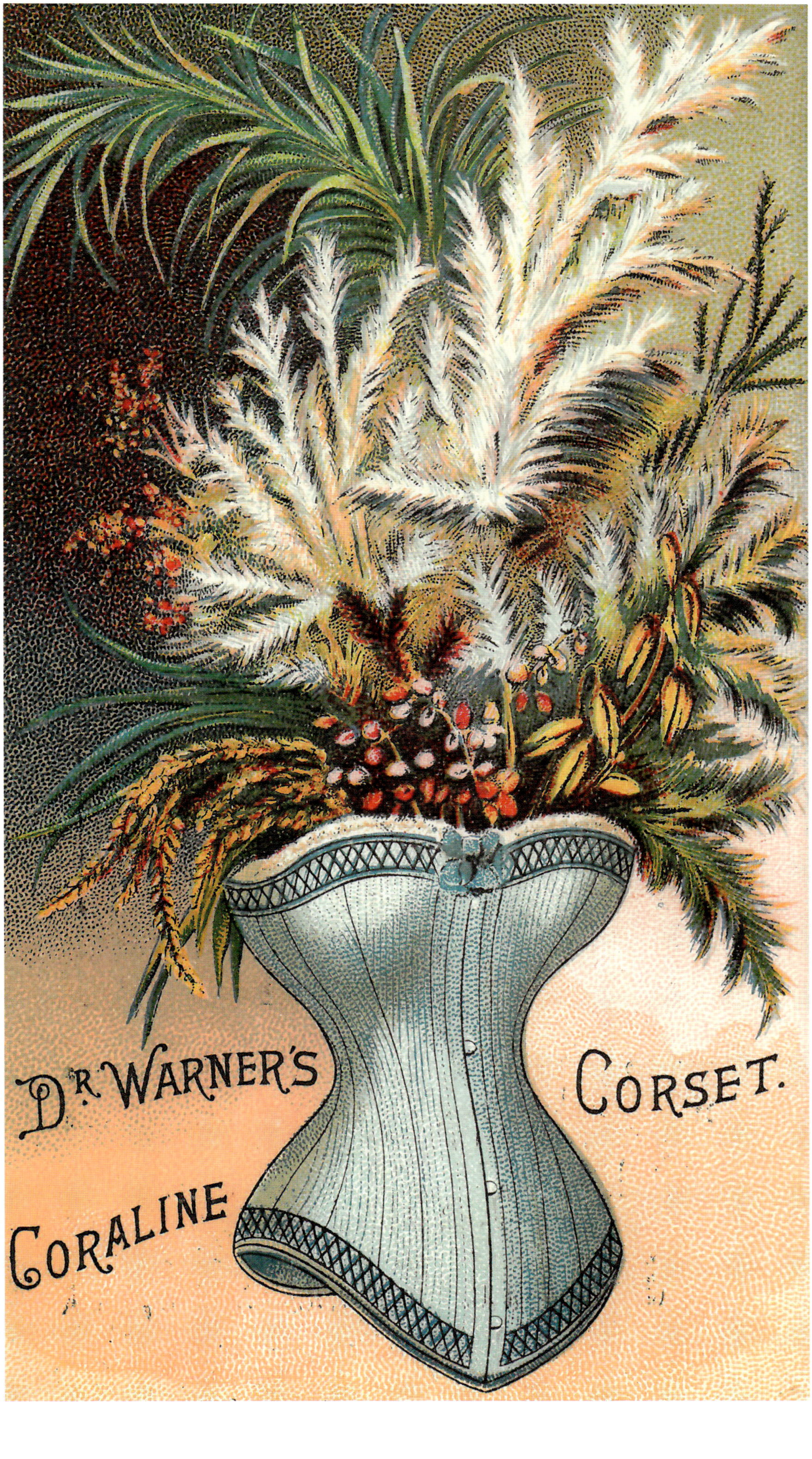

DR. WARNER'S
CORSET.
CORALINE

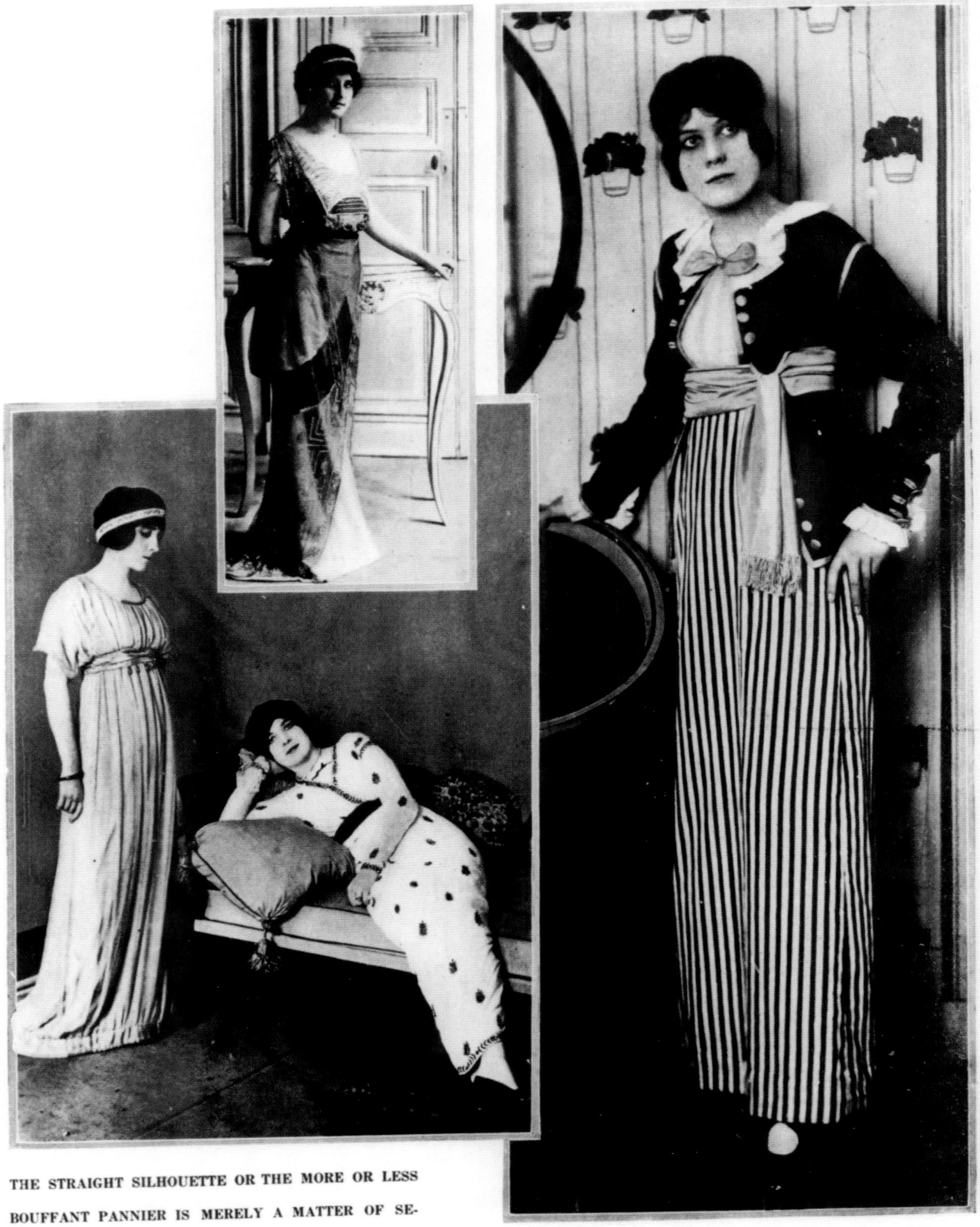

THE STRAIGHT SILHOUETTE OR THE MORE OR LESS BOUFFANT PANNIER IS MERELY A MATTER OF SELECTING ONE'S COUTURIER — CERTAIN DESIGNERS OF NOTE REFUSE TO CONSIDER A SINGLE BROKEN LINE, WHILE OTHERS ARE ALL FOR DRAPERIES

For descriptions see page 92

By the turn of the twentieth century, the same graded sizes of patterns had been integrated into nascent ready-to-wear production. With the advent of other new production technologies such as industrial sewing machines and automated fabric-cutting machines, all of the elements that would enable the mass mechanization of garment manufacturing had fallen into place. But the shift from custom-made to ready-made clothing was neither seamless nor instantaneous. Fit remained an issue that was negotiated through a network of alteration services, dressmakers, and amateur home sewers during an awkward period of transition that lasted through the 1920s.[9]

THE TWENTIETH CENTURY
TOWARD GREATER SPECIALIZATION

It would be the streamlining of the fashionable silhouette that finally enabled the shift from mass customization to mass manufacturing.[10] As the rigid lines of the Gilded Age gave way to the more softly draped styles that fell into vogue in the early 1900s, mass manufacturing became more financially and technologically viable because patterns had grown simpler. Rather than attempting to fit a tightly corseted hourglass shape, patterns were now cut on more or less straight lines. American manufacturers thus began to embrace the idea that "garments could be made en masse . . . for anonymous bodies, according to a limited set of predetermined sizes."[11]

By 1910, American women could buy a variety of cheap, ready-made garments—from corsets to shirtwaists to suits—in a range of standard sizes from mail-order catalogues and department stores. Yet, even as retailers advertised perfect fits, there always seemed to be limits to perfection. For instance, while accurate bust measurements were guaranteed, it was assumed that hemlines could easily be lengthened or shortened. Additionally, "standard" sizes, which typically ranged from thirty-two to forty-two inches at the bust, were relatively narrow in scope. Individuals whose bodies fell outside standard ranges were therefore instructed to purchase from custom departments at an additional cost.[12] Although America's ready-made clothing industry held the promise of leveling class distinctions and making Americans the "best dressed average people in the world,"[13] not unlike the paper-pattern industry that preceded it, it was hampered by flawed assumptions and inefficiencies.

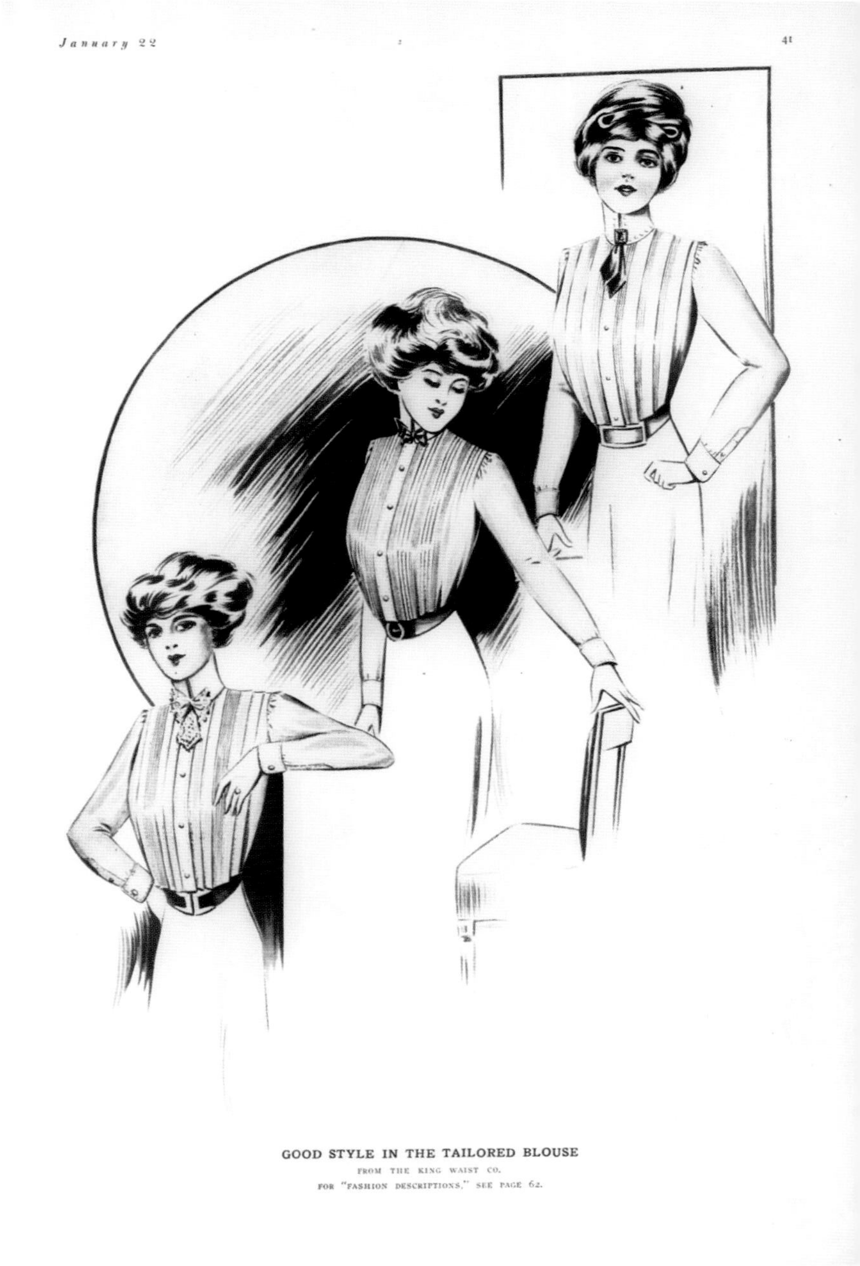

above Illustration from "Fashion: Good Style in the Tailored Blouse," *Vogue*, January 22, 1910.

opposite Page from "Fashion: The Straight Silhouette," *Vogue*, September 15, 1912.

4 *Women's Wear* Friday, July 9, 1915

Scientific Specialization in Stouts

A. Malsin Believes That It Is Impossible to Fit All Types of Stouts According to a Single Standard.

Creates Three Distinct Types of Stouts for Ready-Mades Base on Actual Measurements of 4,000 Women.

GRANTED, as a thing obvious to any observer, that there are many stout women among the possible customers of the ready-to-wear garment stores, what is their approximate proportion to the number of the regulation size customers? What are the laws of nature in shaping the stout figures? What are the proportions and correlations of the bust and waist measurement of stouts? Finally,—what is a stout?

A number of years ago Albert Malsin, established already as manufacturer and retailer of maternity garments under the style of Lane Bryant, set out to solve these questions in an uncontrovertible way, arriving at conclusions on which he has faith enough to base his entire business at the present

To be able to estimate demand on any article in the percentage of the number of customers would be a great benefit both to manufacturer and retailer alike, as fore knowledge of such facts would regulate production and reduce waste, in the shape of left over stock, to the minimum.

No Ordinary Grading Possible in Stouts.

"People ready to start manufacturing or selling ready-made garments for stouts must bear one thing in mind, above all," says Mr. Malsin, "namely, that it is impossible to make such garments by the ordinary process of grading, as it is in use for regulation sizes. To satisfy myself on this point. gave orders to a number of designers to make stouts by ordinary 'grading.' The results were ridiculous. Sizes of 50 bust, for instance, had the shoulder reaching way down to the upper part of the arm with sleeves fit for an elephant.

Exact Measurements of 4,000 Stout Women.

"I soon found out that I would have to approach the problem of manufacturing ready-to-wear garments for stouts from a different angle and, after measuring 4,000 stout women customers of mine to all detail necessary in building a garment, I was able to evolve a grading system, different from that in use for regulation size garments.

Three Main Types of Stout Figures.

The measurements thus conducted for years brought out facts which made him believe that it is impossible to fit all types of stouts by the same system, and accordingly he classified stout figures into three principal types, according to their make-up, with a different set of patterns introduced for each type. While the types were suggested by the difference in the proportions of the body, Mr. Malsin says, the demarcational line between them was arbitrary for the sake of convenience, as well as selecting the bust measurement as a basis for the entire system, has been arbitrary.

The three types, as used by him in his work shop are:

Type A—The woman with a big bust and comparatively small hips and abdomen;

Type B—Women who are stout all around;

Type C—Women with flat bust and large abdomen and hips, as often found in those of advanced age.

How Stout figures Are Shaped.

With a propensity for mathematics (he was an engineer before starting in the garment manufacturing business) Mr. Malsin figured out the proportion of the different sizes among the stout figures.

In bust size 44 inches,
actual measurement;......—of Type A 35 per cent have 34 1-2 waist.
—of Type B 37 per cent have 36 inch waist.
—of Type C 28 per cent have 38 1-2 waist.

In bust size 46 inches,
actual measurement;......—of Type A 32 per cent have

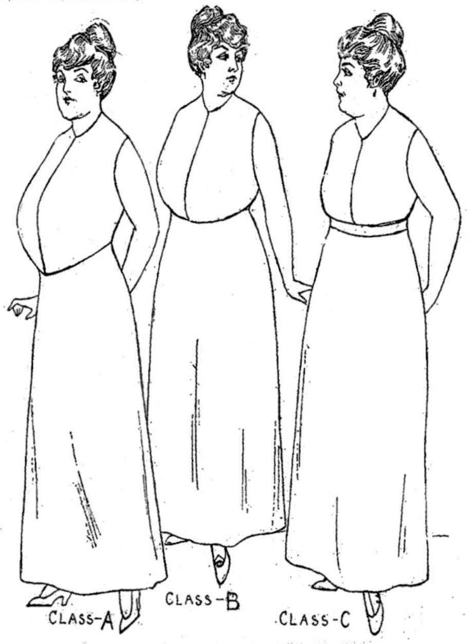

Three Principal Classes of Stout Figures as Graded by Albert Malsin

Table of Grading for Stouts

CLASS "A."

Bust.	Waist.	Hips.	Waist front.	Waist back.	Bust pts.	Shldrs.
42	32½	46	18¾	15	12¾	5¼
44	34½	48	18¾	15	12¾	5¼
46	36	50	19½	15¾	13	5½
48	27½	52	20¼	16	13⅜	5½
50	39¼	53	21	16½	13¾	5¾
52	40½	54½	31¼	17	13¾	6
54	42	56	22	17	14	6
56	43½	57½	23	17	14¼	6⅛
58	45	59	23	17	14¾	6½

CLASS "B."

Bust.	Waist.	Hips.	Waist front.	Waist back.	Bust pts.	Shldrs.
42	32	45	16¾	15	10½	5¼
44	33	46	17	15	10¾	5¼
46	34	47	17	15	11¼	5½
48	35	48	17½	15	11½	5½
50	36	49	17½	15¼	11¾	5¾
52	37	50	17½	15¼	12¼	6
54	38	51	18	15¼	12½	6
56	39	52	18	15½	14¾	6⅛
58	40	53	18½	15½	15¼	6⅛

CLASS "C."

Bust.	Waist.	Hips.	Waist front.	Waist back.	Bust pts.	Shldrs.
42	35	45	16	14½	10	5¼
44	36½	50	16	14½	10	5¼
46	38	52	17	15	10½	5½
48	39½	54	17½	15½	10¾	5½
50	41½	55	18½	16	11	5¾
52	42½	56½	19½	16½	11½	6
54	44	58	20	16½	11¾	6
56	45½	60	20	16½	11¾	6⅛
58	47	62	20	16½	11¾	6⅛

A key problem was the fact that, well into the twentieth century, a thirty-six-inch bust remained the standard measure from which all other sizes were graded. In industry trade journals, this base measurement was grudgingly referred to as the "perfect thirty-six" because, as one manufacturer explained to *Women's Wear Daily* in 1917, it was "an idealist's conception of a perfectly formed woman." He continued to explain how garment manufacturers continued to produce garments "based on the false premise that there are living De Milos to whom to sell perfect 36s." As a result, it was estimated that upwards of ten percent of mail orders were returned and ninety percent of ready-made garments required aftermarket alterations (the cost of which was absorbed by shops and department stores that guaranteed perfect fits).[14] Although the cost burden had shifted from manufacturers to consumers by the late 1920s,[15] perfunctory alterations wasted time and labor and also made for unhappy consumers who were increasingly expecting a perfect fit off the rack.

These expectations, of course, were set by retailers who continued to promise perfect fits in advertising and marketing materials even as they acknowledged behind the scenes that the fleshy body was ill-suited to the practices and conventions of mass manufacturing. Indeed, as Peter Corrigan observes, in an industry underpinned by theories of scientific management, and which aimed to increase efficiency (and therefore profits) through standardization, the body proved to be a pressure point because "ready-made clothing [demanded] ready-made bodies."[16] Yet, even

above "Scientific Specialization in Stouts," *Women's Wear*, July 9, 1915.

as mass manufacturing proved to be poorly equipped for dealing with the diversity of American bodies, there occurred a crucial, if subtle, shift in the first decades of the twentieth century. As suggested by *Vogue* in a 1923 beauty column about the rise of the slender beauty ideal, this shift occurred precisely in 1908 when, Parisian designers (figuratively) issued the edict, "You must be slender, Madame." The growing popularity of mass-manufactured, one-piece dresses in the first decades of the twentieth century all but necessitated a svelte, youthful physique. As a result, *Vogue* claimed that, seemingly overnight, fashion magazines began filling up with advertisements for weight-loss products as women began trying to fit their bodies to their clothes, rather than fitting their clothes to their bodies.[17]

Although there was no shortage of quick fixes and cure-alls that promised to help women "reduce" so they could fit their bodies into the era's fashionably streamlined silhouettes, a number of manufacturers, having realized that good fit remained out of reach of most American women, set out to create new, ever-more-specialized sizing systems to accommodate a wider range of body shapes and sizes. Albert Malsin—an early pioneer of "stoutwear," or the precursor to what is today referred to as "plus-size fashion"—was one such innovator who set out to solve problems in fit for the estimated thirty-three percent of American women whose bodies exceeded the largest standard sizes. After measuring as many as one thousand "stout" women in 1915, he created a tripartite sizing system that accommodated proportionate, top-heavy, and bottom-heavy body shapes with bust measurements that ranged from forty-two to fifty-six inches.[18] While stoutwear enjoyed great success throughout the 1910s and '20s, when the fashionable, tubular silhouette was more accommodating of larger bodies, with the return of more body-conscious silhouettes in the 1930s, the stoutwear industry fell into decline and with it, a great deal of knowledge was lost to history.

Throughout the twentieth century, various government entities conducted large-scale sizing surveys with the hope that more data would lead to more accurate sizing systems. In 1939, for instance, the Department of Agriculture conducted a national survey of fifteen thousand American women in order to solve issues in sizing that, as *Time* magazine observed, were costing the American apparel industry upwards of $10 million annually—the reasons for which included, among other things, customer returns.[19] This survey was flawed—for instance, only white women, many of whom were girdled, were measured—and its applications were limited. It produced, however, the key insight that the majority of American women stood under five feet five inches, spurring manufacturers to begin making petites.[20] In 1958, a coordinated effort between the Department of Commerce and garment manufacturers resulted in a commercial standard for women's apparel, but the system was never enforced. As reported in *Women's Wear Daily* that same year, manufacturers were highly critical of the attempt to standardize sizes, citing the cost of overhauling their production methods and fears of alienating loyal consumers.[21] With little industry support, the Department of Commerce officially withdrew the commercial standard in 1983, leaving manufacturers once again to determine their own sizing and grading systems—a move that would lead to a rampant increase in so-called vanity sizing, the practice whereby manufacturers falsely assign smaller sizes to garments to appeal to customers' vanity and thus increase sales.

BEYOND THE "STANDARD" BODY

The history and evolution of standardized sizing in the United States has been defined by attempts to make and remake a system that, at its foundations, is based on a false premise of a "standard" body. Caught in the crosshairs of attempts to correct and refine methods for sizing, grading, and labeling garments, consumers—especially women—gradually became inured to using sizing as a litmus for measuring overall health, beauty, and well-being.

Indeed, alongside other twentieth-century technologies of the body, from scales to height and weight charts, clothes sizing functions as yet another tool for measuring and categorizing bodies as either "normal" or "deviant."[22] Throughout the nineteenth and twentieth centuries, sizing systems reinforced the idea that "normal" bodies were proportionate with a balanced bust-waist-hip ratio, and that they gained weight with mathematical regularity. Bodies that flouted these conventions were therefore relegated to segregated "petite" and "plus-size" departments or were reflexively punished by so-called fat taxes (premiums charged for the supposed extra cost of materials used for larger sizes) and the cost burden of alterations.

Although attempts to standardize and correct the flaws of proportional-sizing systems fell under the purview of tailors and government agencies throughout much of the twentieth century, today, high-profile designers like Christian Siriano and Rihanna, as well as more mass-market retailers like Universal Standard and Lane Bryant, have led the charge in conceiving of more inclusive approaches to sizing. In addition to consistently using a diverse and inclusive cast of models in his fashion shows, Siriano produces

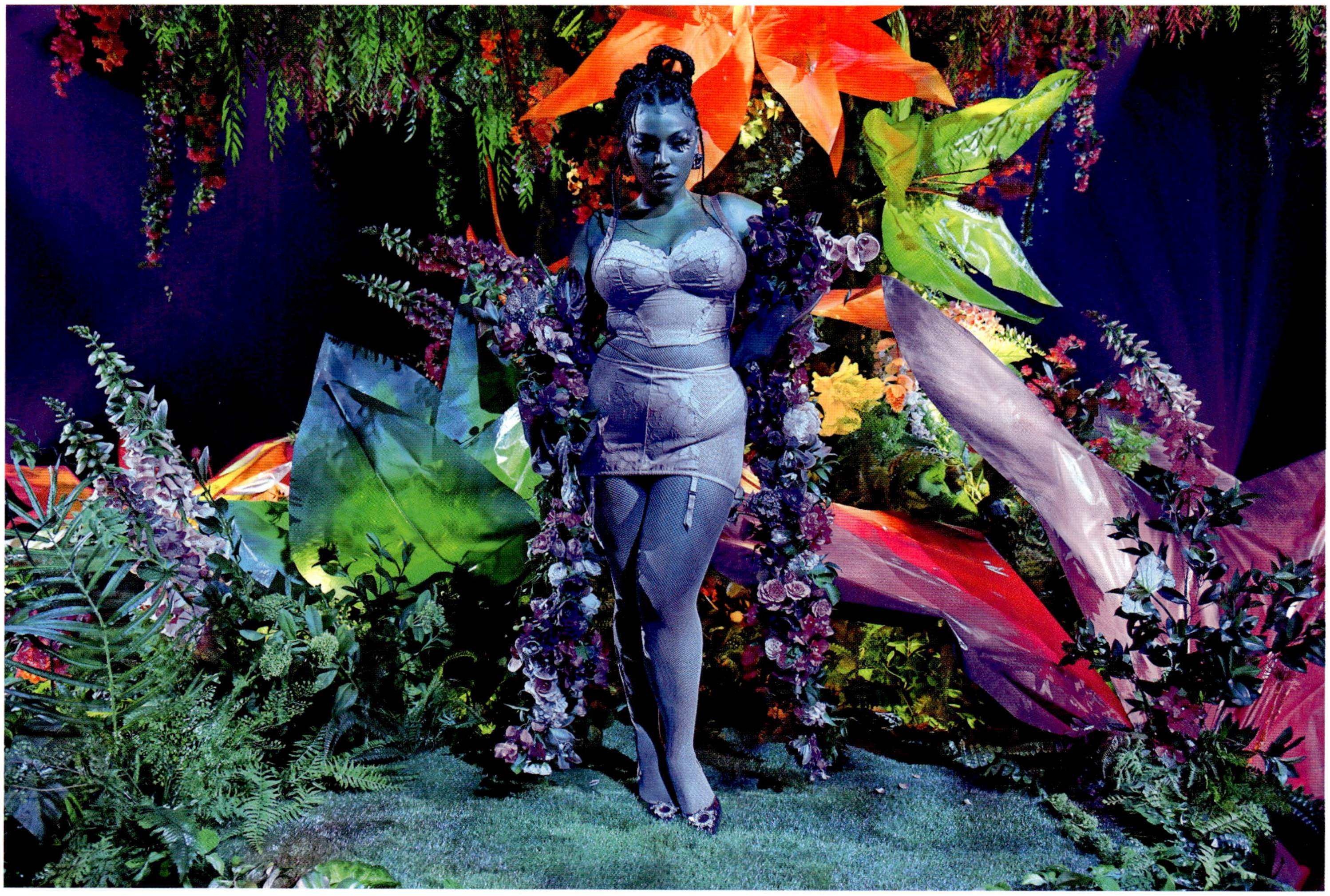

his ready-to-wear line in sizes zero to twenty-eight without any divisions between "straight" and "plus" sizes. He has even worked with retailers such as Moda Operandi to reprogram the luxury e-commerce site's interface so that it can offer a greater range of sizes. Rihanna offers her lingerie line across size divisions and has used the runway to celebrate diverse bodies in dynamic performances that are part fashion show and part concert. Harkening back to old ways of sizing garments, Lane Bryant has recognized that a truly inclusive approach to sizing addresses both size and *shape*. With three different fits available in all of their denim styles, the brand guarantees in their marketing copy that women, no matter where they carry their weight, can achieve a precise and comfortable fit.

Despite these popular examples, there still remains a clear bias toward the thin body in fashion—in the design studio, on the runway, in ad campaigns, on the retail floor, and in fashion schools. If true progress is to be made, the fashion industry, in collaboration with fashion educators, must commit to rethinking the most foundational, seemingly objective assumptions that are made about sizing and garment fit. A key starting point for change is recognizing that the American sizing systems never worked in the first place; they were focused more on ideals and averages than on the fit needs of a heterogeneous population of consumers. Once those working behind the scenes acknowledge this crucial fact, sizing might become a site for innovation (rather than one of consternation) that could lead to better fits, less waste, and more contented consumers overall.

With their prominent places on the global fashion stage, New York City and its biannual fashion weeks have become significant hubs of size diversity. Likewise, across the country in Silicon Valley, 3D body-scanning technologies, mass customization, and virtual fit avatars being built and tested in the labs of tech startups all offer tantalizing glimpses into the future of highly individualized sizing. Perhaps just as the United States gave birth to mass sizing technologies, it can also play a key role in finding a way beyond them.

above Savage X Fenty Fashion Show, Volume 2, 2020.

NOTES

1 Claudia B. Kidwell, *Cutting a Fashionable Fit: Dressmakers' Drafting Systems in the United* States (Washington, DC: Smithsonian Institution, 1979), 28.

2 Claudia B. Kidwell and Margaret C. Christman, *Suiting Everyone: The Democratization of Clothing in America* (Washington, DC: Smithsonian Institution, 1974), 109.

3 Kidwell and Christman, *Suiting Everyone*, 108.

4 Emma M. Hooper, "Hints for Home Dressmakers," *Ladies' Home Journal*, March 1888, 11.

5 Hooper, "Hints for Home Dressmakers."

6 Mrs. Ralston, "What the New Patterns Will Be," *Ladies' Home Journal*, January 1905, 54.

7 Anonymous, "How to Measure for Patterns," *Ladies' Home Journal*, April 1906, 83.

8 Hooper, "Hints for Home Dressmakers," 13.

9 Winifred Aldrich, "History of Sizing Systems and Ready-to-Wear Garments," in *Sizing in Clothing: Developing Effective Sizing Systems for Ready-to-Wear Clothing*, ed. Susan P. Ashdown, 1–56 (Cambridge: Woodhead, 2007), 21.

10 Kidwell, *Cutting a Fashionable Fit*, 98.

11 Nancy L. Green, *Ready-to-Wear, Ready-to-Work: A Century of Industry and Immigrants* (Durham, NC: Duke University Press, 1997), 30.

12 Kidwell and Christman, *Suiting Everyone*, 107–9.

13 Kidwell and Christman, *Suiting Everyone*, 15.

14 "Who's to Blame for Alterations?" *Women's Wear*, August 29, 1917, 25.

15 "Large Majority of Stores Charge for Alterations, Discussions Show—Operation of This Department, However, Generally Result in Loss," *Women's Wear*, May 14, 1926, 8, 39.

16 Peter Corrigan, *The Sociology of Consumption* (London: Sage, 1997), 64.

17 "As You Were, 1892," *Vogue*, January 1923, 172.

18 "Scientific *Specialization* in Stouts," *Women's Wear*, July 9, 1915, 4.

19 "Women: No Boondoggling," *Time*, December 25, 1939.

20 "Let's Standardize Our Size Range," *Women's Wear Daily*, May 24, 1945, 26.

21 Earl Dash, "See Little Chance of Trad O.K. of Government Size Standards," *Women's Wear Daily*, July 28, 1958, 16.

22 Ingrid Jeacle, "Accounting and the Construction of the Standard Body," *Accounting, Organizations and Society* 28 (2003): 357.

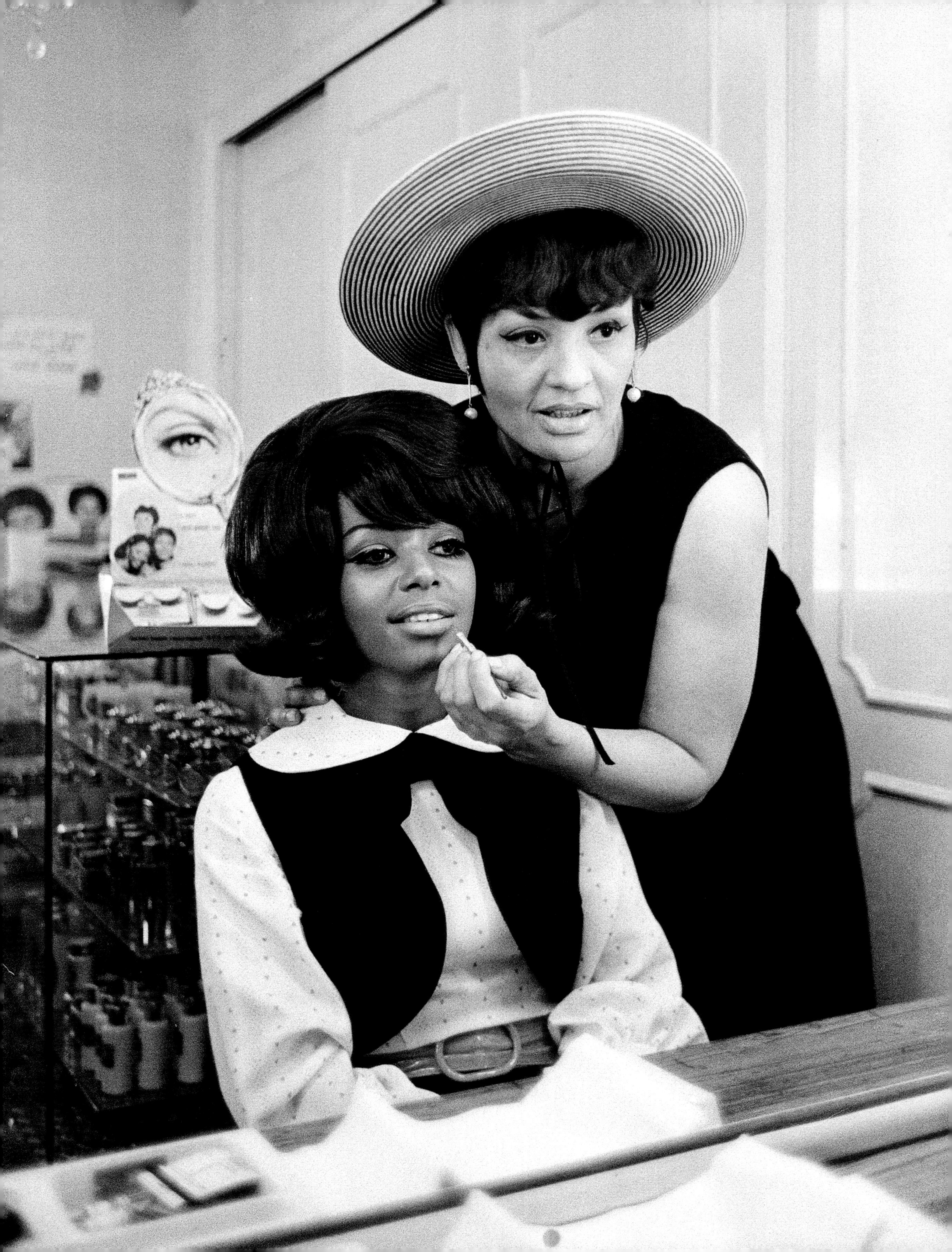

Refashioning the World

WHITENESS, RACIAL PLAGIARISM, AND DIVERSIFYING THE FUTURE

Xuxa Rodríguez

Martine Gutierrez's *Girl Friends (Rosella & Palma)* (2014, printed 2020) is a haunting black-and-white photo series that presents an imagined, undefined relationship between two women, a masculine figure, and the lush villa in which they find themselves. Across the photographs, the women—one Gutierrez in character, the other a mannequin—are shown sharing intimate moments: lying in a bed of hydrangeas in a garden, clad in light-colored lace dresses in bright midday light; standing on the landing of a grand double staircase while wearing dark evening gowns; in repose on the checkerboard floor of a dark room in silky evening slips, illuminated by the light of a door opened to reveal their presence; and sitting together in the garden wearing silk robes and nightgowns as morning streams in through the trees behind them.

All photographs commercially processed in North America beginning in the 1950s would be developed and printed with light balanced to fair and white skin, rendering subjects of color lighter than they actually were.

Each image is a carefully curated scene of leisurely, opulent glamour, with both the light and camera's focus lingering on the women's faces, clothes, hair, and hands as they tuck a lock of hair behind their ears, appear to adjust each other's clothing and coifs, or tenderly place a hand on the other's knee, all in an ambiguously orchestrated dance of touches that could be interpreted as familial, platonic,romantic, or anything in the range of feelings experienced during other intimate relationships or encounters. One image in the series features the human protagonist gazing dramatically at a figure left mostly outside the photo's frame, with its only visible features—a small hand and sculpted draping gown—a kind of shorthand suggesting a statuette of a saint or the Virgin Mary. In the blurred haze of

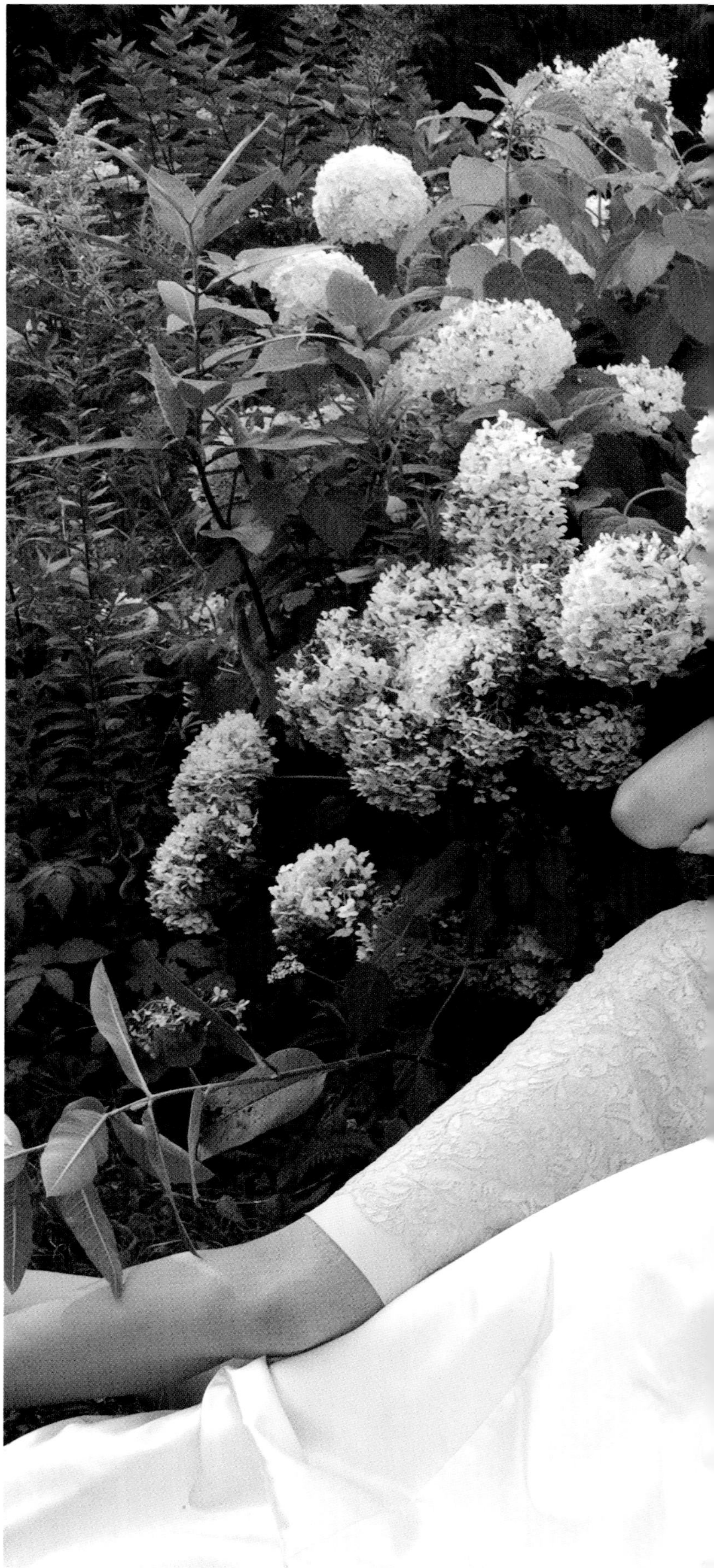

right and pages 142–47 Martine Gutierrez, *Girl Friends (Rosella & Palma)*, 2014 (printed 2020). Archival inkjet print mounted on foamboard, four of seven parts, 9 ½ × 14 ⅛ in. (24.1 × 35.9 cm). Crystal Bridges Museum of American Art, Bentonville, Arkansas, 2020.74.

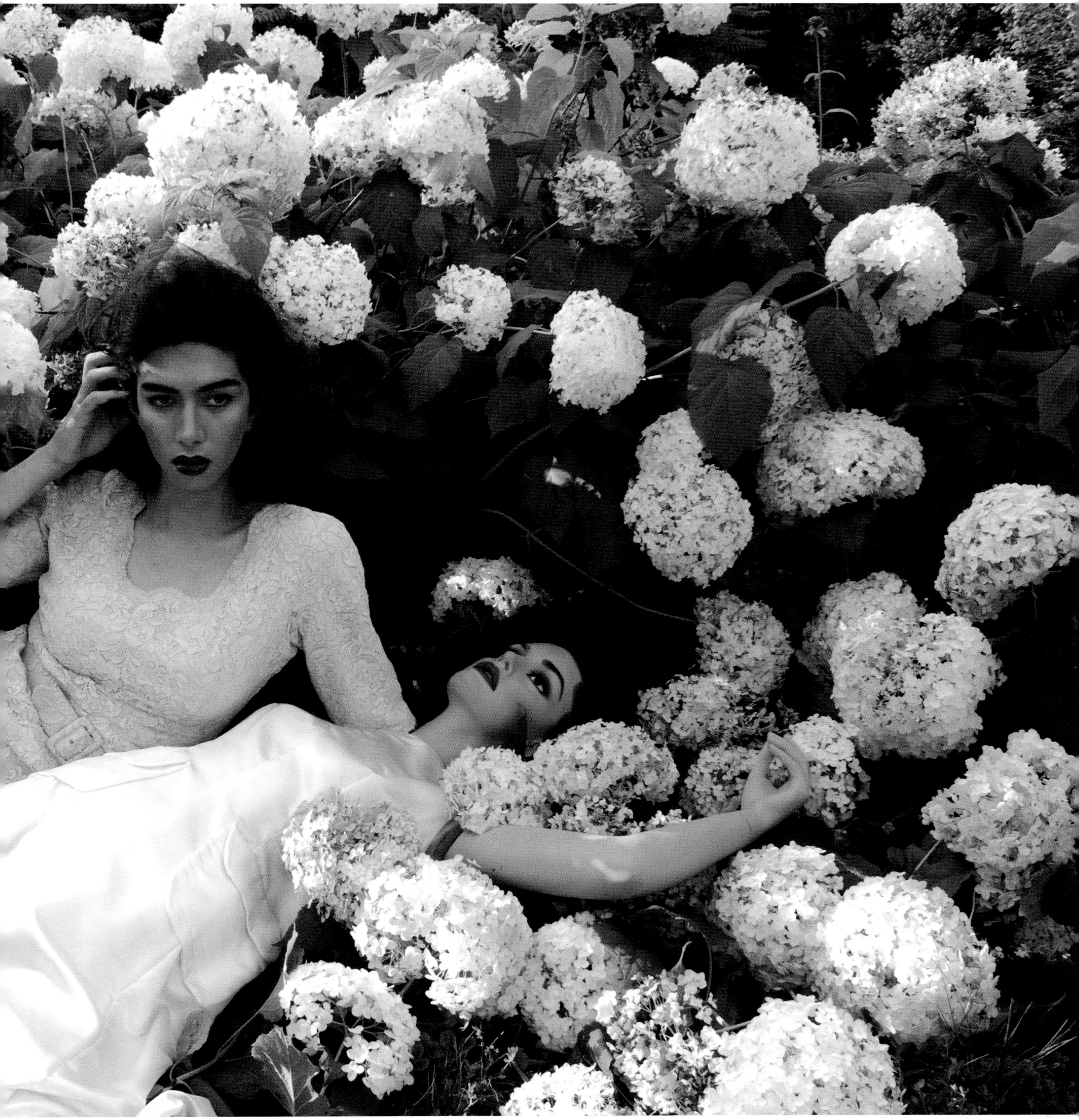

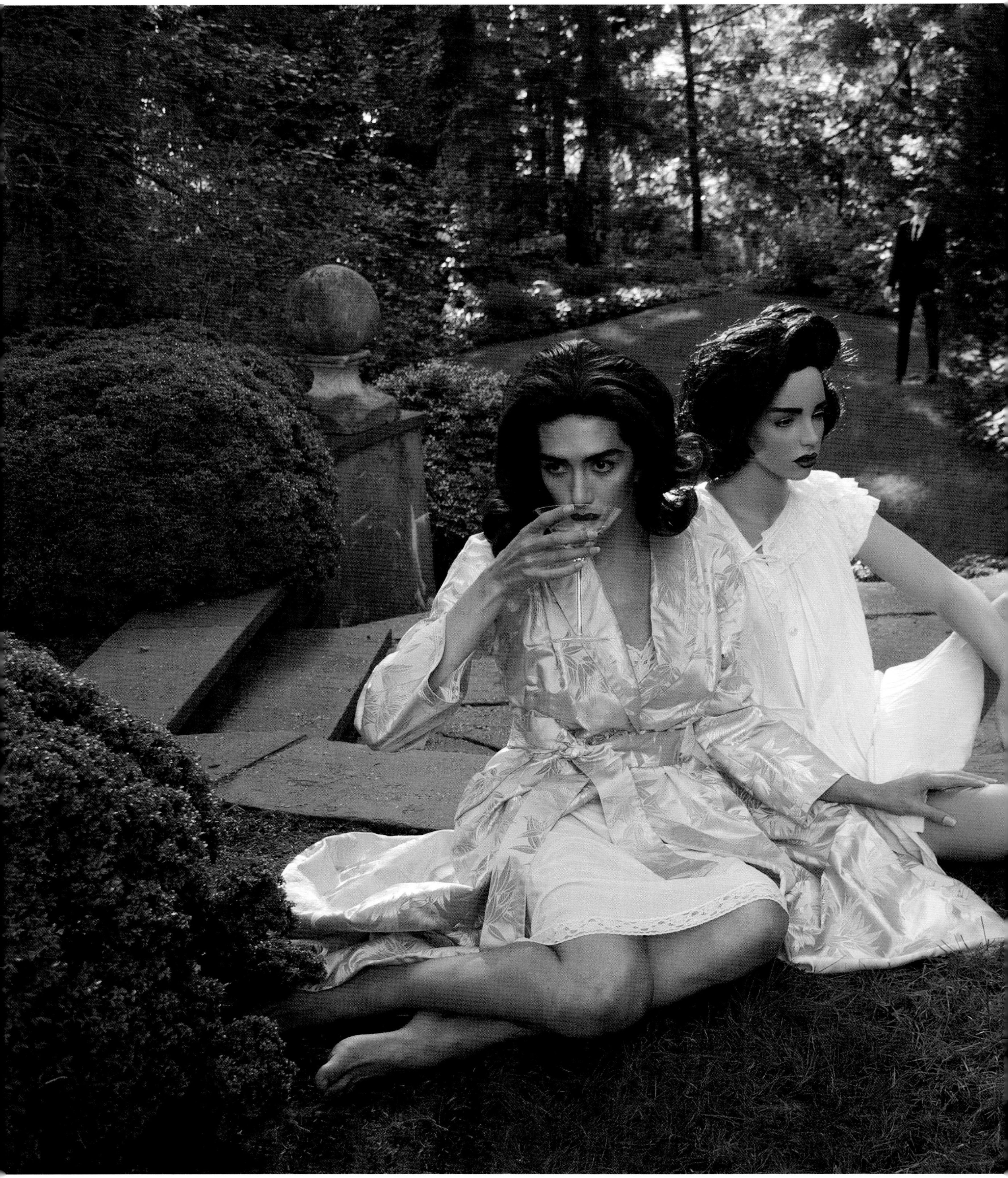

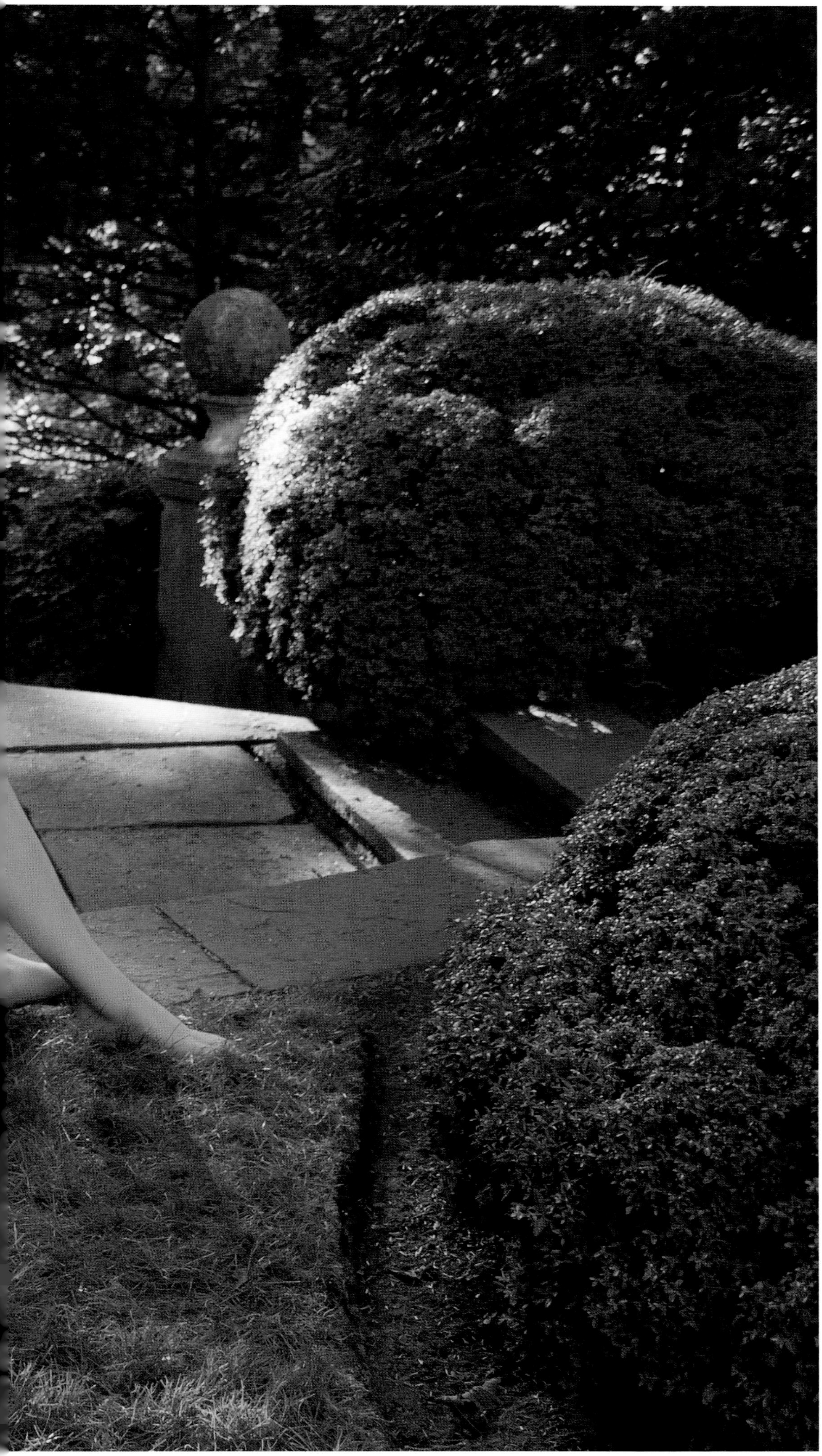

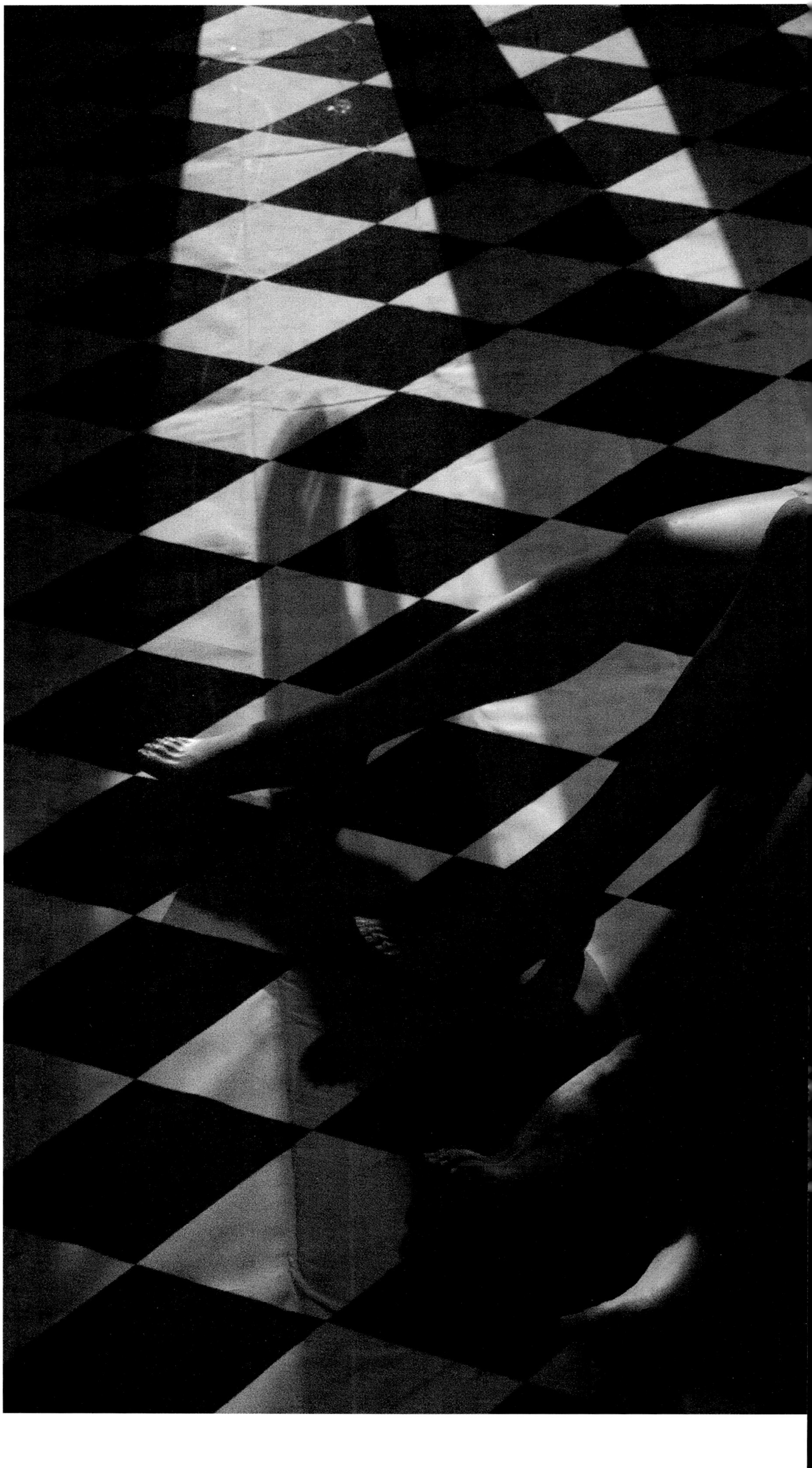

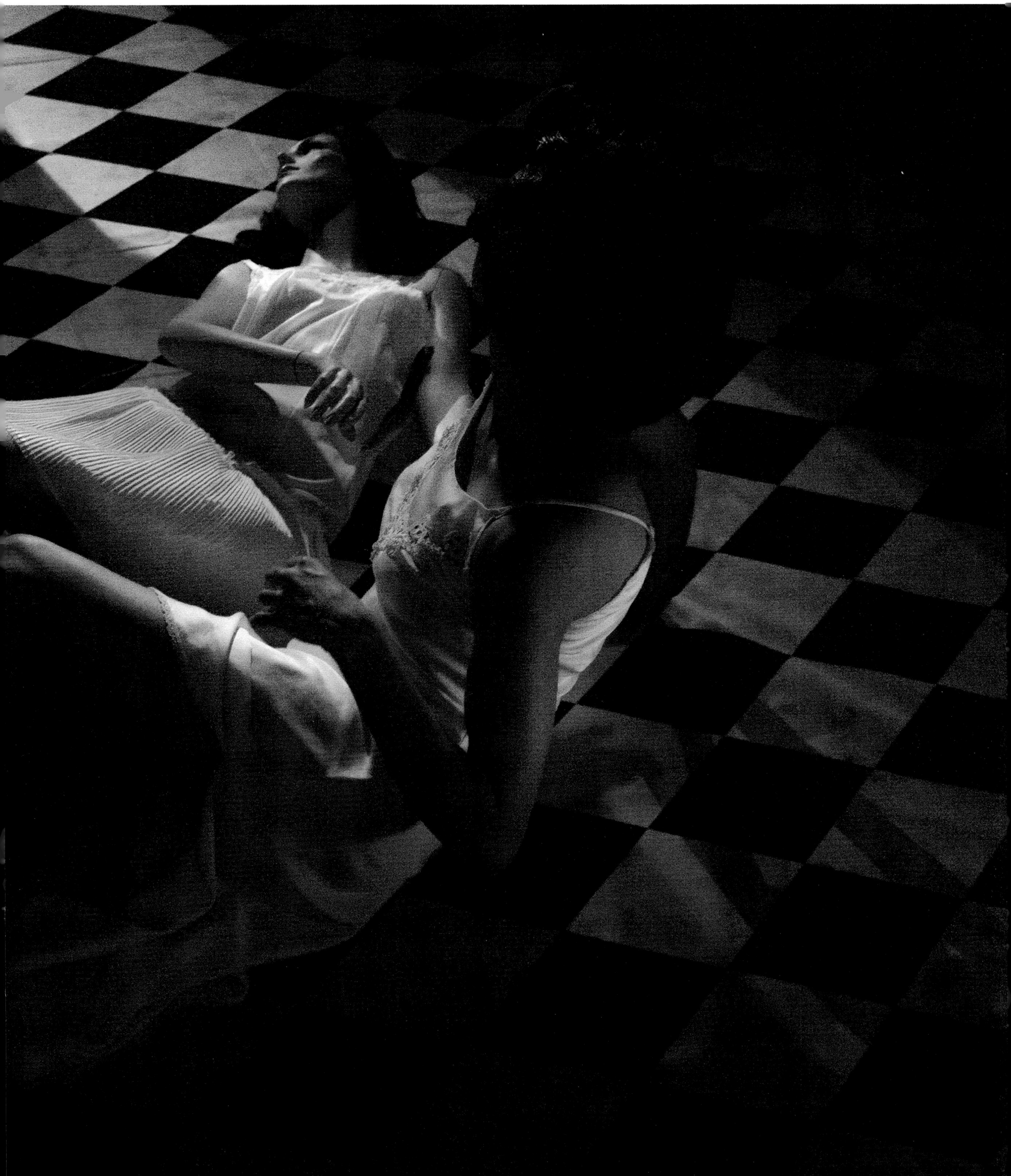

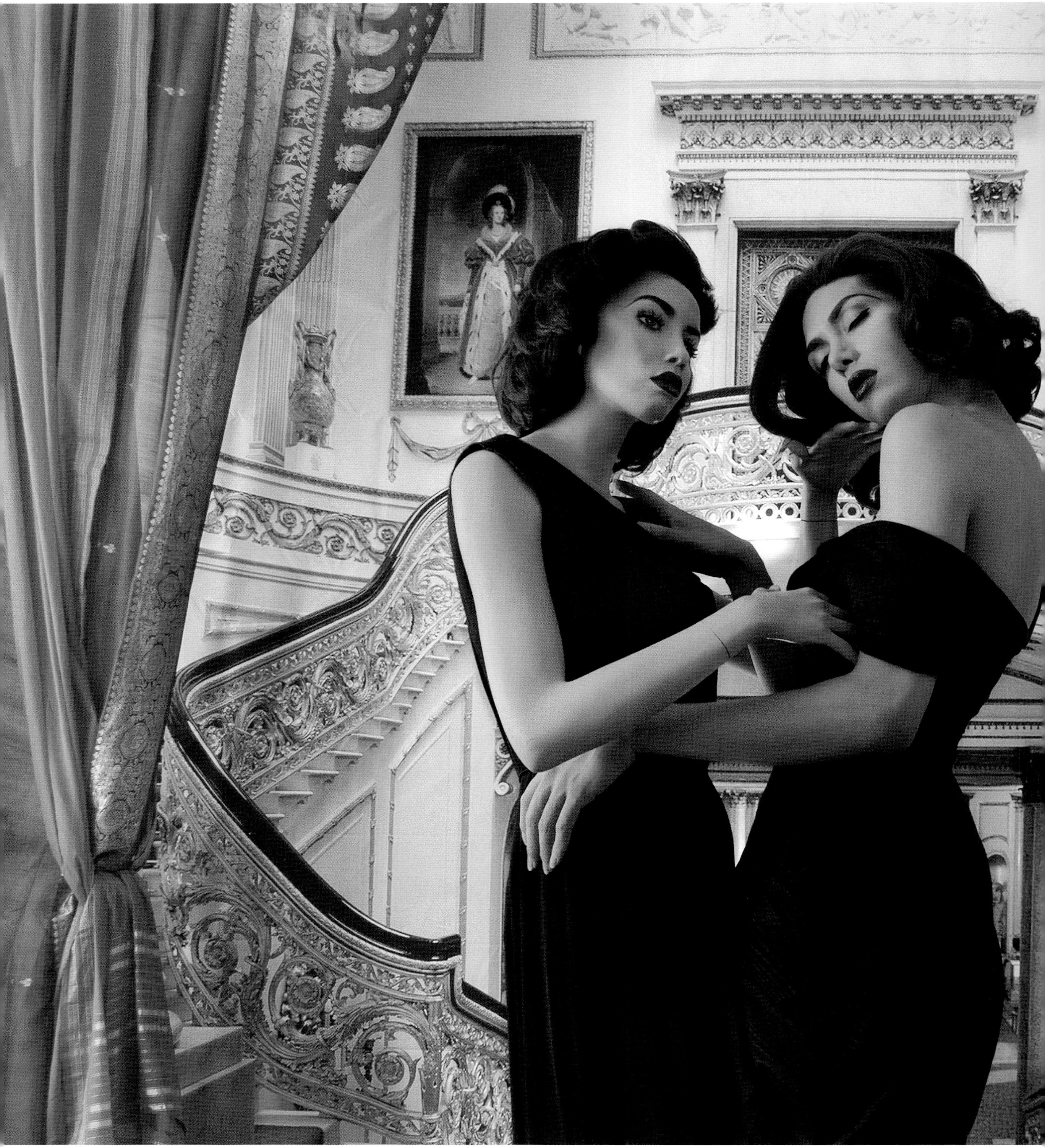

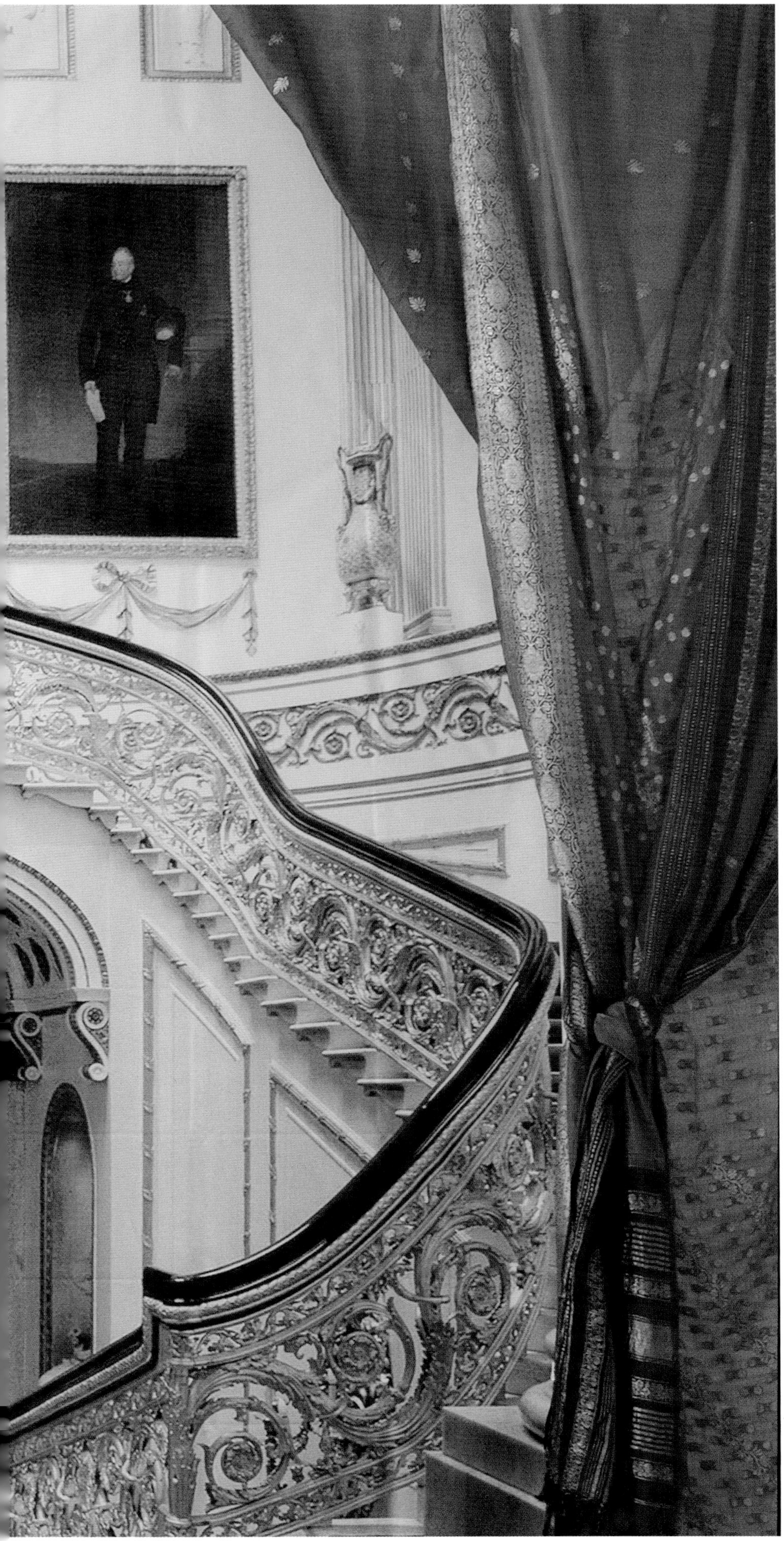

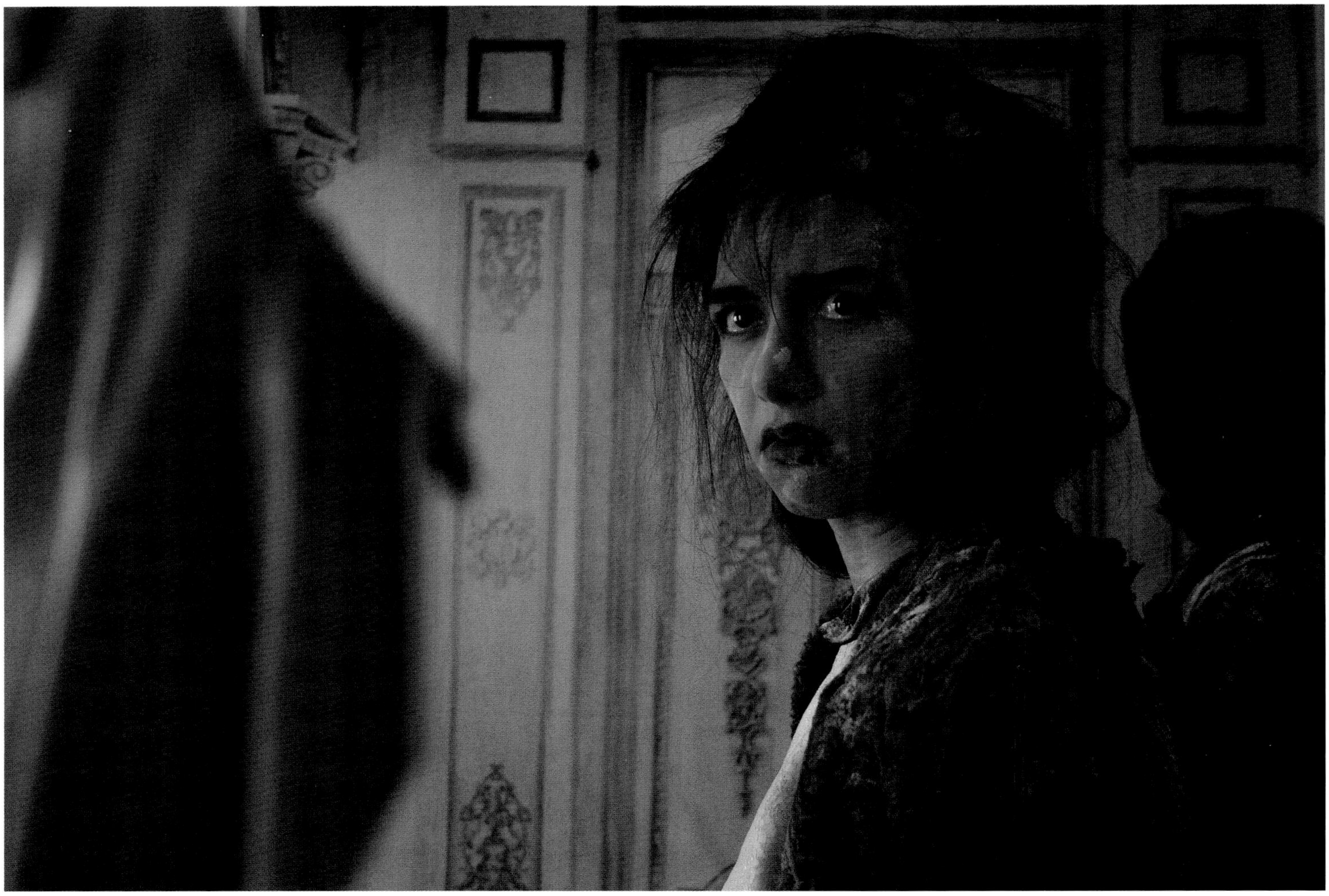

a shallow depth of field, the camera focuses intently on the Gutierrez's messily pulled-up hair; its appearance is uncharacteristically raw, perhaps just loosed from the day's long-secured style or mussed from a freshly arisen bedhead.

This singular image stands in contrast to the others in the series, calling attention to the laborious styling needed to produce the glamourous figures in the other photos. It also alludes more forcefully than the others to Cindy Sherman's *Untitled Film Stills*. The seventy images of Sherman's now-canonical series are black-and-white photographs across a slew of imaginary films' scenes that reference generic visual cinematographic tropes.[1] Despite the overarching sense of déjà vu across the series, Sherman's characters are never identified as specific personages; like Gutierrez's women, they exist within unknown spaces and sometimes engage with an unidentified character just beyond the photograph's frame. By contrast, Gutierrez's protagonists have names, Rosella and Palma, that suggest Latinx or Hispanic identities. Neither of these categories point toward a particular race or ethnicity, and the subtitle of the series is as close to a specific identification as the photos will allow. Whereas Sherman's *Untitled Film Stills* omit all identificatory information and present the subjects as a kind of everywoman or blank slate, Gutierrez's *Girl Friends* parenthetical inclusion of the presumed protagonists' names asks viewers to imagine more specific identities for them. And, by way of contrast, it suggests we return to Sherman's series and ask the same questions: Exactly who are these characters? What are their relationships to each other? Where are they? Where have they come from? What are their stories? If Gutierrez's characters are named, why aren't Sherman's, and what does that say about the imagined subject?

above Martine Gutierrez, *Girl Friends (Rosella & Palma)*, 2014 (printed 2020). Archival inkjet print mounted on foamboard, one of seven parts, 9 ½ × 14 ⅛ in. (24.1 × 35.9 cm). Crystal Bridges Museum of American Art, Bentonville, Arkansas, 2020.74.

opposite Cindy Sherman, *Untitled Film Still*, 1978. Gelatin silver print.

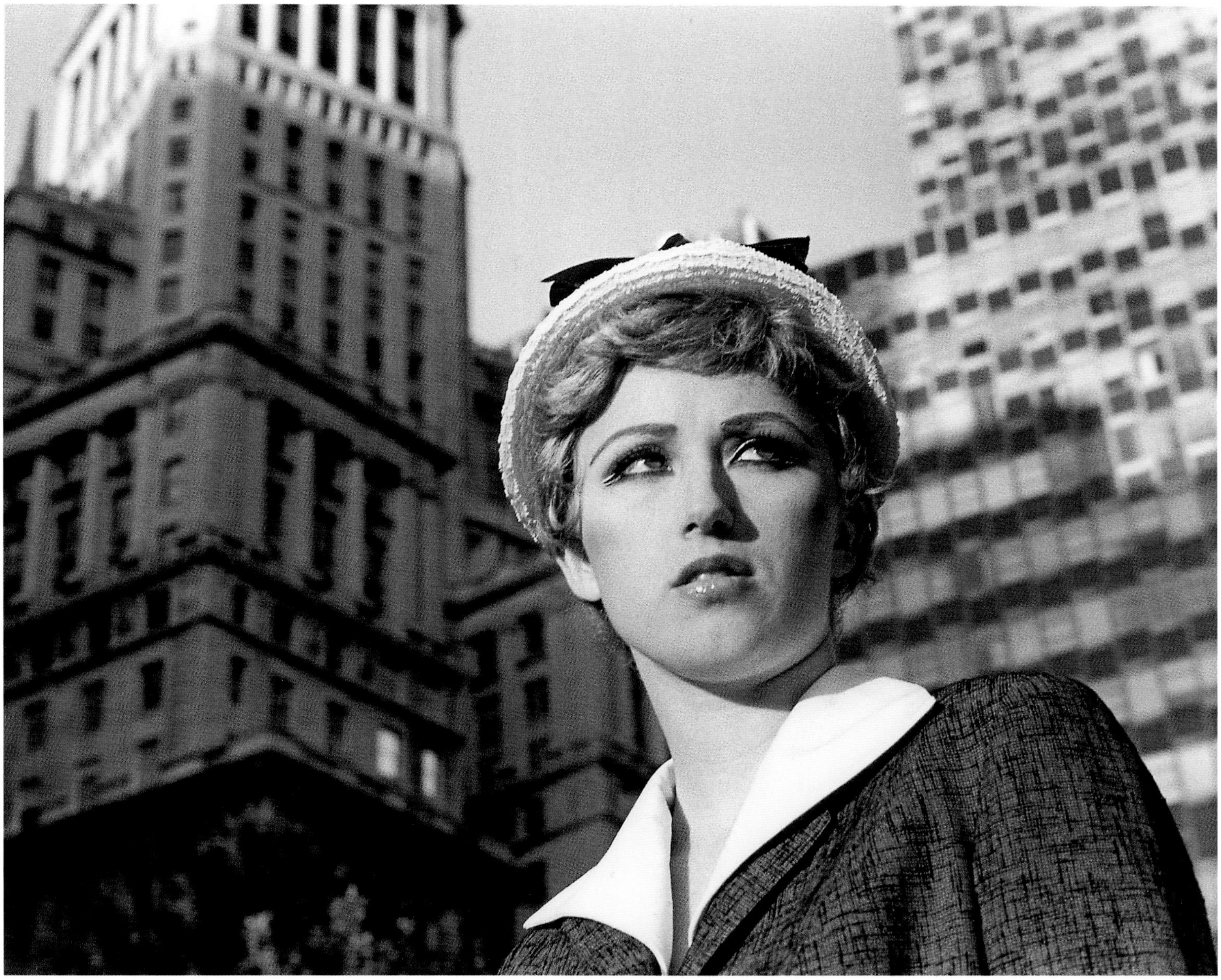

Gutierrez's *Girl Friends* asks us to interrogate the way that the characters in Sherman's *Untitled Film Stills* are presented as a normative default. Sherman's characters just *are*. They have no names to suggest an origin or history; they simply exist, as women, as people. Film scholar Richard Dyer has identified this positioning as the norm for whiteness:

> As long as race is something only applied to non-white peoples, as long as white people are not racially seen and named, they/we function as a human norm. Other people are raced, we are just people.
>
> There is no more powerful position than that of being "just" human. The claim to power is the claim to speak for the commonality of humanity. Raced people can't do that—they can only speak for their race. But non-raced people can, for they do not represent the interests of a race. . . .
>
> Whites are everywhere in representation. Yet precisely because of this and their placing as norm they seem not to be represented to themselves as whites but as people who are variously gendered, classed, sexualized, and abled. At the level of racial representation, in other words, whites are not of a certain race, they're just the human race.[2]

Sherman's use of the title *Untitled* for her black-and-white photographs of unspecified, normative characters calls to mind the history of Shirley cards. Named after Shirley Page, the model who posed for the first version of the images, Shirley cards were images distributed by Kodak when the company held a near-monopoly on film technology in the United States. They were produced to help film developers calibrate their printers—under a rubric defined by an image of a fair-skinned white woman.[3] Communication studies scholar Lorna Roth notes that, in essence, regardless of the subject's skin tone, all photographs commercially processed in North America beginning in the 1950s would be developed and printed with light balanced to fair and white skin, rendering subjects of color lighter than they actually were.[4] Roth points out that Shirley's whiteness as a norm reflected ideals assumed by the photo industry:

> From a more technical perspective, evidence has been accumulating that the reason for these deficiencies [in reproducing skin-tone variations] is that film chemistry, photo lab procedures, video screen colour balancing practices, and digital cameras in general were originally developed with a global assumption of "Whiteness" embedded within their architectures and expected ensemble of practices. What had become a "White"-biased international standard for the ideal flesh tone had been used as a barometer against which the flesh tones of Blacks, Asians, First Peoples, and other "peoples of colour" had been read negatively as an aggravation—a deviation from this invisible norm. This, along with the cross-cultural skin-colour-preference tests conducted by film manufacturers such as Kodak and Fuji, had confirmed an international preference for light complexions within the global consumer photo markets.[5]

Although Roth writes that Kodak researchers began noticing problems with the film's ability to properly capture a range of skin tones even in the 1950s because of contrast issues that rendered dark-skinned students' features illegible in class and graduation photos, it wasn't until the 1960s and '70s that company chemists began working to expand the range of tones that their film would capture—based on complaints from chocolate and furniture companies, who had problems capturing the brown tones of their products.[6] In 1995, Kodak introduced its first multiracial Shirley cards, which featured Asian, Black, and white models in a group pose, at long last allowing commercial photograph developers to produce a range of skin tones that better reflected the diversity of the images' subjects.[7] Yet, this solution to the fifty-five-year-old bias in color balancing didn't end the problem of whiteness as the visual norm: even Instagram, our contemporary moment's beloved digital photo- and video-sharing app, has been called out by users for the way its filters lighten skin tones and whitewash people of color.[8]

While Shirley cards at long last became more diverse at the end of the twentieth century, mainstream fashion's optics have still been trying to catch up in the twenty-first. The presumption of whiteness as the norm has been on full display in some of the ugliest moments in fashion's recent history, such as the spate of models appearing in blackface or with otherwise darkened skin in numerous international magazine photo spreads in the late 2000s and early 2010s. Some examples include *Vogue France*'s October 2009 editorial with model Lara Stone photographed by Steven Klein; *V* magazine's December 2009 spread featuring models Heidi Mount and Sasha Pivovarova photographed by Mario Sorrenti; and *Numéro* magazine's March 2013 "African Queen" story with model Ondria Hardin photographed by Sebastian Kim.[9] *Vogue Italia*'s March 2014 spread with model Saskia de Brauw photographed by Steven Meisel and May 2018

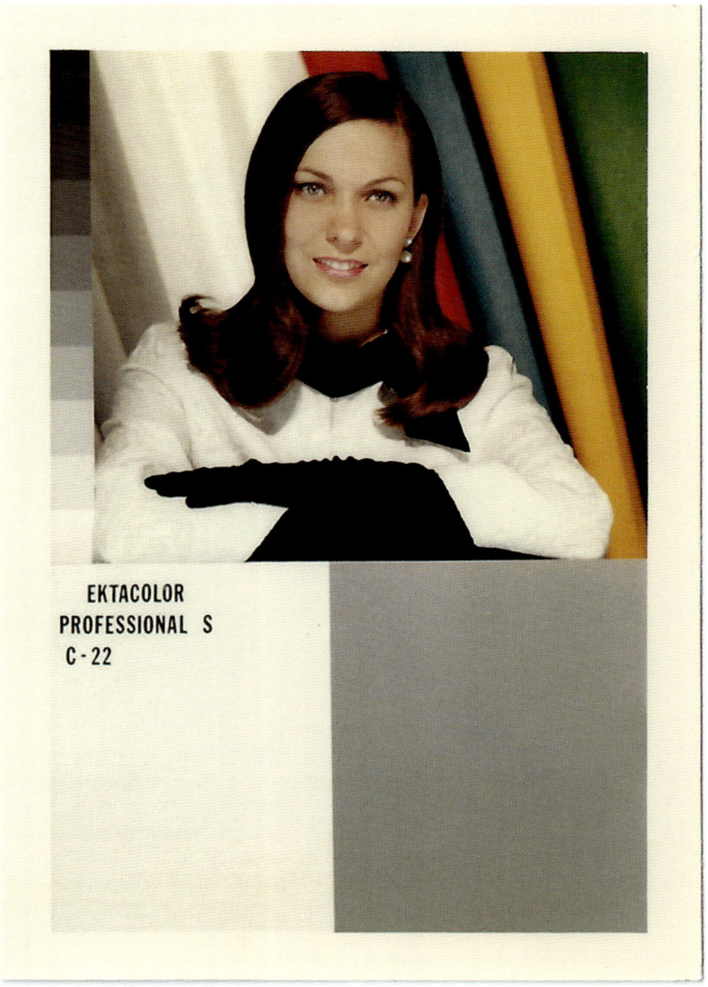

spread with model Gigi Hadid shot by Steven Klein continued the alarming pattern. All of this occurred despite increased activism for dismantling racism in fashion, including designer Maxwell Osborne's 2016 open letter in *W* magazine calling for the industry to self-educate, increase campaign and runway diversity, and deploy their "designs for the public good."[10] Dodai Stewart's response to the October 28, 2009, episode of *America's Next Top Model*, in which models were made up to look biracial, could apply to any of these incidents: "Race is not silver eyeshadow, a bubble skirt or couture gown. It's not something you put on for a photo shoot to seem 'edgy.' "[11]

And perhaps it's exactly the lack of specificity, the non-racialized normativity inherent to whiteness as a visual category that Dyer described, that also has supported fashion in using culturally specific forms of self-adornment and dress as runway décor and styling. Media and fashion studies scholar Minh-Ha T. Pham offers the concept of "racial plagiarism" as a framework for understanding how fashion fails when it sources adornment from racially and culturally specific beauty ideals and forms:

> Racial plagiarism highlights the racial relationships and inequalities that are obscured by terms like cultural appropriation, cultural appreciation, and piracy. In the fashion context, racial plagiarism occurs when a designer copies racial and indigenous styles, forms, practices, and knowledges without permission and without giving adequate (or any) attribution to the source model and community.[12]

As an example of racial plagiarism, Pham offers Marc Jacobs's presentation of their Spring/Summer 2017 collection in fall 2016, in which Jacobs's models wore pastel-colored yarn dreadlocks. The show's stylist, Guido Palau, identified singer Boy George, the

above Kodak Shirley card, 1968.

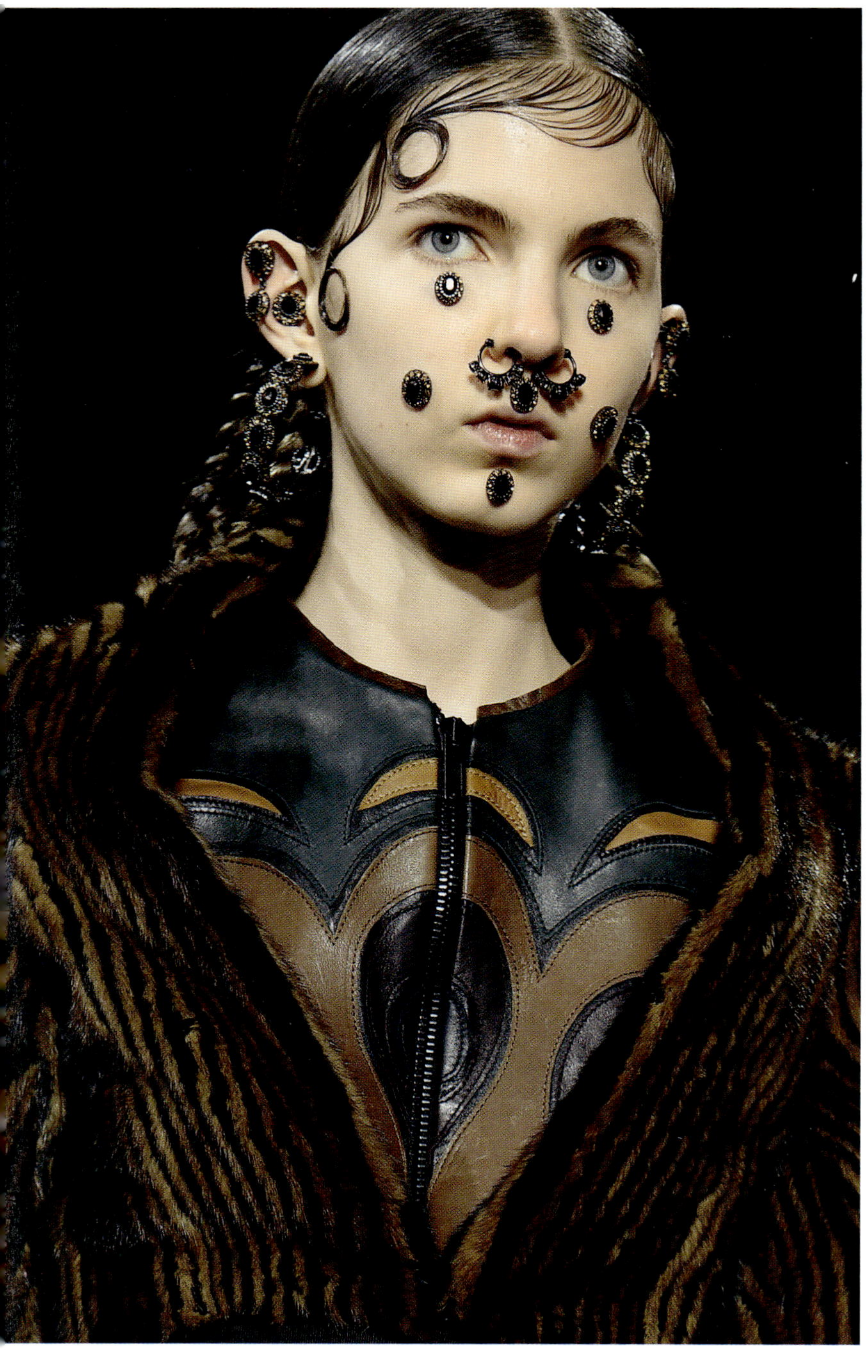

above Givenchy's "Chola Victorian" aesthetic for the fashion house's Fall 2015 collection.

opposite Pauline Trigère, 1962.

Harajuku fashion district in Tokyo, raver culture, and the 1980s in general as inspirations for the hairstyles while also denying any connection to Rasta culture, despite the Black cultural specificity of the hairstyle.[13] Racial plagiarism per Pham's definition can be seen elsewhere in fashion, such as Givenchy's presentation of its Fall 2015 collection in the spring of that year. Riccardo Tisci, the French fashion house's creative director, identified the makeup and styling for the show as "Chola Victorian," for the way it combined Victorian-inspired clothing with the ornately gel-styled baby hairs and bold jewelry style that Black and Latinx femmes have historically worn with pride, despite their being categorized as "hood," "ghetto," or "unprofessional" as a way to devalue aesthetic practices that are self-affirming and empowering on their own terms.[14] Gender and women's studies scholar Jillian Hernandez identifies this devaluing of Black and Latinx aesthetics as a product of "modernist European stylistic values [that] . . . linked racial and gendered inferiority to so-called aesthetic indulgences"[15]:

> These aesthetic theories have traveled from Europe to the U.S. through the institutionalization of canonical histories of Western art and design, and they found contemporary life in the negative, racializing assessments of working-class Black and Latina women and girls—whose elaborate embodiments situate them as the antithesis of high style and therefore as sexual others, according to both modernist and classical Western discourse. . . .
>
> After all, the embodiments, iconographies, and objects created by racialized and colonized peoples are the canvases upon which Euro-American modernism articulated itself—via Picasso's abstracted masks inspired by his visits to ethnographic museums in Paris, Adolf Loos's infamous Josephine Baker house, and, later, Keith Haring's graffiti-inspired works that stemmed from his erotic attraction to poor and working-class Black and Latinx young men in New York City.[16]

While the aesthetic movements of people of color have long been used as drapery for white fashion display and design, Black and Latinx designers and models have resisted this appropriation and stereotyping across the venues to which they have had access. In 1961, Marylin Bender reported in the *New York Times* that Beverly Valdes had become the first Black woman hired as an in-house model for a major fashion label, Trigère.[17] Other Black models working major New York fashion shows at the time included LaJeune Hundley, Helen Williams, and Bani Yelverton.[18] In the article, Bender notes that Valdes had studied at Ophelia

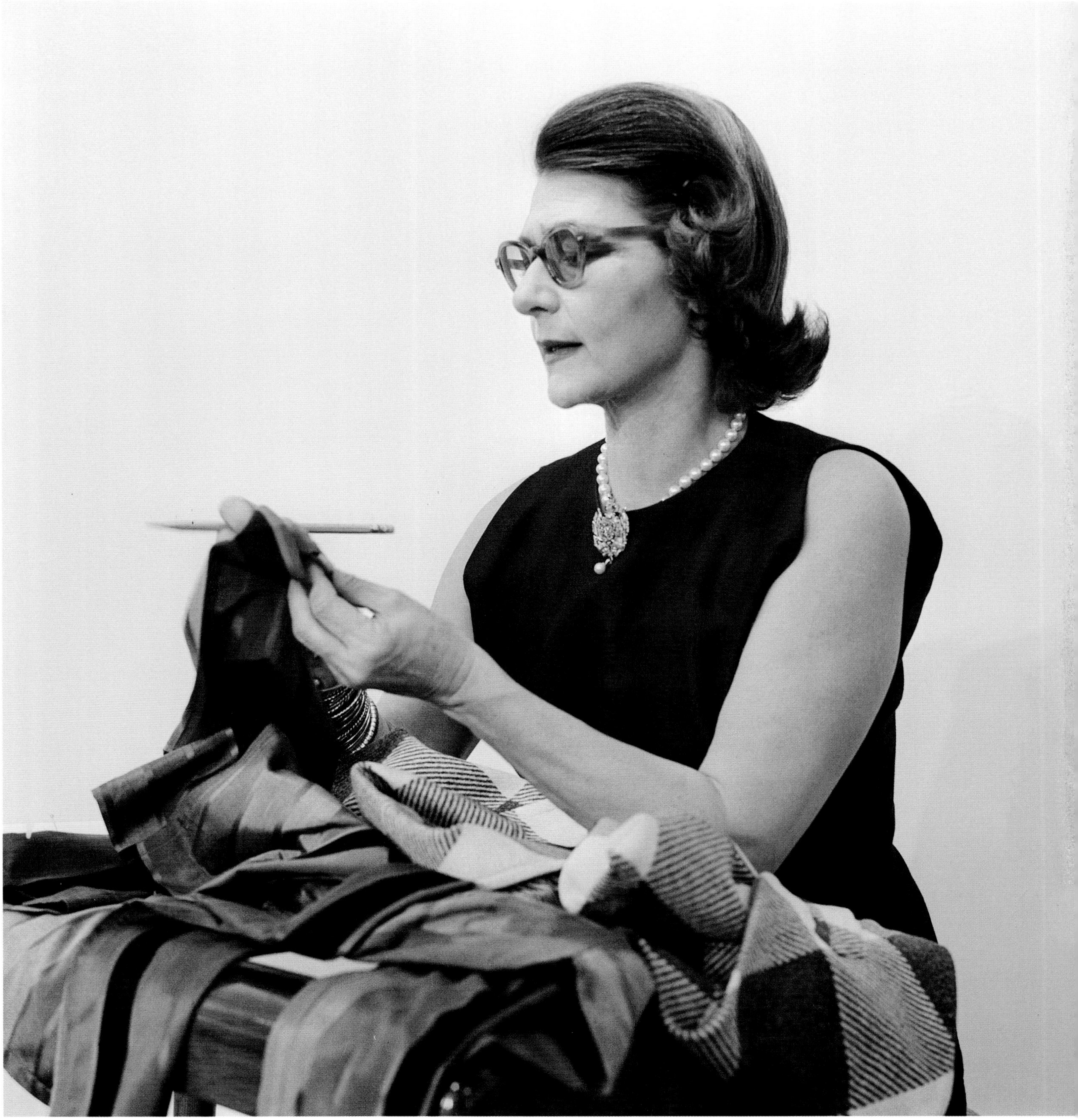

DeVore's Charm School. DeVore, who herself had been the first Black graduate of Vogue's School of Modeling in New York, dedicated her life to advancing Black models' careers through her school and the Grace del Marco agency, which she cofounded.[19] Black and Latinx designers rose to prominence throughout the 1970s, 1980s, and 1990s: Adolfo (Sardiña), Carlota Alfaro, Alvin Bell, Stephen Burrows, Dapper Dan (Daniel Day), Fabrice (Simon), Oscar de la Renta, Carolina Herrera, Jay Jaxon, Patrick Kelly, Willi Smith, and Isabel Toledo became known for their work in couture, craft, evening glamour, prêt-à-porter, and streetwear.[20] More recently, the designer Virgil Abloh created Free Game, a webpage collecting resources and tutorials for emerging designers to build their brands and practices, on subjects including how to market one's work, set up a website, and implement online shopping to help them get a business off the ground.[21] In 2020, Abloh established the "Post-Modern" Scholarship Fund in partnership with the Fashion Scholarship Fund to support Black, African American, or African descendent students' school tuition to help diversify the fashion industry.[22]

Even with fashion designers and models on the front lines advocating for and creating inroads for diversity in the industry, the journey toward equity and inclusion in fashion is long and challenging. A 2021 report on diversity, equity, and inclusion in the industry by the Council of Fashion Designers of America and PVH Corp. found that only 23 percent of Black employees had received referrals for their jobs, in contrast to 57 percent of white employees.[23] Additional findings included the fact that 37 percent of Black employees needed to supplement their industry income while only 23 percent of white employees did; that 26 percent of BIPOC employees were negatively impacted by their race for raise and promotion considerations compared to 1 percent of white employees; and that 36 percent of BIPOC employees received mentorship compared to 47 percent of white employees. The report concluded with a tool kit designed to help track, hire, and retain a diverse range of employees, offering analytics and solutions for expanding the pipeline, such as conducting pay-equity audits, providing housing stipends for interns in major metropolitan areas, and creating promotional pathways for employees to ascend the career ladder. Such findings help us name systemic problems in the fashion industry that need to be addressed to ensure that careers are open to BIPOC workers. As in the case of Martine Gutierrez's *Girl Friends* series, naming the subject marks the difference from the historically assumed norm.

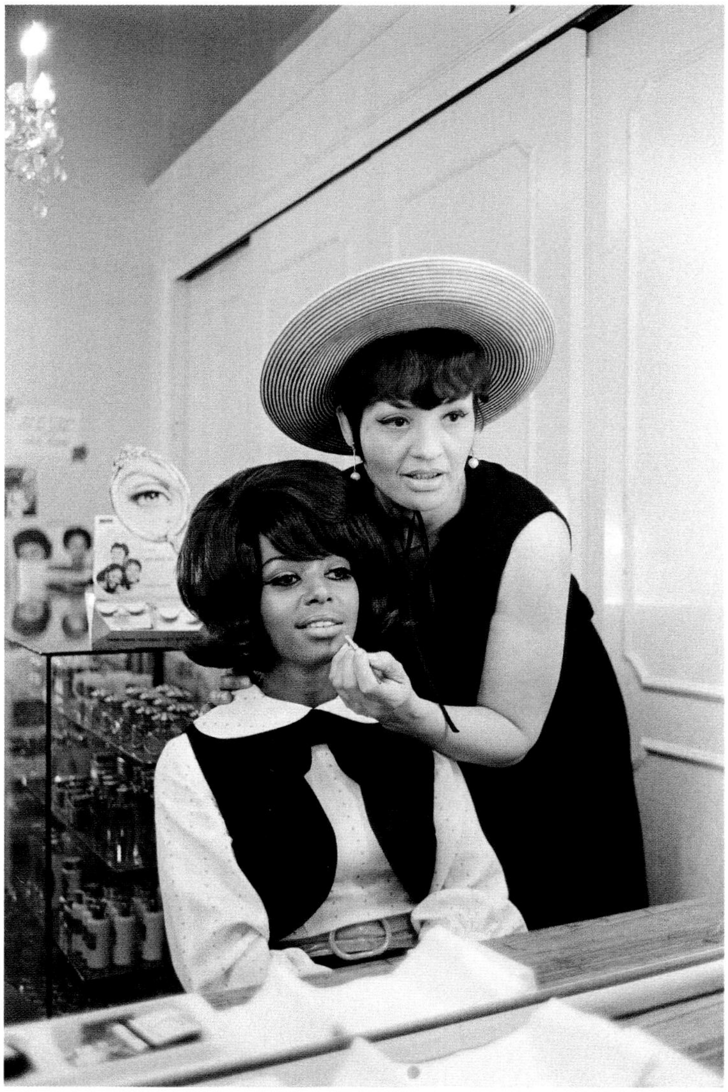

Ophelia DeVore demonstrating makeup techniques with Barbara Barnes.

NOTES

1 Benedetta Ricci, "Portraits of America: Cindy Sherman's *Untitled Film Stills*," *Artland*, accessed December 12, 2021, https://magazine.artland.com/portraits-of-america-cindy-shermans-untitled-film-stills/.

2 Richard Dyer, "The Matter of Whiteness," in *White Privilege: Essential Readings on the Other Side of Racism*, ed. Paula S. Rothenberg (New York: Worth Publishers, 2005), 10–11.

3 Lorna Roth, "Looking at Shirley, the Ultimate Norm: Colour Balance, Image Technologies, and Cognitive Equity," *Canadian Journal of Communication* 34 (2009): 112. Shirley Page is named in Mandalit del Barco's article "How Shirley Cards Set Photography's Skin-Tone Standard," NPR, November 13, 2014, https://www.npr.org/2014/11/13/363517842/for-decades-kodak-s-shirley-cards-set-photography-s-skin-tone-standard.

4 Roth, "Looking at Shirley," 116.

5 Roth, "Looking at Shirley," 117.

6 Roth, "Looking at Shirley," 118–20.

7 Roth, "Looking at Shirley," 122; and Sarah Lewis, "The Racial Bias Built into Photography," *New York Times*, April 25, 2019, https://www.nytimes.com/2019/04/25/lens/sarah-lewis-racial-bias-photography.html.

8 Morgan Jerkins, "The Quiet Racism of Instagram Filters," *Racked*, July 7, 2015, https://www.racked.com/2015/7/7/8906343/instagram-racism; Bridgette L. Hylton, "We Must Stop Using Filters to Whitewash Our Faces If We Want to Be Seen," Medium, July 11, 2020, https://medium.com/the-kickstarter/we-must-stop-using-filters-to-whitewash-our-faces-if-we-want-to-be-seen-6da0a07e4a.

9 Many thanks to Dodai Stewart for tracking these phenomena in near real time during her tenure at *Jezebel*. Articles there and elsewhere include Jenna Sauers, "Oh No They Didn't: French *Vogue* Does Blackface," *Jezebel*, October 12, 2009, https://jezebel.com/oh-no-they-didnt-french-vogue-does-blackface-5379708; John Kennedy, "V Style: Is Blackface the New Black?" *Vibe*, November 3, 2009, https://www.vibe.com/lifestyle/style/v-style-blackface-new-black-47767/; and Dodai Stewart, "The Truth about Using a White Girl in the 'African Queen' Fashion Shoot," *Jezebel*, March 1, 2013, https://jezebel.com/the-truth-about-using-a-white-girl-in-the-african-queen-5987856.

10 Barbara-Shae Jackson, "Vogue Spread Strikes Racial Chord," *Atlanta Black Star*, March 10, 2014, https://atlantablackstar.com/2014/03/10/vogue-spread-strikes-racial-chord; Tahmina Begum, "Gigi Hadid Apologises for Vogue Italia Cover after 'Blackface' Accusations," *Huffington Post*, May 4, 2018, https://www.huffingtonpost.co.uk/entry/gigi-hadid-vogue-italia-cover_uk_5aec1d1ae4b0c4f19320f2ad; and Maxwell Osborne, "Why I Stand With Black Lives Matter," *W*, July 14, 2016, https://www.wmagazine.com/story/black-lives-matter-maxwell-osborne-public-school-dkny-open-letter.

11 Dodai Stewart, "*ANTM* Models in Oh-So-Trendy Blackface Shoot," *Jezebel*, October 28, 2009, https://jezebel.com/antm-models-in-oh-so-trendy-blackface-shoot-5391756.

12 Minh-Ha T. Pham, "Racial Plagiarism and Fashion," *QED: A Journal in GLBTQ Worldmaking*, 4, no. 3 (Fall 2017): 69.

13 Pham, "Racial Plagiarism," 67–68.

14 Givenchy's Fall 2015 fashion show was widely covered across popular online media and news sites. Critical reports of the show included Madelyn Chung, "Here's Why Givenchy's 'Chola Victorian' Theme Is Problematic," *Huffington Post*, March 10, 2015, https://www.huffpost.com/archive/ca/entry/givenchy-chola_n_6838656; Alice Newell-Hanson, "What's the Big Deal with Baby Hair?" *i-D*, March 9, 2015, https://i-d.vice.com/en_uk/article/7xv49y/whats-the-big-deal-with-baby-hair; Phillip Picardi, "The Underlying Issue with That Epic Givenchy Show," Refinery 29, March 9, 2015, https://www.refinery29.com/en-us/2015/03/83536/givenchy-fall-2015-runway-chola-inspiration; and Gina Vaynshteyn, "This Givenchy 'Victorian Chola' Runway Look Is All Kinds of Problematic," Hello Giggles, March 10, 2015, https://hellogiggles.com/lifestyle/givenchy-victorian-chola/.

15 Jillian Hernandez, *Aesthetics of Excess: The Art and Politics of Black and Latina Embodiment* (Durham, NC: Duke University Press, 2020), 9.

16 Hernandez, *Aesthetics of Excess*, 9–10.

17 Marylin Bender, "Fashion Designer Hires Negro Model: Beverly Valdes Said to Be First of Race to Work on 7th Ave. Magazines, Ad Agency Officials Hesitant to Employ Negroes," *New York Times*, June 23, 1961, https://timesmachine.nytimes.com/timesmachine/1961/06/23/98440578.html?pageNumber=33.

18 For deeper dives into the histories of Black fashion models, see Barbara Summers, *Skin Deep: Inside the World of Black Fashion Models* (New York: Amistad Press, 1999); Ben Arogundade, *Black Beauty: A History and Celebration* (New York: Thunder's Mouth Press, 2001); and Marcellas Reynolds, *Supreme Models: Black Women Who Revolutionized Fashion* (New York: Harry N. Abrams, 2019).

19 Margalit Fox, "Ophelia DeVore-Mitchell, 92, Dies; Redefined Beauty," *New York Times*, March 13, 2014, https://www.nytimes.com/2014/03/13/nyregion/ophelia-devore-mitchell-91-dies-redefined-beauty.html. More on DeVore can be learned from Alina Mitchell's *The Color of Beauty: The Life and Work of New York Fashion Icon Ophelia DeVore* (self-pub., 2019).

20 Tonya Blazio-Licorish, "12 of Fashion's Most Influential Latinx Designers," *WWD*, September 22, 2020, https://wwd.com/fashion-news/designer-luxury/most-influential-latinx-hispanic-fashion-designers-1234588826/; Anne-Marie Schiro, "Fabrice Simon, 47, Designer of Glittery Evening Clothes," *New York Times*, August 5, 1998, https://www.nytimes.com/1998/08/05/nyregion/fabrice-simon-47-designer-of-glittery-evening-clothes.html; and Jake Silbert, "Willi Smith Made Streetwear before the Word Existed," Hypebeast, July 8, 2020, https://hypebeast.com/2020/7/willi-smith-williwear-black-fashion-designer-history.

21 Virgil Abloh, "Free Game," VirgilAbloh.com, accessed February 3, 2022, https://virgilabloh.com/free-game/.

22 Virgil Abloh, "Post-Modern," Virgil Abloh's official website, accessed February 21, 2022, https://virgilabloh.com/postmodern/; and "Virgil Abloh™ 'Post-Modern' Scholarship Fund," Fashion Scholarship Fund, accessed February 21, 2022, https://www.fashionscholarshipfund.org/virgil-abloh.

23 Joseph Corchado Maglieri, "CFDA and PVH Release the State of Diversity, Equity and Inclusion in Fashion Study and Report," Council of Fashion Designers of America, February 1, 2021, https://cfda.com/news/cfda-pvh-release-the-state-of-diversity-equity-inclusion-in-fashion-study-report.

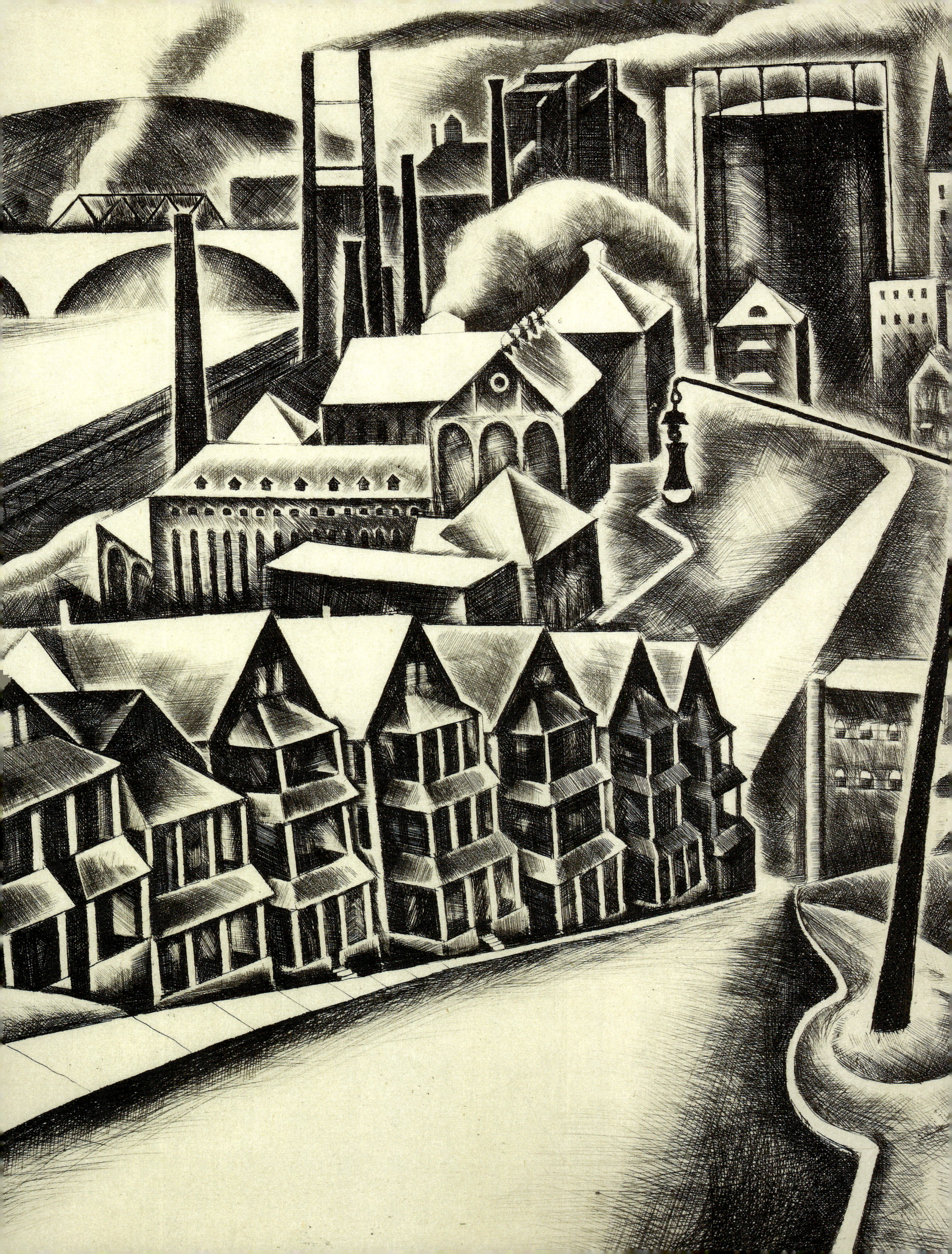

Hidden in the Seams

A FAMILY ACCOUNT OF DOMINICAN IMMIGRATION TO MASSACHUSETTS

Angely Mercado

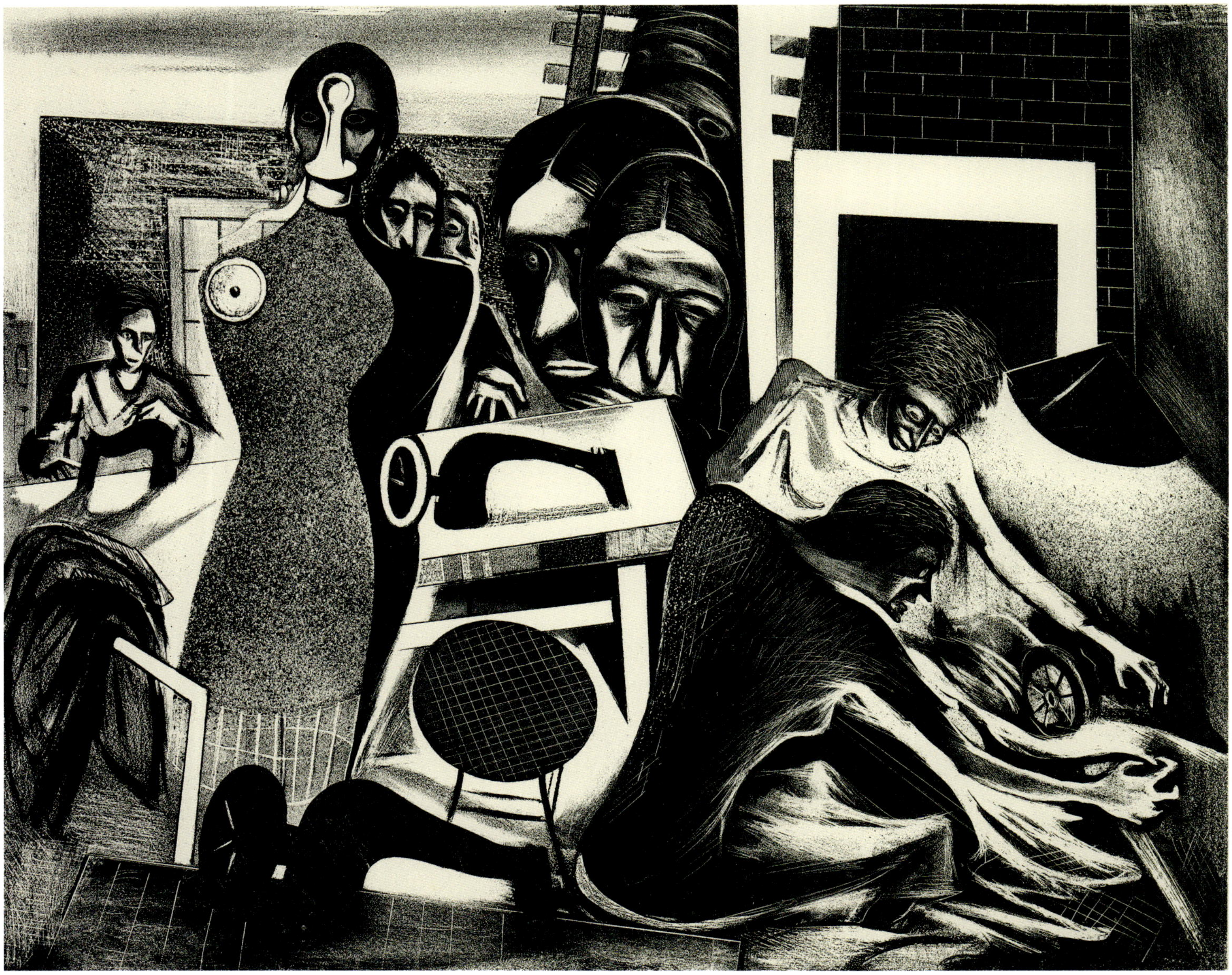

I grew up spending weekends with my mother's side of the family in Haverhill, Massachusetts, and shopping in and around the neighboring towns of Lawrence and Lowell. My friends at home in New York would be surprised when I explained that some parts of the state were home to Dominican enclaves.

They would ask: "Why did they go way up there, when NYC and New Jersey had larger Caribbean populations and public transportation?"

The answer to this question, as with so many questions, is economics.

My godmother and godfather (who are also my uncle and his wife, on my mother's side) moved to Massachusetts from the Dominican Republic in the 1980s. My godmother worked in a bank in the Dominican Republic, but when she emigrated, she took a job sewing decorative details onto shoes. She doesn't fully remember how long she worked at the shoe factory.

According to my godmother, the shoe factories offered training for new workers, which made them accessible to the recently arrived. New workers didn't have to speak perfect English; they just had to show they could learn on the job and follow safety guidelines. My mother likes to relate the tale of how, on one trip to visit my godparents when she still lived in the Dominican Republic, my godmother took her to the factory to work with her, and my mother was trained and earned money that same day.

above Boris Gorelick, *Sweat Shop*, ca. 1935. Lithograph; image: 11 ¾ × 15 ⅜ in. (29.8 × 39.1 cm). Crystal Bridges Museum of American Art, Bentonville, Arkansas, 2012.12.

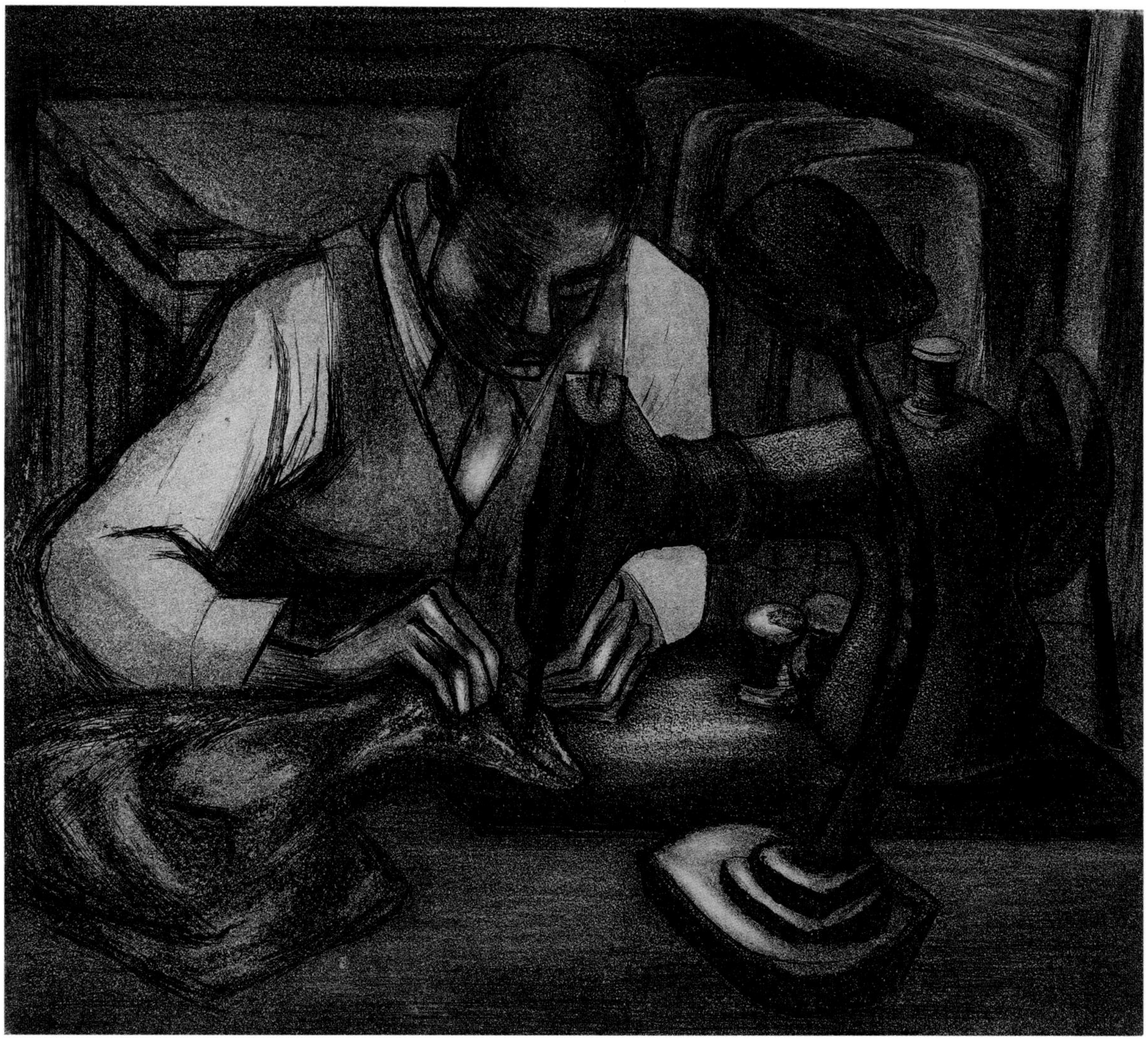

She continued to work there for about two weeks while she was visiting. I asked my mom if it was hard work. She remembers it being repetitive, but she was able to go shopping thanks to those earnings, so it wasn't a bad temporary gig.

Throughout the 1980s, other relatives began to arrive in Massachusetts and many of them worked in local factories, including a bread factory that still operates in Haverhill today. I recently learned that my grandfather, who never really learned English, was also briefly employed in the bread factory.

I thought of my godmother and her coworkers when I saw Boris Gorelick's lithograph *Sweat Shop* (ca. 1935) and Will Barnet's etching *Swing Shift* (1937), both in the Crystal Bridges Museum of American Art's collection. In *Sweat Shop*, the black-and-white images are semi-abstract—large sewing machines, laborers using them, a mannequin just off center, and floating heads and eyes surveying it all. I wondered if the column of eyes in the background belonged to other workers, those in need of a job during the Great Depression, or supervisors. It was a little jarring to see, and I tried to imagine what that environment must have been like over the years. The imagery, along with the image of an African American man toiling at a sewing machine under dim lamplight in *Swing Shift*, anchored my conceptions of some of my mother's and godmother's stories of sewing in the factory.

above Will Barnet, *Swing Shift*, 1937. Etching and aquatint; image: 9 11⁄16 × 10 5⁄8 in. (24.6 × 27 cm). Crystal Bridges Museum of American Art, Bentonville, Arkansas, 2012.48.

I wondered if the prints were inspired by real people. I wondered if those people were worried or excited when they started a new job. I wanted to know if they were paid a living wage, if they were treated well, and if there were any safety guidelines in their workplaces.

I imagined my mother at a machine sewing shoes. I asked her if she saw other Dominicans there at the factory (my godmother recalls the company being called Davco, though information about it is hard to find). Both she and my godmother remember seeing several Dominicans and a few Latinxs from other countries working alongside them. Such a cohort fit a pattern of emigration to the United States from the Dominican Republic. My godmother hand-sewed adornments on hundreds of pairs of shoes a year alongside many other Latin American immigrants.

Immigration to the United States from the Dominican Republic surged in the early 1960s after the country's longtime dictator, Rafael Leónidas Trujillo Molina, was assassinated in 1961. What followed was political turmoil. A military coup occurred, and the United States eventually invaded the country to prevent "another Cuba"—the establishment of a leftist government near American shores. The culture began to shift. The post-Trujillato years eventually brought about democracy, with the first free elections taking place in the early 1960s, and with them, growing pains that became pronounced by the early to mid-1980s. Unrest took place in 1984, for example, when the country's government raised prices for basic necessities like food and medication to lower the country's deficit in hopes of securing a $400 million loan from the International Monetary Fund. As a result, Dominicans rioted in cities across the country, and thousands were arrested. Issues with the cost of living and access to food continued: in 1990, the country experienced gasoline and sugar shortages, and protests against the rising cost of living and austerity measures occurred. But the early 1990s and early 2000s saw significant change for the country. Unemployment decreased and the economy saw tremendous growth for over a decade.

Beginning in the 1960s, immigration from the Caribbean to the United States, especially from the Dominican Republic, began to increase dramatically. From the early 1970s to the early 1980s, the Dominican immigrant population in the United States almost tripled, rising from approximately sixty-one thousand to more than a hundred sixty thousand. In 1989, Dominican musician Juan Luis Guerra released the song "Visa para un sueño"—in English, "A visa for a dream"—which compared hopeful immigrants waiting for their visas to livestock waiting to be slaughtered. In 1992, Guerra discussed the cost of living in "El costo de la vida," pointing out that perhaps no one cared about certain countries because their inhabitants didn't speak English.

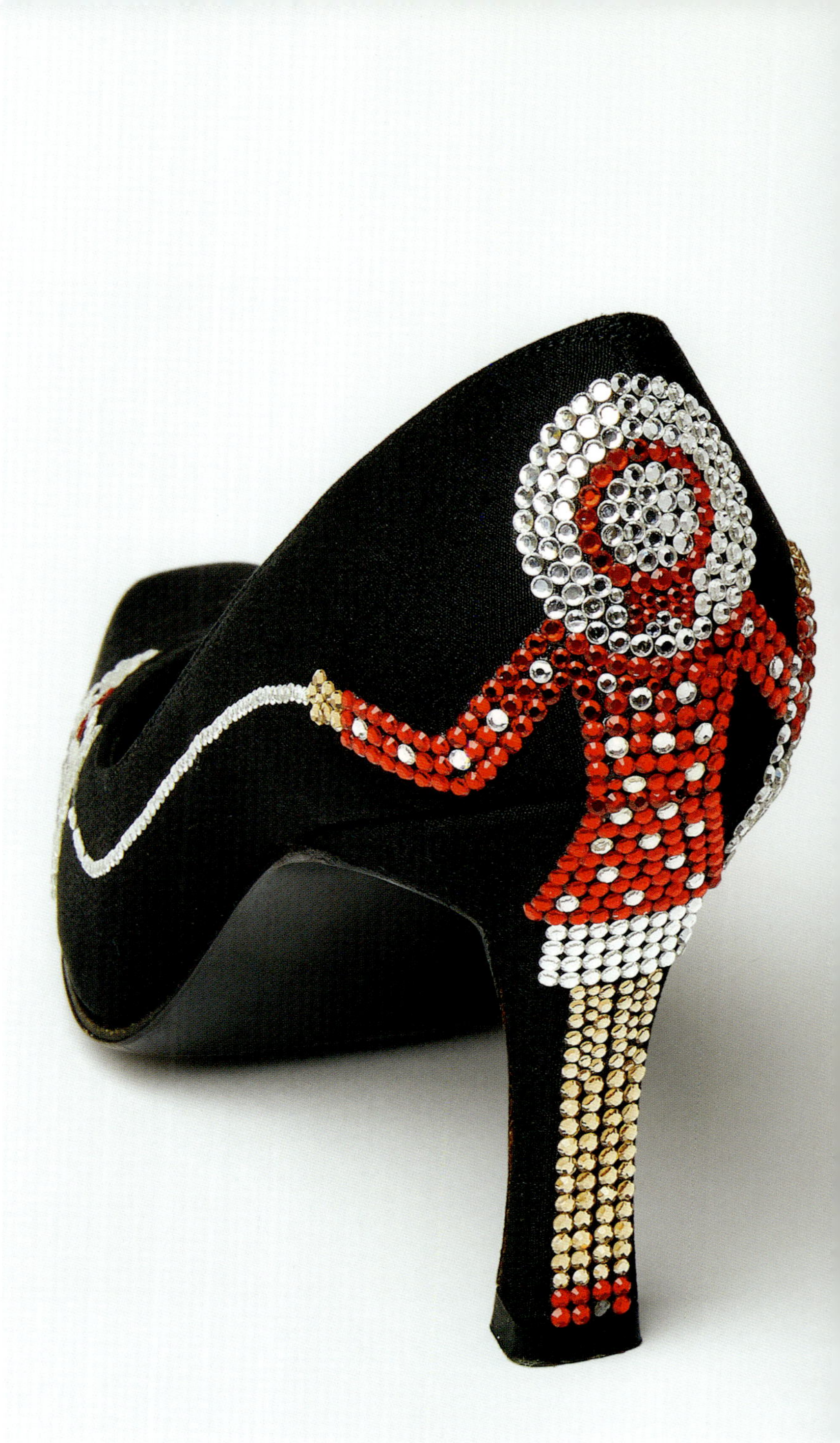

I asked my godmother if the pay was good at the shoe factory. Was it worth the move and the switch from working in a bank?

"It was minimum wage or something like that," she told me. "But they had so much work we could get overtime if we wanted to.Sometimes they even gave me work to take home with me for more money."

Jobs paid a little more in the United States than they did in the Dominican Republic, and from what my family remembers, the work was consistent and reliable.

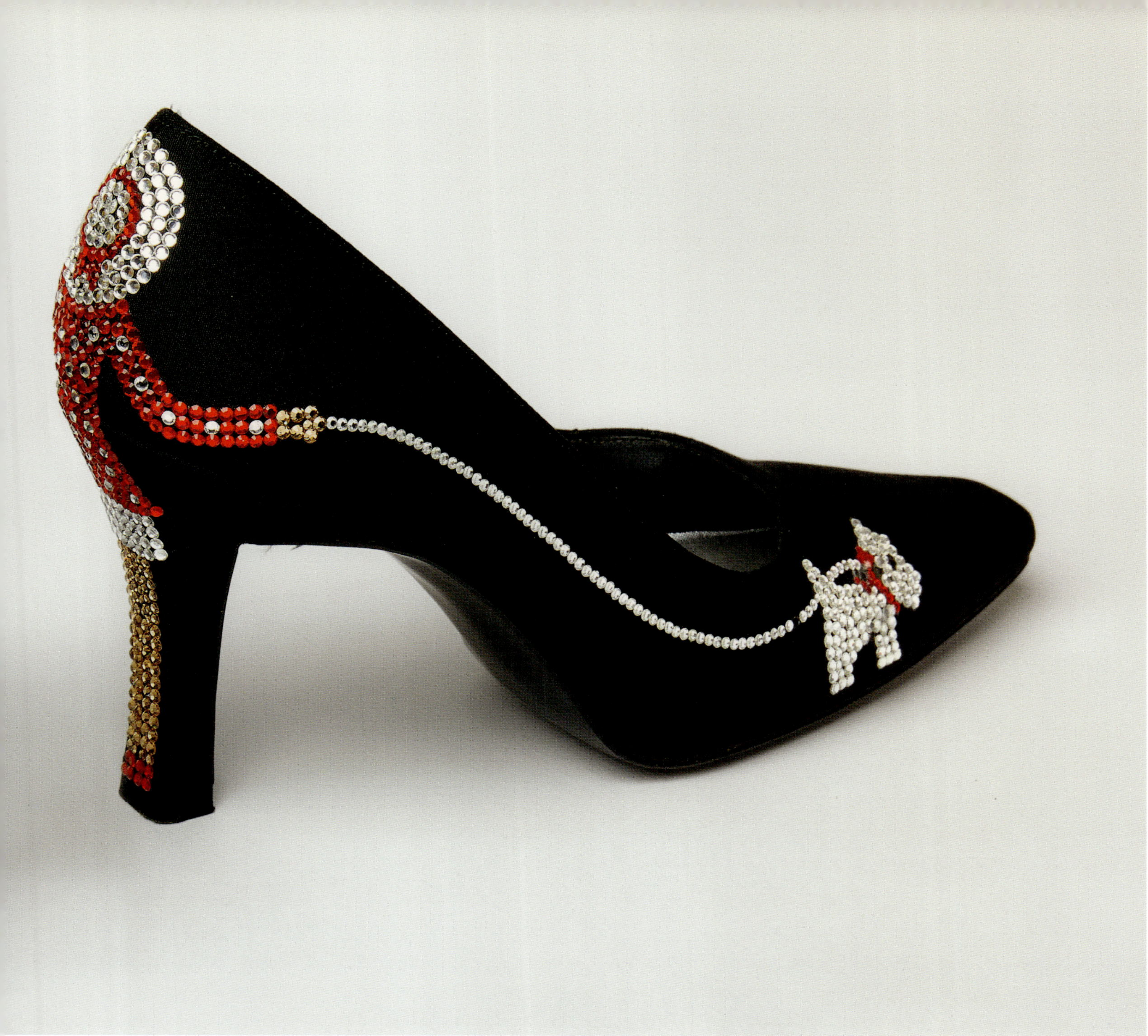

The Dominican side of my family is part of the 1980s wave of migration north. Much of that migration ended up in towns like Lawrence, Methuen, Lowell, and Haverhill, the last of which was once one of the country's top shoe producers, for a time bearing the nickname Queen Slipper City. In the early 1900s, Haverhill had what were then some of the largest shoe factories in the country, in the Burgess and Lang Buildings. Luxury shoe designer Stuart Weitzman had his start in his father's shoe factory, Seymour Shoes, which was also based in Haverhill.

Haverhill and several neighboring towns now feature corner bodegas that blast *bachata* classics and sell domino tables with the Dominican national coat of arms, which bears the credo *Dios, Patria, Libertad*: God, Country, Liberty. My godmother and a few uncles said that when they arrived, the area was mainly populated by "Americanos," and the population of Caribbean people, especially Dominicans, began to grow around them. They learned and practiced English phrases with neighbors and made friendly acquaintanceships with the people they saw regularly. Before the decline of textile and shoe manufacturing in the area

above Stuart Weitzman, "Walking the Dog" shoes, early 1990s. Leather, satin, and crystal. Jimmy Raye Collection, Salem, Massachusetts.

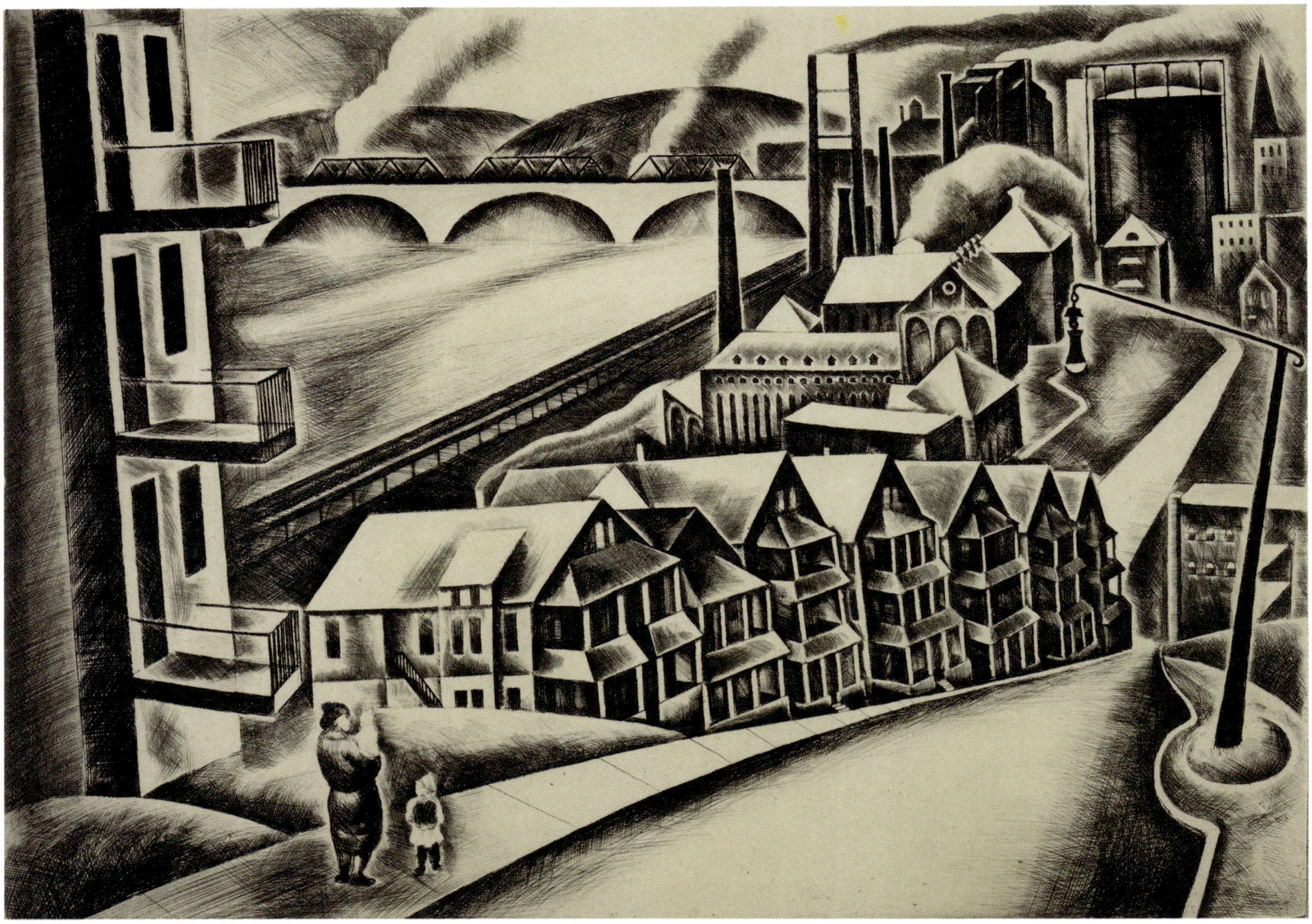

(which had already begun before my family even arrived in Massachusetts), it felt like there was an abundance of jobs. "I had heard from other people that if you walked by some factories, the boss would be standing by the door and they'd ask if anyone needed a job," my godmother told me.

Had they decided on New England versus New York or Florida like so many other Caribbean immigrants because they had heard about the jobs in textile and shoe factories? I asked her. Why did they settle there?

"We knew there would be work," she explained, I could practically hear her shrugging on the other end of the call, "and when we got here, there was work."

In the 1990s, the textile industry, along with other manufacturing, began to decline more steeply in the area, but the Dominicans who had worked in the clothing factories created their own small businesses. Among them were those I grew up referring to collectively as "the *platano* bus," which in fact were a number of independent transit companies that connected Washington Heights in Upper Manhattan—one of the largest Dominican communities outside the country itself—to Massachusetts and elsewhere.

"There was a better service when you were younger," my mom recently told me. "The bus would pick you up right in front of your door."

My grandparents (along with many of my aunts and uncles) would never become very fluent in English. Some workers at the factories and the workers on the bus routes mainly spoke Spanish. They existed within their own ecosystem and managed to make lives for themselves in New England.

In the decades that followed my relatives' move, they went on to raise kids, run in-home daycare centers, own bodegas, and work in hotels; some have now retired back to the Dominican

above Howard Norton Cook, *New England City*, 1930. Etching; image: 6 ⅞ × 9 ¾ in. (17.5 × 24.8 cm). Crystal Bridges Museum of American Art, Bentonville, Arkansas, 2012.86.

Republic. There are remnants of factories throughout the region, with the old manufacturing buildings in Haverhill that were for years boarded up today becoming loft apartments, breweries, and restaurants.

The *platano* buses are still running. One of my siblings lived near Lawrence while he was attending trade school. He had visited New York one weekend and didn't want to take a bus to Boston and then have to pay for a cab to get to his apartment. So we drove him up to Washington Heights, and one of the buses I used to take to visit my godparents dropped him off near his apartment.

Before the decline of textile and shoe manufacturing in the area, it felt like there was an abundance of jobs. "If you walked by some factories, the boss would be standing by the door and they'd ask if anyone needed a job."

By the early 2000s, Lawrence became the first Latino-majority city in all of Massachusetts. Today, a large Latin American community has opened small businesses throughout the small city. Before the pandemic, I visited relatives and we stopped by an independent coffee shop and bookstore that sold bilingual books and had items like *cafe con leche*, Mexican macchiato, and the popular Dominican brand Embajador hot chocolate on the menu. A lot of the factories are gone, but many of the children and grandchildren of those who labored in them are now restaurant workers, local politicians, community organizers, and small business owners.

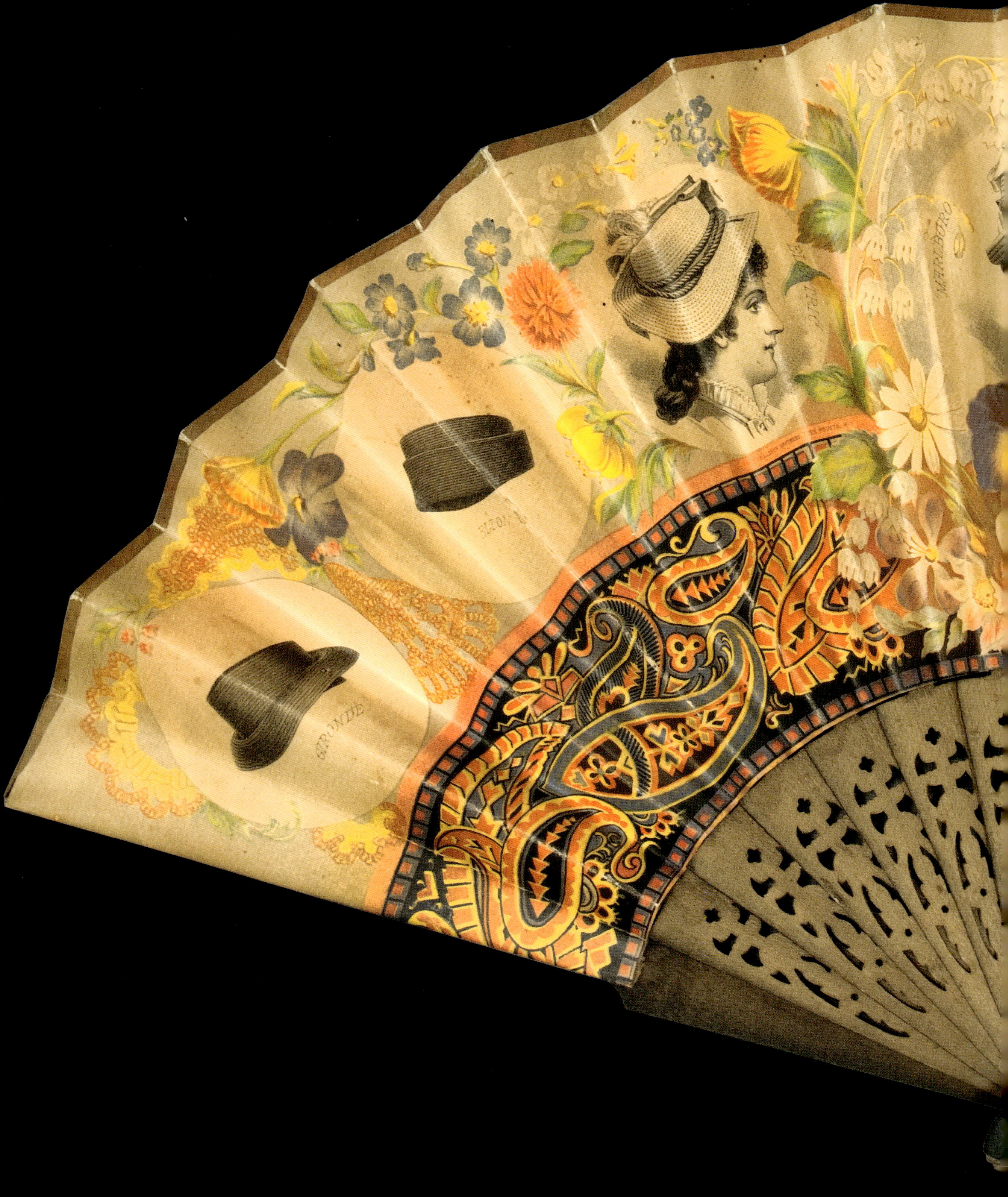
GIRONDE

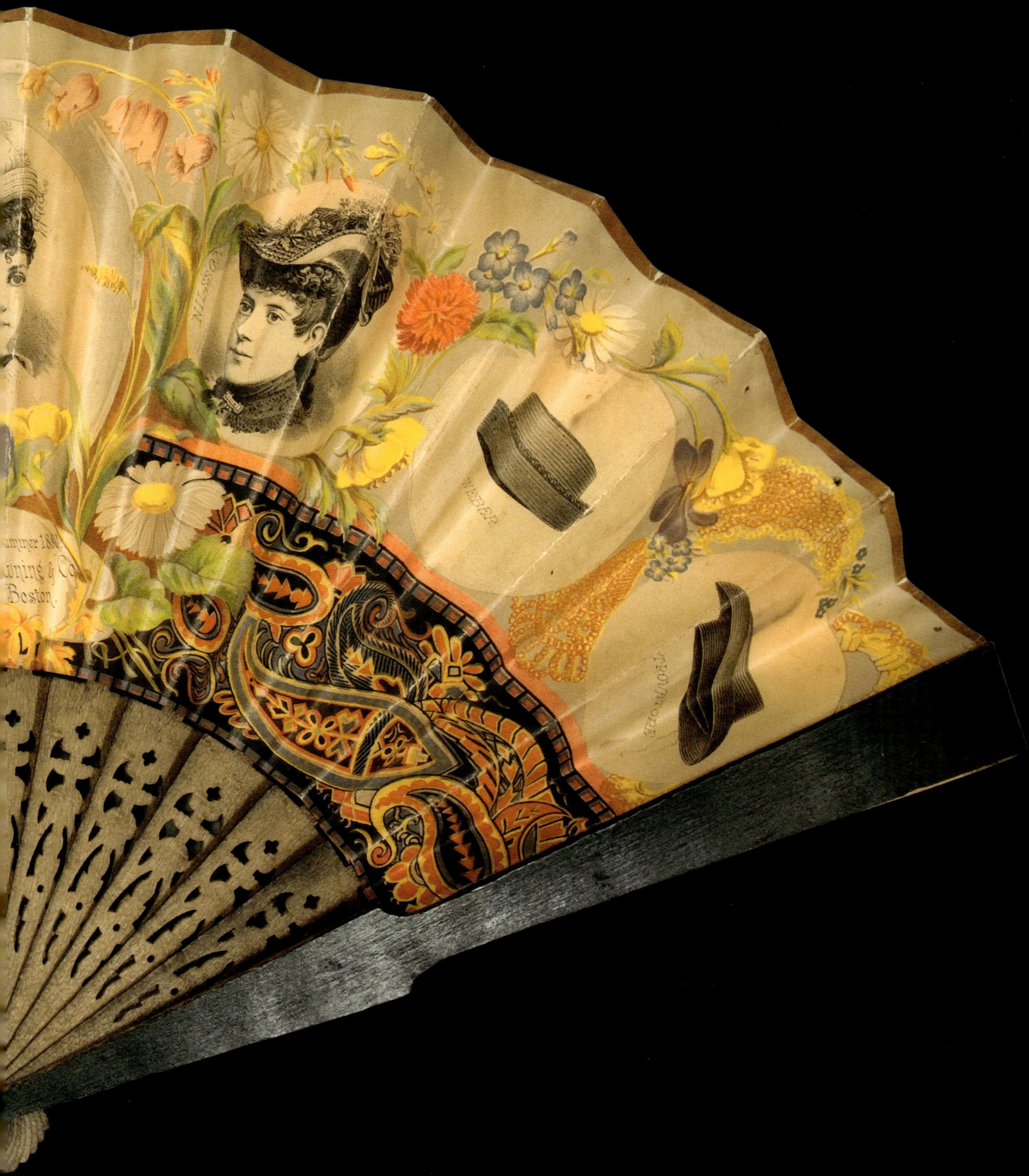
Boston.
WEBER

SELECTED BIBLIOGRAPHY AND SUGGESTED READING

Abrego, Sonya. *Westernwear: Postwar American Fashion and Culture.* London: Bloomsbury, 2022.

Aldrich, Winifred. "History of Sizing Systems and Ready-to-Wear Garments." In *Sizing in Clothing: Developing Effective Sizing Systems for Ready-to-Wear Clothing*, edited by Susan P. Ashdown, 1–56. Cambridge: Woodhead, 2007.

Anayanwu, Obi. "Kerby Jean-Raymond on Reinventing the System." *Women's Wear Daily*, November 5, 2019. https://wwd.com/fashion-news/designer-luxury/kerby-jean-raymond-on-reinventing-the-system-1203360152/.

Bean, Susan S. *Yankee India: American Commercial and Cultural Encounters with India in the Age of Sail, 1784–1860*. Salem, MA: Peabody Essex Museum/Mapin Publishing, 2001.

Biron, Gerry. *A Cherished Curiosity: The Souvenir Beaded Bag in Historic Haudenosaunee (Iroquois) Art*. Saxtons River, VT: Gerry Biron, 2012.

Blanks, Tim. *The World of Anna Sui.* New York: Abrams, 2017.

Chilvers, Simon. " 'Hip, Rebellious, Even a Bit Sinister': How Andy Warhol Made Pop Art Fashion." *Guardian*, March 2, 2020. https://www.theguardian.com/fashion/2020/mar/02/hip-rebellious-even-a-bit-sinister-how-andy-warhol-made-pop-art-fashion.

Corn, Wanda M. *Georgia O'Keeffe: Living Modern*. Brooklyn, NY: Brooklyn Museum, 2017.

Corrigan, Peter. *The Sociology of Consumption*. London: Sage, 1997.

Daves, Jessica. *Ready-Made Miracle: The Story of American Fashion for the Millions.* New York: G. P. Putnam's Sons, 1967.

Day, Daniel R. *Dapper Dan: Made in Harlem; A Memoir.* New York: Random House, 2020.

Del Barco, Mandalit. "How Shirley Cards Set Photography's Skin-Tone Standard." NPR, November 13, 2014. https://www.npr.org/2014/11/13/363517842/for-decades-kodak-s-shirley-cards-set-photography-s-skin-tone-standard.

Dyer, Richard. "The Matter of Whiteness." In *White Privilege: Essential Readings on the Other Side of Racism*, edited by Paula S. Rothenberg. New York: Worth Publishers, 2005

Ferragamo, Salvatore. *Shoemaker of Dreams: The Autobiography of Salvatore Ferragamo.* London: George G. Harrap & Co., 1957.

Ferrari, Mary. " 'Obliged to Earn Subsistence for Themselves': Women Artisans in Charleston, South Carolina, 1763–1808." *South Carolina Historical Magazine* 106, no. 4 (October 2005): 235–55.

Finamore, Michelle Tolini. *Hollywood before Glamour: Fashion in American Silent Film*. London: Palgrave Macmillan, 2013.

Ford, Tanisha C. *Dressed in Dreams: A Black Girl's Love Letter to Fashion.* New York: St. Martin's Press, 2019.

Friedman, Vanessa. "A Black American Designer Disrupts the French Couture." *New York Times*, July 11, 2021. https://www.nytimes.com/2021/07/11/style/pyer-moss-couture.html.

Gamber, Wendy. "Reduced to Science: Gender, Technology, and Power in the American Dressmaking Trade, 1860–1910." *Technology and Culture* 36, no. 3 (July 1995): 465–66.

George-Warren, Holly. *How the West Was Worn*. New York: Harry N. Abrams; Los Angeles, Autry Museum of the American West, 2001.

Giedion, S. (Sigfried). *Space, Time, and Architecture: The Growth of a New Tradition*. Cambridge, MA: Harvard University Press, 1954.

Givhan, Robin. *The Battle of Versailles*. New York: Flatiron Books, 2015.

Glasrud, Bruce A., and Michael N. Searles. *Black Cowboys in the American West: On the Range, on the Stage, behind the Badge*. Norman: University of Oklahoma Press, 2016.

Green, Nancy L. *Ready-to-Wear, Ready-to-Work: A Century of Industry and Immigrants*. Durham, NC: Duke University Press, 1997.

Harris, Michael. *Jeans of the Old West: A History*. Altglen, PA: Schiffer Publishing, 2016.

Hartman, Saidiya. *Wayward Lives, Beautiful Experiments: The Intimate Lives of Riotous Black Girls, Troublesome Women, and Queer Radicals*. New York: W. W. Norton, 2019.

Hawes, Elizabeth. *Fashion Is Spinach*. New York: Random House, 1938.

Hilfiger, Tommy, with Peter Knobler. *American Dreamer: My Life in Fashion and Business*. New York: Ballantine Books, 2016.

Jerkins, Morgan. "The Quiet Racism of Instagram Filters." *Racked*, July 7, 2015. https://www.racked.com/2015/7/7/8906343/instagram-racism.

Jones, Kevin, and Christina M. Johnson, with Kirstin Purtich. *Sporting Fashion: Outdoor Girls, 1800 to 1960*. Munich: Prestel; New York: American Federation of Arts, 2021.

Kapoun, Robert W. *Language of the Robe: American Indian Trade Blankets*, 1st ed. Salt Lake City: Peregrine Smith Books, 1992.

Kasson, Joy S. *Buffalo Bill's Wild West: Celebrity, Memory, and Popular History*. New York: Hill and Wang, 2001.

Kidwell, Claudia B., and Margaret C. Christman. *Suiting Everyone: The Democratization of Clothing in America*. Washington, DC: Smithsonian Institution, 1974.

Kimmerer, Robin Wall. *Braiding Sweetgrass: Indigenous Wisdom, Scientific Knowledge, and the Teachings of Plants*. Minneapolis, MN: Milkweed Editions, 2013.

Kouwenhoven, John A. " 'What Is Vernacular?' " In *Made in America: The Arts in Modern Civilization*, 15–53. New York: Doubleday, 1948.

Kramer, Karen. *Native Fashion Now: North American Indian Style*. Munich: Prestel; Salem, MA: Peabody Essex Museum, 2015.

La Chapelle, Peter. "All That Glitters: Country Music, Taste, and the Politics of the Rhinestone 'Nudie' Suit." *Dress* 28, no. 1 (January 2001): 3–12.

Lambert, Eleanor. *World of Fashion: People, Places, Resources*. New York: R. R. Bowker, 1976.

Lewis, Sarah. "The Racial Bias Built into Photography." *New York Times*, April 25, 2019. https://www.nytimes.com/2019/04/25/lens/sarah-lewis-racial-bias-photography.html

Lucero, Helen R. *Chimayó Weaving: The Transformation of a Tradition*. Albuquerque: University of New Mexico Press, 1999.

Mallis, Fern. *Fashion Lives: Fashion Icons with Fern Mallis*. New York: Rizzoli, 2015.

Manns, William. *Cowboys and the Trappings of the Old West*. Santa Fe, NM: Zon International Publishing, 1997.

Marguerite, Ann Tartsinis. *An American Style: Global Sources for New York Textile and Fashion Design 1915–1928*. New York: Bard Graduate Center, 2013.

Marshall, Amani T. " 'They Are Supposed to Be Lurking about the City': Enslaved Women Runaways in Antebellum Charleston." *South Carolina Historical Magazine* 115, no. 3 (July 2014): 188–212.

Martin, Richard. *American Ingenuity: Sportswear, 1930s–1970s*. New York: Metropolitan Museum of Art, 1988.

McClendon, Emma. *Denim: Fashion's Frontier*. New Haven, CT: Yale University Press; New York: Fashion Institute of Technology, 2016.

McCormick, Jennifer. "Tobias and Christiana Scott: The Road to Freedom." Charleston Museum News and Events (blog). https://www.charlestonmuseum.org/news-events/tobias-and-christiana-scott-the-road-to-freedom/.

McGinnis, Vera. *Rodeo Road: My Life as a Pioneer Cowgirl*. New York: Hastings House, 1974.

Metcalfe, Jessica. "Native Designers of High Fashion: Expressing Identity, Creativity, and Tradition in Contemporary Customary Clothing Design." PhD diss., University of Arizona, 2010.

Millar Williams, Susan. "The Fan Master." *Charleston Style and Design Magazine*, July 9, 2018. https://charlestonstyleanddesign.com/the-fan-master/.

Morgan, Philip D. *Slave Counterpoint: Black Culture in the Eighteenth-Century Chesapeake and Lowcountry*. Chapel Hill: University of North Carolina Press, 1998.

Myers, Amrita Chakrabarti. *Forging Freedom: Black Women and the Pursuit of Liberty in Antebellum Charleston*. Chapel Hill: University of North Carolina Press, 2011.

Newton, James E., and Ronald L. Lewis. "Appendix: Directory of Occupations Held by Black Artisans and Craftsmen Prior to 1865." In *The Other Slaves: Mechanics, Artisans, and Craftsmen*, edited by Newton and Lewis. Boston: G. K. Hall, 197

Nudie, Jamie Lee. *Nudie: The Rodeo Tailor*. Salt Lake City: Gibbs Smith, 2004.

Olwell, Robert. *Masters, Slaves, and Subjects: The Culture of Power in the South Carolina Low Country, 1740–1790*. Ithaca, NY: Cornell University Press, 1998.

Ortiz, Virgil. "Indigenizing Fashion: Reclaim Ownership of Our Cultural Imagery." Soundboard, Walker Art Center, June 6, 2019. https://walkerart.org/magazine/soundboard-indigenizing-fashion-virgil-ortiz.

Paredes, Américo. *Folklore and Culture on the Texas-Mexican Border*. Austin: CMAS Books, Center for Mexican American Studies, University of Texas at Austin, 1993.

Paterek, Josephine. *Encyclopedia of American Indian Costume*, Denver: ABC-CLIO, 1994.

Phillips, Ruth B. *Identities: The Souvenir in Native American Art in the Northeast, 1700–1900*. Montreal: McGill-Queens University Press; Kingston: University of Washington Press, 1998.

Rennolds Milbank, Caroline. *New York Fashion: The Evolution of American Style*. New York: Abrams, 1989.

Ricci, Benedetta. "Portraits of America: Cindy Sherman's *Untitled Film Stills*." *Artland*. https://magazine.artland.com/portraits-of-america-cindy-shermans-untitled-film-stills/.

Richards, Florence S. *The Ready-to-Wear Industry, 1900–1950*. New York: Fairchild Publications, 1951.

Roshco, Bernard. *The Rag Race: How New York and Paris Run the Breakneck Business of Dressing American Women*. New York: Funk & Wagnalls Company, 1963.

Roth, Lorna. "Looking at Shirley, the Ultimate Norm: Colour Balance, Image Technologies, and Cognitive Equity." *Canadian Journal of Communication* 34, no. 1 (2009): 111–36.

Schöpf, Johann David. *Travels in the Confederation (1783–1784)*. Edited by Alfred J. Morrison. 2 vols. Baltimore: The Lord Baltimore Press, 1911.

Spivack, Emily. *Worn Stories*. New York: Princeton Architectural Press, 2014.

Square, Jonathan Michael. "Slavery's Warp, Liberty's Weft: A Look at the Work of Eighteenth- and Nineteenth-Century Enslaved Fashion Makers and Their Legacies." In *Black Designers in American Fashion*, edited by Elizabeth Way, 29–46. London: Bloomsbury, 2021.

Stewart, Dodai. "*ANTM* Models in Oh-So-Trendy Blackface Shoot." *Jezebel*, October 28, 2009. https://jezebel.com/antm-models-in-oh-so-trendy-blackface-shoot-5391756.

Tashjian, Rachel. "King Kerby: Inside the World of Pyer Moss." *Garage*, February 5, 2019. https://garage.vice.com/en_us/article/vbwe7x/pyer-moss-kerby-jean-raymond.

Toledo, Isabel. *Roots of Style: Weaving Together Life, Love, and Fashion.* New York: Penguin/Celebra, 2012.

Way, Elizabeth, ed. *Black Designers in American Fashion.* London: Bloomsbury, 2021.

Wieser, Kimberly G. *Back to the Blanket: Recovered Rhetorics and Literacies in American Indian Studies*. Norman: University of Oklahoma Press, 2017.

Wilson, Laurel. "American Cowboy Dress: Function to Fashion." *Dress* 28, no. 1 (January 2001): 40–52.

CONTRIBUTORS

SONYA ABREGO is a New York–based design historian specializing in American fashion of the twentieth century. She holds a PhD in decorative arts, design history, and material-culture studies from Bard Graduate Center. Abrego takes an interdisciplinary approach to examining the interconnections among dress, popular culture, and modern art and design, publishing in both scholarly and popular venues. She has presented at conferences across North America and is the author of *Westernwear: Postwar American Fashion and Culture* (forthcoming).

AMBER-DAWN BEAR ROBE (Siksika Nation) is assistant faculty of art history in the museum studies department at the Institute of American Indian Arts and fashion-show program director for the Southwestern Association for Indian Arts, both in Santa Fe, New Mexico. Bear Robe received an MA in American Indian studies and an MA in art history, both from the University of Arizona, and she was awarded regional Emmys in 2020 and 2021 as producer for two documentary short films on Indigenous fashion. She is an acting trustee for the Western States Arts Federation and the Wheelwright Museum of the American Indian, Santa Fe.

MICHELLE TOLINI FINAMORE, PhD, is a Salem, Massachusetts–based fashion curator and historian. She curated *Gender Bending Fashion* (2019), *#techstyle* (2016), *Hollywood Glamour* (2015), and *Think Pink* (2014) at the Museum of Fine Arts, Boston. Her books include *Gaetano Savini: The Man Who Was Brioni* (2015), *Hollywood before Glamour: Fashion in American Silent Film* (2013), and *Jewelry by Artists: In the Studio, 1940–2010* (2010). She has lectured widely and written for both the scholarly and popular press, including *European Drama and Performance Studies*, *Modern Magazine*, *Fashion Theory*, and *Gastronomica*. She has taught courses on film, fashion, and design history at Northeastern University, Rhode Island School of Design, Massachusetts College of Art and Design, and the Fashion Institute of Technology.

TORREN GATSON is an assistant professor of history at the University of North Carolina at Greensboro and codirector of the Black Craftspeople Digital Archive. Gatson is a public historian and scholar of the history of the American South, focusing on nineteenth- and twentieth-century African American built environments and material culture, and a historic preservationist who has produced numerous projects throughout the South. In 2020, Gatson guest-edited the *Journal of Early Southern Decorative Arts*' special edition on African American material culture.

EMMA McCLENDON is a fashion historian and curator based in New York. She has curated numerous exhibitions, including *Power Mode: The Force of Fashion* (2019), *The Body: Fashion and Physique* (2017), and *Denim: Fashion's Frontier* (2015). McClendon holds an MA Hons. in art history from the University of St. Andrews and an MA in the history of dress from the Courtauld Institute of Art, and she is currently completing her PhD at the Bard Graduate Center. Her research focuses on the power dynamics inherent in clothing, with a particular interest in body politics, technology, and standardized sizing.

ANGELY MERCADO is a lifelong New Yorker who works as a researcher, independent fact-checker, and writer. Her work focuses on environmental justice, climate science, social justice, tech, and her experiences as a member of the Caribbean American diaspora in the United States. Her writing has appeared in the *New York Times*, the *Nation*, *Gizmodo*, *Popular Science*, and the *Guardian*, among others.

TIFFANY MOMON is a public historian and assistant professor of history at Sewanee: The University of the South. She earned her PhD in public history from Middle Tennessee State University, working with the Center for Historic Preservation. Momon is the founder and codirector of the Black Craftspeople Digital Archive, a digital humanities project that centers Black craftspeople, their lives, and their artistry. Recent notable publications include "John 'Quash' Williams, Charleston Builder" in the *Journal of Early Southern Decorative Arts* (2020) and "The Spatial Geographies of Skilled Black Labor: The Creation of the Black Craftspeople Digital Archive" in the *Southern Quarterly* (forthcoming).

LAUREN DOWNING PETERS, PhD, is assistant professor of fashion studies and director of the fashion study collection at Columbia College Chicago. Her research focuses on the history of plus-size fashion, the lived experience of fat sartorial embodiment, and transformed and inclusive fashion studies pedagogies. Her work has been published in *Fashion Theory*, *Design Issues*, *Critical Studies in Fashion and Beauty*, *International Journal of Fashion Studies*, and the *Journal of Curatorial Studies*, among others. Her first book, *Fashion before Plus-Size: Bodies, Beauty and the Birth of an Industry*, is forthcoming.

XUXA RODRÍGUEZ is assistant curator of contemporary art at Crystal Bridges Museum of American Art. A critical race and intersectional feminist art historian, Rodríguez is responsible for modern and contemporary American art in the museum's collection, spanning the areas of Latinx and Latin American art, African diasporic art, feminist and queer art, time-based media, and the work of transnational artists. Her research has been supported by Luce / American Council of Learned Societies, the Smithsonian Institution, and the US Department of Education's Foreign Language and Area Studies Program. She holds a PhD in art history from the University of Illinois at Urbana-Champaign.

ELIZABETH WAY is associate curator of costume at the Museum at the Fashion Institute of Technology, New York. Her research focuses on the intersection of African American culture and fashion. Past exhibitions include *Head to Toe* (2021), *Fabric in Fashion* (2018), and *Black Fashion Designers* (2016). She edited *Black Designers in American Fashion* (2021), and her recent publications include "Dressing to Pass During the Harlem Renaissance: Fashion in the Novels of Jessie Redmon Fauset and Nella Larsen" in *Fashion Theory* (2020). She holds an MA in costume studies from New York University.

IMAGE CREDITS

Section-opener images

Page 7: Detail of Patrick Kelly day dress, Fall/Winter 1986–87. Photograph courtesy of the FIDM Museum at the Fashion Institute of Design & Merchandising, Los Angeles, CA
Page 8: Ralph Lauren, evening ensemble, "September" collection, Fall 2016. Model Luna Bijl. Photograph © Marcelo Soubhia
Page 12: Teri Greeves, *Abstraction: Kiowa by Design*, 2014 (detail). © Teri Greeves. Photography by Edward C. Robison III
Page 46: Made in Native America® insignia. Photograph © Virgil Ortiz, all rights reserved
Page 60: I. Miller shoe, mid-1920s. Photograph by Joel Benjamin
Page 82: Detail of Tobias Scott fan, ca. 1875. Photograph courtesy of The Charleston Museum, Charleston, South Carolina
Page 90: Kerby Jean-Raymond for Pyer Moss, Typewriter Dress, Fall 2021. Courtesy of the Hinton Group
Page 102: Detail of sleeve from Manuel Cuevas's Chimayo blanket coat, 1980. Courtesy of the FIDM Museum at the Fashion Institute of Design & Merchandising, Los Angeles, CA
Page 112: Battle of Versailles Fashion Show at the Palace of Versailles, 1973. Detail of photograph by Alain Dejean / Sygma via Getty Images
Page 124: Crotty & Richards, corset, 1872. Cotton, metal, and bone. Agefotostock / Alamy Stock Photo
Page 138: Ophelia DeVore demonstrating makeup techniques with Barbara Barnes. William E. Sauro / The New York Times
Page 156: Detail of Howard Norton Cook's *New England City*, 1930. © Estate of Howard Norton Cook. Photography by Edward C. Robison III
Pages 164–65: Donaldson Brothers for C. A. Browning & Co., advertising fan, ca. 1880. Printed paper, carved wood, and metal. Courtesy of the FIDM Museum at the Fashion Institute of Design & Merchandising, Los Angeles, CA

Page 14 (top): Photograph by Kasia Wandycz / Paris Match via Getty images
Page 16: Photography by Edward C. Robison III
Page 17: Photograph by Ron Sachs-Pool / Getty Images
Page 18: © Teri Greeves. Photography by Edward C. Robison III
Page 19: Photograph courtesy of Gerry Biron
Page 20: Courtesy of the FIDM Museum at the Fashion Institute of Design & Merchandising, Los Angeles, CA
Page 21: Artwork courtesy of the Norman Rockwell Family Agency. Photography by Dwight Primiano
Page 22: Photograph by Raoul Gatchalian / Thomas Lau. Courtesy of Anna Sui
Page 23: acc no. 1973.61. Photograph by Allen Philips. Courtesy of the Wadsworth Atheneum
Page 24: Photography by Edward C. Robison III
Page 25: Photograph by Joel Benjamin
Page 26: Courtesy of the FIDM Museum at the Fashion Institute of Design & Merchandising, Los Angeles, CA
Page 27: Photograph by Joel Benjamin
Page 28: Photograph by Joel Benjamin
Page 29: Bettmann / Getty Images
Page 30: Courtesy of the New York Public Library
Page 31: Photograph by Johnny Nunez / WireImage
Page 32: Photograph © Eric Johnson
Page 33: Photograph by Micaiah Carter. Courtesy of Olivia Anthony
Page 34: Courtesy of the FIDM Museum at the Fashion Institute of Design & Merchandising, Los Angeles, CA
Page 35: Photograph by Mike Coppola / Getty Images for MTV
Page 36: Photograph by Claire R. Greenway / Getty Image
Page 38: Photograph by Robert Rausch. Courtesy of Alabama Chanin
Page 39: Photograph by Sofia Brogi. Courtesy of IED Istituto Europeo di Design S.p.A.
Page 40: Photograph by Rog Walker. Courtesy of Ikiré Jones
Page 41: Photograph by Jessica Onesto with Cheers Babe Photo. Courtesy of Praise Santos McKenna
Pages 42–43: Photograph © Jora Frantzis
Page 44: Photograph by Lev Radin / Pacific Press / LightRocket via Getty Images
Page 46: Photograph © Virgil Ortiz, all rights reserved
Page 51: Photograph by Danielle Picerne. Courtesy of Fashion by Robert Black
Pages 52–53: Photograph by Robert Mesa. Courtesy of Patricia Michaels
Page 55: Photograph by Kari Rowe
Pages 56–57: Photograph © Virgil Ortiz, all rights reserved
Page 58: acc no. 2011.42.A,B © Jamie Okuma. Photograph © Nelson Gallery Foundation
Page 63: 1958.482A,B. Photograph by Allen Philips. Courtesy of the Wadsworth Atheneum
Page 64: Courtesy of the FIDM Museum at the Fashion Institute of Design & Merchandising, Los Angeles, CA
Page 65: Photograph courtesy of the Abraham Lincoln Presidential Library and Museum
Page 66: acc no. 1933.99a-c. Photograph by Allen Philips. Courtesy of the Wadsworth Atheneum
Page 67: Photograph by Joel Benjamin
Page 68: US Patent Office
Page 69: Courtesy of Christina Erteszek

Page 70: Courtesy of the IAIA Archives, Santa Fe, New Mexico
Page 71: Photograph by @sydneyakagiphoto
Pages 72–73: Courtesy of the FIDM Museum at the Fashion Institute of Design & Merchandising, Los Angeles, CA
Page 74: Photograph by Ron Galella, Ltd. / Ron Galella Collection via Getty Images
Page 75: Photograph courtesy of Bob Packert, Peabody Essex Museum
Page 76: Bettmann / Getty Images
Page 77 (top): Photograph by Joel Benjamin
Page 77 (bottom): © Betty Davis / Light in the Attic Records
Page 78: Photograph by George Karger / Getty Images
Page 79: Photograph by Bob Packert. Courtesy of the Peabody Essex Museum
Page 80: Courtesy Ford Foundation, J. Paul Getty Trust, John D. and Catherine T. MacArthur Foundation, Andrew W. Mellon Foundation and Smithsonian Institution
Page 87: Photograph courtesy of The Charleston Museum, Charleston, South Carolina
Page 88: Photograph courtesy of The Charleston Museum, Charleston, South Carolina
Page 92: Photograph courtesy of The Charleston Museum, Charleston, South Carolina
Page 93: Photograph courtesy of The Charleston Museum, Charleston, South Carolina
Page 94: www.metmuseum.org
Page 95: https://www.loc.gov/item/2001705790
Page 97: Courtesy of the Hinton Group
Page 98: Courtesy of the Hinton Group
Page 100: Courtesy of the Hinton Group
Page 105: AFF / Alamy Stock Photo
Page 106: Photograph by 2020 Robe Blake
Page 109: Courtesy of the FIDM Museum at the Fashion Institute of Design & Merchandising, Los Angeles, CA
Page 110: Photograph courtesy of Levi Strauss & Co. Archives
Page 115: © courtesy of Trigère. Photograph courtesy of the Kent State University Museum
Page 116: Photograph by Arrigo Coppitz. Courtesy of Museo Salvatore Ferragamo, Florence
Page 118: © John Valadez. Photography by Edward C. Robison III
Page 119: Courtesy of the FIDM Museum at the Fashion Institute of Design & Merchandising, Los Angeles, CA
Pages 120–21: Photograph by Alain Dejean / Sygma via Getty Images
Page 122: Photograph by Olivier Turpin
Page 126: CBS Photo Archive / Contributor
Page 127: Ovidiu Hrubaru / Alamy Stock Photo
Page 128: Library of Congress
Page 131: Courtesy of the FIDM Museum at the Fashion Institute of Design & Merchandising, Los Angeles, CA
Page 134: © 1915 Fairchild Publishing, LLC
Page 136: Photograph by Kevin Mazur / Getty Images for Savage X Fenty Show Vol. 2 Presented by Amazon Prime Video
Page 149: © Cindy Sherman. Courtesy of the artist and Hauser & Wirth
Page 151: © Kodak
Page 152: Photograph by Pascal Le Segretain / Getty Images
Page 153: Bettmann / Getty Images
Page 154: William E. Sauro / The New York Times
Page 158: Photography by Edward C. Robison III
Page 159: © 2022 Will Barnet Trust / Licensed by VAGA at Artists Rights Society (ARS), NY. Photography by Edward C. Robison III
Pages 160–61: Photograph by Joel Benjamin
Page 162: © Howard Norton Cook Estate. Photography by Edward C. Robison III

INDEX

Note: Entries for images are italicized.

C

D

E

H

I

N

O

P

Q

R

S

T

Crystal Bridges
Museum of American Art

ACQUAVELLA

Crystal Bridges publications are sponsored by
Acquavella Galleries

ISBN: 978-1-68226-217-7
eISBN: 978-1-61075-785-0

26 25 24 23 22 5 4 3 2 1

Manufactured in the United States of America

Designer: Jena Sher Graphic Design
Editor: Domenick Ammirati

The paper used in this publication meets the minimum requirements of the American National Standard for Permanence of Paper for Printed Library Materials Z39.48-1984.

Library of Congress Cataloging-in-Publication Data

Names: Finamore, Michelle Tolini, editor. | Crystal Bridges Museum of American Art, organizer, host institution.
Title: Fashioning America: grit to glamour / edited by Michelle Tolini Finamore.
Description: Fayetteville: Crystal Bridges Museum of American Art; The University of Arkansas Press, 2022. | Includes bibliographical references and index. | Summary: "The companion volume to Crystal Bridges Museum of American Art's first fashion exhibition, Fashioning America: Grit to Glamour celebrates the history of American attire, from the cowboy boot to the zoot suit"—Provided by publisher.
Identifiers: LCCN 2022017101 (print) | LCCN 2022017102 (ebook) | ISBN 9781682262177 | ISBN 9781610757850 (ebook)
Subjects: LCSH: Clothing and dress—Social aspects—United States—Exhibitions. | Fashion—Social aspects—United States—Exhibitions.
Classification: LCC TT504.4 .F37 2022 (print) | LCC TT504.4 (ebook) | DDC 746.9/20973—dc23/eng/20220524
LC record available at https://lccn.loc.gov/2022017101
LC ebook record available at https://lccn.loc.gov/2022017102

Cover: photograph © Jora Frantzis
Back cover: detail of photograph © Virgil Ortiz, all rights reserved